WITHDRAWN

Behavior
Theory and Learning

Selected Papers

Kenneth W. Spence

State University of Iowa

PRENTICE-HALL, INC.

Englewood Cliffs, N. J.

1 9 6 0

Library of Congress
Catalog Card No.: 60-14658

07315—C

❖❖❖❖❖❖❖❖❖❖❖❖❖❖❖❖❖❖❖❖❖

Preface

The following collection of papers, while mostly theoretical in nature, includes a number of experimental articles that have served as vehicles for elaborating the behavior theory approach of the writer.   Consisting of twenty previously published articles and two new papers, the volume offers a kind of behavior or activity sample of a psychologist who has not only been concerned with attempting to bring the kind of order into psychological phenomena that theories provide, but has also had an abiding interest in the nature and role of theory *per se* in this scientific endeavor.

This latter interest is reflected especially in the papers that have been grouped into Part I of the book.   Primarily concerned with philosophical and methodological problems of psychology, *i.e.,* its philosophy of science, these articles discuss both empirical questions relating to the requirements that scientific concepts must fulfill in order to be both testable and significant and the nature and role of theoretical structures in providing for scientific explanation in psychology.   For the most part, the first three articles provide an exposition and analysis of the views of learning theorists as to the function of the theoretical constructs in their formulations.   For example, in the first article, Hull's theorizing of the late thirties was revealed as not being of the type that began with the introduction of an axiomatic system which was later coordinated to empirical concepts as he thought, but as being essentially similar in nature to Tolman's intervening variable approach.   Following the appear-

iii

ance of this article Hull acknowledged that his theory was of this type and he explicitly employed intervening variables in his *Principles of Behavior*.

As far as the concept of intervening variables is concerned these three earlier articles were primarily expository in nature, attempting merely to present the views of Hull and Tolman as to the nature and function of this type of theoretical concept. The writer's own interpretation of the function that the intervening variables serve in present day psychology is presented in the two final papers of Part I, particularly in the third section of the last paper. Acknowledged as being primarily abstractive in nature, intervening variables—when used in conjunction with the laws interrelating them and the so-called composition rules (laws)—are nevertheless regarded as having "surplus meaning" in the sense that they permit the derivation of laws concerning phenomena quite different from those in which they originated. Abstracted from investigations of simple classical and instrumental conditioning, the intervening variables of behavior theory, in conjunction with composition laws, provide for derivations concerning more complex behavior, such as is involved in selective (discrimination) learning, paired associate learning, etc. The final article in Part I also presents the author's conception (methodological behaviorism) of the empirical basis of a scientific psychology and contrasts it with the diametrically opposed empathic approach of Allport.

Part II contains a heterogeneous collection of papers concerned both with the basic theoretical structure of learning phenomena developed by the author from simple conditioning studies and with extrapolations of this theory to more complex types of behavior such as are involved in simple T-maze, complex serial mazes, and paired associates learning in humans. The first previously unpublished paper (No. 6) contrasts the development of Hull's and the author's views on reinforcement and then extends the theoretical model presented in the writer's Silliman Lectures (*Behavior Theory and Conditioning*) to some of the phenomena resulting from non-reinforcement and partial reinforcement. Several papers (Nos. 8–12) representative of the writer's theoretical and experimental studies of the role of drive (D) in determining performance level in simple (eyelid conditioning) and more complex learning tasks (paired associates) are also included.

One feature of this latter theory is the manner in which it goes beyond the intervening variable type of theorizing and attempts to offer a speculative theory as to the processes underlying the intervening variable, in this instance the hypothetical emotional response (r_e) as the basis for general drive level, D. The extent to which the writer has engaged in this dual type of theorizing has not always been recognized. For example, in addition to this hypothesis concerning D, the writer has also introduced the hypothetical concepts of the fractional anticipatory goal response (r_g) as the basis of the incentive motivational variable K, and the fractional anticipatory frustration response (r_f) as playing an important motivational and directing role in the phenomena of extinction and partial reinforcement.

The final paper in Part II is one in which the author attempted to compare cognition and S-R theories of learning. In addition to pointing out the few genuine differences of principle between the two viewpoints and the many differences that are merely a matter of emphasis or interest, the article attempts to show in a schematic fashion how one S-R theorist would deal with perception.

In Part III of the volume, three early theoretical articles on discrimination learning, the phenomenon of transposition, and the continuity-noncontinuity issue are followed by representative empirical studies concerned with testing of the theoretical schema. The final two articles represent more recent theoretical developments in this area. One (No. 21) deals briefly and in a preliminary fashion with the more complex types of discrimination behavior involving various kinds of patterning. The other (No. 22) is a new, previously unpublished paper which, after surveying the different theories of discrimination learning, describes two different conceptual models of selective behavior that have been used by Hull and the writer in the past. A third, new model which includes some features of Tolman's sowbug and which provides for predictions concerning vicarious trial and error (VTE) behavior at the choice point as well as per cent correct choices is also described briefly.

A number of the papers were written in collaboration with

colleagues and former students. I wish to thank all of them for permitting me to include these joint pieces. Aside from minor editorial changes the papers are reprinted as they originally appeared.

In the case of the two new papers, I am indebted to Leonard E. Ross for the preparation of the graphs and to my secretary, Helen G. Stone, for the typing of the manuscripts. Mrs. Stone also aided in the editorial changes made in the reprinted articles.

Kenneth W. Spence

Autumn, 1960

Table of Contents

Part III: Discrimination Learning

◇◇◇◇◇◇◇◇◇◇◇◇◇◇◇◇◇◇◇◇◇◇◇◇◇◇◇

Acknowledgments

The author wishes to acknowledge with thanks permission to reprint the following articles:

Operationism and Theory in Psychology. *Psych. Rev.*, 1941, *48*, 1–14.

The Nature of Theory Construction in Contemporary Psychology. *Psychol. Rev.*, 1944, *51*, 47–68.

The Postulates and Methods of Behaviorism. *Psychol. Rev.*, 1948, *55*, 67–68.

Mathematical Formulations of Learning Phenomena. *Psychol. Rev.*, 1952, *59*, 152–160.

The Empirical Basis and Theoretical Structure of Psychology. *Philosophy of Science*, 1957, *24*, 97–108.

The Relation of Response Latency and Speed to the Intervening Variables and N in S-R Theory. *Psychol. Rev.*, 1954, *61*, 209–216.

A Theory of Emotionally Based Drive (D) and its Relation to Performance in Simple Learning Situations. *Amer. Psychol.*, 1958, *13*, 131–141.

Learning and Performance in Eyelid Conditioning as a Function of Intensity of the UCS. *J. exp. Psychol.*, 1953, *45*, 57–63.

UCS Intensity and the Associative (Habit) Strength of the Eyelid CR. *J. exp. Psychol.*, 1958, *55*, 404–411.

Performance in Eyelid Conditioning Related to Changes in Muscular Tension and Physiological Measures of Emotionality. *J. exp. Psychol.*, 1959, *58*, 417–422.

The Relation of Anxiety (Drive) Level to Performance in Competitional and Non-Competitional Paired-Associates Learning. *J. exp. Psychol.*, 1956, *52*, 296–310.

A Study of Simple Learning under Irrelevant Motivational-Reward Conditions. *J. exp. Psychol.*, 1950, *40*, 539–551.

The Order of Eliminating Blinds in Maze Learning by the Rat. *J. comp. Psychol.*, 1932, *XIV*, 9–27 (copyright owned by Williams & Wilkins).

Cognitive Versus Stimulus-Response Theories of Learning. *Psychol. Rev.,* 1950, *57,* 159–172.

The Nature of Discrimination Learning in Animals. *Psychol. Rev.,* 1936, *43,* 427–449.

The Differential Response in Animals to Stimuli Varying Within a Single Dimension. *Psychol. Rev.,* 1937, *44,* 430–444.

Continuous Versus Non-Continuous Interpretations of Discrimination Learning. *Psychol. Rev.,* 1940, *47,* 271–288.

Gradual Versus Sudden Solution of Discrimination Problems by Chimpanzees. *J. comp. Psychol.,* 1938, *25,* 213–224 (copyright owned by Williams & Wilkins).

The Basis of Solution by Chimpanzees of the Intermediate Size Problem. *J. exp. Psychol.,* 1942, *31,* 257–271.

The Nature of Response in Discrimination Learning. *Psychol. Rev.,* 1952, *59,* 89–93.

PART I

Methodological Basis of Psychology

1

Operationism and Theory in Psychology[1]

I

During the last decade psychologists have become increasingly aware of the methodological problems of their science. This trend of thought has been but a part of the larger movement of Scientific Empiricism, which in turn gained momentum through the integration of the ideas developed in England (Russell) and on the Continent (the Vienna Circle) with the pragmatist tradition in this country. In psychology, as in other sciences, these methodological analyses have stressed two different aspects of scientific enterprise. A number of psychologists, Tolman (*17*), Skinner (*13*), and Stevens (*14*), stimulated by the writings of Bridgman (*3, 4*) have centered their efforts largely on the *empirical component* of scientific method. Under the watchword of operationism, they have carefully considered and laid down the requirements that scientific concepts must fulfill in order to insure testability and thus empirical meaning. The second aspect, the *formal (theoretical) component* of scientific endeavor has been brought to the forefront in psychology principally through the writing of Hull (*6, 7, 9*) and Lewin (*11, 12*). By

[1] This article, written in collaboration with Gustav Bergmann, is an elaboration of two papers read by the authors in a symposium on Current Aspects of Behavior Theory at the 1940 meeting of the Midwestern Branch of the American Psychological Association in Chicago.

his persistent attempts to fit articulate theoretical structures to certain realms of behavioral data, the former has tried to show the essential rôle that formal systematization plays in scientific explanation. The latter has likewise emphasized the rôle of theory in his writings but has not as yet attempted rigorous theory construction.

In the broader framework of Scientific Empiricism the complementary nature of these two components of scientific method has been clearly recognized. It might even be said that one of the main achievements of this philosophic movement has been the methodologically correct evaluation and allocation of the respective rôles of these two modes of scientific thinking. Unfortunately in psychology there has not always been a proper appreciation of the incompleteness of an approach which neglects either one of these supplementary procedures in science. The present paper deals with some of the problems which have arisen in psychology with attempts to develop these two aspects of scientific method.

II

No body of empirical knowledge can be built up without operational definition of the terms in use. This basic methodological requirement is clearly recognized by the present writers. We should like, however, to call attention here to a certain tendency to use this "operational criterion" illegitimately as a means of criticizing theoretical attempts which are, at least, *methodologically* sound. Very often the real basis of such criticism has been nothing but a healthy skepticism as to the scientific value of the theories under examination. There should, of course, be no hesitation at voicing such doubts whenever the generalizations of a scientist seem overdrawn or if his theories do not look promising. But to express such doubts as a methodological argument only confuses the issue. Even sterile or rash theories should be eliminated by proper means, for otherwise there is the danger that promising theories will also be ruled out for no good reason at all. At the present state of the discussion, therefore, it might be useful to restate rather carefully the limits and the legitimate scope of operational analysis.[2]

Even before a scientist can set out to study some aspects of the phenomena he is interested in, *e.g.*, animal maze learning or human rote learning, he must have at least some tentative ideas as to what the "relevant factors" might be, that is to say, as to what the determinants of the phenomena studied are. These ideas, of course, are drawn from his knowledge and his theoretical frame of reference. In a more advanced state, if such a relevant factor has become quantifiable, it is called a variable. Sometimes the term "condition" is also used in this context, and we speak of the conditions under which the phenomena occur. One important point that must be made here is that there is no methodological principle, no "operational recipe" which guarantees that no relevant factor has been overlooked. A statement such as this, then: Operationism requires that all the conditions be taken into account, can be quite misleading. For a construct which unwittingly leaves out a relevant factor (or determining condition) just leads to a different formulation of the empirical laws. For example, by telling us what manipulations he performs, what pointers he reads (weighing and measuring cubic content), and what computations he carries out with the numbers thus obtained (division, W/V), a primitive physicist would give us a methodologically correct definition of his *empirical construct* "density of a liquid." And this in spite of the fact that he might not have given any attention to the temperature in his laboratory, one of the conditions upon which, as we know, and as he might not know at that state of his investigation, the result of his manipulations and computations depends. The point is that we are able to trace back the terms of his language to the immediately observable. He has laid down all the conditions under which he is going to say: "This liquid has the density 1.3." Therefore, we know what he means, and that is all general methodology can insist upon at this level of the so-called *operational definition of empirical constructs.*

---

[2] Stevens' recent paper (*15*) on the subject is distinguished by a very cautious and circumspect attitude in this respect. The paper's main concern, however, is to integrate the methodological discussion within psychology with modern philosophy of science, a subject taken up by one of the present writers (*1, 2*).

Historically and psychologically, then, the creation of helpful concepts is a very essential part of a scientific achievement. From the standpoint of methodological analysis, however, if the scientist has defined his concepts, he has only prepared his tools. Explanatory work proper starts, and can start, only after the empirical constructs have been laid down. And this work, of course, consists in nothing else but finding the *empirical laws*, *i.e.*, the functional relationships between the variables. "Finding" in this context means inductive generalization from observation and experimentation. In this way, our hypothetical physicist, for instance, might become aware of the fact that the density of liquids, as defined by him, varies with temperature. He will then set out to establish the functional relationship between these two variables. But whether a more complete law would have to be established between his two variables and the further one of pressure, is again a pragmatic and no methodological question. We add two further remarks in elaboration of this cardinal point.

First, it must not be overlooked that many empirical laws consist only in the finding that different "classes of operations" lead, within certain ranges, to the *same* result. The operations are then said to define the *same* empirical construct. The classical example for such an empirical law is furnished by the alternative ways of measuring length either with a yardstick or by triangulation. Operational analysis has made us alert to the tentative and empirical character which such "identification," often uncritically and sometimes unjustifiably assumed, shares with any other empirical finding.[3]

Secondly, suppose that the scientist of our example, still ignorant of the relation between temperature and density, desired to ascertain whether his empirical construct "density" could be employed as an identifier of liquids. Upon discovery

[3] In order to comply with the more rigorous distinctions of Scientific Empiricism, one should speak here of "reduction chains" (Carnap) rather than of "classes of operations." A further prosecution of these points, however, leads directly into the investigation of the rules governing our use of "thing-names" and of the spatio-temporal frame of reference. Fascinating as this problem is, it does not seem that methodological clarification in psychology needs to go so far back into epistemology and logical analysis proper; the less so, as practically all psychologists agree that only physical phenomena are the material that psychology, like any other natural science, is concerned with.

of the fact that the "same" liquid gives different "density-values" under different temperatures he would realize that this cannot be done.   But then he might try to identify liquids by recording their density at a given standard temperature.   Strictly speaking, this "standard density" is a new construct.[4]   The point is that, even if this new construct proves satisfactory for our physicist's present purposes, he has not yet stated all the conditions simply because there is always, at least theoretically, an infinite number of them.   He might, however, have got hold of all the factors relevant for his purpose: *i.e.*, within the range of specification and variation determined by his experiments and their intended generalization.   The proof of the pudding is in the eating and not in any particular operational criterion. We see that even at the level of the empirical laws the scientist cannot derive any help from operationism.   He will have to rely upon his own ingenuity and whatever help he might be able to get from an articulate theory.

Having formulated this limitation of operationism so strongly, it is only fair to state the real and sound scientific basis of the demand for careful consideration of "all the conditions."   In the less complex and more mature fields of natural science (physics, chemistry) we are reasonably confident that we know and control *practically* all the variables necessary for the complete functional description attempted.   In the biological and social sciences, on the other hand, this is not the case.   Here, complexity of the situation and insufficiency of knowledge tend to preclude successful segregation of a set of variables which is reasonably complete.   This is a shortcoming which limits the importance of most of the "empirical laws" and of theorizing

---

[4] It is worth while mentioning, though, that these two constructs are in an hierarchical relation, *i.e.*, that the class of operations (reduction chain) leading to one of them is a subclass of that leading to the other.   The same holds true for concepts in psychology like learning criterion and retention criterion.   There is, of course, a manifold factual interdependence between constructs and laws.   Still we believe that the sharp analytical distinction between empirical constructs and empirical laws made in this paper is justifiable within scientific methodology, and might prove especially helpful for a clear appreciation of the operational viewpoint in present day psychology.   At the level of logical analysis, however, the disentanglement of the thoroughgoing interdependence between the terms and the whole system of hypotheses constitutes one of the main tasks of scientific philosophy.

in these fields at their present stage of development. The difficulty should be clearly recognized and it is to the credit of the operationists in psychology that they insist upon ultra-cautiousness and skepticism in these matters. But again it must be emphasized that the difficulty is not a methodological one. The question whether the individual variables are adequately and properly defined should be carefully distinguished from the question as to whether a set of variables sufficiently complete for a satisfactory functional description has been ascertained.

Before turning to the discussion of theory, there is still one further point to be made regarding the definition of "empirical constructs," the only aspect with which, as we have seen, operationism is properly concerned. The language of any science contains a whole hierarchy of interlocked empirical constructs— mass, acceleration, momentum, energy, or stimulus trace, excitatory potential, and so on. None of these particular constructs, of course, is "observable," in the sense in which a physical thing is observable. Nevertheless they are just as empirical as length, duration, weight, stimulus and all other such terms which are sometimes thought of exclusively as being operationally defined. All scientific terms are derived terms, derived from and retraceable to what one might call "the hard data," the "immediately observable," or what Stevens calls the "elementary operation of discrimination." [5] Any attempts then to divide this hierarchy of constructs into sheep and goats, *i.e.*, operational constructs and theoretical constructs, is of necessity arbitrary. Actually much of what is usually called theorizing in empirical science consists, as will be discussed later, in the creation of these organizing empirical constructs during the search for the empirical laws. And for this reason some of them are sometimes referred to as theoretical constructs. This is all that can be meant by this distinction.

III

Turning now to the discussion of the theoretical aspects of

[5] Again, in the stricter language of Scientific Empiricism, all these expressions are rather objectionable and would have to be replaced by the syntactical term "primitive predicates." On this level of analysis the names of physical things themselves can be considered as "derived terms." For all these problems Carnap's *Testability and Meaning* should be given as a general reference (5).

scientific method in psychology, one of the most important tasks would seem to be the clarification of the terms "hypo-thetico-deductive method" and "postulational technique." A certain amount of confusion is apt to arise, and indeed has arisen, from an ambiguity in the meaning of these terms. In logic and mathematics they have reference to a formal language system developed as the consequence of a basic set of relations (called postulates or implicit definitions) between otherwise undefined terms. Hilbert's Axiomatics is an outstanding example of such a formal system. Interpretation by means of co-ordinating definitions relating the formal terms with empirical constructs makes this method a feasible one for scientists.

That is to say, the theoretical scientist can start from a set of undefined terms, a, b, c, state his postulates (implicit definitions) which relate them, and then show that by virtue of these few postulates, the terms a, b, c themselves or certain compound terms x, y, z, defined by means of them, fulfill exactly the formulæ which represent the empirical laws. This formal system may then be "interpreted" by co-ordinating a basic class of empirical constructs (experimental variables) either to the original terms a, b, c (phenomenological theory), or to the compound terms x, y, z (non-phenomenological theory). Actually there are few, if any, instances of such a method being exclusively relied upon in the development of the empirical sciences. As a matter of fact, even in geometry, the postulational method was a late achievement, born out of the need for systematic organization and epistemological clarification.

In actual scientific practice and particularly in recent psychological discussions (Hull) the term "mathematico-deductive" has been used in a meaning different from that of the formal logico-geometrical term just defined, although the distinction has not always been apparent. As the scientist usually understands the term, mathematico-deductive method consists in making guesses or hypotheses as to the choice of constructs (variables) and the mathematical relationships holding between them, and the further notion, not always followed in actual practice by psychologists, of strict and complete deductive elaboration of the consequences implied in these assumed relationships. Obviously, such a procedure is not necessarily hypo-thetico-deductive in the first sense.

This distinction is especially important for a proper understanding of the theoretical systems put forward by Hull, which we will therefore use as an exemplification of the general principles laid down in the preceding paragraphs. One can find the most divergent statements concerning various aspects of Hull's theories. Thus one writer (12) states that Hull's terms (concepts) are more or less well defined operationally, but that they are lacking in conceptual properties. At the other extreme one hears that his constructs are too highly theoretical and completely lacking in any empirical reference. These conflicting points of view appear to have arisen from Hull's terminology, particularly from his use of terms like "mathematico-deductive," "undefined concepts," and "postulates."

Misunderstanding might have been avoided if there had always been clear recognition of the fact that Hull's theorizing is hypothetico-deductive only in the second meaning outlined above. Hull does not begin with a set of purely formal terms, having no other meaning than that imparted to them by a set of implicit definitions, from which are then derived new terms and theorems made testable by means of co-ordinating definitions. Instead he actually begins with terms directly operationally defined. Unfortunately, he called them "undefined concepts," and thus created the erroneous impression that he started with purely formal terms which are never given the necessary co-ordinations to empirical constructs. A careful examination of these so-called "undefined concepts," however, will show that they are nothing but what one would call in a less sophisticated language the basic experimental variables, *i.e.,* the variables manipulated and observed in the laboratory.[6]

---

[6] In the recent monograph on rote learning Hull (9) uses the terms "undefined concepts" and "definitions" (defined concepts). Both undefined and defined concepts consist largely in what might be described as directly operationally defined concepts and there is no essential methodological difference between them. Apparently the idea underlying Hull's distinction between these two categories is that the undefined concepts are those most directly point-at-able, *i.e.,* involve the shortest defining sentences. Having selected these, he employs them in the definitions of the more complex defined notions. The whole system of definitions and postulates exhibits the mixture of explicit definitions and reduction chains characteristic of empirical science.

It should be mentioned that U6, U7 and U8 should not have been included among the undefined concepts of the rote learning monograph. They are elu-

The essential point to be noted, however, is that Hull's postulate systems do not contain implicit definitions relating these initial variables (concepts). Indeed, his postulates are nothing but definitions which define new constructs by stating them as mathematical functions of the initial variables (concepts). For example, in a recent modified formulation of his theory of simple adaptive behavior, Hull (*8*) gives as a postulate, what is really a definition of his term stimulus trace (*ṣ*):

$$(1) \qquad \dot{s} = a \log S(1 - e^{-hT}) e^{-kT'},$$

where S is the intensity of the physical stimulus; T the time of duration of S; T' the time since the termination of S; a, h, and k being empirical constants. Here the term stimulus trace has been newly created out of the independent variables S, T, and T' by means of a mathematical technique.[7]

Several questions now arise concerning the scientific status of such "postulates," the answers to which will reveal a characteristic feature of psychological theory. Are these formulæ guesses as to the empirical laws of psychology? Obviously not in the same sense as the gas law or Newton's attraction formula, for there is no independent empirical referent, so far, for the newly defined variable. What then is the possible use of such *a priori* constructions?

For a satisfactory answer to this latter question we must examine the basic task of psychology. Like every other science, psychology conceives its problem as one of establishing the interrelations within a set of variables, most characteristically between response variables on the one hand and a manifold of

---

cidations regulating the use of derived terms defined later in the postulates. This has been recognized by Hull, himself, in a later section of the monograph (p. 306). By and large, however, operationists will correctly interpret Hull by substituting "operationally defined" for his expressions "undefined concepts" and "definitions."

[7] It should be clearly understood that, in spite of the use of such terms as stimulus trace, excitatory potential, etc., no physiological referents for these arbitrarily defined terms are implied. Attention should also be called to the point that by this very procedure these derived terms become themselves empirical constructs, or if one prefers, they are indirectly operationally defined. They are methodologically comparable to the physicist's concepts of momentum, energy, etc.

environmental variables on the other. Or, in the usual mathematical denotation:

$$(2) \quad \begin{aligned} y_1 &= f_1(x_1 \ x_2 \bullet \bullet \bullet x_n) \\ &\overline{- - - - - - - -} \\ y_m &= f_m(x_1 \ x_2 \bullet \bullet \bullet x_n) \end{aligned}$$

The problem here is two-fold: (1) the obtaining of the empirical curves and (2) the determination of their mathematical form, *i.e.*, the specific nature of functions $f_1, f_2 \bullet \bullet \bullet f_m$. In solving this problem, physics is able to start out with assumptions as to the specific form of the f's describing elementary situations, *i.e.*, situations of simple structure with a very limited number of variables, for it is possible to generalize or hypothesize these functions from experimental observation. More complex situations can then be adequately handled by deduction from and combination of these basic formulæ. In the course of this elaboration the physicist sometimes finds it convenient to employ new auxiliary terms (*e.g.*, force in mechanics) defined out of the original variables.

In psychology, on the other hand, the number of variables entering into even the simplest behavior situation that can be experimentally produced is so great and the structure of their interrelationship is so complex that we are unable to make even a first guess as to the mathematical form of the equations directly from the empirical data without some auxiliary theoretical device.[8] *The terms defined by Hull's postulates provide just such a device.* They attempt to bridge the gap between the two sets of variables, those manipulated by the experimenter and those measuring the observed responses. Technically, they aim at providing the means for ascertaining a rational fit to the empirical curve.

This aspect of our analysis can perhaps be best illustrated by a brief consideration of Hull's most recent formulation of simple behavior theory (*8*). The figure attempts to give a graphic representation of the hierarchic order of the terms involved.

---

[8] The securing of empirical data under concomitant variation of several variables is only beginning in psychology.

The basic (directly operationally defined) variables from which the construction starts, as shown at the left, are:

T_1 = the time of duration of S_1,
S_1 = the intensity of a physical stimulus, *e.g.*, buzzer, lever,
S_2 = reinforcing (goal) stimulus, *e.g.*, food,
T_2 = starvation time,
T_3 = time between response to S_1 and occurrence of S_2,
N = number of presentations of $S_1 - S_2$ sequence, *i.e.*, trials.

Moreover there are the various measurable aspects of the response shown at the right:

$$R_1 = \text{amplitude of response,}$$
$$R_2 = \text{latency of response, etc.}$$

Hull now proceeds to the task of specifying the mathematical form of the empirical laws relating these two classes of variables. He attempts to do this by defining new terms out of the original variables so that in the final formulation of the empirical laws only the end members of this chain of intervening variables appear. This is accomplished in the manner schematically illustrated in the figure. The dotted lines indicate that these

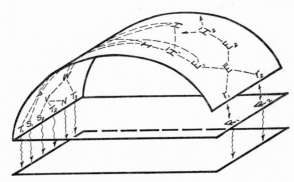

intervening variables, shown on the bridge, are derived in stepwise fashion from each other. To go into any detail would be beyond the scope of this paper. It is sufficient to indicate here that the final rational equations would express the response variables as a function of the just preceding intervening variable, excitatory potential ($\bar{E}$). It will also be noted that the response variables appear twice in the diagram; once on the bridge as derived, intervening constructs ($r_1\ r_2$) and once as independently operationally defined variables ($R_1\ R_2$).

These two sets of formally different terms (r's and R's) are then identified and the success of the construction depends upon whether this identification is borne out by the experimental data. If so, the gap at the right end of the bridge is closed and the desired formulation of the empirical law has been attained. Finally, to complete the description of the diagram, the wavy lines leading down to the base symbolize the completion of the operational tie-up with the "immediately observable." [9]

For the sake of methodological completeness attention should be called here, perhaps, to a point of considerable importance (one somewhat obscured by the present emphasis) in regard to the determination of the final and complete rational form of the empirical law. By "final and complete" is meant the precise specification of each and every function connecting the two sets of variables. However, many deductions as to shapes and trends of behavior curves can be drawn if only some of the mediating functions (postulates) are specified, provided that the remaining non-specified functions hold to the general pattern assumed. As a matter of fact, many of the testable deductions made by Hull from this particular set are of this kind, for so far he has only roughly indicated the type of functions beyond the term H in the above scheme.

IV

In concluding this analysis it may be of some interest to indicate how this theoretical structure of Hull's relates to the conception of the nature of psychological theory outlined by Tolman in his presidential address (*18*) and earlier papers (*16, 17*). Tolman begins with equation system (2) and like Hull

---

[9] This latter feature of the diagram follows the method of graphical representation suggested by Feigl and Koch in their clarification of the relation between empirical and formal language in psychology (*10*).

and any other methodological behaviorist conceives the task of psychology as one of determining the form of the functions (see page 12). In his scheme the independent variables $(x_1 \, x_2 \cdot \cdot \cdot x_n)$ are split into two classes, environmental and individual difference variables, and the dependent variables are some aspects of behavior. As to the form of the functions, he states that "It is in fact so complicated that we at present seem unable to state it in any single simple statement. We find, rather, that we have to handle it by conceiving it as broken down into successive sets of component functions. These component functions connect the independent variables to logically constructed 'intervening variables,' and then connect these intervening variables in their turn to one another and to the final dependent behavior" (*17*, p. 91).

Clearly this description is fully in line, indeed identical, with the picture of Hull's actual procedure as outlined by our preceding analysis, and it is to Tolman's credit that he has been one of the first in psychology to outline this general methodological scheme. His actual theorizing, however, has always moved on a very general, programmatic level and has not gone beyond suggesting and cataloguing the various possible intervening variables and showing how they provide for the definition and use of mental terms (demands, hypotheses, etc.) in a behavioristic psychology. Such essential convergence between two theoretical viewpoints which are often regarded as being far apart strongly suggests that essential agreement on this level of general methodology is about to be reached in psychology. The most imperative task would now seem to be the persistent pursuit of attempts to formulate articulate theories in closest contact with the experimental data.

REFERENCES

1. BERGMANN, G. On some methodological problems of psychology. *Philos. Sci.*, 1940, *7*, 205–219.

2. ——. The subject matter of psychology. *Philos. Sci.*, 1940, 7, 415–433.

3. BRIDGMAN, P. W. *The Logic of Modern Physics.* New York: The Macmillan Company, 1928.

4. ——. *The Nature of Physical Theory.* Princeton: Princeton University Press, 1936.

5. CARNAP, R. Testability and meaning. *Philos. Sci.*, 1936, *3*, 419–471; 1937, *4*, 1–40.

6. HULL, C. L. Mind, mechanism, and adaptive behavior. *Psychol. Rev.*, 1937, *44*, 1–32.

7. ——. The problem of stimulus equivalence in behavior theory. *Psychol. Rev.*, 1939, *46*, 9–30.

8. ——. Memoranda concerning behavior theory. 1940–41, p. 55. (On file in Yale University Library.)

9. ——, HOVLAND, C. I., ROSS, R. T., HALL, M., PERKINS, D. T., & FITCH, F. B. *Mathematico-Deductive Theory of Rote Learning.* New Haven: Yale University Press, 1940.

10. KOCH, S. The logical character of the motivation concept. M.A. Thesis, State University of Iowa, 1939.

11. LEWIN, K. The conceptual representation and the measurement of psychological forces. *Contrib. Psychol. Theory, I,* No. 4. Duke University Press, 1938.

12. ——. Formalization and progress in psychology. In *University of Iowa Studies: Studies in Child Welfare.* 1940, *16,* No. 3, pp. 9–42.

13. SKINNER, B. F. The concept of the reflex in the description of behavior. *J. gen. Psychol.*, 1931, *5*, 427–458.

14. STEVENS, S. S. The operational definition of psychological concepts. *Psychol. Rev.*, 1935, *42*, 517–527.

15. ——. Psychology and the science of science. *Psychol. Bull.*, 1939, *36*, 221–263.

16. TOLMAN, E. C. Psychology vs. immediate experience. *Philos. Sci.*, 1935, *2*, 356–380.

17. ——. Operational behaviorism and current trends in psychology. *Proc. 25th Amer. Celebration Inaug. Grad. Stud.*, Los Angeles: The University of Southern California, 1936, pp. 89–103.

18. ——. The determiners of behavior at a choice point. *Psychol. Rev.*, 1938, *45*, 1–41.

2

The Nature of Theory Construction in Contempory Psychology[1]

I. Introduction

The task of the scientist has been described as that of attempting to discover ever more generalized laws by which the observable events within his field of study may be brought into interrelation with one another. To this end he develops and refines (mainly in the direction of quantitative representation) his concepts or variables, arranges highly controlled (experimental) conditions of observation and introduces theoretical constructions. While it is not the primary purpose of this paper to attempt a methodological analysis of these components of scientific method, it is necessary to begin our discussion by calling attention to two somewhat different roles or functions that one of them, construction of theory, plays in different fields of science or in the same field at different stages of development.

In some areas of knowledge, for example present day physics, theories serve primarily to bring into functional connection with one another empirical laws which prior to their formulation had been isolated realms of knowledge. The physicist is able to isolate, experimentally, elementary situations, *i.e.,* situations in

1 The writer is greatly indebted to Dr. Gustav Bergmann for reading the manuscript and making valuable suggestions.

which there are a limited number of variables, and thus finds it possible to infer or discover descriptive, low-order laws.   Theory comes into play for the physicist when he attempts to formulate more abstract principles which will bring these low-order laws into relationship with one another.   Examples of such comprehensive theories are Newton's principle of gravitation and the kinetic theory of gases.   The former provided a theoretical integration of such laws as Kepler's concerning planetary motions, Galileo's law of falling bodies, laws of the tides and so on.   The kinetic theory has served to integrate the various laws relating certain properties of gases to other experimental variables.

In the less highly developed areas of knowledge, such as the behavior and social sciences, theory plays a somewhat different role.   In these more complex fields the simplest experimental situation that can be arranged usually involves such a large number of variables that it is extremely difficult, if not impossible, to discover directly the empirical laws relating them.   Theories are brought into play in such circumstances as a device to aid in the formulation of the laws.   They consist primarily in the introduction or postulation of hypothetical constructs which help to bridge gaps between the experimental variables.   Examples of such theoretical constructs are legion in psychology, *e.g.,* Tolman's "demand," Hull's "excitatory potential," Lewin's "tension system," and a host of other mentalistic and neurophysiologically-sounding concepts.   It is the purpose of this paper to examine the attempts of psychologists to discover general laws of behavior, particularly the auxiliary theoretical devices they have employed in doing so.

II. Theoretical Constructs in Psychology

Like every other scientist, the psychologist is interested in establishing the interrelations within a set of experimental variables, *i.e.,* in discovering empirical laws.   At the present stage of development the variables (measurements) studied by the psychologist and between which he is attempting to find functional relations appear to fall into two main groups:

(1) *R*-variables: measurements of the behavior of organisms; attributes of simple response patterns (actones), complex achieve-

ments (actions) and generalized response characteristics (traits, abilities, etc.).   These are sometimes referred to as the dependent variables.

(2) S-variables: measurements of physical and social environmental factors and conditions (present and past) under which the responses of organisms occur.   These are sometimes referred to as the independent, manipulable variables.

While not all laws are quantitative, science typically strives to quantify its constructs and to state their interrelations in terms of numerical laws.   The numerical laws the psychologist seeks may be represented as follows:

$$R = f(S).$$

The problem here is two-fold: (1) to discover what the relevant S variables are, and (2) to ascertain the nature of the functional relations holding between the two groups of variables.

In general, two radically opposed positions have been taken by scientists, including psychologists, as to the best procedure to follow in solving this problem.   On the one hand are those who propose the introduction of theoretical constructs as described above.   On the other there are the more empirically minded persons who attempt to refrain from the use of such inferred constructs and try to confine themselves entirely to observable data.   An excellent defense of this latter viewpoint, along with a constructive proposal as to how such an approach can hope to discover general quantitative laws in psychology, is contained in the recent presidential address of Woodrow to the American Psychological Association (23).   We shall leave consideration of the method proposed by Woodrow until later; certain criticisms he offers of the theoretical approach provide an excellent introduction to this method of discovering laws.

Beginning with the conception, more or less the same as that expressed at the start of this paper, that explanation in science consists in nothing more than a statement of established relationships of dependency (for psychology in terms of laws between measurements of environment and behavior) Woodrow goes on to protest that most psychologists seem to have been entirely too interested in postulating intermediate events occurring within the organism to explain the obtained measurements. The difficulty with such speculative constructs, he thinks, is that they cannot be measured because it is not possible to observe the interior of organisms.   The result is that their specification must be left to the imagination.   And as he says:

> . . . our imaginations have not failed us.   The things we have stuck within the organism in the hope thereby of explaining behavior are almost without limit in number and variety.   They include mental sets and cortical sets, traces, residues, synaptic resistances, inhibitory and excitatory substances, inhibitory and excitatory tendencies, determining tendencies, mental attitudes, sentiments, wishes, tensions, field forces, valences, urges, abilities, instincts, and so on and on.   Very popular indeed is the animistic type of explanation (23, p. 3).

While it must be admitted with Woodrow that many of the theoretical constructs employed by psychologists have never been too satisfactorily specified, one must protest the lumping together of all theoretical constructs in such a completely indiscriminate manner.   As a matter of fact, Woodrow has included in his list certain conceptions which were never meant to be explanatory concepts.   Thus such terms as set, attitude, sentiment, and in some instances drive, are what Carnap (3) has termed *dispositional predicates or concepts,* because they refer to the disposition of an object to a certain behavior under certain conditions.   They usually serve as names for events which do not appear in observable experience but instead are introduced into the scientist's language in terms of conditions and results which can be described in terms that refer directly to observable experiences.   Such concepts are prevalent in all fields of science and serve a useful purpose.

Then, again, Woodrow has failed to distinguish in his list between what turn out upon analysis to be very different kinds of theoretical constructs.   While some of them are little better than the animistic notions of primitive man, others have qualified as quite satisfactory in the sense that they have led to the formulation of behavioral laws.   We turn now to the consideration of the different kinds of theories (theoretical constructs) that have been proposed in psychology.

III. Four Types of Theoretical Constructs

Theoretical constructs are introduced, as we have said, in the form of guesses as to what variables other than the ones under control of the experimenter are determining the response. The relation of such inferred constructs (I_a) to the experimental variables, measurements of S and R, is shown in the following figure. Here we have assumed an over-simplified situation for purposes of exposition.

S-variables	I-variables	R-variables
X_1	I_a	R_1

FIG. 1. Intervening variables.

If under environmental conditions X_1 the response measure R_1 is always the same (within the error of measurement) then we have no need of theory. Knowing that condition X_1 existed we could always predict the response. Likewise if, with systematic variation of the X variable, we find a simple functional relation holding between the X values and the corresponding R values we again would have no problem, for we could precisely state the law relating them. But unfortunately things are not usually so simple as this, particularly in psychology. On a second occasion of the presentation of condition X_1, the subject is very likely to exhibit a different magnitude of response, or in the second example there may be no simple curve discernible between the two sets of experimental values. It is at this point that hypothetical constructs are introduced and the response variable is said to be determined, in part by X_1, and in part by some additional factor, or factors, I_a, I_b $\cdots$, i.e., $R = f(X_1, I_a, I_b \cdots)$. The manner in which these theoretical constructs have been defined by different psychologists permits a grouping of them into four categories: (1) animistic-like theories in which the relations of the construct to the empirical variables are left entirely unspecified, (2) neurophysiological theories, (3) theories involving constructs defined primarily in terms of the R variables and (4) theories involving constructs intervening between the S and R variables.

1. *Animistic conceptions.*

Little need be said about such instances of psychological speculation. They are included here merely for the purpose of completing the record. The invoking of such general concepts as the "soul," "mind," "élan vital," "entelechy," "idea," "libido," not to mention many more specific instances (*e.g.*, insight, instinct [2]) in order to account for the apparent capriciousness of the behavior of organisms has been all too prevalent in psychology. When not safe from disproof by reason of the fact that their locus is usually specified to be in some region within the organism unaccessible to observation, these concepts are rendered invulnerable by failure to specify what relations they might have either to the S or R variables. While such vagueness renders them unverifiable, it does insure them a vigorous and long career among certain types of thinkers. Needless to say, such vague conceptions receive little attention today among scientific-minded psychologists.

2. *Neurophysiological theories.*

The extent to which neurophysiological concepts, defined in terms of the operations and instruments of the neurophysiologist, are employed in psychological theorizing is not nearly so great as is sometimes thought. As a matter of fact, if we employ such variables to help us out in our formulation of behavior laws we are not, strictly speaking, theorizing for such concepts are not hypothetical, but are empirically defined. In such instances we have stated a law interrelating environmental, organic and behavioral variables. As yet we do not have very many such laws, except in the case of the simplest kinds of behavior (sensory responses, reflexes, etc.).

There are, of course, many theoretical constructs in psychology which are supposed to represent hypothetical neurophysiological processes, but whose properties are defined either in terms of the response variables (type 3 theory), in terms of environmental factors and the response variables (type 4 theory), or just assumed to be operating without making any specification

---

[2] Such terms, of course, when used as dispositional predicates serve the useful function of providing a name for the phenomenon.

of their relations to either the environmental or response variables (type 1 theory). Examples of these are Köhler's construct of brain field (*12*) to explain perceptual and memory phenomena (type 3), Pavlov's constructs (*16*) of excitatory and inhibitory states (type 4), and certain neural trace theories of learning (type 1).

It will be seen that this category really cuts across the other three. Further consideration of some of these theories will be given in our discussion of the final two classes of theory.

3. *Response inferred theoretical constructs.*

The fact that the behavior of organisms varies even though the objective environmental condition remains unchanged has led some psychologists to assert that the laws of such behavior cannot be formulated in terms of objective environmental variables even though additional hypothetical constructs are employed to bolster the effort. These writers have insisted that behavior must be accounted for in terms of the psychological situation. Thus Lewin (*13*) in his book *Dynamic Theory of Personality* refers to what he describes as the complete failure of such German writers as Loeb, Bethe and other objectivists to develop an adequate theoretical interpretation of behavior in terms of the objective situation, *i.e.,* the physical situation as described by the operations of measurement of the physicist and/or the objective social situation as described by the sociologist. It is always necessary, he insists, to describe the situation as the subject sees or perceives it, *i.e.,* in terms of what it means to him. Typical quotations from Lewin's writings indicate the positive tone taken by such writers:

For the investigation of dynamic problems we are forced to start from the psychologically real environment of the child (*13,* p. 74). Of course, in the description of the child's psychological environment one may not take as a basis the immediately objective social forces and relations as the sociologist or jurist, for example, would list them. One must rather describe the social facts as they affect the particular individual concerned (*13,* p. 75).

One of the basic characteristics of field theory in psychology, as I see it, is the demand that the field which influences an individual should be described not in "objective physicalistic" terms, but in the way in which it exists for that person at that time (*15,* p. 217).

As Lewin implies in the last quoted excerpt it would seem that this type of "psychological" approach to the theoretical constructs of psychology is characteristic of the self-styled field theorists or Gestalt psychologists. Thus Koffka (*10*) makes use of the construct of "behavioral environment" and the more inclusive construct of "psychophysical field" which includes the former and the physiological field, while Köhler (*11, 12*) refers to "phenomenal field" and to "brain field." Koffka and Köhler differ slightly from Lewin in that they introduce a physiological terminology in the description of the properties of some of their behavior-determining fields whereas Lewin does not. The methods of determining the structure and properties of these fields whether "brain field," "behavioral environment" or "life space" are, however, essentially the same, and as we shall see later, involve extensive use of the phenomenological type of introspection.

S-variables   I-variables   R-variables

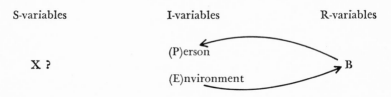

X ?

(P)erson

(E)nvironment

B

FIG. 2.   Lewin's theoretical constructs.

The nature of this type of theorizing may be made clearer by attempting to show how it fits into the schema we have already employed. Figure 2 makes use of the constructs of Lewin, who has been the most articulate of this group of writers so far as the exposition of the formal nature of his theorizing is concerned. Lewin employs the concept of life space to represent the totality of facts which determine the behavior (B) of an individual at a certain moment. The life space includes two groups of constructs, the person (P) and the psychological environment (E). Use is then made of certain concepts from geometry (topology and hodology) and dynamics to represent the existing relationships.[3] By means of what Lewin calls co-

---

[3] There is considerable reason to doubt whether Lewin does much more than take over the terms of topology, making little if any use of the postulates (im-

ordinating definitions these constructs are said to be related to empirical concepts.

Without going into detail, Figure 2 reveals an interesting fact.   It is that little, if any, use is made of the S-variables in Lewin's theorizing.[4]   The question immediately arises then as to what kinds of laws, if any, does Lewin arrive at.   The functional relationship which frequently appears in his writings, $B = f(P, E)$, is obviously not a law of the type that psychologists were said to be interested in, *i.e.*, $R = f(S)$.   But if it is not this kind of a law, what kind is it?   Some writers have implied that Lewin really does not attain any laws at all.   They call attention to the fact that laws are statements of relations between *independently defined variables* and they ask what are the two sets of independent variables in Lewin's formula.

The answer to this question is not easy, and the writer is of the opinion that it has not been met in all instances of field theory.   However, an examination of the methods employed by Lewin and his students in determining the structure and properties of their fields reveals that they depend heavily upon the phenomenological introspections of their subjects or themselves.   If we now think of these as a kind of verbal response or "perceptual" response, in which the subject tries to describe his own particular way of perceiving the objective situation, we see that Lewin's theory really does provide us with laws mediat-

plicit definitions) of this formal system. Koch, after making a very thorough analysis of Lewin's formulations, states that Lewin "finds it expedient to abstract from the postulates (of topology) the properties with which they implicitly endow the constructs, instead of fully stating the postulates" (*9*, p. 148). In this sense, then, it may be said that Lewin employs very fragmentary parts of sub-systems of topology. As for the formal system of dynamics it remains thus far closeted, to use Koch's happy description, in Lewin's mind. Like so many of these field theorists, Lewin sets up a most attractive program for theory. Taken in conjunction with his interesting experiments the illusion is nicely created that there is some connection between them.

[4] Lewin states that the objective physical and social surroundings "have a relation to the life space similar to that which 'boundary conditions' have to a dynamic system" (*15*, p. 217). He believes that physicalistic behaviorism has made the mistake of treating such variables as if they were parts of the life space. Attention should be called here to the fact that Koffka concerned himself much more extensively with the objective environmental variables or the geographic environment as he called it. He discussed at some length the relations between the geographic and the behavioral environments—the traditional problem of perception (*10*).

ing between independent variables, *i.e.*, between two different responses of the subject, or as in some cases, between the experimenter's own perceptual responses and the subjects' subsequent response.   Thus Lewin discovers what amount to laws of the following type: $R_1 = f(R_2)$.

Of course, such theorists do not always rely on such phenomenological introspections.   Once certain laws of the above type have been formulated it is possible to formulate further laws between purely overt behavior items, neither of which are of this introspective, verbal type.   There are also instances in which from the pattern of the observed response the theorist makes an inference as to the nature of the hypothetical field; and then by means of his postulates as to what happens in these fields he is able to make certain predictions as to subsequent behavior.   An excellent example of the latter is Köhler's theoretical treatment (*12*) of perceptual problems involving reversible figures and the effects of prolonged inspection in certain types of simple perceptual situations.   Thus in the light of perceptual behavior to reversible figures, he formulated the hypothesis that percept processes are associated with fields of electric currents in the nervous system.   Then by means of postulates based on knowledge about electrolytical conduction he was able to predict other perceptual behavior.

By and large, however, the field theorist depends heavily upon phenomenological introspection in introducing his theoretical constructs.   In order to understand the field of the subject he asks him to describe how he perceives the situation, or he infers it on the basis of his own introspections.   With engaging frankness Snygg has made an appeal for the recognition of the important role that phenomenological introspection plays in these theories.[5]   Thus he writes in connection with the problem of prediction:

By postulate *B* the determining locus of action is the behaver's p.f. [phenomenological field].   This is not open to direct observation by an outside observer.   The process of prediction therefore involves two steps: (1) the

[5] Snygg also admits another obvious characteristic of such theoretical systems which some of its proponents have not always willingly acknowledged.   Reference is made here to the fact that such systems are anthropomorphic.

securing of an understanding of the subject's field by inference or reconstruction, (2) the projection of the future field.

The first operation is of the common "Now why did he do that?" or
"Under what circumstances would I have done that" character. Much of
the topological work of Lewin is of this type and essentially the same procedure was used by Shepard when from the behavior of his rate he inferred
the existence of floor cues which he himself was unable to experience (17,
p. 413).

That this field approach to the problems of psychology has
been fruitful and valuable is amply supported by the experimental contributions it has made, although in the writer's
opinion, the theoretical superstructure has played a much less
significant role than is sometimes credited to it.   Furthermore,
the phenomenological approach has its advantages, particularly
in the complex field of social behavior of the human adult.   It
is obviously much easier to gain some notion as to the relevant
variables determining such complex behavior by asking the
individual to verbalize than it is to employ the procedure of
trying to hypothesize them from knowledge of past history.
Usually the latter is not available in sufficient completeness to
make it even worthwhile to try to theorize as to the nature of
such historical laws.[6]

A final point of no little importance is the failure of such field
theories to provide us with laws which will enable us to control
and manipulate the behavior-determining psychological field.
Such laws are obviously a basic prerequisite to successful clinical
therapy.   While it may be true, as Snygg claims (17), that psychiatrists and teachers find the phenomenological approach most
valuable in diagnosing behavior disorders, it is difficult to understand how the response-response laws it provides can be of
much use in guiding therapeutic treatment.   The latter requires a knowledge of what to do to the individual, what changes
in his physical and social environment to arrange, in order to
bring about the desired behavior changes.   The laws telling us
how to proceed in such matters are historical laws and involve
as an important component of them objective variables repre-

[6] The situation in the case of animal behavior is somewhat different. Here
one usually does have a pretty good record of the past history relevant to the
present environmental situation.

sentative of past and present factors in the physical and social environments. Psychiatrists and clinical psychologists who employed a purely phenomenological approach might or might not be successful at diagnosis; it is difficult to see how they could ever prescribe satisfactory reëducative procedures.[7]

4. Theoretical constructs as intervening variables between S and R variables.

In sharp contrast to these response inferred theories with their emphasis upon the phenomenological approach is the point of view that theoretical constructs in psychology are to be regarded as "intervening variables" which bring into relation with one another the dependent R variables on the one hand and the independent S variables on the other. As Bergmann and Spence (2) have previously pointed out, two psychologists in particular, Hull and Tolman, have advocated, each in his own individual way, this type of psychological theory. In a little known paper Tolman (22) has presented an excellent account of such a theoretical program, while in his book *Principles of Behavior* Hull (7) has demonstrated in actual practice how such intervening variables provide us with a formulation of the basic principles or laws governing simple learning behavior. The following discussion makes no attempt to give a systematic account of this theoretical procedure. Instead we shall merely outline very sketchily its main features and then single out one or two aspects of it for more detailed examination.

According to Hull and Tolman, theoretical constructs, or intervening variables have to be introduced into psychology either

---

[7] Bergmann has summed up this difficulty most succinctly in the form of the following questions:—"But even so, what is the predictive value of the suggestive metaphor 'psychological environment'? Is it not the business of science to ascertain which objective factors in the past and present states of the organism and its environment account for the difference in response, so that we can actually predict it instead of attributing it, merely descriptively and after it has happened, to a difference in the psychological environment?" (1).

Mention should perhaps be made here of the fact that the theoretical constructs (factors) that Spearman (18), Thurstone (20), and other factor analysts arrive at are response derived and hence fall into this class. These men do not, of course, use the phenomenological method, but beginning with response intercorrelations (empirical $R - R$ relations) they arrive at hypothetical factors by various methods of mathematical analysis. Like the phenomenologists their theoretical factors have no tie-up with the S variables.

when we do not know all the important variables entering into a set of experimental events, or the precise nature of the inter-relating function is not known.   Consider, for example, the data obtained from conditioning experiments.   These investigations have presented us with a wealth of data showing how the response variable changes or varies with the manipulation of certain other experimental variables.   That is to say, various measurable aspects of response are studied as functions of the manipulable environmental variables and the data so obtained are plotted in the form of various curves.

The task of the psychologist here is to discover the precise nature of the interrelations holding within this set of variables. Instead of knowing merely that the response, R, is some function of the variables X_1, X_2, X_3, $\cdots$ X_n, he desires to know the precise function.   But in such a situation, involving as it does a large number of variables, the function relating the dependent and independent variables is so complicated that we are unable to conceive of it directly.   It is necessary, say Hull and Tolman, to proceed by conceiving of it as broken down into successive sets of simpler component functions.   These component functions begin by introducing new intervening constructs defined in terms of the independent variables.   Further intervening variables are then introduced by stating them as functions of the first set of intervening constructs, until finally the dependent behavior variable is postulated to be a function of one or more of the intervening variables.

Thus Tolman, beginning with the empirical data that the response measure is some function (f_1) of two groups of independent variables (environmental variables and individual difference variables), writes:

In place of the original f_1 function, I have introduced a set of intervening variables, I_a, I_b, I_c, etc., few or many, according to the particular theory. And I have conceived a set of f_2 functions to connect these intervening variables severally to the independent variables on the one hand, and an f_3 function to combine them together and connect them to the final dependent variable on the other (*21*, p. 9).

It is characteristic of Tolman's theorizing, however, that it never gets beyond the programmatic stage.   In his writings

Tolman has merely shown how such a theoretical device as the "intervening variable" can provide for the definition and proper utilization within psychology of such mentalistic terms as "demands," "hypotheses," "traits," "discriminanda," etc., but he never actually reaches the point of formulating a specific theory. In the present context this would, of course, require the precise specification of the various functions relating the intervening variables to the independent and dependent experimental variables.   Instead of risking guesses on such matters, however, Tolman seems to prefer to ascertain them empirically by a series of what he calls "standard experimental set-ups."   He believes the data from these studies will mirror the functions obtaining between the experimental (empirical) and intervening (theoretical) variables.[8]

Quite in contrast to such an approach, Hull has ventured to make guesses as to the precise nature of the functions introducing the intervening variables in his theoretical formulations. Thus he has attempted to formulate the basic laws of simple adaptive behavior (learning) by introducing a number of intervening variables.[9]   Beginning with the experimental variables, he has introduced by means of specific mathematical functions such symbolic constructs as stimulus trace (s), habit strength $(_sH_R)$, the limit of habit strength (M), excitatory potential $(_sE_R)$, inhibitory potential (I_R), effective excitatory potential $(_s\bar{E}_R)$, and so on.   Ultimately the observable response variable, R, is stated to be some function of the final intervening variable (e.g., $R = f(_s\bar{E}_R)$).   Despite the neurophysiological tone of some of the terms that Hull employs to designate these constructs, the mistake should not be made of interpreting them as physiologi-

[8] Tolman has been accused (and he has usually made no denial) of employing the phenomenological method in his psychology, and, because he has worked with animals, of being guilty of anthropomorphism.   The present writer's interpretation is that it is Tolman, the experimentalist, who uses phenomenological introspection; Tolman, the theorist, introduces his intervening variables in terms of objectively defined variables.   The difference between Lewin and Tolman on this point is interesting.   Lewin, as we have seen, employs the phenomenological method primarily in his theoretical efforts, whereas Tolman uses it chiefly in the formulation of experimental problems.

[9] Reference is made here to Hull's latest writings in which the "intervening variable" technique is made more explicit.   As Bergmann and Spence (2) have pointed out, Hull's earlier miniature systems (5, 8) really involved the definition of such mediating constructs.

cal concepts. Their scientific meaning is given only by the equations introducing them, and in this respect they are strictly comparable to many similar, abstract, mathematical constructs employed by the physicist in his theorizing. The use of neuro-physiological terms and such additional statements as Hull sometimes makes as to their possible locus in the nervous system merely serve the purpose of providing experimental hints to persons interested in such matters. It may or may not turn out that they represent actual neurophysiological states or conditions that will some day be measurable by independent neuro-physiological procedures.

An example of the specific manner in which Hull introduces his theoretical constructs is shown by the equations which he employs to define the two constructs, habit strength ($_sH_R$) and the limit of habit strength (M). With all experimental variables except the number of reinforced trials (N) and the length of the delay of the goal reinforcement (L) constant, the two equations are:

$$_sH_R = M(1 - e^{-iN})$$
$$M = 100e^{-kL}.$$

Grice (4) has recently shown how such precisely defined theoretical constructs may be tested. He employed several mazes of different absolute lengths involving a shorter and longer path to the goal and ran different groups of rats on each maze. On the basis of the above two equations the following rational equation was then derived mathematically to describe the rate of learning the mazes:

$$\left[N = b \, \log \left(\frac{e^{-kL} - e^{-kHL}}{e^{-kL} - e^{-kHL} - a} \right) \right].$$

Where N = number of pairs of trials on the two paths to learn the maze.
  L = length of short path to goal.
  H = ratio of long to short path length.
  k, a, b = empirical constants.

This rational equation was then shown to fit the experimental data, whereas another equation

$$\left[N \;=\; b \ \log \left(\frac{\operatorname{Log} H}{\log H - C} \right) \right]$$

derived from a logarithmic postulate [10] as to the relation of M to L was shown not to be in agreement with the experimental data.

One really does not have a scientific theory, until constructs are introduced in some such precise fashion as Hull employs, for it is only under such conditions that the possibility of verification or refutation exists. Unfortunately, much of what has passed for theory in psychology has been sadly lacking in this respect, a state of affairs which is largely responsible for many of the "theoretical" controversies, and for the low regard in which theory is held in some quarters in psychology. That theory construction has not always been intelligently pursued, however, is no reason for doing without theory. Without the generalizations which theories aim to provide we should never be in a position to predict behavior, for knowledge of particular events does not provide us with a basis for prediction when the situation differs in the least degree. The higher the level of abstraction that can be obtained the greater will be both the understanding and actual control achieved.

IV. The Ultra-Positivistic Approach

All the methods of ascertaining the laws of psychology we have discussed so far have agreed, in principle at least, that it is necessary to introduce some type of symbolic construct. It is also apparent that agreement ceases as regards the extent to which the proponents of these different views have insisted on rigorous and objective specification. We turn now to a quite different approach to the same problem—that of the ultra-positivist or empiricist, who tries to eschew all types of theoretical constructs. Usually the writings of such persons are

[10] $M = 100 - K \log L.$

limited to negativistic, critical attacks on all theory. Recently, however, Woodrow has come forward with a constructive proposal as to how general mathematical laws of psychology may be discovered by a method which he believes avoids the necessity of introducing theoretical constructs.

Woodrow's method consists in an attempt to obtain by mathematical curve fitting a general equation describing a wide variety of experimental facts. Thus, after plotting a series of experimental curves of such widely varying situations as learning to abstract, learning to associate numbers and letters, learning a maze, reaction time to different intensities of stimulation, the forgetting of monosyllabic words, brightness and pitch discrimination, the growth of intelligence, etc., Woodrow sought to fit these empirical curves by means of a single general equation. He found that such an equation could be found and that it took the following form:

$$Y = a + \sqrt{p^2 + k^2(1 - f^{X+d})^2}.$$

This equation states a law between two experimental variables, a dependent response variable Y, e.g., errors, successes, latencies, etc., and an independent manipulable variable X, e.g., number of practice periods, intensity of the stimulus, preparatory interval, etc. But it will be noticed further that the law includes more than these two variables. It also involves certain constants or unknowns, termed parameters, the a, p, k, f, and d in the equation. We cannot stop to discuss these parameters in too great detail here. Suffice it to say that the specific shapes of the different empirical curves determine what parameters it is necessary to assume. Two of them, a and b, have no particular psychological significance, they merely express the fact that either one or both variables may have been measured by scales with an arbitrary zero. The parameter, k, is introduced because all his curves exhibit a limit to improvement, no matter how favorable the status given the environmental variable. Another parameter, f, is determined by the rate of approach of the curve to this limit and p, finally, is introduced to take care of the fact that the lower part of the curve sometimes shows positive acceleration.

As Woodrow himself points out, these parameters may be thought of, if one so wishes, as representing hypothetical states or factors within the organism.[11] Woodrow prefers not to do so, for as he argues, it really makes little difference what the internal referents are since they cannot at present be independently measured anyway. From the point of view of finding a general equation or law that will fit the experimental data the important thing, Woodrow states, is to determine how many parameters are required and the mathematical function of each.

While in general sympathy with Woodrow's mathematical approach and his view that it is unnecessary to specify the factors or complexes of factors inside the organism which determine the values of the parameters, the writer is, nevertheless, of the opinion that such an equation as Woodrow obtains by his analysis is, on the whole, rather barren and sterile. Its defect is not that the factors *within* the subject are not specified, but rather that it fails to give any indication whatever of the conditions or variables even *outside* the subject which determine these parameters. In this respect Woodrow's approach is similar to the field theorists'. We shall have occasion later to point out other resemblances between these two approaches.

This criticism can be made clearer, perhaps, by contrasting the end result of Woodrow's empirical procedure with Hull's rational approach to the same problem. Woodrow's law specifies but a single experimental variable determining the response:

$$Y = f(X_1).$$

Hull's theorizing culminates in a much more comprehensive law. Thus in the case of his theoretical formulation of simple adaptive behavior (learning) his derivation involves the following series of steps:

[11] Woodrow writes, "Now these parameters may refer to anything whatsoever, conscious, physiological, environmental, psychic, or purely imaginary. Here one is free to follow his predilections, whether for motives, excitatory and inhibitory substances, field forces, states of disequilibrium, inertia of the nervous system, abilities, or what not" (*23*, p. 4).

$$(1) \quad \boxed{M} = f(T, G)$$
$$(2) \quad \boxed{H} = f(\boxed{M}, T', N)$$
$$(3) \quad \boxed{D} = f(T'')$$
$$(4) \quad \boxed{E} = f(\boxed{D}, \boxed{H})$$
$$(5) \quad \boxed{I} = f(N, W, F)$$
$$(6) \quad \boxed{E} = f(\boxed{E}, \boxed{I})$$
$$(7) \quad R = f(\boxed{E}).$$

Here the squared symbols are intervening variables or hypothetical constructs. The other symbols represent the dependent response measure (R) and the various manipulable, environmental variables $(T, G, T',$ etc.). By substituting in the successive equations, a single equation stating R as a function of seven environmental variables is obtained.[12]

$$R = f(T, G, T', N, T'', W, F)$$

The latter procedure thus comes much closer to achieving the goal of the scientist, that of discovering all of the experimental variables determining the response measure and the nature of the functional interrelations holding between them. If this is achieved, the parameters become known functions of these experimental variables and thus become experimentally manipulable. Woodrow's formulation, on the other hand, provides us with very little more information than we had when we started.

It is also interesting to note that a strong case can be made out for the position that Woodrow's method is really not a great deal different from those theoretical approaches which infer

[12] The reader may ask, "Why have a series of equations that introduce intervening variables? Why not write the single equation from the beginning and avoid the hypothetical constructs?" One obvious reason, of course, is that it is just not possible to conceive of such a complex function all at once. As Tolman says, one can arrive at it only by breaking it down into a series of simpler functions. The reader is referred to a recent article by Hull in which he gives other reasons for using intervening variables with multiple equations rather than a single equation (6).

their constructs from the characteristics of the response.   In introducing his parameters Woodrow is, in effect, assuming or postulating some kind of hypothetical factor.   Thus, on noticing that some of his curves show an initial period of positive acceleration, Woodrow assumes a factor, p, "whose influence is greatest when the magnitude of the environmental variable is small" (23, p. 7).   This factor is inferred, we see, from the characteristics of the response curve and is therefore in a certain sense akin to the hypothetical constructs of the field theorists which, as we have seen, are also inferred from the response characteristics.   The important difference is that in arriving at these hypothetical factors Woodrow does not make use of the introspective report associated with a response but rather bases his constructs on the mathematical properties of a curve of successive response measures.

V. Conclusions

In summary, the present paper has stated the task of the psychologist to be that of discovering the general laws of behavior, and has attempted to present a brief and critical outline of five different methods of approaching this task.   The conclusions that the writer believes may be drawn from this survey are:

1. That theory is still at a very primitive level in psychology, concerning itself primarily with the discovery of low-order laws rather than the integration of different realms of laws.

2. That there is a variety of different theoretical procedures possible in psychology.

3. That some psychologists substitute, often quite unconsciously, phenomenological introspection and anthropomorphic thinking for theorizing.   There is, of course, nothing wrong with such introspection; it has often served as a means of formulating interesting and valuable experiments.   In such instances, however, the credit should not be given to a theory.

4. That many theories in psychology have provided us with response-response (R-R) laws rather than stimulus-response (S-R) laws.

5. That the most promising theoretical technique, especially from the point of view of discovering the historical stimulus-

response laws, is the so-called "intervening variable" method proposed by Hull and Tolman.

REFERENCES

1. BERGMANN, G. Psychoanalysis and experimental psychology: A review from the standpoint of scientific empiricism. *Mind,* 1943, *52,* 122–140.

2. ——, & SPENCE, K. W. Operationism and theory in psychology. *Psychol. Rev.,* 1941, *48,* 1–14.

3. CARNAP, R. Testability and meaning. *Philos. Sci.,* 1936, *3,* 419–471; 1937, *4,* 1–40.

4. GRICE, G. R. An experimental study of the gradient of reinforcement in maze learning. *J. exp. Psychol.,* 1942, *30,* 475–489.

5. HULL, C. L. Mind, mechanism and adaptive behavior. *Psychol. Rev.,* 1937, *44,* 1–32.

6. ——. The problem of intervening variables in molar behavior theory. *Psychol. Rev.,* 1943, *50,* 273–291.

7. ——. *Principles of Behavior.* New York: D. Appleton-Century Co., 1943.

8. ——, HOVLAND, C. I., ROSS, R. T., HALL, M., PERKINS, D. T., & FITCH, F. B. *Mathematico-deductive Theory of Rote Learning.* New Haven: Yale University Press, 1940.

9. KOCH, S. The logical character of the motivation concept. II. *Psychol. Rev.,* 1941, *48,* 127–154.

10. KOFFKA, K. *Principles of Gestalt Psychology.* New York: Harcourt, Brace & Co., 1935.

11. KÖHLER, W. *Gestalt Psychology.* New York: Liveright Publishing Corp., 1929.

12. ——. *Dynamics in Psychology.* New York: Liveright Publishing Corp., 1940.

13. LEWIN, K. *A Dynamic Theory of Personality.* (Trans. by D. K. Adams and K. E. Zener) New York: McGraw-Hill Book Co., 1935.

14. ——. *Principles of Topological Psychology.* (Trans. by Fritz and Grace Heider.) New York: McGraw-Hill Book Co., 1936.

15. ——. Field theory and learning, pp. 215–242. In *Forty-First Yearbook National Society for the Study of Education,* Part II. Bloomington, Illinois. Public School Publishing Co., 1942.

16. PAVLOV, I. P. *Conditioned Reflexes: an Investigation of the Physiological Activity of the Cerebral Cortex.* (Trans. and ed. by F. C. Anrep.) London: Oxford University Press, 1927.

17. SNYGG, D. The need for a phenomenological system of psychology. *Psychol. Rev.,* 1941, *48,* 404–424.

18. SPEARMAN, C. *The Abilities of Man.* New York: The Macmillan Company, 1927.

19. SPENCE, K. W. Theoretical interpretations of learning. In *Comparative Psychology,* rev. ed. (F. A. Moss, ed.), Englewood Cliffs, N. J.: Prentice-Hall, Inc., 1942, Chap. II.

20. THURSTONE, L. L. *The Vectors of Mind.* Chicago: University Chicago Press, 1935.

21. TOLMAN, E. C. The determiners of behavior at a choice point. *Psychol. Rev.,* 1938, *45,* 1–41.

22. ——. Operational behaviorism and current trends in psychology. *Proc. 25th Anniv. Celebration Inaug. Grad. Stud.* Los Angeles: The University of Southern California, 1936, pp. 80–103.

23. WOODROW, H. The problem of general quantitative laws in psychology. *Psychol. Bull.,* 1942, *39,* 1–27.

3

The Postulates and Methods of "Behaviorism" [1]

There was a time when the term "behaviorism" in the title of a speech required no further specification. Every psychologist at least knew the referent to be that new brand of psychology, introduced by Watson, which proposed to break with tradition and deny that psychology had anything to do with either a mentalistic entity called consciousness or a method known as introspection. Today the situation is not so simple. The term "behaviorism" may, on the one hand, merely imply a very general point of view which has come to be accepted by almost all psychologists and thus does not point to any particular group or theoretical position. Or, on the other hand, it may refer to any one of several varieties of behaviorism which have been offered as supplementations or modifications of the original formulation of Watson (*e.g.,* molecular behaviorism, molar behaviorism, operational behaviorism, purposive behaviorism, logical behaviorism—to mention only some of the varieties). While these current formulations usually acknowledge some debt to Watson, for various reasons which we cannot stop to discuss they almost invariably take great pains to differentiate themselves from what has come to be known as "Watsonian

[1] This article was an address given at the Symposium on "The Postulates and Methods of Gestalt Psychology, Behaviorism and Psychoanalysis" given at the Conference on Methods in Philosophy and the Sciences in New York City, November, 1946. Some minor changes have been made in the paper itself and a list of references has been added.

Behaviorism" or "Watsonianism." In fact, so far as I know, there are no proponents today of the original Watsonian version. Proper care should be taken to note, however, that this statement holds true only for the particular pattern of assumptions that Watson advanced. Many of the basic postulates of his formulation are to be found in the present-day varieties of behaviorism and, what is more important, probably, in the underlying working assumptions of the great majority of present-day American psychologists.

Now that I have taken the precaution to differentiate the behaviorisms of today from the original version of behaviorism, I should like to call attention to the further interesting fact that—with the possible exception of Tolman—very few, if any, current psychologists ever seem to think of themselves, or at least explicitly refer to themselves, as behaviorists. Such labeling, when it occurs, is usually the contribution of psychologists who consider themselves opposed to behaviorism. Undoubtedly, one of the reasons underlying this absence or lack of "old-school-tie" spirit is that a large majority of present-day American psychologists just take for granted many of the behavioristic assumptions and, occupied as they have been with the details of developing and applying their specific research tools, they have had little time or inclination to give much thought to the more general methodological and systematic problems of their science.

Even the more theoretical-minded of the behavioristically-oriented psychologists seem to have been too preoccupied with matters of detail to get around to the consideration of a more general theoretical framework. Instead of attempting to formulate a complete system of psychology, these theorists have been more concerned with the elaboration of relatively specific hypotheses concerning rather limited realms of data—*e.g.*, theories of simple learning phenomena, motivational theories, theories of personality development, etc. As a consequence we find that instead of being built up around the symbol "behaviorism," allegiances tend to become attached to such labels as associationism, conditioning, reinforcement theory, frustration hypothesis, etc. It seems, in other words, that these psychologists have outgrown the stage of schools.

Under these circumstances, I cannot and I shall not undertake to present a fixed set of articles of faith, articulately and self-consciously held by a group of men calling themselves behaviorists. Instead, I shall attempt to formulate a few methodological principles that are, I believe, exemplified in the work of certain contemporary psychologists who would undoubtedly acknowledge a heavy historical debt to that earlier formulation known as the school of behaviorism.

The first problem that I shall discuss has to do with the behavior scientist's conception of the nature of psychological events.   In the older, classical psychologies, whether of the structural or act varieties, the point of view taken was that psychology, if it was a natural science, was, to say the least, a somewhat unique one.   Instead of being conceived like physics, for example, as concerning itself with events mediated by or occurring in the consciousness or immediate experience of the observing scientist, psychology was said to be concerned with observing and analyzing, by a kind of inner sense, immediate experience *per se*. Sensations, emotions, thoughts were regarded as observable aspects of direct experience rather than systematic constructs which, like the physicist's atoms and electrons, were inferred from immediate experience.

Fortunately, the relationship of immediate experience (consciousness) to the data and constructs of science has been considerably clarified in recent years by the writings of several different groups of thinkers.   The philosophers of science, particularly the logical positivists (1, 5, 6, 7), philosophically-minded scientists such as Bridgman (3) and within psychology, such writers as Boring (2), Pratt (15), and Stevens (18) have succeeded, I believe, in making the point that the data of all sciences have the same origin—namely, the immediate experience of an observing person, the scientist himself.   That is to say, immediate experience, the initial matrix out of which all sciences develop, is no longer considered a matter of concern for the scientist qua scientist.   He simply takes it for granted and then proceeds to his task of describing the events occurring in it and discovering and formulating the nature of the relationships holding among them.

Boring stated this matter very clearly for psychologists in his book of some years ago, *The Physical Dimensions of Consciousness.* He wrote:

Thus the events of physics, as Wundt said, are mediate to experience, which stands in the background as the dator of scientific data, unrealizable as reality except inductively. In the same way psychology must deal with existential reals which are similarly mediate to experience. There is no way of getting at "direct experience" because experience gives itself up to science indirectly, inferentially, by the experimental method (2, p. 6).

More recently Pratt, in his *Logic of Modern Psychology* (*15*), has hammered home this same point with considerable effectiveness. As he points out, the subject matter of psychology is exactly the same in kind as all other sciences; any differentiation among the sciences is merely a matter of convenience, a division of scientific labor resorted to as the amount of detailed knowledge increases beyond the capacity of a single person's grasp.

I think that it is of some historical interest to note in connection with this point that in the first of his articles introducing the behavioristic position, Watson took essentially the same stand. He wrote:

It [psychology] can dispense with consciousness in a psychological sense. The separate observation of "states of consciousness" is, on this assumption, no more a part of the task of the psychologist than of the physicist. We might call this the return to a non-reflective and naive use of consciousness. In this sense consciousness may be said to be the instrument or tool with which all scientists work (*21*, p. 176).

Acknowledging, then, that the psychologist conceives his task as that of bringing order and meaning into the realm of certain events provided by immediate experience, we now turn to the question of what these particular observed events are. In attempting to answer this question, attention should first be directed to the fact that the sense events in the experience of the observing scientist may depend upon or result from two different classes of conditions, intra-organic and extra-organic, the former exciting the interoceptors and the latter, the exteroceptors. The physical sciences, it should be noted, moreover, deal only with events of an extra-organic origin—*i.e.,* those received through the exteroceptors. The data of classical psychology, on the other hand, were regarded as involving primarily sense events initiated through the interoceptors. These latter were regarded as being stimulated by such internal mental activities as thinking, desiring, emotional reactions, perceiving, etc., and hence were thought of as providing primary data concerning them.

It is apparent, however, that these internally initiated experiences differ rather markedly from the externally aroused ones in the extent to which they are publicly controllable and communicable. At least, if we can judge from the interminable disagreements of the introspective psychologists themselves, this class of experiences does not meet too well the requirements of social verification and acceptance demanded by the scientist. It was in the face of this difficulty that Watson made his suggestion that the psychologist, like all other scientists, should confine himself to those segments of his experience which have their origin in extra-organic conditions. In other words, the events studied by the psychologist, Watson held, should consist in observations of the overt behavior of *other* organisms, other persons than the observing scientist himself, and not in the observation of the scientist's own internal activities.

As everyone knows, however, most behavior scientists have continued more or less to make use of this latter type of material in the form of the objectively recordable verbal reports of their subjects. Indeed, the scientist himself, in certain circumstances, may assume a dual role and serve as both subject and experimenter. In this event his own introspective report is recorded as a linguistic response and becomes a part of the objective data. To some critics of the behavioristic viewpoint, this acceptance of the verbal reports of their subjects as a part of the data has seemed to represent an abandonment of the strict behavioristic position and a return to the conception that psychology studies *experiential* events as well as overt behavior.

Such a contention, it seems to me, fails to note a very important difference in the two positions. The introspectionist, it should be recalled, assumed a strict one-to-one relationship between the verbal responses of his subjects and the inner mental processes. Accordingly, he accepted these introspective reports as *facts* or *data* about the inner mental events which they represented. The behavior scientist takes a very different position. He accepts verbal response as just one more form of behavior and he proposes to use this type of data in exactly the same manner as he does other types of behavior variables. Thus he attempts to discover laws relating verbal responses to environmental events of the past or present, and he seeks to find what relations they have to other types of response variables. He also makes use of them as a basis for making inferences as to certain hypothetical or theoretical constructs which he employs. In contrast, then, to the introspectionist's conception of these verbal reports as mirroring directly inner mental events, *i.e.*, facts, the behaviorist uses them either as data in their own right to be related to other data, or as a base from which to infer theoretical constructs which presumably represent internal or covert activities of their subjects. We shall return later to the use made of such language responses in the theorizing of the behaviorist.

From this all too cursory discussion of the initial data of the behavioristic psychologist, I should like now to turn to a consideration of the nature of the concepts which he employs to record and describe these events. I do not believe it is necessary for me to discuss at any length the position of the behaviorist with respect to the movement known as operationism. The insistence of the early behaviorists on a thoroughgoing operational analysis of the traditional mentalistic concepts was really nothing more than an anticipation of this somewhat overemphasized program. That a body of empirical knowledge cannot be built up without providing for verifiability of the terms in use is simply taken for granted by the behaviorist. Instead, then, of talking about operational definition of psychological concepts, I should like to discuss certain matters related to a second criterion of acceptability of a scientific concept—namely, its *significance*.

One often hears criticisms to the effect that behavioristic concepts are too elementaristic, too atomistic, or that they fail to portray the real essence or true meaning of man's behavior. These latter critics often complain bitterly about the impoverishment of the mind, and of the lack of warmth and glowing particulars in the behaviorist's picture of psychological events.

Some of these criticisms merely reflect, of course, a lack of appreciation on the part of some "psychologists" as to the difference between scientific knowledge of an event on the one hand and everyday knowledge, or the kind of knowledge the novelist or poet portrays, on the other. Either by reason of training or because of their basically non-scientific interests, these critics have never really understood the abstract character of the scientific account of any phenomenon. The only reply that can be made to such a critic is to point out that the scientist's interests are quite different from his. There are, of course, other legitimate interpretations of nature and man than the scientific one and each has its right to be pursued. The behavior scientist merely asks that he be given the same opportunity to develop a scientific account of his phenomena that his colleagues in the physical and biological fields have had. If there are aspects of human or animal behavior for which such an account cannot ever be developed, there are not, so far as I know, any means of finding this out without a try. Unfortunately, the attitudes of too many psychologists with regard to this matter are not such as are likely to lead them to the discovery of such knowledge. The difficulty, I fear, is that too many persons whose interests are non-scientific have become psychologists under the mistaken impression that psychology is one of the arts.

As to the criticisms that the behaviorist's concepts are too elementaristic, I must confess to the belief that the term "elementarism" is merely one of those stereotypes, or "rally-round-the-flag" words which the Gestalt psychologist has used in the defense and exposition of his holistic doctrines. However fervently the Gestalt psychologist may claim that he deals only with wholes, with total situations, the fact remains that if he is interested in discovering uniformities or scientific laws he must, of necessity, fractionate or abstract out certain features of the total events he observes. Such uniformities or laws describe ways in which events repeat themselves. Total concrete events, however, are seldom if ever repeated. Only certain features of events are repeated and since this is the case science must always abstract.

The problem here is really one of the size of the "units of description" that the scientist is to employ and this brings us back to the criterion of acceptability of a scientific term which we referred to as *significance*. By the *significance* of a scientific concept is here meant the extent to which a concept or variable aids or enters into the formulation of laws. Significant concepts in science are those which are discovered to have functional relations with other concepts. Unfortunately, there are few if any rules for deciding *a priori* which concepts will and which ones will not be significant. Whether elementaristic concepts or units of description which, like the Gestaltists, are nearer the "meaningful" common sense level, are to be chosen is entirely a pragmatic matter of which ones are most successful—*i.e.*, which ones lead to the discovery of laws. This can be ascertained only by trying them out.

Attention might also be called here to the further fact that it is entirely conceivable that different sizes or levels of descriptive units may be employed for the same set of events. The physical sciences provide us with numerous instances of this sort of thing and we see examples of it in psychology both in the description of behavior and stimulus events. Thus, employing the terms of Brunswik (4) and Heider (8), we may make use of either a proximal or distal account of the stimulus situation, and behavior may be described either in terms of movements (muscular patterns) or in terms of gross achievements. The particular alternative chosen, molecular or molar, depends upon the interest and purpose of the scientist, the kind of law he expects to find or use. As Hull (11) has pointed out in discussing this matter, some of the seeming disagreements among current psychologists are merely that one prefers to use more molar concepts than another.

Such different descriptions, however, do not necessarily represent fundamental disagreements. If the two systems of concepts should each be successful in leading to the discovery and formulation of laws, it should also be possible to discover coordinating definitions which will reveal the interrelations of the two systems. Or, as Hull (11) suggests, the postulates or primary assumptions of those working at a more molar level may ultimately appear as theorems in a more molecular description.

To sum up, then, the position which the behavior scientist takes with respect to the selection of the descriptive concepts to be employed in his science, recognizes (a) that the *significance* of a concept is to be measured in terms of the extent to which it leads to the formulation of laws about the phenomena; (b) that a scientific law is always, in some greater or less degree, abstract in the sense that it refers only to certain properties of the events or sequence of events it describes and ignores other properties which are irrelevant to the particular momentary purpose; (c) that the method of elementary abstraction or analysis has been highly successful in all fields of science. While the disentanglement of the great complexes of properties and relations (sequences) among psychological events is undoubtedly much more difficult than in the case of physical phenomena, the difference between them need not be regarded as more than one of degree. On the basis of this assumption there would seem to be little reason for abandoning the method of abstraction or analysis.

We have said that the primary aim of the behavior scientist is to bring order and meaning into the particular realm of events he studies. Ordering a set of observable events for the scientist consists in discovering relationships between the events or, as we say, in the finding of empirical laws. The scientist seeks to establish laws relating his concepts or variables because they make possible explanation and prediction.

In the case of such areas of science as physics, the finding of empirical laws has involved chiefly the process of inductive generalization from observation and experimentation. In other words, in physics it has been possible to isolate sufficiently simple systems of observation to arrive at such laws in this manner. The situation in psychology and the other behavior sciences is quite different. Primarily because of the greater complexity of psychological as compared with physical phenomena, the psychologist has either been unable to isolate, experimentally, simple systems, or he has not found satisfactory means of measuring all of the relevant variables in the system under observation. In this circumstance he has resorted to guesses or postulations as to the uncontrolled or as yet unmeasurable factors. As a result of this difference the term "theory" has, as I have pointed out elsewhere (*17*), come to have a very different connotation in psychology from that which it has in physics.

Theories in physics are constructions which serve primarily to integrate or organize into a single deductive system sets of empirical laws which previously were unrelated. The classical example is, of course, the Newtonian integration of the previously unconnected areas of mechanics and astronomy by the gravitational theory. Other well-known examples are the electro-magnetic theory of light and the kinetic theory of gases.

In psychology, on the other hand, theories serve primarily as a device to aid in the formulation of the empirical laws. They consist in guesses as to how the uncontrolled or unknown factors in the system under study are related to the experimentally-known variables. To these hypothetical constructs Tolman (20) has applied the very appropriate term "intervening variable" because they are assumed to intervene between the measurable environmental and organic variables, on the one hand, and the measurable behavior properties on the other.

The manner in which the behavior scientist has used these hypothetical, intervening constructs may be shown by considering the various kinds of laws which the psychologist seeks to discover. Confining ourselves for the moment to laws which do not involve any hypothetical components, we find that the variables studied by the behavioristic psychologist fall into two, or possibly three, main groups:

(1) Response variables: measurements of behavior properties.
(2) Stimulus variables: measurements of properties of the physical and social environment.
(3) Organic variables: measurements of neuroanatomical or neurophysiological properties of the organism.

The different types of empirical relationships or laws in which psychologists have been interested are as follows:

$$1. \; R = f \; (R)$$
$$2. \; \overline{R = f \; (S)}$$
$$3. \; \overline{R = f \; (O)}$$
$$4. \; O = f \; (S)$$

Type 1 laws are laws of association of behavior properties. A great deal of use is made of the statistical constant, the coefficient of correlation, in the formulation of these laws and, as is well known, this type of law is investigated extensively in the field of psychological testing.

Type 2 laws may be concerned with the present environment or with past environmental events. Thus in the case of the typical perception experiments, we are interested in the effects of variation of aspects or features of the environmental stimulus on the perceptual or discrimination responses of the subject. Best examples of laws relating behavior to past events in the environment are laws of learning, laws of secondary motivation, etc.

For the most part the present-day behavioristic psychologists tend to concentrate their energies on these two classes of laws and and to a very considerable extent they have favored the use of the molar rather than molecular concepts. A few psychologists whose interests have been in mediational problems have concerned themselves with type 3 and type 4 laws. These latter are obviously in the field of neurophysiological psychology and have in the main been concerned only with the simplest kinds of behavior phenomena—*e.g.,* sensory responses. Indeed, our inability to develop measures of this class of events (*i.e.,* organic variables) in the case of the more complex behavior phenomena has been one of the factors underlying the substitution of the hypothetical intervening constructs in their place.

Figure 1 continues this analysis of the laws of psychology. In this diagram I have attempted to portray, in addition to the four types of empirical laws which we have been discussing, the new hypothetical or guessed-at types of relationships which are involved in the introduction of the hypothetical intervening constructs. These latter are indicated as I_a and I_b and are represented as *hypothetical state variables* (enclosed within the rectangle). The environment or world situation at three different time intervals is represented by $S_t - n$ (past) $S_t = o$ (present) $S_t + n$ (future). These S's and also the R's represent empirical variables. I have also represented the class of experimental neurophysiological variables of the first figure by the symbol O, to the left of the rectangle. The four classes of empirical laws, listed at the right side of the figure, are represented by the solid curved lines. The guessed-at or postulated laws relating the hypothetical state variables (I_a, I_b, etc.) to the various experimental variables are represented by the dotted lines. Thus No. 5 type of "law" defines or introduces the intervening variables in terms of past events; No. 6 type relates them to the present en-

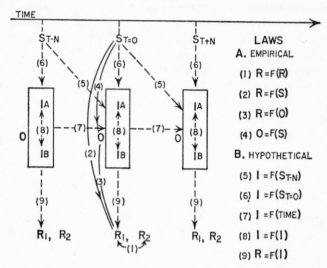

FIG. 1. Showing different kinds of laws.

vironmental variables and No. 7 to time; No. 8 "laws" present interrelations assumed between these intervening variables, and, finally, the relations represented by No. 9 relate the intervening variables to the response variables. That is to say, these dotted lines should be thought of as representative of different classes of postulated relationships, not the usual notion of an S–R connection.

Those who are acquainted with the theoretical constructs of Hull (*11*) will recognize specific examples of these hypothetical laws. Thus his postulate or definition of the construct habit strength, or $S^H R$, as a function of the number of past reinforcements is a good example of class No. 5 "law." His assumption of the nature of the manner in which H and D interact to determine E falls in Class No. 8 and his postulate as to how the construct of reactive inhibition (I_R) is assumed to change (disintegrate) with time is an instance of No. 7 type of "law." Incidentally, it will be noted that this last relationship is the only one which is similar to the so-called dynamic or process laws of physics. This type of law states or describes the laws governing the changes that occur within a system in time.

A question concerning these theoretical constructs that invariably seems to arise is whether they represent some kind of internal, presumably neurophysiological, process or state. The persistence with which misunderstanding arises on this point is truly surprising. It is probably to be explained in terms of the difficulty and resistance we have in shedding old, familiar meanings of words. In this connection it is not a little amusing to note that whereas Hull is usually accused of stuffing the organism with mythological brain states, Tolman, whose theoretical concepts have exactly the same formal structure as those of Hull—*i.e.,* intervening variables defined in terms of independent environmental events—is often charged with the guilt of dreaming up mentalistic ghosts. The explanation of this situation is readily seen when we recall the terms employed by these two men to designate their intervening variables. Thus Hull used such words as habit, drive, excitatory potential and inhibitory potential while Tolman named his theoretical constructs, demands, sign-Gestalt-expectations, hypotheses, etc.

The only meanings that these theoretical intervening constructs have *at the present time* is provided by the equations which relate them to the known experimental variables—the environmental measurements on the one hand and the behavior measures on the other. Such equations constitute the definitions of these terms.

The present role of these theoretical constructs we have said is to aid the psychologist in his search for the empirical laws relating behavior to the conditions determining it. In this sense they are a kind of calculational device which helps us to write the complete law describing the interrelations between all of the relevant experimental variables. In a recent article (*17*) on this problem of theory construction in contemporary psychology I called attention to the point that it is possible in the case of the theoretical formulation of simple learning behavior developed by Hull to substitute in the successive equations introducing the intervening theoretical constructs and obtain a single equation which states the response measure as a function of the several antecedent environmental variables. In this equation the intervening theoretical variables are represented among the parameters of the equation.

While both Tolman and I have emphasized the heuristic value of this type of theoretical construction in the formulation of the complete form of the laws, Hull (12) has called attention to another use which these constructs serve. Such constructs as habit and excitatory potential also provide, he claims, convenient, quantitative representations or indices of the particular complex of experimental variables for which they stand. Thus instead of having to state that the subject has had so many reinforcements in the situation under conditions in which the goal was of such-and-such a magnitude and was delayed for such-and-such a period, it is possible to substitute the calculated value of habit strength.

Finally, there remains the possibility, at least, that these intervening constructs may turn out to have their counterparts somewhere under the skin of the organism. Hull in particular has been quite prone to accept this possibility and has not hesitated to add further statements about these constructs which suggest their possible locus and functioning in the nervous system. His justification, however, has always been that such conjectures provide experimental hints to persons interested in making such coordinations of our knowledge. His main theoretical efforts have been primarily at the molar-behavioral level.

In concluding this discussion of the theoretical framework of the behavioristic psychologist, I should like to emphasize that it is as yet only in a very primitive state of development, a fact which has unfortunately been lost sight of by many of the current critics of this position. The theorist in this field apparently has to choose between attempting to lay down the general theoretical framework of the whole range of behavior phenomena or working out the detailed nature of one small realm of data. Tolman has, for the most part, chosen the former alternative with the consequence that his treatment is characterized by an obvious lack of detailed specification of his theoretical constructs. Hull, on the other hand, has elected to follow the second method. His book, *Principles of Behavior*, dealt only with the most *simple* instances of laboratory learning phenomena, classical and instrumental conditioning, and he and his students are now engaged in extending the fundamental laws there discovered to the major phenomena of individual behavior.

So far as theoretical constructs are concerned, it is obvious that the simple behavior phenomena dealt with by Hull and other behavioristic-oriented psychologists have not required (to any great extent) a whole class of hypothetical intervening variables that must ultimately be postulated. Thus the theoretical constructs in Hull's book—habit, excitatory and inhibitory potential, drive, etc.—are what might be referred to as *state variables*. Each of these constructs represents a hypothetical condition or state of the organism which is assumed to have resulted from and is defined in terms of the past interactions of the organism and its environment. In contrast the new theoretical constructs referred to above will represent, not states, but hypothetical, non-observable responses, implicit processes, occurring in the individual. Thus, in dealing with the more complex types of animal and human behavior, implicit emotional responses, covert verbal responses and not easily observable receptor-exposure and postural adjustments will have to be postulated in addition to these state variables. As yet only a bare beginning has been made in the use of such theoretical constructs—*e.g.*, anxiety reactions and their secondary reinforcing effects (*14*), fractional anticipatory goal reactions as the basis of purposive behavior (*9, 10*).

It is in this realm of theorizing that the verbal reports of human subjects are likely to be of most use to the behavior theorist, for presumably these reports can be made the basis on which to postulate the occurrence of these inferred activities. There are, of course, many pitfalls in the use of such verbal reports and considerable caution needs to be exercised in their use. However, careful control and checking in terms of other, non-verbal responses should provide a means of detecting distortions, both deliberate and otherwise, in this source of data (*16*).

A discussion of behaviorism, especially when it occurs in conjunction with a symposium which includes Gestalt psychology, requires at least some comment on the distinction often made between field and non-field theories in psychology. The Gestalt psychologists, in particular, have been very fond of this contrast and they have not hesitated to imply that their theoretical structures are similar in some respect to the type of field theory in physics represented by the Maxwell electromagnetic theory and Einstein's gravitational theory. In some instances the further implication has been made that behavioristic theories are a mechanical type of theory and as such are just as outmoded as the mechanistic theories of physics. Now I have often wondered what our theoretical brethren from the field of physics would think of these claims if perchance they were ever to take a serious look at these two groups of theories. Certainly the behavioristic theoretical structure I have been talking about uses neither the mechanical models—*i.e.*, particles with their attracting forces—nor the type of mathematical equations that characterize a mechanical theory. Nor do I believe that there is anything even remotely resembling the field equations of Maxwell and Einstein in the theoretical formulations of the Gestalt psychologists. In the sense, then, in which the theoretical physicist understands the dichotomy, mechanical versus field theory, no such distinction, in my opinion, exists in psychology today.

If, on the other hand, the concept of field refers in psychology essentially to the notion of a system of interdependent variables, with its implication that the behavior of an organism at any moment is a resultant of the totality of relevant variables, then there is not to my knowledge any behavioristic theory today which would not also be a field theory. Furthermore, if we accept the additional notion that it is the pattern of interrelationships between the determining variables that is the crucial factor differentiating psychological field theories from non-field theories, I do not believe that the behavior theories which I have been describing would fail to qualify as field theories. The hypothetical equations which Hull (*11*) postulates in the introduction of his theoretical constructs provide in precise mathematical form these very patterns of interrelationship. Finally, as to the characteristic of field theory emphasized by Lewin (*13*) under the principle of contemporaneity—namely, that the behavior at any moment is a function of the situation *at that moment only* and not a function of past or future situations,—I find it difficult to believe that any present-day psychologist believes that other conditions than those of the present moment determine the behavior of this moment. Even the psychoanalyst never held, as Lewin sometimes seems to imply, that past events somehow jump through time to determine the present behavior, but, instead, conceived of these past events leaving their effects in the organism and through them determining the behavior of the moment. The behaviorist takes exactly the same view of the matter.

The development of our science has not been helped, in my opinion, by such distinctions as field and non-field theory. A much more useful procedure would be to examine in detail these differing theoretical positions with a view to ascertaining to what extent they differ in the particular variables they believe to be relevant in a particular instance and what differences, if any, exist in their postulation as to the pattern of the interrelationships involved—*i.e.,* in the form of the hypothetical laws they assume. It is my personal belief that if this procedure were followed there would be much less in the way of specific disagreements to settle than is usually thought. I base this prediction not only on the well-known fact that the Gestaltists, psychoanalysts and behaviorists have to a considerable extent been interested in very different realms of psychological phenomena and that hence their theories are not in competition with one another, but also on the fact that very little real theorizing, particularly in the matter of specifying the precise form of the interrelations between the variables, has actually been done. It is most imperative that psychologists attempt to formulate their theories in as precise and articulate a manner as possible, for it is only by means of such theorizing that psychology can hope, finally, to attain full-fledged scientific statehood.

REFERENCES

1. BERGMANN, G. The subject matter of psychology. *Phil. Sci.,* 1940, 7, 415–433.

2. BORING, E. G. *The Physical Dimensions of Consciousness.* New York: The Century Company, 1933.

3. BRIDGMAN, P. W. *The Logic of Modern Physics.* New York: The Macmillan Company, 1928.

4. BRUNSWIK, E. The conceptual focus of some psychological systems. *J. Unified Sci. (Erkenntnis)*, 1939, *8*, 36–49.

5. CARNAP, R. Testability and meaning. *Phil. Sci.*, 1936, *3*, 419–471; 1937, *4*, 1–40.

6. ——. *Philosophy and Logical Syntax.* London: Kegan Paul, Trench, Trubner, 1935.

7. FEIGL, H. Operationism and scientific method. *Psychol. Rev.*, 1945, *52*, 243–246.

8. HEIDER, F. Environmental determinants in psychological theories. *Psychol. Rev.*, 1939, *46*, 383–410.

9. HULL, C. L. Knowledge and purpose as habit mechanisms. *Psychol. Rev.*, 1930, *37*, 511–525.

10. ——. Goal attraction and directing ideas conceived as habit phenomena. *Psychol. Rev.*, 1931, *38*, 487–506.

11. ——. *Principles of Behavior.* New York: D. Appleton-Century, 1943.

12. ——. The problem of intervening variables in molar behavior theory. *Psychol. Rev.*, 1943, *50*, 273–291.

13. LEWIN, K. Defining the "field" at a given time. *Psychol. Rev.*, 1943, *50*, 292–310.

14. MOWRER, O. H. A stimulus-response analysis of anxiety and its role as a reinforcing agent. *Psychol. Rev.*, 1939, *46*, 553–565.

15. PRATT, C. C. *The Logic of Modern Psychology.* New York: The Macmillan Company, 1939.

16. SKINNER, B. F. The operational analysis of psychological terms. *Psychol. Rev.*, 1945, *52*, 270–278.

17. SPENCE, K. W. The nature of theory construction in contemporary psychology. *Psychol. Rev.*, 1944, *51*, 47–68.

18. STEVENS, S. S. The operational definition of psychological concepts. *Psychol. Rev.*, 1935, *42*, 517–527.

19. TOLMAN, E. C. *Purposive Behavior in Animals and Men.* New York: The Century Company, 1932.

20. ——. The determiners of behavior at a choice point. *Psychol. Rev.*, 1938, *45*, 1–41.

21. WATSON, J. B. Psychology as the behaviorist views it. *Psychol. Rev.*, 1913, *20*, 158–177.

4

Mathematical Formulations of Learning Phenomena [1]

I

The present paper is concerned with some problems that arise in connection with the attempts of psychologists to formulate precise quantitative theories about learning phenomena. Before turning to the mathematical aspects of our topic, however, I should like to do two things: (a) to discuss, very briefly, the experimental phenomena with which we are to be concerned and (b) to consider the purposes that theories serve at the present stage of development of the field of learning. The experimental studies on learning that have provided data sufficiently precise to invite the use of mathematical functions in their description and interpretation have employed relatively simple behavior situations such as classical and instrumental conditioning, simple trial-and-error learning, discrimination learning and serial or maze learning.

The basic data provided by these different kinds of learning experiments consist in a set of empirical functions relating various response measures to a number of experimentally manipu-

[1] This paper was given originally in a symposium on "Statistical Problems and Psychological Theory" jointly sponsored by the American Psychological Association, Psychometric Society and Institute of Mathematical Studies at the annual meeting of the American Statistical Association in Chicago, 1950.

latable environmental variables. The following represent some of these discovered relationships for one experimental situation, classical conditioning:

(1) $R = f$ (Number of trials—N)
(2) $R = f$ (Intensity of the conditioned stimulus—S_c)
(3) $R = f$ (Intensity of the unconditioned stimulus—S_u)
(4) $R = f$ (Time interval between S_c and $S_u - T_{s_c-s_u}$)
(5) $R = f$ (Time between successive trials — T_R)
(6) $R = f$ (Amount of work involved in $R - W$)
$\quad R = f \ (N, \ S_c, \ S_u, \ T_{s_c-s_u}, \ T_R, \ W, \text{ etc.})$

The so-called learning curve, representing the changes that occur in the performance measure as a function of the successive practice occasions, is listed as the first of these functions. While this is the function or law in which learning psychologists have shown the most interest, the other relationships are equally important for the complete description of the behavior of the subject.

As the result of our experimental studies, then, we arrive at a series of empirical laws relating each response measure in the various types of learning situations to N and to the several other determining variables. Assuming that we can obtain such sets of laws for each of the learning situations, why, one may ask, do we introduce theories? What do theories add or what do they provide that the sets of laws do not?

There are psychologists who take the position that all we need to do is to discover such sets of empirical laws and that theorizing, at least at the present stage of development of the field of learning, is not necessary. Actually, if one were satisfied to confine one's study of learning phenomena to *one* particular response measure in a *single* experimental situation, *e.g.*, the frequency measure in classical conditioning, there possibly would be no need for theory. Thus, if it were, in fact, found that a single equation fitted the various curves of frequency obtained in the conditioning experiment under different values of the other experimental variables (S_c, S_u, T_{s_u}, etc.), then one would have a single law that consistently and adequately described all of the curves.[2]

But now let us suppose that when we employed other measures of the conditioned response, *e.g.,* amplitude or resistance to extinction, we found that the curves of learning for these measures took quite different forms from that of the frequency measure. Or suppose on turning to other experimental situations such as the discrimination box, the maze, etc., we found that still different types of learning curves were obtained. We would thus have a series of more or less specific laws for each particular learning situation and, in some instances, even different laws for each different response measure in the same experimental situation. Anyone familiar with the nature of learning data at the present time will readily recognize that this picture is by no means a construction of my imagination, but represents a fairly accurate portrayal of the existing state of our knowledge in this field.

Confronted with such a state of affairs, the theory-oriented psychologist has attempted to integrate these isolated, particular sets of laws into a more comprehensive system of knowledge by means of his theoretical formulations. The more empirical-minded psychologist, on the other hand, has typically not been interested in such integration, believing such attempts to be premature and wasteful at the present stage of development of knowledge in the field. There is, of course, no recipe or set of rules that will tell us precisely when any realm of empirical facts is ready for such attempts at theoretical integration. Undoubtedly, differences among psychologists in regard to this predilection for engaging in theory construction reflect differences in personal attitudes, special skills, etc., that lie quite outside the scope of the present discussion. Most learning psychologists will be found to fall somewhere in between the radical empiricism of Skinner (9) and the sometimes purely mathematical model building of Rashevsky (8).

---

[2] The fact that such a psychologist as Skinner (9) finds little or no need for theory in learning is probably not unrelated to the fact that he has confined his interest in learning data largely to one measure in a single learning situation, *i.e.,* rate of responding in operant conditioning.

One of the most highly developed quantitative theories of learning phenomena at present is that of Clark Hull (6). Basing his theory on data from classical and instrumental conditioning experiments, Hull has been engaged for a number of years in an attempt to show how the particular laws found in the different learning situations may be derived from this theoretical structure. Other quantitative theories similar in principle to Hull's, in that they are based on data from learning experiments themselves rather than on experimental findings in other fields such as neurophysiology, etc., are those of Thurstone (12), Gulliksen and Wolfle (4), Graham and Gagné (2), Pitts (8), Estes (1) and Spence (10).

A second type of quantitative theorizing that has developed in the field of learning has had a quite different origin. Instead of being instigated by the diversity of curves of learning obtained in different types of experiments, this kind of theorizing has attempted to develop a mathematical theory based on neurological foundations. I have reference, of course, to the work of Rashevsky and his students (8). These two theoretical approaches do not, as is sometimes thought, represent competing formulations but are complementary to each other. The development by the behavior theorists of a more comprehensive theory consisting of a fewer number of general principles instead of a multitude of diverse laws that have no obvious relation to one another simplifies the problem for the neurophysiological theorist. Instead of having to derive a number of diverse experimental facts based on special conditions, he can direct his theory to the derivation of these more general learning principles.[3]

---

[3] Considerable confusion has arisen from a failure to realize that these two types of quantitative theories of learning phenomena are, or can be, entirely independent of another class of learning theories, namely, those concerned with the nature of the reinforcing process. Whereas the former theories attempt to provide guesses as to the laws governing the course of development of the hypothetical learning changes that occur with successive practice occasions, the latter are concerned with the conceptions as to how the unconditioned or reinforcing stimulus provides for the hypothetical change. The mathematical learning theorist can employ any one of these latter conceptions he wishes or he can completely ignore them. Thus he can be a reinforcement theorist of whatever variety (need-reduction, drive stimulus reduction, satisfier, etc.) or a contiguity theorist of whatever type he desires.

With this discussion of the nature of learning data and the general aim or purpose lying behind the attempts at quantitative theorizing about them as background, I now wish to turn more specifically to the role of mathematical functions in the description and interpretation of learning phenomena. We shall not stop to discuss at any length the fitting of learning curves by empirical equations. In the decade following World War I there was a flurry of such activity on the part of psychologists and a number of different mathematical functions were employed, among them the hyperbola, arc-cotangent, Gompertz, logarithmic, logistic and exponential functions. For the most part these equations were selected merely because of a resemblance between the learning curve and the mathematical function. However, the logistic and exponential functions were favored not only on this basis but also because their proponents believed that they provided a kind of explanation of the learning process. Following the reasoning of some of the biologists in their treatment of similar curves of body growth, these psychologists postulated either (1) that the learning process was one in which the rate of development of the process was proportional to the amount still to be developed, or (2) that the rate of learning was proportional to the product of the amount already developed and the amount of the process still to be developed. Integration of the first of these assumptions (both of which can be expressed as differential equations), leads to the exponential function; [4] integration of the second leads to the logistic function.[5]

Such "deductions" of the empirical curve of learning do not, as some psychologists seem to have thought, represent any real advance in our knowledge of the learning process. Actually

---

The almost identical nature of the mathematical portion of Estes' treatment (1) of classical conditioning within the framework of Guthrie's contiguity position with the mathematical portions of Hull's reinforcement treatment points up convincingly the independence of these two areas of theorizing in learning.

[4] $Y = a(1 - e^{-ix})$, where $Y =$ some measure of attainment or performance, $X =$ measure of practice, $a =$ limit of attainment, $i =$ parameter determining rate of approach to attainment asymptote.

[5] $Y = \dfrac{b}{ce^{-abX} + 1}$, where $Y =$ some measure of attainment or performance, $X =$ measure of practice, $a =$ parameter dependent upon individual learner and/or task to be learned, $b =$ limit of attainment, $c =$ constant of integration.

such "theoretical" treatments, whether they begin with the differential equation or start directly with the integral function, represent *ad hoc* assumptions that both begin and end with the original empirical curves. A genuine theoretical attempt to account for these learning curves would begin with assumptions concerning underlying hypothetical factors that lead to, rather than follow from, the original learning data.

That mathematical theories, the basic assumptions of which have their origin in laws concerning neurophysiological processes, offer the possibility of providing satisfactory noncircular explanations of learning data is readily accepted by almost all psychologists, regardless of whether or not they have any understanding of the mathematics involved. There is, however, less readiness to accept mathematical theories of learning that do not make reference to any underlying physiological mechanisms, but instead introduce hypothetical constructs or intervening variables (*e.g.*, habit strength) as mathematical functions of the variables of learning experiments themselves.

When one examines the objections given to this latter intervening variable type of mathematical theory, the one most frequently met is similar to that just given in connection with our discussion of the interpretations based on the properties of empirically fitted learning curves, namely, that they are purely *ad hoc* or entirely circular in character. They start and end with the same empirical data. Such an objection to the intervening variable type of learning theory, however, reveals a serious misunderstanding of its nature and purpose. I should like to attempt to correct this misunderstanding and to outline the nature of this type of theorizing as I understand it.

It is true that this kind of theory does begin with learning data, including curves of learning. But the theory does not stop with the treatment of the data on which it is based. To do so would, of course, leave it open to the criticism that it is purely an *ad hoc* affair that begins and ends with the same empirical data. Once formulated on the basis of one set of learning data, however, such theories are subsequently applied to other data either from the same situation or other learning situations. Rational equations representative of relationships to be expected in the new data are derived on the basis of the original constructs and principles. If the empirical findings do not agree with these derived equations, the theory is shown to be wrong and it must either be abandoned or modified in some manner. Any modification to meet the new data must, of course, meet the test of working satisfactorily for the original phenomena.

The particular type of learning that one selects as a basis for the beginning of such theorizing is, of course, purely arbitrary. On the assumption that the simplest kind of learning situation is probably the best source in which to discover a set of basic constructs and principles that not only will work for these data but also serve as a basis for accounting for other learning experiments, Hull and I have started with the data from simple conditioning studies (conditioning, extinction, generalization, etc.). We have assumed that this type of situation provides the best source of evidence for making inferences as to the course of change that occurs during practice in the strength of a hypothetical stimulus-response connection or excitatory tendency. The more complex learning situations, it is assumed, are complicated by the presence or competition between a number of simultaneously occurring excitatory tendencies; hence data from them reflect only very indirectly the changes that occur in these S-R tendencies.

It should be noticed, however, that curves of classical conditioning do not provide an unequivocal picture as to their form. While some are negatively accelerated, others, particularly those using frequency of response as the measure of performance, show an initial phase of positive acceleration followed by a negative phase. Which of these functions are we to choose as representing the course of development of our hypothetical learning construct (habit, associative strength, etc.)? Unfortunately, a somewhat incorrect impression of the procedure that is followed at this stage of theory construction was gained by some psychologists as the result of Hull's treatment in his *Principles of Behavior*. On the basis of three experimental studies from his laboratory that had provided negatively accelerated curves of learning, Hull decided to assume that habit strength $(_sH_R)$ develops according to this type of function. Actually, of course, even if every experimental study gave conditioning curves in which the *response measure* increased in some particular manner, it would still be entirely possible for the theorist to assume that some other function described the development of his hypothetical learning factor $(_sH_R)$. As a matter of fact, in an earlier theoretical attempt Hull chose to assume a linear function in the face of essentially the same experimental evidence.

The point is that in postulating this hypothetical learning process the theorist is free to choose whatever assumption he wishes. Actually the theoretical model typically consists of a number of assumptions, and it is the implications of the complete model (not one particular portion of it) that must agree with the selected data from which the theory starts.

Having fashioned his theoretical model on the basis of one particular set of experimental data, the theorist, as described earlier, must now attempt to apply it to new data and new situations. Ideally this would involve the derivation of rational equations representative of relationships to be found in the new situation on the basis of the same hypothetical constructs and postulates employed in connection with the original data. While this is possible in some instances, as one attempts to apply the theoretical model to more and more complex situations, additional assumptions involving newly introduced experimental variables usually become necessary. One of the major problems faced in such theorizing is to find a way to introduce these new assumptions on some other than a purely *ad hoc* basis. When this cannot be done and the theorist makes the necessary new assumption such that it will account for some of the new findings, then the theory must again be tested by employing this new assumption to predict other findings in the same or similar situations. The new assumptions must also be introduced without altering the old ones except as the new variables are assumed to produce interaction effects that would change them.

The nature of this type of theorizing may be shown by the following development of a theoretical model based on data from classical conditioning. Our treatment is patterned closely after that developed by Hull in his *Principles of Behavior*. Figure 1 presents the variables, experimental and hypothetical, that are involved. At the top are shown some of the experimental variables that have been shown to affect response strength in classical conditioning experiments. We are primarily interested in the relation assumed between H, the hypothetical learning change, and N, the number of conditioning trials. We have followed Hull in postulating that the function relating H to N is the exponential, $A(1 - e^{-bN})$. A and b are parameters that determine, respectively, the limit to which H will grow and the rate at which it approaches this limit. Presumably these parameters vary for different individuals, *i.e.*, fast and slow conditioners. We shall assume that the conditions determining inhibition, I, are negligible and hence can be ignored. In such a response as the eyelid there is probably very little work inhibition involved, especially if the intertrial interval is not too brief.

EXPERIMENTAL VARIABLES

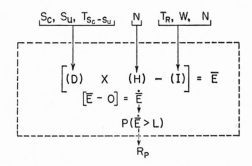

Fig. 1. Showing the relation between the experimentally manipulatable variables in classical conditioning, the hypothetical intervening variables in the rectangle, and the empirical response measure, per cent of conditioned responses R_p.

The variables S_c, S_u, $T_{s_c - s_u}$ are assumed to determine a hypothetical construct, D, that we shall term drive level. D and H are assumed to multiply each other to determine, after subtraction of any I, the intervening variable, $\bar{E}$, effective excitatory potential. Finally, one further hypothetical factor, an oscillating inhibitory factor designated by the symbol O, is postulated. This oscillatory potential is assumed to vary in amount from instant to instant according to a normal probability distribution, the range and sigma of which are constant. It is subtracted from E to give $\dot{\bar{E}}$, momentary effective excitatory potential.

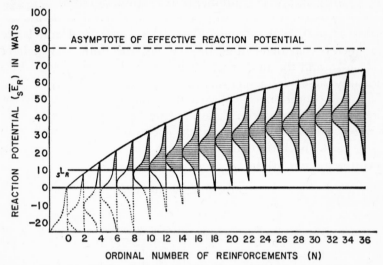

FIG. 2. Hull's diagram showing how with growth of effective excitatory potential, the proportion of superthreshold, momentary effective excitatory potentials [$P(\dot{\bar{E}}>L)$], represented as shaded portions of the upended normal distributions, increases.

Figure 2, taken from Hull (6, p. 327), shows how effective excitatory potential, $\bar{E}$, is conceived to develop as a function of the conditioning trials. The upended normal distributions represent the oscillatory potential. The shaded area in each of these distributions represents the probability that the momentary effective excitatory potential will, on the particular trial, be greater than a threshold value, L, necessary for a response occurrence, i.e., $P(\dot{\bar{E}}>L)$. Returning to Fig. 1 we see that this final theoretical variable, P, is identified or coordinated with the empirical response measure, frequency or percentage of response occurrences (R_p).

If we plot these hypothetical P values as a function of N for a number of different values of the parameters (D and A) that determine the level to which effective excitatory potential will grow, we obtain the family of curves shown in Fig. 3. In other words, these curves represent theoretical frequency curves of conditioning for subjects in which $\bar{E}$, either because of greater learning ability or a combination of both, develops at different rates. In an attempt to ascertain the extent to which experimental data agree with these theoretical frequency curves of conditioning we determined frequency curves for three groups of more or less like subjects. From 100 subjects run in an eyelid conditioning setup, three groups were selected on the basis of the total number of CR's made in 100 conditioning trials. The group curves for nine subjects (Group A) who gave between 71 to 80 CR's, 15 subjects (Group B) who gave a total of 50 to 58 CR's and 11 subjects (Group C) who gave from 32 to 40 CR's are shown in Fig. 4. As the differences between the subjects in each group are very slight, there is probably very little distortion resulting from the grouping of the data. Moreover, the form of the curve is not a product of the distribution of individual scores as is often the case in learning curves based on group data.

It will be seen that the data agree very well with the theoretical curves thus showing the applicability of the hypothetical model to them. It is, of course, possible to develop alternative sets of hypotheses that would fit the data equally well. The value of such theorizing, however, does not lie in the success with which it can fit the data on which it is based but rather in whether and to what extent it permits the derivation of rational equations that describe other empirical functions to be expected in this and other experimental situations.

As it stands, of course, the mathematical model described above is not sufficiently complete to provide predictions about learning situations. It is presented here merely as an example of this type of model construction. Hull has gone considerably beyond the above described theory in that he has included hypothetical constructs and principles relating a number of other experimental variables, *e.g.*, his assumptions about work inhibition, motivation, generalization, stimulus interaction, etc. On the other hand, it should also be emphasized that in his *Principles of Behavior* Hull has not gone much beyond the stage of the initial construction of the theoretical model. Except for a few scattered instances (*e.g.*, the derivation of behavior in the simple choice situation involving differential delays of reward, the derivation of law of least work) he did not, in the *Principles,* attempt to show that his theoretical model could be employed to deduce the data of other, more complex learning situations.

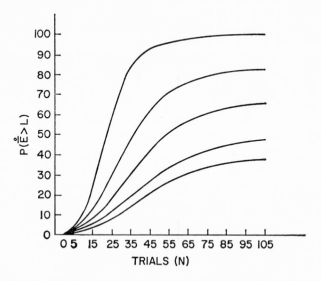

Fig. 3.   Family of theoretically derived curves of the proportion of superthreshold, momentary effective excitatory potentials [$P(\bar{E}>L)$] as a function of number of training trials for different growth curves of excitatory potential ($\bar{E}$).

Two anticipations of this type of application of Hull's theory to other learning situations, than conditioning are those of Grice (*3*) and Thompson (*11*).   Hull and other members of his group are at present engaged in further attempts of this type. There have been very few instances of genuine derivation of rational equations predictive of laws in the field of learning. Other outstanding examples are those of Thurstone (*12*) in the field of maze learning, Gulliksen and Wolfle (*4*) in the area of discrimination behavior and most recently, Estes' (*1*) derivation of laws concerned with latency and rate measures in simple operant conditioning.

     There are a number of important problems that arise in connection with the application of a theoretical model.   Because of the confusion that apparently exists in this matter, I should like to mention at least one problem.   The point I have in mind is the necessity in the testing of a theory for making the experimental setup, including the subjects, conform to the specifica-

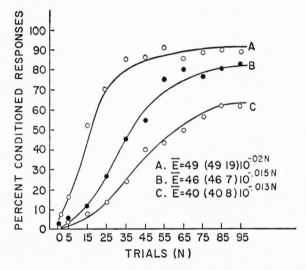

Fig. 4.   Curves of conditioning for three groups of "like" subjects as described in text. The response measure is the per cent of conditioned responses occurring in successive blocks of 10 trials. The points on the abscissae represent the midpoints of the successive 10 trial bocks. The equations are exponential functions describing the growth of $\bar{E}$ from which the solid theoretical curves passing through the empirical points (circles) were derived by means of a table of normal probability values.

tions of the theoretical model.   Failure to meet this requirement precludes the possibility of drawing any worthwhile conclusions either pro or con, other than the trite one that the model is not sufficiently complete to deal with these data.   Thus a theoretical model developed specifically in connection with behavior phenomena exhibited in discrimination learning of non-articulate organisms, *i.e.*, animals, is not disproved by the failure of human subjects to behave according to the theoretical prediction.   While it is true that the theory does not account for the human behavior, nevertheless, it may be a perfectly adequate theory for the realm of phenomena for which it was intended. Unfortunately this type of "disproof" of a theory is all too prevalent in psychology.

REFERENCES

1. ESTES, W. K. Toward a statistical theory of learning. *Psychol. Rev.*, 1950, *57*, 94–107.
2. GRAHAM, C. H., & GAGNÉ, R. M. The acquisition, extinction and spontaneous recovery of a conditioned operant response. *J. exp. Psychol.*, 1940, *26*, 251–281.
3. GRICE, G. R. An experimental study of the gradient of reinforcement in maze learning. *J. exp. Psychol.*, 1942, *30*, 475–489.
4. GULLIKSEN, H., & WOLFLE, D. L. A theory of learning and transfer. I and II. *Psychometrika*, 1938, *3*, 127–149, 225–251.
5. HOUSEHOLDER, A. S., & LANDAHL, H. D. Mathematical Biophysics of the Central Nervous System. *Mathematical Biophysics Monograph, Series I*. Bloomington, Indiana: The Principia Press, Inc., 1945.
6. HULL, C. L. *Principles of Behavior.* New York: Appleton-Century, 1943.
7. PITTS, W. A general theory of learning and conditioning. *Psychometrika*, 1943, *8*, 1–18, 131–140.
8. RASHEVSKY, N. *Mathematical Biophysics.* Chicago: University of Chicago Press, 1938.
9. SKINNER, B. F. Are theories of learning necessary? *Psychol. Rev.*, 1950, *57*, 193–217.
10. SPENCE, K. W. The nature of discrimination learning in animals. *Psychol. Rev.*, 1936, *43*, 427–449.
11. THOMPSON, M. Learning as a function of the absolute and relative amounts of work. *J. exp. Psychol.*, 1944, *34*, 506–515.
12. THURSTONE, L. L. The learning function. *J. gen. Psychol.*, 1930, *3*, 469–493.

5

The Empirical Basis and Theoretical Structure
of Psychology [1]

I

In accepting the invitation of your society to discuss some aspects
of the philosophy of science, particularly as they might bear on
the problems of an experimental psychologist, I should like
from the start to make it very clear that I do not consider myself
a philosopher, not even an amateur one. Like most empirical
scientists, particularly of the laboratory variety, I usually take
it for granted that my world is real and that the things I perceive
as existing in it can be investigated by my empirical methods.
I seem to get along quite well with this unpremeditated, common-sense realism, and, for the most part, I go along minding
my own experimental business. As the psychologists among
you may know, however, every once in a while I seem to have to
abandon this happy, naive state and let myself get involved in
questions *about* my science, the kinds of questions that are more
properly the business of the philosopher of science.

II

The first of two methodological aspects of present-day psychology that I should like to take this opportunity to discuss is

[1] An address given to a joint meeting of philosophers and psychologists of the
Southern Society for Philosophy and Psychology, Asheville, March, 1956.

concerned with the point that experimental psychologists, at least most of those residing in this country, conceive of the subject matter of their science as being the same in kind as other sciences. This position assumes that there is a kind of ascertainable knowledge about the behavior of humans and animals that has the same empirical basis and logical characteristics as the knowledge sought in the natural sciences.

Strange as it now seems, the first empirically oriented psychologists did not take this position. Reference is made here, of course, to the so-called classical psychologists, whether of the structural or act varieties. Influenced by their philosophical views, particularly their ontological biases, the point of view of these men was that psychology, if it were a natural science, was a somewhat unique one. Thus instead of being concerned, like physics, with events mediated by or derived from the immediate experience of the observing scientist, psychology was said to study immediate experience itself. Much was made of the point that psychology had a unique method of its own—introspection, which was regarded as a kind of inner sense that provided for a special kind of observation and analysis of consciousness *per se*. According to this conception, psychology studies the mind, whereas the subject matter of the natural sciences was matter.

It was Watson, of course, who broke with this classical conception of psychology. He insisted instead that the science of psychology, to quote him directly, "is a purely objective experimental branch of natural science which needs introspection as little as do the sciences of chemistry and physics" (*17*, p. 176). In this original formation Watson did not take the extreme stand that he did later—as, for example, denying consciousness and rejecting all mentalistic terms even from the theoretical language of psychology. Instead, he argued for returning to a "non-reflective and naive use of consciousness" in which the psychologist, like other natural scientists, takes immediate experience for granted and goes on to describe and interrelate the observed happenings it provides. According to this view the initial data of all sciences are the same, namely certain observable characteristics in the experience of the scientist.

For the most part psychologists in this country have accepted this view point with respect to the relation of psychological concepts to immediate experience and they have gone ahead with the development of an objective study of the behavior of living organisms, as Watson proposed. Primarily interested as they have been, however, in carrying out their empirical program of research, psychologists have not concerned themselves too extensively with the philosophical assumptions underlying their endeavors. Fortunately, as the philosophers among you know, these basic problems have been the object of intensive study in recent years by a group of philosophers of science known as the logical empiricists.[2] This group has not only been interested in the logical analysis of psychology but more generally they have attempted a logical reconstruction of all science.

Following in the tradition of the positivistic philosophers, Hume, Mach, and Russell, the method employed by the logical empiricists may be briefly described as consisting in the logical analysis of the language of science. Without attempting in the least to get involved in any of the subtle technical issues that arise among different members of this group, and confining ourselves to the immediate problem of the relation of the concepts of science to its evidential basis—the data of experience—the general position of this group may be described very briefly as follows.

Empirical science, aiming as it does at general principles that will provide for the explanation and integration of particular events, has evolved comprehensive systems of terms (concepts) and sentences that may be arranged in a hierarchy. Highest in the hierarchy of the language of any science are the abstract terms and statements that provide for theories of wide scope and great precision. These theoretical concepts, if they are to serve this function, must be connected in one manner or another to the terms lower in the hierarchy, and ultimately to a class of elementary, undefined terms and sentences that have direct experiential reference. Another manner of stating this is to say that all abstract, defined terms, defined, that is, in the broad sense that includes conditional definitions, must be traceable to a basic set of descriptive or observational terms.

2 The main figures in this movement of interest to psychologists are Gustav Bergmann, Rudolph Carnap, Herbert Feigl and Carl Hempel.

One of the indecisions among the logical empiricists that is of interest to scientists, especially psychologists, is the question as to which of two alternative classes or sets of terms should constitute this basic, descriptive vocabulary.   In the initial phase of logical empiricism, as represented b.y the early writings of Carnap (5), the basis chosen, particularly when the discussion involved epistemological considerations, was a phenomenalistic one.   Examples of these observable psychological predicates, as Carnap termed them, are "perceiving red," "having a feeling of anger," "thinking about the H bomb," and so on.   Such terms, or expressions containing them, were said to designate items or aspects of experience that referred to the perceptions or sensations of the observing person.   However, certain difficulties of such a strictly phenomenalistic language basis subsequently led Carnap (6, 7), under the influence of Neurath and Popper, to propose what he called a physicalistic language basis.   According to this conception the basic descriptive vocabulary of a science, indeed, of all sciences consists of terms that Carnap refers to as "observable physical predicates of the thing language." These terms are said to designate certain directly observable characteristics of physical objects, i.e., their properties and the relations among them.   The following are examples of sentences containing such observable physical terms.   "This object is green," "this space-time point is warm," "object A is above object B," and so on.   From the point of view of science the main advantage of such a physicalistic language basis over the phenomenalistic one is that its terms designate the kind of observed experiences for which there is a high degree of intersubjective agreement.

At the risk of revealing my naivete in such matters, I cannot refrain from expressing my puzzlement over certain aspects of this formulation of Carnap.   I recognize, of course, that Carnap's primary aim was that of providing an analysis of scientific language.   Nevertheless the juxtaposing of language bases that refer to such ontological categories as physical objects on the one hand, and psychological (mental) events like perceiving, feeling and thinking, on the other, must, it seems to me, have led many persons to misconstrue his position as another form of ontological doctrine.   While in complete accord with the preference of Carnap for so-called physicalistic terms as the basic observation vocabulary of all sciences, I should prefer, *as a scientist,* to keep as far away as possible from metaphysical issues. Leaving aside all epistemological considerations, then, I would propose to accept as the criterion for the selection of this basic vocabulary of psychology the methodological requirement that its terms designate a class of observations (items or aspects of experiential data) that display the highest possible degree of intersubjective consistency. By degree of intersubjective consistency is meant the extent to which there is agreement among observers concerning a particular observable datum.

The experiential data designated by Carnap's physicalistic terms, common-sensical observations of things and their properties, meet this criterion quite satisfactorily. In such instances it is possible to obtain conformity of report from observer to observer, and highly intercorrelated changes in the reported observations with experimental manipulation of the environment. Such objective data or *public* experiences are to be contrasted with the subjective data or *private* experiences that are obtained by the kind of observation that psychologists call introspection or self-observation. These latter experiences, particularly our feelings and moods, thoughts and memories, do not satisfactorily meet the criterion of intersubjective observational consistency. In the case of these events, observers are not able to confirm one another's reported experiences. Thus the terms designating this class of private experiences do not provide a *basic* observational vocabulary that will adequately provide for the confirmation and testing of scientific laws and theories.

There is one subclass of our observations, the coincidences of spacetime points, that best meets this scientific requirement of inter-subjective agreement among a society of observers. While other observable qualities or properties of things, such as color, hardness, etc., are sometimes employed by scientists, *e.g.,* the color of the contents of the chemist's test tube, progress has been most rapid when the phenomena being studied could be specified in terms of pointer readings involving the observation of the coincidence of points in space or time. As historians of science have pointed out, the great advances made in physics by

Galileo were in large part the result of his decision to delimit the observations that he would admit for study to those represented by such pointer readings.

Modern experimental psychology is part and parcel of such an objective, public venture. Much of the behavior of living organisms may be described in terms of the same types of pointer readings employed in physics. Indeed practically all of the observations of psychologists who employ animals as subjects in their studies are of this type, *e.g.*, the time required to run down an alley, the rate of depressing a lever, the amplitude of a conditioned leg flexion, etc. Similarly, in our laboratory investigations of the behavior of human subjects, extensive use is made of physical measuring techniques. In addition to these physical measures, psychologists have also developed their own objective (*i.e.*, reliable) methods of quantifying the properties of behavior and its effects that involve the same reduction basis as employed in the other biological and physical sciences. It is readily agreed, I believe, that those portions of present-day psychology that employ these objective methods of observation fall within Carnap's "unified science," the different branches of which are united in terms of a common language basis, the so-called physical-thing language.

But while experimental or laboratory psychology undoubtedly qualifies as a branch of such a unified science, what about all the remaining areas of psychological study? In particular what is to be said concerning the more complex aspects of human personality? What methods of observation and hence kinds of concepts are applicable to phenomena represented by such terms as feeling, the self or ego, motives, values, intentions and a host of others? If one examines the beliefs and attitudes of psychologists themselves on these questions, widely divergent views will be found.

At one extreme are those who decry what they regard as the fetishistic emulation of the physical sciences by psychologists. Pessimistic about the application of the strict operational criteria of concepts such as we have been discussing to the investigation of personality as a complex structure, or frankly believing that an entirely different, emergent kind of subject matter is involved, these psychologists embrace the conception that objective, purely behavioristic methods are inadequate to a full understanding of such phenomena. Rather than align psychology, or at least that part of it concerned with personality, with the natural sciences, this group prefers to view it as being one of the mental or cultural sciences. The objects investigated in these cultural sciences are further said to possess an intrinsic meaningfulness which require for their understanding the method of empathic insight or introspection.

One of the foremost and most vigorous exponents of this viewpoint in this country is Professor Gordon Allport. The following statements of Allport's position, taken from his recent Terry Lectures entitled *Becoming: Basic Considerations for a Psychology of Personality*, clearly indicate his attitude on these problems:

Precisely here we find the reason why so many psychologists fail to take an interest in the existential richness of human life. Methods, they say, are lacking. Or, more exactly stated, the methods available fall short of the stringent requirements laid down by modern positivism. In their desire to emulate the established sciences psychologists are tempted to tackle only those problems and to work on only those organisms, that yield to acceptable operations. For this reason we find animal psychology and mathematical psychology highly developed. So dominant is the positivistic ideal that other fields of psychology came to be regarded as not quite reputable. Special aversion attaches to problems having to do with complex motives, high-level integration, with conscience, freedom, selfhood (*1*, p. 11–12).

Allport then goes on to indicate what he believes is needed if we are ever to develop a psychology of personality. He writes:

The outlines of the needed psychology of becoming can be discovered by looking within ourselves; for it is knowledge of our own uniqueness that supplies the first, and probably the best, hints for acquiring orderly knowledge of others . . . it is by reflecting upon the factors that seem vital in our own experience of becoming that we identify the issues that are important (*1*, p. 23).

Before giving my own reaction to this point of view, let me turn first to a brief presentation of a position that is at the opposite pole in that it seeks to keep the investigation of personality within the realm of the natural sciences. The position is that of the logical empiricists, whose views as applied to the special field of psychology have been called by Hempel (9) logical behaviorism. This formulation, it should be clearly understood, is not a theory *within* the field of psychology but rather is a logical theory *about* the propositions of psychology. Unlike Watsonian behaviorism, it does not take the position that mentalistic terms like intention, thought, goal idea, feeling must not be introduced at any level into the language employed by the psychologist to systematize his observations. On the contrary the viewpoint of logical behaviorism is that such mentalistic terms are quite permissible so long as they are not among the elementary, undefined terms of the basic observational vocabulary, but rather are *defined* terms, again in the broad sense that includes both partial and conditional definitions.

These mentalistic terms are to be defined ultimately, of course, in terms of a class of undefined terms that enter into the definitions of physical science. Many of these psychological terms are of the type known as dispositional predicates. Such concepts, *e.g.*, the emotion of anger, depressed feelings, ego threat, are, as Carnap and Hempel have shown, reducible to a physicalistic basis if we can but specify a set of environmental conditions and observable effects or results characteristic of each in terms of observable thing predicates. In the case of psychological terms these conditions and their results consist, on the one hand, of a description of the physical or social environment, and on the other, of a description of the behavior in terms of physiological processes, such aspects of overt behavior as can be observed, or the effects on the environment of the organism's activity. That there are such defining procedures which reveal stable symptom patterns is readily apparent, for otherwise we should never be able to apply such abbreviatory psychological terms to another person on the basis of our observation of his behavior, as we obviously do in everyday life.

This formulation of logical behaviorism represents essentially, I believe, the methodological position of most present-day experimental psychologists. Certainly the operational behaviorism of Tolman follows closely this conception, and the behavior theory of Hull and myself is based on such a methodological approach. Skinner's formulation is another obvious instance.

Now, undoubtedly, as Allport's statement quoted earlier implies, it is easier for psychologists whose research interests have been concerned with such relatively simple phenomena as animal learning and simple conditioning, or even the acquisition of motor and verbal skills in human subjects, to hold to the criteria that such a methodological behaviorism demands. Unquestionably the more rapid progress that has been made in the study of these simpler events, as compared with the more complex aspects of human personality, is due, in part, to the fact that the simpler phenomena have readily lent themselves to study by acceptable operations, whereas such methods have not been so available in the case of complex phenomena.

One must also agree with Professor Allport that we objectivists have tended to concentrate our efforts in these simpler areas; not however, as he implies, because we have any special aversion to the problems of personality and certainly not because we have a preference, to quote him, "for externals rather than internals, for elements rather than patterns, for geneticism, and for a passive or reactive organism rather than for one that is spontaneous and active" (1, p. 12). The explanation of our interests is, I think, much simpler. As scientists we are interested in discovering and formulating a body of knowledge concerning the behavior of living organisms that is continuous with and has the same properties, empirical and logical, as the knowledge sought in the other natural sciences. Since the attainment of such knowledge requires methods of observation that assure publicly verifiable concepts, we have naturally insisted on the use of such techniques.

While insistence on the meeting of this methodological requirement has been one factor determining the particular aspects of behavior that we have chosen to investigate, the primary criterion that has guided us in any priorities that we have given to various areas of psychological study has been our estimate of the likelihood of successful accomplishment of our aim of discovering scientific laws about the phenomena. Being guided by such purely scientific objectives, and not having any special interests, humanitarian, religious, social betterment or otherwise, no particular area of human or animal behavior is seen as more important than another.   We have chosen to investigate simpler phenomena first because we are of the belief that progress in the formulation of psychological laws and theories will be more rapid in this area than in the case of more complex behavior.   We also believe that many of the variables and laws isolated in the study of simpler forms of behavior will be operative in more complex instances, interacting presumably with the additional factors introduced into these more complex situations.   If such is the case it would appear to be more efficient in the long run to investigate the simpler phenomena first.

From what has just been said, however, it should not be inferred that I would recommend that we neglect for the present the more complex aspects of personality.   Quite to the contrary, I am of the belief that our attempts to investigate such behavior phenomena by objective means have been reasonably encouraging.   Human adjustment, conflict and anxiety, complex motives, attitudes and interests, problem solving and reasoning are all now being studied by purely objective methods of observation.   To a considerable extent progress in these matters will depend on our success in developing methods for studying and analyzing the language behavior of our human subjects.   As yet we have made only the barest beginning in this important area of behavior.   Whether there will be aspects of human activity, such things as Allport designates by the terms selfhood, conscience and freedom, that are not susceptible to investigation by our objective techniques is an empirical question, the answer to which can only be ascertained by trying.   Psychologists who know *a priori* that such efforts are doomed to failure are relying on something other than scientific judgment.[3]

Finally, it should be evident that any body of knowledge concerning phenomena that is based on introspective observation or empathic projection is a kind of knowledge that differs from

---

[3] So far as areas that depend primarily for their data on language reactions are concerned, for example clinical psychology, the strict physicalistic position described here is as yet only programmatic and not something that is assured of unlimited success. While, from a practical viewpoint, it may be advantageous in such areas to begin with a less strict objectivism, my plea here is for the encouragement of research in such areas entirely within the framework of the strict physicalistic position.

scientific knowledge. If there are persons who are desirous of developing such knowledge about human personality, one can have no objection. It should be clearly understood, however, that such a formulation does not meet the criteria of the natural sciences and hence should not be represented as being one of them. My own preference would be to avoid using the term science (*e.g.,* cultural science) in connection with such formulations, for this will only lead to confusion. Perhaps we also ought to set off scientific psychology by the use of some such terms as biopsychology or possibly psychobiology.

III

From this discussion of the basic observational terms of the language of science in general and psychology in particular, I should like to turn now to the terms at the opposite end of the hierarchy—namely the so-called theoretical concepts. I shall begin by discussing these concepts as they are used in the more highly developed natural sciences, particularly physics. First, with regard to the function they serve, theories are introduced by the scientist for the purpose of providing a more comprehensive understanding or explanation of the observed phenomena. They do this by providing for the deduction of previously unrelated empirical laws and as yet unknown laws, thus unifying and extending our knowledge.

For our present purpose such theories in physics may be divided into two classes. In the first class, which I shall refer to as the *empirical construct type* of theory, the theoretical structure consists of a set of abstract concepts that are organized into a system of general laws (postulates) from which other empirical laws may be deduced as theorems. The constructs of such theories, it should be noted, are a part of the hierarchy of empirical concepts, being among the most highly abstract. One example of this type of theory is Newton's gravitational theory, which provided for the unification of the previously unrelated areas of astronomy and terrestrial mechanics. Bergmann has also cited Maxwell's electromagnetic theory of light as a further example of a theory lying, to quote him, "entirely within the realm of the empirical constructs" (2, p. 338).

The second class of comprehensive theories in physics is best represented by the atomic theories. Such theories, which I shall designate as *axiomatic-model* theories, employ an axiomatic system or scientific calculus. Very briefly, they consist of a system of postulated relations (implicit definitions) between empirically undefined terms or primitive signs. Further terms are then introduced by means of explicit definitions, and theorems are logically deduced. Finally, some of the terms of this calculus, preferably defined terms, are identified by what are called co-ordinating definitions with certain terms in an empirical system. Examples of such axiomatic-model theories are the Maxwell-Boltzman theory of gases and the various quantum theories.

I have identified these two types of theories in physics so that I might contrast them with what passes for theory in psychology. It should be noticed that such comprehensive physical theories, whether of the first or second class, are formulated only after there is available a considerable body of empirical laws relating concepts of a fairly abstract nature *i.e.*, highly generalized laws. It would hardly seem necessary to have to say that no such comprehensive, highly abstract theories exist today in psychology, for the simple reason that we do not even have a well developed body of very general laws in any area of our field. And yet, as you well know, one finds frequent reference to axiomatic-model types of theory in psychology today. Apparently the so-called hypothetico-deductive systems formulated in the late thirties and early forties by Hull and Lewin are primarily responsible for the mistaken notion that such theories exist in psychology. However, as Bergmann and I pointed out some years ago, Hull's miniature theoretical systems, despite appearances to the contrary, were not of the type that began with the introduction of a formal calculus which was later coordinated to an empirical system of concepts (3). Rather, as we showed, his theory was of the intervening variable type in which new, abstract concepts were introduced, *i.e.*, defined, in terms of the basic experimental variables. Following this analysis Hull explicitly acknowledged this conception of his theorizing, and he employed it in his *Principles of Behavior* (10). Needless to say, Lewin's formulations also possessed only the trappings of such theories.

A proper understanding of the nature and function of psychological theories is to be found in the present status of our knowledge in psychology.   If one examines the various fields of psychology it will be readily apparent that many areas are as yet in a very primitive state of development.   For example, the study of complex personality is still only in the initial stages of scientific inquiry.   Psychologists in this area are just beginning to discover technical concepts that show promise of being significant, *i.e.,* of leading to laws.   Other segments of psychology would appear to be at a more advanced stage, one in which it has not only been possible to identify and measure a goodly number of the relevant variables, but also to determine fairly precisely laws relating them.   Except possibly for the areas concerned with the sensory processes, however, these laws have not been very general, but have tended rather to be highly specific to each particular situation.   The laws in the area of learning are a particularly good example of this specific type of lower-order relation.   Thus we find that curves of learning tend to take a different form in each particular learning situation, and even in the same situation with different response measures.

Being primarily in this stage of discovering and formulating laws, the theorizing of psychologists is chiefly concerned, then, either with (1) guessing at what the as yet unknown, relevant variables might be, or (2) in the more advanced areas, attempting to integrate relatively circumscribed sets of lower order laws. The latter, as we shall see, has involved the introduction of auxiliary concepts, *i.e.,* intervening variables, in the form of theoretical schemata that attempt to provide for the deduction and hence integration of the specific, law-order laws.

An adequate and comprehensive analysis of all of the various types of theorizing current in psychology today would require much more time than is presently at my disposal.   Hence, I shall attempt here only to deal with one example of psychological theorizing, that represented by the use of intervening variables, in connection with the phenomena of simple learning. The nature of this type of theorizing is not, I fear, very well understood, and I must admit that a rereading of some of my own earlier attempts (12, 13), to describe it appear to me now to be somewhat unsatisfactory.   Nor do I think that the recent discussions of intervening variables by Ginsberg (8) and MacCorquodale and Meehl (*11*) have been very helpful. The former apparently had little appreciation of the primitive nature of psychological laws, while MacCorquodale and Meehl let their concern over physiological reduction carry them away to such an extent that they were unable to see what possible function intervening variables might serve. Let us turn then to an examination of the intervening variable type of theory as it has been developed in the field of learning.

The first psychologist to suggest the need for intervening variables in psychology was Tolman. In an article entitled "Operational Behaviorism and Current Trends in Psychology," Tolman called attention to the point that in our experimental investigations various measurable aspects of behavior are studied as functions of the manipulable environmental variables, and the data so obtained are plotted in the form of various curves or families of curves. Typically, as Tolman further pointed out, these laws are rather complex, in the sense that a number of determining variables is involved and consequently the function $R_1 = f(X_1, X_2, X_3, \cdots X_n)$ is a very complicated one, one that is very difficult to formulate. As I interpreted Tolman, he proposed intervening variables as a theoretical device to aid in the discovery and formulation of such complicated functions (*12*). Thus he wrote:

> It (*i.e.*, this type of function) is in fact so complicated that we at present seem unable to state it in any single simple statement. We find, rather, that we have to handle it by conceiving it as broken down into successive sets of component functions. These component functions connect the independent variables to logically constructed "intervening variables," and then connect these intervening variables in their turn to one another and to the final dependent behavior (*16*, p. 91).

Whether this interpretation of Tolman's conception of the function of his intervening variables is correct or not, I have never known. Tolman has never commented on it, and since he never got around to being specific about his intervening variables, it has not been possible to analyze them, as it were, in action, and thus see what function they served in his system. Actually, the introduction of intervening variables will not lead to the *discovery* of the nature of such complex functions. There is but one way to ascertain the nature of these laws and that is to conduct experiments in which two or more of the independent variables are manipulated concomitantly. While intervening variables might aid in guessing at such compound laws, they will not provide for their derivation in the sense of prediction. Once discovered by experimentation, intervening variables can, of course, provide for simpler formulation of such laws.

More recently Tolman has rejected intervening variables with the following statement:

> I am now convinced that "intervening variables" to which we attempt to give merely operational meaning by tying them through empirically grounded functions either to stimulus variables, on the one hand, or to the response variables, on the other, really can give us no help unless we can also imbed them in a model from whose attributed properties we can deduce new relationships to be looked for (4, p. 49).

The important requirement of an adequate theory, Tolman now claims, is that *specific intrinsic properties* must be ascribed to the theoretical model.

That Tolman should have come to this view after all these years is certainly surprising. When one reads further that the models contemplated were to be, as he termed them, brain or "pseudo-brain" models, one cannot help but begin to share Skinner's scepticism of theories and theorists in psychology. My own attitude on this particular matter is probably best summed up in the following quotation from an eminent psychologist: "But the psychological facts and laws have also to be gathered in their own right. A psychology cannot be explained by a physiology until one has a psychology to explain" (16, p. 92). This statement, as the reference indicates, is taken from Tolman's article in which he originally introduced the concept of intervening variables. In my own opinion it is, perhaps unfortunately, just as pertinent today as when written 20 years ago.

This brings us, finally, to my own conception of the role of intervening variables. The formulation to be presented is based on my understanding of what Hull and I have been attempting to accomplish in the area of learning. I say "my understanding," because Hull's emphasis has been somewhat different from mine in that he has tended to include in his use of intervening variables their physiological connotations. On the other hand, I have emphasized only their mathematical specifications.

The type of theoretical schema that employs intervening variables, as I conceive it, is primarily concerned with integrating and bringing into deductive relation with one another the different, specific laws found in the various kinds of learning situations (14, 15). That is, the objective is to introduce a set of concepts which, in combination with the experimental variables and the particular initial and boundary conditions of the environment and the organism, will provide for the deduction of the many different, specific empirical relations that are found in the several kinds of learning situations.

Examination of the current fields of learning phenomena reveals the fact that the laws, e.g., the curves of learning, take different forms in different situations and in the same situation with different response measures. Indeed, even the same response measure in the same learning situation may give quite different curves under variation of such conditions as the motivational level. For example, we have found that frequency curves of eyelid conditioning obtained in our laboratory with comparable, homogeneous subjects under different levels of puff intensity consistently give two quite different kinds of functions: subjects conditioned with a strong puff give a negatively accelerated curve, whereas subjects conditioned with a weak puff give an S-shaped curve.

At this point it seems to me that we are confronted with a choice of being a radical empiricist or a theorist. We can, on the one hand, fit two different functions to such curves and be satisfied to state two quite different, unrelated laws for this measure of conditioning under two levels of puff intensity. This presumably is what an empiricist such as Skinner is content to do. On the other hand we can, as Hull and I have attempted, try to provide a theoretical schema that will derive these two different curve forms as special cases depending upon the particular initial and boundary conditions employed. Similarly, the same theoretical schema is employed to derive the many other kinds of learning curves that are obtained with other response measures in various types of learning situations. That is, this type of theory attempts to provide for the unification of what, without the theory, would be a multiplicity of isolated, specific laws.   It is, in effect, a primitive form of the empirical-construct type of theory described earlier, in which the auxiliary (theoretical) concepts, *e.g.*, habit strength (H), excitatory potential (E), oscillatory inhibition (I_o) etc., like the concepts of force and energy in mechanics, are defined out of the original experimental variables.

Like these latter concepts, the intervening variables of learning theory serve as general or abstract terms that are applicable to a variety of situations.   The difference between such a psychological theory and the empirical-construct type of theory in physics (*e.g.*, Newton's theory) is in the range of knowledge that is unified.   Unlike the theory of gravitation, which served to integrate laws dealing with situations of widely diverging appearance, our learning theory is concerned only with very low-order laws in a relatively circumscribed area of observation. The field of learning is as yet only in the early period of Galileo, not that of Newton.

REFERENCES

1. ALLPORT, G.   *Becoming: Basic Considerations for a Psychology of Personality.*   New Haven: Yale University Press, 1955.

2. BERGMANN, G.   Outline of an empiricist philosophy of physics (Concluded).   *Amer. J. Physics.*   1943, *11*, 335–342.

3. ———, & SPENCE, K. W.   Operationism and theory in psychology.   *Psychol. Rev.*, 1941, *48*, 1–14.

4. BRUNER, J. S. & KRECH, D.   *Perception and Personality.*   Discussion by Tolman, pp. 48–51.   Durham: Duke University Press, 1950.

5. CARNAP, R.   *Der logische Aufbau der Welt.*   Leipsig: F. Meiner, 1928.

6. ———.   *The Unity of Science.*   London: Kegan Paul, Trench, Trubner, 1934.

7. ———.   Testability and meaning.   *Philos. Sci.*, 1936, *3*, 419–471, 1937, *4*, 1–40.

8. GINSBERG, A.   Hypothetical constructs and intervening variables.   *Psychol. Rev.*, 1954, *61*, 119–131.

9. HEMPEL, C. G.   The logical analysis of psychology.   Reprinted in Feigl, H., & Sellers, W.   *Readings in Philosophical Analysis.*   New York: Appleton-Century-Crofts, 1949.

10. HULL, C. L.   *Principles of Behavior.*   New York: D. Appleton-Century, 1943.

11. MacCorquodale, K., & Meehl, P. E.   On a distinction between hypothetical constructs and intervening variables. *Psychol. Rev.*, 1948, *55,* 95–107.

12. Spence, K. W.   The nature of theory construction in contemporary psychology. *Psychol. Rev.*, 1944, *51,* 47–68.

13. ———.   The postulates and methods of behaviorism. *Psychol. Rev.*, 1948, *55,* 67–78.

14. ———.   Mathematical formulations of learning phenomena. *Psychol. Rev.*, 1952, *59,* 152–160.

15. ———.   Mathematical theories of learning. *J. gen. Psychol.*, 1953, *49,* 283–291.

16. Tolman, E. C.   Operational behaviorism and current trends in psychology. *Proc. 25th Anniv. Celebration Inaug. Grad. Stud.* Los Angeles: The University of Southern California, 1936, pp. 89–103.

17. Watson, J. B.   Psychology as the behaviorist views it. *Psychol. Rev.*, 1913, *20,* 158–177.

PART II

Behavior Theory

6

The Roles of Reinforcement and
Non-reinforcement in Simple Learning[1]

In the presentation of my theoretical views concerning classical
and instrumental conditioning (29) given in the Silliman Lectures at Yale University a few years ago, little or no attention
was given to the phenomenon of inhibition or response decrement that occurs with non-reinforcement. The limitation of
seven lectures necessitated confining the discussion primarily
to the role of motivational and reinforcement variables in the
acquisition of a CR and to the theoretical constructs relative to
them. While some hint as to the nature of my theorizing concerning such inhibitory phenomena was provided in connection
with the discussion in these lectures of the delay of reinforcement variable, I do not seem to have been able to find an opportunity to present a more extensive treatment of them. In the
present paper, then, the theoretical schema of classical and instrumental conditioning formulated in the Silliman Lectures
will be extended to include the behavioral effects of non-
reinforcement. Not only will the role of non-reinforcement in
experimental extinction be discussed, but consideration will also
be given to its function in the acquisition of a conditioned response under partial reinforcement schedules.

By way of background I should like to begin by considering,

[1] Presented with some variations in Colloquim talks at the Universities of
Alabama, Michigan, and Maryland.

historically, the views that Hull and I have had as to the role of reinforcement and non-reinforcement in simple learning. My reason for starting out in this manner is that many psychologists, particularly the younger ones, have not always been sufficiently aware either of the different conceptions that Hull held at various times with respect to the role of these variables in learning or of the differences that existed between his views and mine concerning them.

First it is important to realize that as far as learning theory is concerned, there were two Hulls—Hull of the 1930's, and Hull of the 1940's and after. Apparently many psychologists have either never realized or have lost sight of the fact that in his theoretical articles in the *Psychological Review* in the thirties Hull did not think of himself and was not regarded as being a reinforcement theorist (*c.f. 13, 14, 15, 16*). In these early articles Hull was primarily interested in the possibility of extending the quantitative laws of behavior discovered in simple conditioning experiments to more complex instances of learning, such as trial and error learning, maze learning, and human rote learning. It was during this period that I became associated with Hull and, paralleling his work, I attempted to show how these same laws could be employed to derive behavioral phenomena exhibited in visual discrimination learning, such as, for example the phenomena of position habits or "hypotheses" and transposition behavior (*23, 24*).

The emphasis in such theorizing was on the quantitative aspects of the behavior and, as I have pointed out on a number of occasions (*c.f. 28*), this kind of quantitative theory can be developed quite independently of such theoretical issues as reinforcement versus contiguity, drive or stimulus reduction versus stimulus onset, etc. For the most part this type of theorizing proceeded from the empirical law-of-effect, which merely summarized a relation observed to hold between two sets of events; on the one hand, the kind of outcome or effect (reinforcer or non-reinforcer) a response produces, and on the other, the subsequent probability of occurrence of that response. That is, in this type of formulation, empirical response measures such as probability of occurrence, response amplitude, speed of response, etc., are first specified as some function of the excitatory tendency of an S to arouse an R. The further basic assumptions are then made that the strength of this excitatory tendency increases on each occasion that R is followed by a reinforcer (as empirically determined) and decreases when not accompanied by a reinforcer. By making certain quantitative assumptions concerning the magnitude of these increments and decrements with successive reinforcements or non-reinforcements such a theory was able to derive various implications about the growth or decline in strengths of the net or effective excitatory tendencies of the response or responses involved.

Such a quantitative, empirical law-of-effect theory, it should be noted, need not take a position on the mechanism of the action of a reinforcer. Thus it could be assumed that the increment in excitatory tendency of the response results merely as a consequence of the occurrence of the response to the S, and that the role of the reinforcer is to insure or maintain this increase in the excitatory strength. This latter, of course, is the position of a contiguity theorist such as Guthrie (11). Actually, neither Hull in his earliest formulations, nor I, took any position on this matter, but merely introduced the quantitative construct, excitatory tendency, that was assumed to increase with a reinforcement and decrease with failure of occurrence of one. That such a theory is not necessarily a reinforcement theory in the sense of Hull's theorizing in his *Principles of Behavior* (17) will become apparent later.

So much for this earlier quantitative, law-of-effect type of learning theory. I should like to turn now to the more recent theoretical formulations of Hull (17, 18, 19) and myself (27, 29), limiting our considerations for the moment to those portions of the theory that deal with instrumental reward conditioning involving appetitional needs such as hunger and thirst.

Hull's Reinforcement Theory of Instrumental Reward Learning

The following equation represents the theory of this kind of learning proposed by Hull in his *Principles of Behavior* (17):

$$R \quad = \quad f(\bar{E}) \quad = \quad \underset{\underset{T_D}{\uparrow}}{D} \quad \times \quad \underset{\underset{N_G, M_G, T_G}{\uparrow}}{H} \quad - \quad \underset{\underset{N_R, T_R, W_R}{\uparrow}}{\dot{I}_R}$$

In this formulation a hypothetical learning or associative factor
(H) was introduced for the first time as a function of the number of occasions that the S-R was accompanied or followed by a
reinforcer (N_G).   Non-reinforcement was definitely assumed not
to lead to any H, and different increments of H were postulated
as a function of the amount (M_G) and delay (T_G) of the reinforcer.   These latter two variables, M_G and T_G, appeared as
parameters in the function relating H to N_G, determining the
asymptote to which H would develop with successive reinforced
trials.   This habit factor, based on reinforcements, was assumed
to combine with a drive factor (D) in a multiplicative fashion to
determine excitatory potential (E) and hence the strength of the
response.

Failure of a reinforcer *as such,* it should be noted, was not
assumed to produce any decremental effect, but an inhibitory
factor, work inhibition (I_R), was introduced in terms of such
variables as the number of successive responses (N_R), the time
between successive trial runs (T_R) and the amount of work involved in the response (W_R).   Extinction of a response presumably took place because, with non-reinforcement, there was
no further growth of H, whereas the work inhibition factor continued to develop, thus weakening the effective excitatory potential ($\overset{i}{E}$).   Conditioned inhibition (s-r) also developed according to Hull's theory and interfered with the learned response.
The symbol $\dot{I}_R$ includes these two kinds of inhibition.

This 1943 theory of Hull's was the kind of theory that will be
referred to as a true reinforcement theory and by such a theory
I mean that an associative factor, habit strength (H), is assumed
to vary with the number of occurrences and other properties of
a reinforcer.   Hull also, of course, had a physiological hypothesis of the mechanism of this reinforcement, conceiving of it in
terms of a reduction in the strength of the existing need or drive
stimulus.

Hull 1952 Reinforcement Theory

In his later, posthumus book, *A Behavior System,* Hull (*19*)
modified his system somewhat as shown in the following equation:

$$R = f(\bar{E}) = \overset{\overset{\displaystyle T_D}{\downarrow}}{D} \times \overset{\overset{\displaystyle M_G, T_G?}{\downarrow}}{K} \times \overset{\overset{\displaystyle N_G}{\downarrow}}{H} - \overset{\overset{\displaystyle N_R, T_R, W_R}{\downarrow}}{\dot{I}_R}$$

The main point to be noted here is that a reinforcer was still specified as a necessary condition for the development of H (i.e., $H = f\ N_G$). However, Hull no longer conceived of the increment of H as being functionally related in any manner to either the magnitude or delay of the reward, but instead substituted an all or none conception for the continuous function he previously assumed.

On the basis of the experimental findings of the effects of varying and shifting reward magnitude, Hull also introduced an incentive motivational variable, K, which he assumed to be a function of the magnitude of the reinforcer (i.e., $K = f\ W_G$). As may also be seen, Hull continued to hold to his concepts of work and conditioned inhibition. Both of Hull's theories of instrumental reward conditioning are thus seen to be reinforcement theories in the sense that the occurrence of a reinforcer is assumed to be *necessary* for the development of the habit strength (H) of the instrumental response.

Spence Theory of Instrumental Reward Conditioning

We come next to the theoretical formulation of this kind of conditioning that I have held since about 1950 and which was presented in the Silliman Lectures (*29*). Examination of the following equation will reveal some of the ways in which it differs from Hull's formulations.

$$R = f(E) = (\overset{\overset{\displaystyle T_D}{\downarrow}}{D} + \overset{\overset{\displaystyle N_G, M_G}{\downarrow}}{K}) \times \overset{\overset{\displaystyle N_R}{\downarrow}}{H} - \overset{\overset{\displaystyle N_G, N_{TG} > O}{\downarrow}}{I_N}$$

First, with respect to the role of a reinforcer, it will be observed that the action of a reinforcer is *not* conceived as affecting the associative factor, H, but instead is assumed to determine the excitatory potential (E) of the instrumental response through the incentive motivational factor, K. That is, the number of times a reinforcer (N_G) follows a response and its magnitude

(M_G) are assumed to determine not H, but the incentive motivational variable, K.   As has been indicated elsewhere the mechanism underlying this concept is assumed to be the classically conditioned fractional anticipatory goal response, r_g.   Or, in other words, K is a quantitative molar variable conceived as reflecting the strength of this anticipatory goal response.   Like the drive variable, D, K is assumed to combine multiplicatively with habit strength (H) to determine reaction potential E. Tentatively, D and K have been assumed to combine in a simple additive fashion.   It is possible that this will have to be changed to some non-linear function.

The habit strength (H) of the instrumental response, it is important to note, is assumed to be a function of the number of occurrences of the response (N_R) in the situation and to be quite independent of the occurrence or non-occurrence of a reinforcer. Thus, if the response occurs there will be an increment in H regardless of whether a reinforcer does or does not result.   This assumption, it is apparent, makes this formulation a contiguity and not a reinforcement theory.   And yet the theory, as is clearly evident, implies that the *excitatory strength* (E) of the response in such instrumental learning situations does depend upon the occurrence and properties of the reinforcer.   Thus the theory is in accord with the *empirical law-of-effect*, which summarizes the experimental evidence that the presence or absence of a reinforcer, and variations in its properties when it is present, do make a difference in the *strength* of the response in such learning situations.

Turning now to the portion of my theory of instrumental reward learning dealing with the concept of inhibition, I have always assumed, quite in contrast to Hull's work or fatigue conception, that failure of occurrence of a reinforcer following an instrumental response is responsible for the development of an inhibitory factor, which I have designated I_n.   With regard to this aspect of the theory Hull and I were at odds for many years. My conception, dating from my 1936 theoretical paper on "The Nature of Discrimination Learning in Animals," has been that inhibition in such reward type learning situations is primarily a *frustration* phenomena.   Indeed, I referred to the principle operating in the case of such non-reinforcements as the principle of "inhibition or frustration" (23, p. 430). My emphasis on the frustration character of the phenomenon stemmed from my early observations of the chimpanzee in discrimination learning situations. Anyone who has observed the behavior of these emotionally expressive animals under circumstances involving non-reinforcement will know to what I am referring. While varying from individual to individual the reaction pattern can best be described as aggression and interpreted as reflecting the emotion of anger.

On the basis of the quantitative findings of these early discrimination experiments (25, 26), I was led to conclude that this inhibitory or frustration effect not only varied directly with the strength of the non-reinforced response tendency, but also that *there was no inhibitory effect present until a certain number of prior reinforcements to the stimulus complex had been received.* In other words, these early experiments suggested that the subject had to learn to *expect* or to *anticipate* a reward upon responding to a stimulus before there would be any inhibition or frustration effect.

As I indicated earlier, except for some brief references in my Silliman Lectures, I have not had an opportunity to elaborate my conception of inhibitory phenomena in print.   In these lectures I did call attention to the point that delay of reinforcement at the terminal end of an instrumental response chain is essentially analogous to experimental extinction.   The latter, in fact, may be thought of as the limiting case of delay of reinforcement, that in which the delay is infinitely long.   From this point of view performance decrements produced by such delays of reinforcement would be regarded as resulting essentially from the same set of factors that are operating in experimental extinction or non-reinforcement.   Accordingly, the constructs I_t and I_n were introduced, depending upon which operation, delay or witholding of reward, was employed.   While the basis of this inhibition was assumed to be frustration-aroused, competing responses that occur with such operations, the molar concepts of I_t and I_n were introduced to represent their quantitative effects.

In elaborating this conception of inhibition here it will be

seen that my ideas about it are very similar to formulations that
have been put forward recently by a number of behavior-theory
oriented writers, including Rohrer (*21*), Adelman and Maatsch
(*1*), and Amsel (*2*).   The latter, in particular, has been especially
active in this area, contributing extensively not only to theory
but also conducting some ingenious experiments to test his ideas
(*3, 4*).   The following brief summary gives the main ideas of my
version of this type of theory:

1. Non-reinforcement of a previously reinforced response results in an emotional state or response which, following the
terminology suggested by Amsel (*2*), is designated as r_f.   This
emotional (anger) response, like the hypothetical emotional
(pain) response, r_e, that I have postulated as resulting from a
noxious stimulus (*30*), is assumed to contribute to the general
drive level, *D,* of the subject.

2. The occurrence of the response, r_f, is assumed to depend
upon the prior development in instrumental reward learning of
the expectation of the reward, or in terms of my theory, when
the fractional anticipatory r_g has been conditioned in some
degree to the stimulus cues in the instrumental chain.   Moreover, it is assumed that a positive relation holds between the
strength of the r_f and the strength of the r_g.   Attention should
be called to the point that these assumptions are in essential
agreement with the earlier postulates made in my discrimination
theory that the inhibitory effect of a non-reinforcement is related to the strength of the response tendency and would be zero
at very low levels, such as presumably would be the case in the
earliest stages of learning.

3. As Amsel (*2*) was the first to suggest and assume, the emotional (frustration) response, r_f, not only would occur at the end
of the response chain, *i.e.,* in the goal box, but, as in the case of
the fractional anticipatory consummatory reaction, r_g, would be
expected to become conditioned to stimulus events earlier in the
response chain.   In other words the animal should also come
to make an anticipatory frustration (emotional) response in the
runway (S_c—r_f).

4. Finally, it is assumed that during experimental extinction
the frustration-aroused response, r_f, through its own response
produced cues, s_f, tends to elicit previously learned or unlearned

overt responses, some of which are incompatible with the learned instrumental response of running forward. Occurring as they do in the goal box, these competing responses should become conditioned to the stimulus cues present there and thus, through generalization, to the highly similar cues of the alley. With repetition of the non-reinforced trials during experimental extinction these incompatible responses would gradually become more strongly conditioned to the situation with the consequence that they would compete more and more successfully with the learned response sequence. The more frequent occurrence of these interfering responses has the effect, of course, of increasing the time required to complete the response chain, thus producing the typical curve of decrement in response strength. As may be seen, this formulation is essentially an interference theory of inhibition.

With this outline of the theoretical schema of inhibition before you, I should like next to show how it may be applied to certain phenomena that have appeared when partial or intermittent schedules of reinforcement have been employed in the original learning. Since Amsel (2) has already shown how this kind of theory is nicely able to account for the well known fact that extinction is much slower following partial reinforcement than after continuous reinforcement, I shall confine the present discussion to a consideration of certain differential effects of varying reinforcement schedules on performance during the *acquisition* period of instrumental learning.

In the case of a partial reinforcement schedule during training we should expect the frustration or emotional response, r_f, resulting from the intermittent non-reinforcements, to become conditioned to the cues of the instrumental situation. Because the anticipatory goal response, r_g, is assumed to be zero at the start and to develop gradually during the course of training, it follows that there will be a lag in the appearance of the conditioned frustration response. As a consequence the response-produced s_f cues will be absent or weak at first and thus will presumably have only weak tendencies to evoke responses incompatible with the to-be-learned instrumental response (principle of stimulus dynamism). Under this circumstance to-be-learned instrumental response would be more likely to occur in

the situation than the competing responses, with the result that
the s_f cues would become conditioned to it.   Thus the animal
would come, though frustrated, to make the required instrumental response (running forward in the runway) rather than
the competing responses as described earlier in the case of experimental extinction (100% non-reinforcement).

Fortunately, there are some fairly clear cut implications of
this rather elaborate theory that permit some experimental tests
of it.   The first results from the fact that a partially reinforced
group, e.g., 50% reinforcement, will have an additional motivational factor present as compared with a continuously reinforced
group.   That is, the conditioned emotional response, r_f, should
add substantially to the general drive level, D, of the partial
group with the consequence that after a considerable amount of
training, its performance should eventually be higher than that
of the continuous group.   The derivation of this implication
requires, of course, that the habit strengths of the instrumental
responses of the 50% and 100% reinforced Ss be equal.   Such
equality does hold, it should be noted, for our theory of instrumental reward conditioning assumes that the habit strength, H,
of such responses is a function of the number of response occurrences (N_R) and not the number of reinforced trials (N_G).   A
problem does exist, however, concerning the values of K for the
two groups.   Unfortunately, we do not have definitive knowledge as to whether partial reinforcement (e.g., 50%) leads to a
lower asymptotic strength of a classical reward CR than when
continuous reinforcement is employed.   If this should be the
case our theory would have to assume that the difference ($K_{100}-
K_{50}$) was less than the difference ($D_{50}-D_{100}$) produced by different
reinforcement schedules.   Should the percentage of reinforcement merely determine the rate of approach to the same maximum asymptotic strength of a classical reward CR, then the K
values for different schedules would become equalized after extensive instrumental reward training.

A number of experimental studies have recently provided
considerable support for this theoretical prediction.   Shown in
Fig. 1 are the results of a Master's thesis recently conducted in
our laboratory by Goodrich (10).   The upper graph presents
curves of speed of starting in a runway for groups reinforced 50

and 100 per cent of the training trials.   The lower graph presents similar curves for a running speed measure also taken in the runway.   As may be seen the 50% group performed faster at the end of training than the continuously reinforced group in the case of both measures.

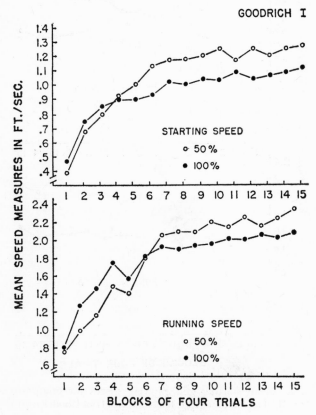

Fig. 1.   Mean starting and running speeds for groups reinforced 50 and 100 per cent trials in Exp. I of Goodrich (*10*).

Fig. 2 presents the results of a second experiment also carried out by Goodrich (*10*) under slightly different conditions.   As may be seen the results are essentially the same as in the first except that the final advantage of the 50% group in the case of measure was even greater than in the first study.   Taken to-

gether the difference in performance at the asymptotes was
highly significant.

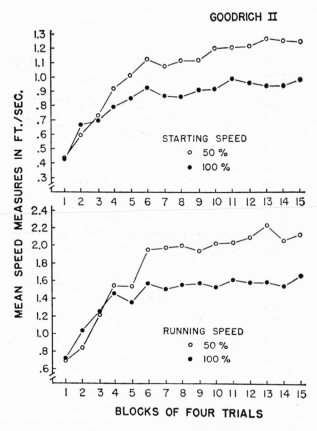

FIG. 2. Mean starting and running speeds for groups reinforced 50 and 100 per cent trials in Exp. II of Goodrich (*10*).

There are a number of further interesting facts to be noted in
these data.   First, it will be observed that the superiority of the
partially reinforced groups was not attained until after a certain
number of training trials.   It will be recalled that this finding
is precisely what the present theory would predict, for the development of the added motivational factor in the first part of
the response chain, the conditioned r_f, must await the prior de-

velopment of the classically conditioned fractional anticipatory goal response, r_g.

A second feature of these data is that there is a remarkably consistent pattern present in all of the graphs. Thus, in each instance the performance level of the 100% reinforced group is above that of the 50% group in the early stages, whereas in the later stages the reverse is the case with the performance curves crossing after approximately 20–24 trials. In the case of the starting speed measure this pattern has been obtained in six independent experiments (9, 10, 12, 33, 35). Two other studies (34, 35) have provided almost identical data except that the initial period of superiority of the 100% group has not been so clear cut. Of eight investigations reporting curves for the running speed measure, four have reported finding this same pattern (9, 10, 33). In the case of the failures, two (35, 36) have not shown clearly the initial advantage of the 100% group, while the other two (12, 34) have not revealed the final advantage of the 50% group. The latter finding is probably related to the fact that the running speed measure has involved the portion of the runway near the goal. There is some evidence to show that measures of performance taken at the end of the response chain (e.g., in goal box) differ greatly from those earlier in the chain in that the 100% group is superior to the 50% group at all stages of training (7, 10).

It is interesting to relate this pattern of results to the widely quoted generalization that Jenkins and Stanley made in their extensive review of the studies on partial reinforcement prior to 1950. Thus they concluded as follows:

Over-all, it can be said with considerable assurance that acquisition proceeds somewhat more rapidly and reaches a higher final training level under continuous reinforcement than under partial reinforcement (20, p. 209).

Examination of the studies reviewed by these writers reveals that this conclusion was based on only three studies that involved instrumental reward conditioning and in two of these only sixteen training trials were given, while in the third thirty partially reinforced training trials were given after ten continuously reinforced trials. Thus Jenkin's and Stanley's generalization would still appear to be supported as far as the early stages of training in instrumental reward learning are concerned. Obviously it does not hold in the later stages of this kind of learning, especially at the asymptote of performance after extended training.

Before leaving these data, attention should be called to the possible explanation provided by this theory of the initial superiority of the 100% reinforcement group over the 50% reinforced group. It is that the classically conditioned fractional anticipatory goal response would develop more slowly in a partial than in a continuously reinforced group and hence the value of the intervening variable, K, would be lower. As was discussed earlier, however, this difference in K might conceivably disappear with prolonged training.

Still another factor that may be operating to produce this initial difference between the 50 and 100% reinforced groups is that even though conditioned frustration has presumably not yet developed in this period, nevertheless, the subject on the non-reinforced trials is in the empty goal box with the consequence that it tends to make turning and other responses that are competitive with the running forward response. Thus these responses would tend to become conditioned to some extent to the goal box cues and with generalization to the similar runway cues. In this connection Goodrich reported finding that during this initial period of inferior performance on the part of partially reinforced subjects, these animals actually made a greater number of competing responses in the runway. Furthermore, he reports the observation that the greater incidence of competing responses on the part of the partial groups tended to disappear at the point at which the response speed curves for the 50 and 100% animals came together.

At this point I should like to call attention to a fact that so far appears to have escaped notice, namely that the findings of studies comparing acquisition performance asymptotes under intermittent and continuous reinforcement are quite different for instrumental reward conditioning than they are for classical aversive conditioning. In Figure 3 frequency conditioning curves obtained by Ross (1959) in our laboratory for groups conditioned with continuous and intermittent (50%) reinforcement are presented. A total of 200 trials was employed in order to insure that asymptotic performance was reached.   As can be seen, the 50% group attained a markedly lower asymptotic level than the continuously reinforced group, the difference being highly significant.   We have partially completed a second study

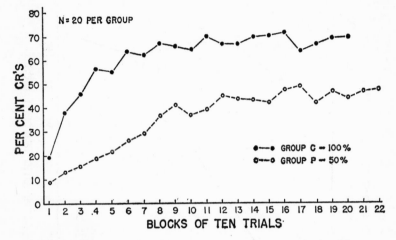

FIG. 3.   Frequency curves of eyelid conditioning obtained by Ross (22) for groups reinforced 50 and 100 per cent of trials.

in which three percentage of reinforcement values, 100%, 50%, and 20%, have been used with essentially the same results.   The three curves appear to be approaching different final asymptotic values.   Grant and Schipper (1950), using 100, 75, 50, and 25% reinforcement, have also obtained results that suggest the same conclusion although these investigators gave only 80 trials to each of their groups.

The difference between the effects of varied schedules of reinforcement in these two types of conditioning experiments is strikingly revealed in Figure 4.   The broken curve with closed circles in this graph depicts the asymptotic speed values for groups trained in a runway with different proportions of reinforced trials as estimated from running speed curves of conditioning reported by Weinstock (1954b).   The solid curve with open circles represents asymptotic percentage of CR values estimated from the frequency curves of eyelid conditioning obtained with groups of human subjects trained with four dif-

ferent percentage of reinforcements reported by Grant and
Schipper (1950). The third, solid curve joining the two open
triangles, shows the actual mean percentage of eyelid CR's obtained by Ross' groups in the block of trials 151–200, a point

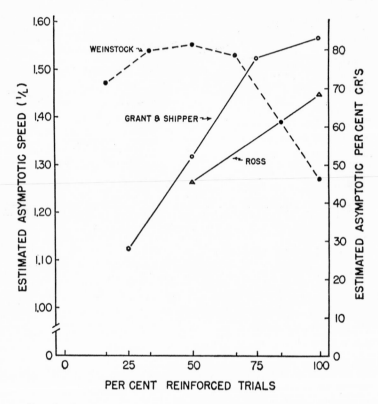

FIG. 4.   Performance limits obtained in instrumental reward
learning (36) and eyelid conditioning (8, 22).

at which the asymptote of the partially reinforced group had
clearly been attained. Since the scales of the two measures,
speed of running and percentage of CR's, are not comparable
the relative heights and slopes of the curves have no significance.
The direction of the curve slopes, however, are meaningful and
they clearly show that in the region between 50 and 100%
reinforcement the relation between response strength in the

instrumental reward situation and proportion of reinforcements is just the opposite to that obtained in classical aversive conditioning.

These divergent findings pose a rather formidable problem for all learning theories and it is interesting to consider, briefly, how they fare with respect to them. The implication of Hull's theory, with its reinforcement assumption that H is a function of N_G and his assumption about work inhibition being a function of response occurrence, may be shown to be that continuous reinforcement would at first lead to a higher level of performance than intermittent reinforcement, but that, eventually, both groups would reach the same performance asymptote. This derivation holds, moreover, for all forms of classical and instrumental conditioning, whether of the reward or aversive type. Obviously, the findings we have described for the instrumental reward and classical defense conditioning situations are quite contrary to these predictions.

Bush and Moesteller (5) have offered a modified reinforcement theory which assumes that probability of responding is increased by reinforcement and decreased by non-reinforcement. Without going into detail as to the derivation it may be shown that this theory leads to the prediction that the larger the percentage of reinforced trials, the greater will be the asymptotic probability of responding and also response speed, which is directly proportional to response probability. It is apparent that while the prediction of this theory is confirmed by the findings in classical aversive conditioning, the data obtained in instrumental reward conditioning are not in accord with it.

With regard to the statistical-association type of contiguity theory originally formulated by Guthrie it would appear that in classical conditioning, at least, continuous reinforcement would be expected to be superior to a partial schedule. This derivation is predicated upon the assumption that the response being conditioned will not occur on some of the non-reinforced trials and consequently the sample of stimulus elements present on such occasions will be disassociated from the response. The greater the proportion of non-reinforced trials the greater should be the number of such response failures and hence disassociations of the sampled stimulus elements. Thus it would be predicted that response probability would be directly related to percentage of reinforced trials in both aversive and reward types of classical aversive conditioning. Unfortunately we do not have satisfactory evidence on the effects of different reinforcement schedules on classical reward (*i.e.*, Pavlovian) conditioning.

In their statistical elaboration of association theory, Estes and Straughn (6) have developed an equation for the type of situation known as verbal conditioning which predicts that the asymptotic probability of making a particular response is the same as the proportion of times that response is reinforced. As Estes has pointed out, however, these equations are not applicable to "left-right discrimination without correction, to free-responding in the Skinner Box, or to Pavlovian conditioning" (6, p. 226). He might have added to this list the straight runway.

Nevertheless, Weinstock (35), one of Estes' students, has applied the more general statistical-association theory to the problem of intermittent reinforcement in the instrumental reward situation. To the usual notion that non-reinforcement leads to unconditioning of the sampled cues from the to-be-learned response that occurs in the situation, Weinstock adds the conception that these competing responses negatively adapt during the training period. Overlooking the incongruous nature of the assumption of negative adaptation within this theoretical framework, the implication of the formulation is that "there should be a direct relation between percentage of reinforcement and asymptotic speed running. The notions advanced, however, would lead us to believe that the differences in final running level . . . should be small" (1954a, p. 321). In a first investigation Weinstock (1954a) did not find significant differences in the asymptotic speeds of animals trained with 30, 50, 80, or 100% reinforcements, although the 30 and 80% groups did run faster than the 100% group. In a second experiment involving more subjects in each group (total 226) and a greater range of reinforcement proportions, Weinstock (1954b) did find the asymptotic runway speeds to be significantly different (.01 level). Indeed, it will be recalled from the previous graph that all partial groups (16.6, 33.3, 50, 66.7, and 83.3%) performed at a higher final level than the group reinforced on every trial.

Needless to say such findings as these and the similar ones of Goodrich and others mentioned earlier are extremely embarrassing not only to the statistical-association theory, but also to Hull's reinforcement theory and to the Bush-Moesteller model. Whether or not any of these theories can be rescued from this predicament is, of course, another matter.   It has been my observation that as Estes has attempted to extend his theory beyond the narrow base of phenomena to which it was originally directed, he has been forced to introduce more and more new, *ad hoc* assumptions.   Indeed, I suspect he is beginning to wish he had not been quite so critical of the extent to which Hull and I have had to make use of similar assumptions as we proceeded to extend our theories to a broader range of phenomena.   At the present primitive stage of development of our science the necessity for doing this is not surprising; only naïveté would lead one to expect anything else.

Returning now to my own theorizing on these matters, those who are acquainted with my Silliman Lectures know that I have tended to favor a kind of two-factor theory in so far as learning involving appetitional needs and aversive emotional states are concerned.   Thus, as we have seen, I have assumed in instrumental reward conditioning that habit strength (H) is not a function of a reinforcer, but only of the occurrence of the instrumental response.   On the other hand in the case of classical aversive conditioning the findings of some recent studies of ours involving different intensities of UCS in eyelid conditioning have led me to conclude that in the case of aversive motivation, habit strength (H) is dependent upon the occurrence and the intensity of the reinforcing stimulus, *e.g.*, the air puff (*31, 32*).

This theoretical schema for classical defense conditioning is shown in the following equation, in which it will be noted that H is assumed to be a function of both the intensity and frequency of presentation of the reinforcing stimulus (S_u).

$$R \quad = \quad \underset{\underset{D}{\downarrow}}{S_u} \quad \times \quad \underset{\underset{H}{\downarrow}}{S_u, N_{Su}} \quad - \quad \underset{\underset{I_n}{\downarrow}}{N_{-su}}$$

Inhibition (I_n), as may be seen, is assumed to be a function of the number of trials the conditioned stimulus is presented without the reinforcing stimulus (N_{-su}).

In the case of partial reinforcement in classical aversive conditioning, omission of the UCS on some proportion of the trials would, according to this theory, imply that, for any given number of trials, habit strength would be less for a partial than a continuously reinforced group. Combined with the inhibition resulting from the non-reinforced trials it would thus be predicted that response strength in this type of situation would be proportional to the per cent of trials that were reinforced. In connection with this derivation it should also be pointed out that I believe the nature of the mechanism lying behind inhibition (I_n) in the case of such aversive conditioning is very different from that in learning situations involving appetitional needs and reward incentives. Indeed it seems rather implausible to me that any frustration is involved in not receiving a noxious UCS. Hence, there would not be the increment in motivation (D) as in the case of reward learning. If this is so it would appear that the basis and hence the laws concerning the development of inhibition in these two types of learning situations should be quite different. Certainly the results of partial reinforcement studies would seem to support such a conclusion.

REFERENCES

1. ADELMAN, H. M., & MAATSCH, J. L.   Resistance to extinction as a function of the type of response elicited by frustration. *J. exp. Psychol.*, 1955, *50*, 61–65.
2. AMSEL, A.   The role of frustrative non-reward in non-continuous reward situations. *Psychol. Bull.*, 1958, *55*, 102–119.
3. ——, & HANCOCK, W.   Motivational properties of frustration: III. Relation of frustration effect to antedating goal factors. *J. exp. Psychol.*, 1957, *53*, 126–131.
4. ——, & ROUSSEL, J.   Motivational properties of frustration.   I. Effect on a running response of the addition of frustration to the motivational complex. *J. exp. Psychol.*, 1952, *43*, 363–368.
5. BUSH, R. R., & MOESTELLER, F.   A mathematical model for simple learning. *Psychol. Rev.*, 1951, *58* 313–323.
6. ESTES, W. K., & STRAUGHN, J. H.   Analysis of a verbal conditioning situation in terms of statistical learning theory. *J. exp. Psychol.*, 1954, *47*, 225–234.

7. FRIEDES, D. Goal box cues and pattern of reinforcement. *J. exp. Psychol.*, 1957, *53*, 361–371.

8. GRANT, D. A., & SCHIPPER, L. M. The acquisition and extinction of conditioned eyelid responses as a function of the percentage of fixed ratio random reinforcement. *J. exp. Psychol.*, 1950, *42*, 97–101.

9. GREENE, J. T. Performance in the runway as a function of the percentage of reinforced trials. Unpublished doctoral dissertation, Univ. of Illinois, 1955.

10. GOODRICH, K. P. Performance in different segments of an instrumental response chain as a function of reinforcement schedule. *J. exp. Psychol.*, 1959, *57*, 57–64.

11. GUTHRIE, E. R. *Psychology of Learning.* New York: Harper, 1935.

12. HAGGARD, D. F. Acquisition and extinction of a simple running response as a function of partial and continuous schedules of reinforcement. Unpublished doctoral dissertation, State Univ. of Iowa, 1956.

13. HULL, C. L. Simple trial-and-error learning: A study in psychological theory. *Psychol. Rev.*, 1930, *37*, 241–256.

14. ———. Knowledge and purpose as habit mechanisms. *Psychol. Rev.*, 1930, *37*, 511–525.

15. ———. The goal gradient hypothesis and maze learning. *Psychol. Rev.*, 1932, *39*, 25–43.

16. ———. The conflicting psychologies of learning—a way out. *Psychol. Rev.*, 1935, *42*, 491–516.

17. ———. *Principles of Behavior.* New York: Appleton-Century, 1943.

18. ———. Behavior postulates and correlaries.—1949. *Psychol. Rev.*, 1950, *57*, 173–180.

19. ———. *A Behavior System.* New Haven: Yale Univ. Press, 1952.

20. JENKINS, W. O., & STANLEY, J. C. Partial reinforcement: A review and critique. *Psychol. Bull.*, 1950, *47*, 193–234.

21. ROHRER, J. H. A motivational state resulting from non-reward. *J. comp. physiol. Psychol.*, 1949, *42*, 476–485.

22. ROSS, L. E. The decremental effect of partial reinforcement during acquisition of the conditioned eyelid response. *J. exp. Psychol.*, 1959, *57*, 74–82.

23. SPENCE, K. W. The nature of discrimination learning in animals. *Psychol. Rev.*, 1936, *43*, 427–449.

24. ———. The differential response in animals to stimuli varying within a single dimension. *Psychol. Rev.*, 1937, *44*, 430–444.

25. ———. Analysis of the formation of visual discrimination habits in chimpanzees. *J. comp. Psychol.*, 1937, *23*, 77–100. (b)

26. SPENCE, K. W. Gradual versus sudden solution of discrimination problems by chimpanzees. *J. comp. Psychol.*, 1938, *25*, 213–224.

27. ———. Mathematical formulations of learning phenomena. *Psychol. Rev.*, 1952, *59*, 152–160.

28. ———. Mathematical theories of learning. *J. gen. Psychol.*, 1953, *49*, 283–291.

29. ———. *Behavior Theory and Conditioning.* New Haven: Yale University Press, 1956.

30. ———. A theory of emotionally based drive (D) and its relation to performance in simple learning situations. *Amer. Psychol.,* 1958, *13,* 131–141.

31. ———, HAGGARD, D. F., & ROSS, L. E. UCS intensity and the associative (habit) strength of the eyelid CR. *J. exp. Psychol.,* 1958, *55,* 404–411. (a)

32. ———, ———, ———. Intrasubject conditioning as a function of the intensity of the unconditioned stimulus. *Science,* 1958, *128,* 774–775. (b)

33. WAGNER, A. R. Motivational effects of non-reinforcement as a function of the reinforcement schedule. Unpublished master's thesis, State Univ. of Iowa, 1957.

34. WEINSTOCK, MARIAN B. A factorial study of some variables effective resistance to extinction under partial reinforcement with spaced trials. Unpublished doctor's dissertation, Indiana Univ., 1957.

35. WEINSTOCK, S. Resistance to extinction of a running response following partial reinforcement under widely spaced trials. *J. comp. physiol. Psychol.,* 1954, *47,* 318–322. (a)

36. ———. Acquisition and extinction of a partially reinforced running response at a 24-hr. intertrial interval. Ph.D. dissertation, Indiana University, 1954. (b)

7

The Relation of Response Latency and Speed to
The Intervening Variables and N in S–R Theory

I

In the *Principles of Behavior* Hull introduced his theoretical constructs (intervening variables) initially in terms of independent environmental variables (*e.g.*, S_c, N, T_d, etc.), and completed the theoretical structure by anchoring them to certain response measures. The latter involved the introduction of specific *ad hoc* postulates that related each of the response measures (*e.g.*, latency, frequency, resistance to extinction, etc.) to one or other of the theoretical constructs. Thus in the case of the response measure (latency) with which we shall be concerned, Hull made the following assumption:

The latency of response (R_t) is a decreasing hyperbolic function of the momentary effective excitatory potential ($\dot{\bar{E}}$), *i.e.*, $R_t = a\dot{\bar{E}}^{-b}$, where a and b are empirical parameters (Postulate 13, p. 344).

Attention has been called elsewhere (*7, 8*) to the point that certain of these postulates are entirely superfluous in that assumptions already a part of the system (*i.e.*, earlier postulates) permit one to derive a necessary relation between these response measures and one or other of the theortical constructs. Thus in the case of the postulate introducing response probability or frequency ($R\%$) as a function of effective excitatory potential

($\bar{E}$), the relation assumed is, as has been shown, derivable from definitions and postulates already made concerning effective excitatory potential ($\bar{E}$), oscillatory inhibition (O) and reaction threshold (L). In this particular instance, the postulate Hull made (normal integral function) happened to be identical with the relation that may be derived from assumptions already a part of the system (6). In the case of the latency measure, however, it may be shown that the postulate he assumed is actually inconsistent with a necessary relation that follows from earlier assumptions. The main purpose of the present article is to consider the implications for this relationship of the assumptions already made concerning $\bar{E}$, O, and L, and to extend their implications to the empirical laws (learning curves) to be expected between response latency and speed, on the one hand, and the variable N on the other.[1]

We need to recall first that momentary effective excitatory potential, $\dot{\bar{E}}$, is equal to $\bar{E} - O$, and that a response is assumed to occur to a stimulus only when (a) $\bar{E}$ is greater than L, and (b) when an O value exists that is sufficiently small to make the value of $\dot{\bar{E}}$ greater than L. Oscillatory inhibition (O), it will be remembered, is assumed to change in value from moment to moment, the distribution of the values being postulated as normally distributed. The problem becomes one, then, of determining the average time, $\bar{t}$, before a momentary O value occurs that will provide an $\dot{\bar{E}}$ value greater than L.

Let P be the probability of occurrence of such an O value. Then the probability that such a value of O will be the first one to occur is P; the probability that such a value will be the second is $(1 - P)P$; the probability that it will be the third is $(1 - P)(1 - P)P$ or $P(1 - P)^2$, etc. Considering now an indefinitely large number of occasions on which the stimulus is presented, and representing the number of occurrences of momentary O values on any occasion by n, we may weight each possible value of n by its probability (expected relative frequency), and thus obtain a mean expected value of n. Estes (1) has shown that this mean value, $\bar{n}$, is equal to $1/P$. In other words, $\bar{n}$ is the

[1] The assumptions made concerning O are those given in Hull's *Principles of Behavior* (3), not those in his later *Essentials of Behavior* (4) and *A Behavior System* (5).

mean expected number of momentary O values that will occur on each stimulus occasion until an O value that provides a super-threshold $\dot{\bar{E}}$ value will occur.

If now we let u' represent the average time or duration of a momentary O, then the average time, $\bar{t}$, for a superthreshold $\dot{\bar{E}}$ value to occur will be the product of the expected number of momentary O values that will occur and the mean duration of a momentary O.

$$(1) \qquad\qquad \bar{t} = \bar{n}u' = \frac{u'}{P}.$$

In terms of an average measure of speed of response evocation $(\bar{v})$, this equation becomes

$$(2) \qquad\qquad \bar{v} = 1/\bar{t} = \frac{P}{u'} = uP,$$

where

$$u = 1/u'.$$

Figure 1 represents two levels of $\bar{E}$ and shows their relation

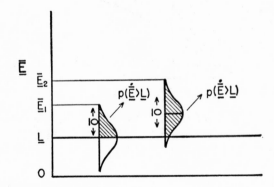

FIG. 1. The shaded portions of the upended normal distribution functions show the probability of E being greater than L for two levels of $\bar{E}$

to L and O. The probability (P) of O being a value that will produce a superthreshold $\dot{\bar{E}}$, which can also be described as the probability that $\dot{\bar{E}}$ is superthreshold, $[p(\dot{\bar{E}} > L)]$, is given by the proportion of the upended normal distribution that is above L. This yields

(3) $$P = p(\dot{\bar{E}}>L) = \int_{-\infty}^{\overline{E}-L-2.5\sigma 0} (O)\ dO.$$

Since $\bar{E}$ is assumed to be an exponential function of N, $i.e.$, $\bar{E} = A\,(1 - e^{-iN})$, it is possible to ascertain the theoretical function that P is of N by means of a table of cumulative probability values of the normal curve.   Figure 2 shows the family of theo-

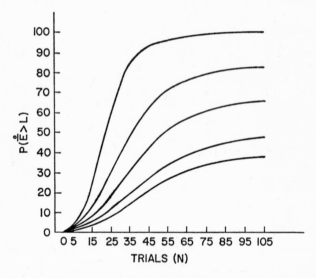

FIG. 2.   Family of theoretical curves of the proportion of superthreshold $\bar{E}$ values as a function of N for different curves of growth of $\bar{E}$

retical curves of the proportion of superthreshold $\dot{\bar{E}}$ values, $p(\dot{\bar{E}} > L)$ as a function of N for different curves of growth of $\bar{E}$. When multiplied by the parameter, u, representing the reciprocal of average duration of a momentary O value, such curves provide a theoretical prediction of $\bar{v}$ as a function of N. The relationship is identical in form, it should be noted, with the theoretical frequency measure in classical conditioning (7) and implies an initial period of positive acceleration, providing that the data represent the major portion of the total possible learning and not just some later part of it.

Now the measure $\bar{t}$, it should be noted, is a measure of the time it takes to get the effector activity initiated. As such it does not involve the time or duration of whatever neuromuscular activity is involved on the part of the subject in the measuring situation. In actual practice, however, any measurement of response latency must also involve the time taken by the action of the effector system. Presumably our so-called latency measures, or measures of response time, represent a summation of these two durations so that, if we let T represent the obtained experimental measure of response time, $\bar{t}$ the measure of action latency, and t' the duration of the effector activity involved in the measuring operation, then

$$(4) \qquad\qquad T = \bar{t} + t'.$$

A similar equation can be derived for a measure of speed of response (V) as follows:

$$(5) \qquad\qquad V = \frac{1}{\bar{t} + t'}$$

The problem immediately arises as to how t' (and its reciprocal, v') vary with $\bar{E}$. The present writer has not been able to derive a relation between t' and $\bar{E}$ from any of the existing postulates of the system. Accordingly, the working hypothesis is made that the relation is the simple hyperbolic one shown in the following equation: [2] $t' = \dfrac{c}{(\bar{E} - L)}$ where c is a constant.

Substituting now in equations 4 and 5, we obtain the following equations as representing the functions relating the experimental measurements of time (T) and speed of response (V) in simple instrumental conditioning to $\bar{E}$:

[2] This implies, of course, that the relation between speed of activity (v') and $\bar{E}$ is linear. $v' = \dfrac{(\bar{E} - L)}{c}$.

(6) $$T = \frac{u'}{P} + \frac{c}{(\bar{E} - L)},$$

(7) $$V = \frac{1}{\frac{u'}{P} + \frac{c}{(\bar{E} - L)}}.$$

An interesting implication of the above theorizing is that the shape of the curve of V as a function of $\bar{E}$, and hence of N, will depend upon the magnitude of the parameter c, which is experimentally manipulable by varying the amount (duration) of motor activity involved in the measurement of the response. Thus in the simple approach type of situation (locomotion in a straight alley), one could vary the value of c by measuring the response for different lengths of runway. When a minimum length of alley was employed, c would approach zero, and equation 7 would become identical with equation 2. Under this condition, the speed measure would provide an initially positively accelerated curve.

As the length of the runway involved in the measurement is increased, the value of c will increase, and the family of speed-of-response (V) curves as a function of N would be expected to vary in their initial phase from positive to negative acceleration. By selecting an appropriate length of runway, one should be able to obtain a curve that is linear in its early course of development. Finally, it should be noted that the theory implies that if the measurement (t') is taken from a point after the activity has started, the curve for speed of running (v') as a function of N should be a negatively accelerated exponential function, *i.e.*,

(8) $$v' = \frac{A (1 - e^{-iN}) - L}{c}.$$

II

The above derivations concerning the relation of the measures, response time and speed of response to N in instrumental learning, assume that the growth of $\bar{E}$ is an exponential one of the type that Hull employed. This assumption, in turn, depends upon the postulate that H grows in this manner and that the other factors determining $\bar{E}$, such as stimulus dynamism Q, drive D, incentive motivation K, and work inhibition I, are *constant* throughout the course of the training period. By means of various experimental techniques, such as distributing the trials, having only a few trials a day (three or four), etc., it is possible to keep Q, D, and I fairly constant. The situation is not so simple so far as the incentive motivational factor, K, is concerned. In recent discussions of theories of learning (6) the writer has suggested that this factor K might represent a stimulus dynamism, that provided by the proprioceptive component (s_G) of the fractional anticipatory goal response (r_G). According to this notion, in instrumental learning involving reward, one also has classical conditioning taking place so that a fractional part of the goal response becomes conditioned to the stimulus situation. With conditioning, this r_G and its cue s_G, by virtue of generalization, move forward in time and thus become a part of the internal stimulus complex determining the strength of the instrumental response. Thus it is a kind of acquired motivating factor, the strength of which depends not only on the conditions of reinforcement (*i.e.*, magnitude and delay of reinforcement), but also on the stage of training, *i.e.*, number of reinforced trials (N).

This hypothesis has a number of important implications, not only for experiments involving different magnitudes and delays of reinforcement, but also for the nature of the learning (performance) curve in simple instrumental learning. Confining our interest here to the latter problem, we shall consider the implication of the variation of K during learning *without taking into account how this motivational variable interacts or combines with the other two motivational constructs, Q and D.*

According to our assumption concerning E, and ignoring D and Q,

(9) $$R = f(E) = (K \times H).$$

Substituting for K and H their postulated relations to N, we obtain the following:

(10)
$$R = f(E) = [B - (B - x)e^{-gN}]$$
$$\times [A - (A - x)e^{-iN}].$$

According to equation 9, the growth of E as a function of N would be initially positively accelerated instead of the negatively accelerated exponential function that would obtain if K were some constant value.   In view of the fact that the curves of learning, *e.g.*, $V = f(N)$ and $v' = f(N)$, are determined in part by the growth of E, it is readily apparent that we need to take this function into account in making any predictions as to the form of these curves.   Thus, one interesting implication of this hypothesis is that if one were to establish K at a maximum (hence constant) value by setting up the classical CR $(S_c - r_a)$ to the sight and sound of the lever (S_c) *prior to the beginning of the instrumental learning,* the growth of E would now be expected to be a negatively accelerated function throughout its course.   Under this condition, the period of positive acceleration of the speed of response evocation curve $\bar{v} = f(N)$ should, other things being equated, be less than under the normal procedure in which the classical conditioning proceeds along with the instrumental learning.

In a similar fashion, one may predict that curves of speed of running $(v' = fN)$ would be a negative growth function only under the condition in which K is a constant, and would tend to exhibit an initial phase of positive acceleration to the extent that K grows from zero to its maximum throughout the course of learning the instrumental response.   It is probably the case that K is, as the result of transfer from past experience, already considerably developed in the simple running situation under normal illumination conditions, with the consequence that the curve of growth of E is distorted only slightly from the negative exponential function that holds when K is constant.

III

In this section some of the problems connected with the experimental testing of these theoretical implications will be discussed.   If one examines the existing data from instrumental learning investigations, it will be found that a variety of curves of speed of response (reciprocal of latency or response duration) have been obtained.   Of some score of curves, both from the literature and from unpublished studies conducted in the Iowa laboratory examined by the writer, it was evident that the majority showed a relatively brief initial period of positive acceleration followed by a period of prolonged negative acceleration to the asymptote. The second most frequently observed type was linear in its early portion (10 to 15 trials), followed by a negatively accelerated approach to the limit. A few curves exhibited negative acceleration throughout their course. It is the writer's impression that the latter type of curve tends to occur when the drive is very high, such as in running to escape an electric shock or under a strong hunger drive.

Unfortunately, these data are not very satisfactory for the reason that they are typically group curves involving the mean or median of a whole group of subjects. The forms taken by such group curves may deviate markedly from the curves of individual subjects, as Hayes (2) has recently so nicely demonstrated. The reasons for this become obvious when we consider that there are marked differences among individual subjects, not only in initial and final levels of performance, but also in their different rates of learning, *i.e.*, their different rates of approach to the performance asymptote.

A number of alternatives to the use of such group curves suggest themselves. One is to employ the data of individual subjects. The notorious variability of individual measures from trial to trial, however, usually necessitates some form of averaging of the individual measures in terms of blocks of trials, a procedure which also often leads to distortion of the curve. Thus if an individual curve that shows an initial phase of positive acceleration within the first 10 trials followed by a negatively accelerated phase is averaged in terms of successive blocks of 10 trials each, the initial period of positive acceleration will be lost entirely. The most satisfactory manner of treating individual measures, particularly measures of speed of response, would appear to be the moving average method with small blocks of trials, *e.g.*, three trials in a block.

As an alternative to these curves based on individual measures and averages of a group of subjects, the writer has employed curves based on "like," or homogeneous, subjects. The homogeneity of the subjects can be ascertained in terms of the likeness of the subjects' performances at different stages of the practice or throughout the total learning period. Thus, in the case of the frequency measure in classical conditioning, the subjects' scores in terms of the total number of CR's occurring in a given number of trials, *e.g.*, 100, can first be determined, and then groups of "like" subjects can be formed in terms of those that fall in a small range of scores, such as from 20 to 30 CR's, or from 50 to 60, etc. The writer has shown that such data from different parts of the distribution of total CR scores provide very smooth, comparable curves with relatively small numbers of subjects. In such curves the form is not a function of the distribution of the individual scores.

There are, of course, further refinements that can be made in this procedure. For example, in terms of the speed measures we have been discussing, one could obtain measures for each subject at the beginning, at some intermediate point, and at the end of the learning, and then form groups of subjects that are alike at all three points rather than alike only on the basis of an over-all performance measure. As psychology moves into a period when testing of its theories requires the evaluation of the empirical data in terms of the precise form of some predicted lawful relation, more refined procedures for ascertaining the nature of the function will have to be made available.

A second point in connection with the testing of these theoretical implications is that the experimenter must define his response measures more precisely. Thus the present theory makes it necessary to differentiate between measures that involve starting of the action, the duration of the activity once set going, and combinations of both. The predicted differences in these various measures provide one of the most feasible ways of testing the theory. Similarly, the motivational conditions, relevant and irrelevant, will have to be carefully controlled and their possible differential effects taken into consideration.

Undoubtedly, the most difficult task will be that of arranging the experimental conditions so that there are no competing responses in the situation; for the theoretical model assumes but a single response, not a number of competing responses. Most instances of instrumental conditioning are really limiting cases of trial-and-error learning in which competing responses, while minimized, still play a more or less important role. Obviously, the occurrence of other competing responses in such simple learning situations involves time and thus importantly affects speed measures. Moreover, it is an unfortunate fact that interference from such competing responses is greatest at the beginning of instrumental learning when the rewarded response is weak. Later in the learning, this response is so much stronger than the competing ones that the latter are unable to interfere.

Elimination of competing responses will necessitate both experimental procedures and objective criteria for eliminating data on trials on which competing responses do occur despite the experimental controls. Particularly important also is control of the response orientation of the subject just prior to the presentation of the stimulus. A procedure that has been found to be quite successful in obtaining such control in a very few trials (two to four) is to employ two doors, one opaque and the other glass, in the starting box of an operant situation such as the straight alley. Each trial is started by the experimenter raising the opaque door first and then, at a fixed interval (three seconds) thereafter, the glass door. The raising of the opaque door serves as a warning signal for the subject, which very quickly comes to be set to respond to the raising of the glass door. Similarly, measuring techniques will have to be as precise as possible, particularly in measuring the speed of response evocation. The stop watch will hardly serve for our present purposes.

Finally, in addition to controlling competing responses, it will be necessary to minimize transfer from past experience so that the strength of the S-R is sufficiently low to provide a picture of the major portion of the total learning. It is particularly important from the point of view of the present theory that a good share of the initial phase of learning be represented in the data.

IV

In the preceding sections we have elaborated some of the implications with respect to the form of the speed of response evocation curve of learning of the original theoretical model put forward by Hull in his *Principles of Behavior*. The present treatment differs somewhat from that given by Hull in that certain implications of his postulates with respect to excitatory potential $(\bar{E})$, oscillatory inhibition (O), and threshold (L) were developed, with the consequence that it was possible to derive the relation to be expected between speed of response evocation $(\bar{v})$ and $\bar{E}$. By means of an assumption relating speed of running (v') to $\bar{E}$, additional implications were drawn concerning measures that involved various combinations of the two measures, speed of response evocation $(\bar{v})$ and speed of running (v'). Also considered were certain problems relating to the obtainment and treatment of experimental data bearing on the theory.

REFERENCES·

1. ESTES, W. K. "Toward a statistical theory of learning." *Psychol. Rev.,* 1950, *57,* 94–107.
2. HAYES, K. J. "The backward curve: a method for the study of learning." *Psychol. Rev.,* 1953, *60,* 269–276.
3. HULL, C. L. *Principles of Behavior.* New York: D. Appleton-Century, 1943.
4. ——. *Essentials of Behavior.* New Haven: Yale University Press, 1951.
5. ——. *A Behavior System.* New Haven: Yale University Press, 1952.
6. SPENCE, K. W. Theories of learning. In C. P. Stone (Ed.), *Comparative Psychology.* (3rd. Ed.) Englewood Cliffs, N. J.: Prentice-Hall, 1951.
7. ——. Mathematical formulations of learning phenomena. *J. exp. Psychol.,* 1952, *59,* 152–160.
8. ——. *Symposium on Relationships Among Learning Theory, Personality Theory and Clinical Research.* New York: Wiley, 1953.

8

A Theory of Emotionally Based Drive (*D*) and Its Relation to Performance in Simple Learning Situations

A number of years ago we instituted at the University of Iowa a series of experiments concerned with the role of aversive motivational factors in learning situations. In addition to the more usual direct manipulation of variables influencing the motivational state of an individual, such, for example, as varying the intensity of a noxious stimulus, degree of motivation was also varied in these studies by employing selected subjects who differed in terms of their performance on a so-called scale of emotional responsiveness or manifest anxiety (*31*). That these experiments have aroused considerable interest among both clinical and experimental psychologists is readily evident, not only from the large number of published studies that have attempted either to check or extend our experimental findings, but also from the not infrequent critical reactions they have elicited. Now, while some of the criticisms directed against our studies undoubtedly have merit, it has been rather dismaying to discover the extent to which many of them reflect a serious lack of understanding of the structure and purpose of the basic theoretical framework underlying the experiments.

While some of the responsibility for this failure to understand the nature and objectives of the theory can be assigned to the critics, I hasten to acknowledge that our theoretical treatments have been quite inadequate. The major difficulty is that the studies have appeared only in experimental journals in which space limitations have required that theoretical discussions be kept to a minimum. Since each article tended to limit the discussion to those portions of the theory relevant to the particular phenomena being reported, the theory has been presented only in a very piecemeal fashion. Apparently our hope that the interested reader, particularly the critic, would familiarize himself with the theory as a whole by considering all of the articles has not been realized.

Theoretical Schema

One of the purposes of this paper is to provide a more systematic presentation of our basic theory, or, to use an expression recently introduced by Cronbach and Meehl (4), of the nomological network underlying our studies. Following this the experimental evidence bearing on the theory will be presented and discussed. Figure 1 presents the main concepts employed, at

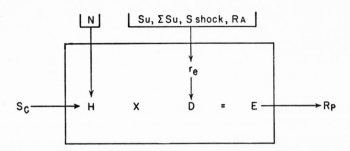

Fig. 1. Diagram representing portion of theoretical schema relevant to data for classical conditioning. (See text for explanation of symbols.)

least in so far as one kind of learning situation, classical conditioning, is concerned. At the top of the figure are shown the experimentally manipulated independent variables such as N, the number of paired conditioning trials; S_u, the unconditioned stimulus; ΣS_u, the number of previous presentations of the unconditioned stimulus; R_A, score on the anxiety or emotional responsiveness scale. The empirical response measure at the lower right-hand corner is the dependent variable. Inside the rectangle are represented the several theoretical concepts (intervening variables) and the interrelations assumed among them. The arrows indicate the functions relating the dependent response measure to the intervening variables, and the latter to the experimentally manipulated variables. Details of the portion of the theory between the intervening variable E and the empirical response measure (R_p), involving such theoretical concepts as oscillatory inhibition and response threshold, have been omitted since our present purpose does not require them. It is sufficient to state that response frequency (R_p) is some positive monotonic function of excitatory potential E.

That the schema presented in Figure 1 conforms to the Cronbach and Meehl concept of a nomological net is readily apparent. Thus to quote these writers: "The laws in a nomological network may relate (a) observable properties or quantities to each other; or (b) theoretical constructs to observables; or (c) different theoretical constructs to one another" (4, p. 290). One may readily find examples in our schema of each of these "laws," or as I would prefer to call them, "relations," since the term "law" typically has a narrower meaning than these authors have given it.

The theory takes its start from Hull's basic assumption that the excitatory potential, E, determining the strength of a response is a multiplicative function of a learning factor, H, and a generalized drive factor, D, i.e., $E = H \times D$ (9). We have assumed, further, that the drive level, D, in the case of aversive situations at least, is a function of the magnitude or strength of a hypothetical response mechanism—a persisting emotional response in the organism, designated as r_e, that is aroused by any form of aversive stimulation. That is, aversive, stressful stimulation is assumed to arouse activity under the control of the autonomic nervous system, which, according to some neurophysiological evidence, may act as an energizer of cortical mechanisms. Those of you who are familiar with the theoretical writings of Miller (13) and Mowrer (14) will recognize that this mechanism is similar to one these writers have postulated in connection with their investigations of acquired motivation. Thus they assumed that aversive stimuli arouse a hypothetical pain (emotional) response which, when conditioned to previously neutral stimulus events, provides the basis for an acquired drive of fear.

On the basis of analogy with overt reflexes to noxious stimulation, there were a number of properties that could be assigned to our hypothetical response mechanism. Three, in particular, will be discussed here. The first and most obvious is based on our knowledge that the magnitude or strength of observable reflexes to noxious stimulation (e.g., the corneal reflex to an air puff, the GSR to an electric shock) varies directly with the intensity or degree of noxiousness of the stimulus. Assuming our hypothetical emotional response, r_e, would exhibit the same property, it followed that the level of drive, D, present in classical defense conditioning would be a positive function of the intensity of the US. From the remaining portion of the theory, it could be deduced that the performance level, e.g., frequency of CR's, would vary positively with the intensity of the US employed. At the time of the original formulation of our theory there was some evidence, in particular an experiment by Passey (15), which supported this implication of the theory.

A second implication of our hypothetical mechanism was based on the adaptive property of observable reflexes to noxious stimuli: namely, that such responses characteristically exhibit adaptation or weakening with repeated stimulation. On the assumption that our hypothetical emotional response would behave in an analogous manner, it followed that, if a series of trials employing the US alone were given *prior* to conditioning, a lower level of D would be present during the subsequent conditioning than if no such adaptation trials were given. But if D were lower, the level of performance in the conditioning situation would also be lower following such adaptation trials than without them. This assumption or hypothesis, if you wish, is represented in Figure 1 by $r_e = f(\Sigma S_u)$. At the time of formulation of the theory, we found a study by MacDonald (12) that gave results precisely in line with this implication.

The third implication of our theoretical mechanism was based on the well-known fact or observation that individuals differ in the magnitude of their reflex responses to a given intensity of stimulation. By analogy, again, we were led to assume that individuals would differ characteristically in the magnitude of this response, r_e, to the same intensity of stressful stimulation. If now there were available some means of assessing differences in this emotional responsiveness of individuals, our theoretical schema would lead to the prediction that highly emotional subjects, as assessed by the measuring device, would exhibit a higher level of performance in aversive forms of conditioning than subjects who scored low on the device.

The problem thus became one of attempting to develop a test for identifying individual differences in the responsiveness of this hypothetical emotional mechanism.   Such a test, of course, would have to be defined independently of the measures that were to be employed in testing the theoretical network, *i.e.*, the measures of performance in conditioning and other learning situations.   It was in connection with this portion of our theory that the Manifest Anxiety or A-scale was developed.   The idea of using a self-inventory test that would differentiate subjects in terms of the degree to which they admitted to possessing overt or manifest symptoms of emotionality was suggested by Taylor in a doctoral dissertation (*30*).

At this point I should like to make a methodological digression and comment on a criticism recently made concerning this aspect of our research.   One pair of critics, inspired, but unfortunately not too enlightened, by the excellent article of Cronbach and Meehl (*4*) on construct validity, insisted that we should have developed our scale for measuring *D* on the basis of a theory so that, and I quote them, "performance on it might be a basis for inferring drive (differences) independently of the outcome of subsequent experiments" (*10*, p. 162).   While there are a number of highly questionable methodological points in the arguments of these critics, I should like to call attention here merely to the fact that it is simply not true that no theorizing guided us in the development of the A-scale.   As has just been recounted, we did have some very definite theoretical notions as to what lay behind differences in level of generalized drive, *D*, especially in the case of classical defense types of conditioning.

This theory, that *D* is a function of the strength of the emotional response made by the organism to the noxious stimulation, had already received considerable support. Its extension in the present instance to the individual difference variable logically demanded that we measure the emotional responsiveness of individuals under comparable environmental conditions. Naturally, so-called physiological indices of emotionality, such as, for example, changes in pulse rate or in the GSR, were indicated; and we have conducted some research along this line. However, it occurred to Taylor that it might be both interesting and valuable to investigate the possibility of making use of the presumed behavioral symptoms of emotionality that clinicians have described. That the questionnaire type of test developed turned out as well as it apparently has is to the credit, I think, of the clinical psychologists who selected the behavioral items as indicative of emotionally over-reactive individuals.

In this connection a further comment is in order concerning a surprising question that was asked by these same critics. Thus the problem was posed as to what the consequences would have been for either the theory or the test had the experiments using the A-scale been negative. The answer to the question, at least regards the theory, should be obvious. The implications of the other portions of our theory with respect to our response mechanism, r_e, were sufficiently well confirmed that we would have had no hesitancy about abandoning the A-scale as being related to D in our theory. Since, however, the implications of this aspect of our theoretical net were confirmed, we have continued to employ the A-scale as one operational definition of this emotional responsiveness variable. That a more satisfactory scale, even one of this questionnaire type, can be developed, I have no doubt. Indeed, I would recommend that some of the time and energy now being squandered in the many distorted, even mendacious, criticisms that seem to find such ready acceptance in our current discussion-type journals be directed at this more constructive task. If the main purpose of these attacks is to discredit and eliminate the theory, they will fail in this objective, for the history of science clearly reveals that a theory is usually discarded only when a better theory is advanced. The same goes for the constructs within a theory.

Experimental Evidence

With these methodological remarks out of the way, let us turn now to the experimental evidence bearing on our theoretical schema.   I shall spend the major part of my limited space presenting and discussing the findings of our eyelid conditioning experiments, for it was in connection with data from this type of learning situation that the schema was originally formulated. With regard to performance curves of conditioning, e.g., frequency curves, the implications of the theory are, as we have seen, that level of performance will be a positive function of (a) the intensity of the US, (b) the level of score on the A-scale, and (c) the intensity of an extra stressful stimulation.   We shall take up the first two of these variables together; since space is so limited, I shall present only those studies which had the largest sample of subjects and hence have provided the most reliable and stable data.

Eyelid Conditioning Experiments

In Figure 2 are presented the findings of two experiments (one unpublished; the other, 27), one of which involved 120 subjects and the other 100 subjects.   Both studies employed two levels of puff intensity, .6 lb. and 2.0 lbs./sq. in., in the one represented in the lower graph; .25 lb. and 1.5 lbs./sq. in., in the upper graph.   Each study also involved two levels of emotionality (upper and lower 20% of subjects on the A-scale).   Examination of the curves in both graphs shows clearly that at each of the four puff intensities, the High A group (shown by solid curves) was well above the Low A group (broken curves).   Statistical analysis over all of the conditioning trials revealed the differences were significant at the .01 level in the lower graph and at the .025 level in the upper.[1]

A second point to be noted in these data is relevant to the assumption that the learning or habit factor (H) and the drive

---

[1] Since unequal numbers of each sex were used in both of these studies and because women consistently exhibit a greater difference than men, the curves have been weighted equally for male and female subjects.

factor (D) combine in a multiplicative manner to determine response strength.   This assumption leads to the further implication that frequency curves of conditioning for different values

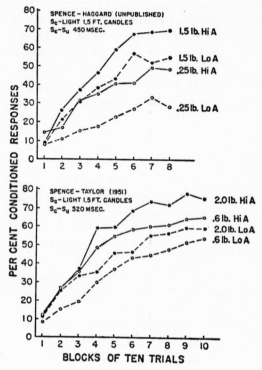

FIG. 2.   Performance in eyelid conditioning as function of
A-score and intensity of US.

of the anxiety variable will exhibit a gradual divergence over the course of training.[2]   That this prediction was borne out may be seen by inspecting the graphs.   Statistical confirmation of the divergence is revealed by the fact that the trials-$\times$-anxiety interaction terms for both sets of data were highly significant (.005 and .025 levels).

The findings with respect to the intensity of US variable also

[2] This prediction must be qualified to the extent that the frequency measure has a ceiling of 100% and thus may not always reflect the continued growth of E. This is particularly the case at high levels of D in which E also is high.

supported the implications of our theory. Thus it may be seen in both studies that the subjects that had the strong puff performed at a higher level than those with the weak puff. The divergence between the curves is also apparent.

As an indication of the stability of our findings involving these two experimental variables, Figure 3 presents data from

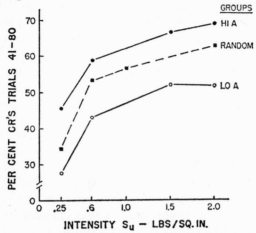

FIG. 3.   Showing relation between conditioning performance and intensity of US for unselected and high and low A-score subjects.

these same two studies along with some relevant data from four other investigations recently conducted in our laboratory (26). Shown on the ordinate of this graph are the percentage of CR's given in the block of Trials 41–80 as a function of the intensity of the unconditioned stimulus employed.   The uppermost curve in this graph represents the results for subjects selected from the high end of the A-scale; the lowest curve, subjects selected from the low end.   The middle curve represents data obtained in four different experiments in which unselected subjects, so far as A-score, were conditioned under highly comparable conditions to those used with the selected subjects (*i.e.*, similar visual CS and very comparable S_c–S_u intervals).   The consistency of the results from experiment to experiment, particularly the relation of the curve for the unselected subjects to those for the High and Low A subjects, is, I believe, quite impressive.

In addition to the data presented in these graphs, four other investigations have reported finding that High A subjects responded at a significantly higher level than Low A subjects in eyelid conditioning (*21, 22, 28, 30*). One additional study (*8*) also found superior performance by High A subjects, although the difference in this instance was not significant. A reasonable interpretation of the failure to obtain a significant difference in this latter study, especially to anyone familiar with the variability of individual conditioning data, is that there were only ten subjects in each group.

Mention was made earlier of the fact that in addition to the anxiety scale we have also attempted to employ a number of physiological measures as further operational definitions of our emotional responsiveness variable. One of the most discouraging aspects of this work has been the lack of consistency, *i.e.,* unreliability from day to day, of such measures. Especially has this been the case with the GSR, on which, unfortunately, we concentrated most of our time and energy. Recently, however, we have obtained results (to be published) with these measures that are rather more promising. Using changes in GSR and heart rate made to a mildly noxious stimulus and converting the measures into a so-called autonomic lability score by means of a formula suggested by Lacey (*11*), two groups of subjects who fell in the upper and lower third of the distribution of such scores were subsequently conditioned. Shown in Figure 4 are the frequency curves of eyelid conditioning for these two groups of subjects. As may be seen, the subjects with the high autonomic lability index performed at a higher level than those with a low index. The difference is significant at the .02 level.

In addition to varying performance by manipulating the A-scale and US variables, it should be possible to produce a higher level of conditioning performance by presenting a strong extra stimulus, such as an electric shock, during the course of conditioning. Similarly, after a subject has experienced a strong electric shock just prior to conditioning, the mere threat of further shocks during the conditioning should arouse a strong and persisting emotional response that would raise the level of *D* and hence the level of performance. We have already published the results of one such experiment with unselected sub-

jects which corroborated, in part, these theoretical expectations
(25).

Recently a further experiment (to be published) studying the
effects of shock threat on High and Low A subjects was com-

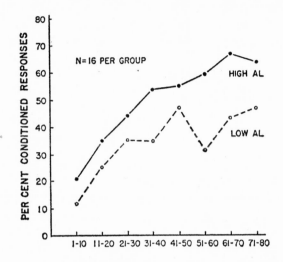

FIG. 4.   Percentage of CR's for the high and low autonomic
lability (AL) groups in blocks of ten trials.

pleted in our laboratory.   Some idea of the nature of the findings can be gained from Figure 5 which presents the frequency
curves of conditioning for four groups of Low A subjects (20th
percentile).   The two top curves in this graph are for subjects
conditioned with a relatively strong air puff (1.5 lbs./sq. in.); the
lower two, for subjects who had a weak puff (.25 lb./sq. in.).   It
will be seen that at both puff levels the threatened group (solid
curve) was consistently above the nonthreatened group (broken
curve) throughout the whole 80 trials.   A similar experiment
with high anxious subjects revealed a difference between the
threat and nonthreat groups throughout the conditioning in the
case of groups which had a weak puff.   In the strong puff
groups, however, the curves for the threat and nonthreat group,
after separating in the early trials, came together in the later
stages of the conditioning (last 40 trials).   This latter effect un-

doubtedly results, in part, from the ceiling imposed by the frequency measure.

Space will not permit a detailed presentation of the experimental evidence with respect to that portion of our theory con-

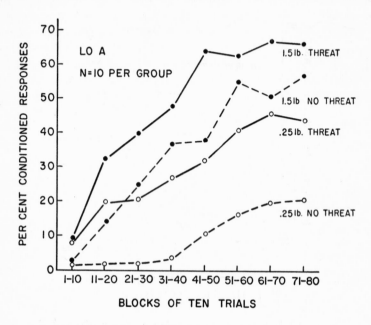

FIG. 5. Percentage of CR's in blocks of ten trials as a function of shock or no-shock threat and intensity of the US for subjects who score low on A-scale.

cerned with the assumption that the emotional response to the noxious US would be weaker if adaptation trials are given prior to conditioning. It is sufficient to state that the original finding of MacDonald (12), that such preadapted subjects exhibited a lower level of performance in conditioning than nonadapted subjects, has been corroborated by Taylor (32). The latter experimenter also found that conditioning performance was inversely related to the intensity of the US employed during the preconditioning adaptation period. Thus the implications of this part of the theoretical network have also received further support.

The final set of conditioning data that I would like to present are concerned with the effect of level of D on differential conditioning. Without going into the theoretical derivation, it may be shown that one of the implications of our theory is that the higher the drive level, D, of the subjects, the greater should be the differentiation between the positive and the negative, *i.e.*, nonreinforced, stimulus in such differential conditioning. Two studies from our laboratory have reported finding that, in five separate comparisons, high anxious subjects showed better discrimination than low anxious subjects *(21, 23)*. Although none of the differences were significant, four closely approached being so. More recently we have investigated the effect of varying the level of D on differential conditioning by direct manipulation of the intensity of the US. The graph in Figure 6 presents

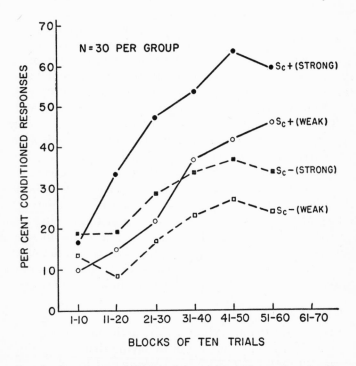

Fig. 6. Percentage of CR's to the positive and negative stimuli for groups conditioned with a strong and weak US.

the findings of this study (*17*) in terms of the frequency of CR's given to the two stimuli, positive and negative. As may be seen, the subjects conditioned with the strong US not only showed a higher level of response to the positive and negative stimuli, but, as predicted from our theory, the difference between the conditioned responses to the two stimuli was greater in the case of the group that had the strong US. Again this latter difference approached, but did not quite reach, statistical significance. Unfortunately, conditioning data are plagued by high individual variability, produced in part by a few subjects who show very little or no conditioning. In an effort to ascertain what the finding would be for subjects who showed considerable conditioning, a separate analysis was made of the upper two-thirds of each of the two groups run in the experiment. In the case of these subjects discrimination was significantly better for the high drive group at the .05 level.

So much for the findings in our eyelid conditioning studies. On the whole, we believe they are in fair accord with our theoretical schema, including the portion of it that involves the A-scale. While not all of the results have met acceptable levels of significance, the fact that the direction of the differences in such instances has almost invariably been in accord with the theory has encouraged us to continue to hold to it. Attention might also be called here to the fact that this theoretical model, particularly the hypothetical emotional response mechanism, has also been quite successful in connection with a wide variety of other behavioral situations involving noxious stimulation with animals. Examples are to be found in the many studies cited by Miller (*13*) on the motivating and reinforcing roles of acquired fear in learning situations. The experiments of a number of investigators on the persisting motivational effects of emotionality aroused by electric shock on the consummatory behavior of rats provide yet another example (*1, 2, 18, 19*).

Complex Human Learning

Turning now to our studies involving the more complex types of human learning, let me begin by saying that it is in this area that the limitations of space in experimental journals for theoretical elaboration have been most unfortunate. Certainly we recognize that these treatments have been quite inadequate, particularly from the point of view of discussing the many factors that complicate efforts at theorizing in this area. By way of example let me mention two important points that need to be recognized but, unfortunately, have not always been so.

First, it should be realized that in order to derive implications concerning the effects of drive variation in any type of complex learning task, it is necessary to have, in addition to the drive theory, a further theoretical network concerning the variables and their interaction that are involved in the particular learning activity. It is perhaps unnecessary to point out here that theoretical schemas for such types of learning are as yet in a very primitive state of development, indeed almost nonexistent. As a consequence of this, one has considerable difficulty in drawing conclusions about the motivational part of the new, combined theory from supposedly negative findings, for the defect may be in the part of the network specifying the action of the variables in the complex learning situation.

The second point is that our theory of the mechanism underlying D was developed in connection with experimental situations involving some form of noxious stimulation. Complex human learning tasks, on the other hand, typically do not involve the use of a noxious stimulus. Whatever stress is present in these situations is usually produced by instructions that aim to create in the subject the desire or need to make as good a showing as possible. While it is true that this stress may be greatly augmented by introducing failure or punishment into the situation, so far as the usual type of human learning experiment is concerned, the question as to whether High A subjects would be more emotional than Low A subjects, and hence have a higher D level, is a moot one. In this connection two alternative subhypotheses have been proposed: (a) the chronic hypothesis: that High A subjects react emotionally in a chronic manner to all situations, whether stressful or not; and (b) the emotional reactivity hypothesis: that High A subjects have a lower threshold of emotional responsiveness and react with a stronger emotional response than Low A subjects to situations containing some degree of stress (16, 20, 25). As may be seen, according to the first of these hypotheses, mild nonthreatening situations would produce a differential drive (*D*) level in subjects scoring at extremes of the scale; whereas according to the second, there would not be a difference. These two examples are sufficient, I believe, to point up the fact that the problems involved in the extension of the theory to these more complex types of learning are quite formidable and that at this stage there necessarily must be a considerable amount of trial and error in our theorizing.

Now it will be recalled that the theoretical schema presented in Figure 1 assumed that in classical conditioning habit strength to but a single response was established to the CS. In this circumstance, as we have seen, an increase in drive level implied an increase in response strength. In more complex, selective learning tasks, on the other hand, there is, typically, a hierarchy of competing response tendencies. Actually most of the complex learning situations employed with humans involve a number or sequence of such response hierarchies which involve competing responses, *e.g.*, a number of choice points in the maze, whether verbal or spatial. To show what the implications of variation of drive level will be in such competing response situations, let us begin by considering the simplest conceivable case: one in which there is but a single response hierarchy involving two alternative responses. The single choice point maze involving turning left or right is one example of such a situation. If now the habit strength of the correct to-be-learned response is, at the beginning of the learning, somewhat stronger than that of the incorrect response, it may be shown that the higher the drive level, *D*, the greater will the difference between the competing excitatory potentials be and, *neglecting all other considerations*, the higher should be the percentage of correct responses at the start of learning, the sooner should the learning criterion be attained, and the smaller should be the total number of errors.[3]

3 As discussed in my Silliman Lectures (*21*), there are a number of other considerations that need to be taken into account in extending the theory to such competing response situations. Thus the particular composition rule (law) assumed in these lectures to describe the manner in which the competing responses interacted with each other led to the implication that the percentage of occurrence of the competing responses is a function, not only of the magnitude of the difference between the competing *E*s, but also of their absolute level above the threshold *L*. As a consequence in the low range of E values, there may actually be an inverse relation between performance level (percent choice of the response with stronger *E*) and the level of drive. Still other considerations involve whether

The reverse situation, that in which the correct response is at the outset weaker than the incorrect one, is, from the theoretical viewpoint, even more complex. In this instance the stronger the drive, the greater will be the percent choice of the wrong response, or, in other words, the poorer will be the performance at this initial stage. But, as training proceeds, sooner or later the habit strength of the correct, reinforced response will overtake that of the wrong, unreinforced response and from this point on the percent choice of the correct response should in general be higher for the high drive group than for the low drive group. In other words, the performance curves should be expected to cross. Precise predictions about the total number of errors, number of trials, etc., in this situation will depend to a considerable extent upon the particular functions and parameter values assigned to the assumed habit and inhibitory factors. Actually we have never got around to working out in detail the implications of the various possibilities for the total learning period even in this simplest case.

Recalling now that such a learning task as the serial verbal or spatial maze involves a number of such competing response hierarchies, we see that the problem of predicting the effect on performance of variation of the drive in such situations becomes even more complicated. On the assumption that anticipatory and perseverative associative tendencies would develop in such a manner as to make the incorrect response the stronger in the case of many of the choice points of a maze, it was hoped that it would be possible to demonstrate that high drive (*i.e.*, High A) subjects would perform more poorly in such serial learning situations than low drive (*i.e.*, Low A) subjects. Two experiments, one with a verbal form of maze (35) and one using a finger maze (5) actually did provide results in agreement with this theoretical expectation. However, as was pointed out at the time, there was a serious discrepancy between the theory

---

habit strength (H) in learning situations is or is not assumed to be dependent on the reinforcer and whether drive strength (D) determines the inhibitory factor (I_n). Different combinations of these alternative assumptions, including even other possible composition rules, lead to different behavior consequences. Critical evaluation of the different conceivable theoretical models will require considerably more empirical data obtained under a wide variety of experimental conditions than is now available.

and the obtained results in these studies in that the anxious subjects made more errors at all but one of the choice points in both studies. In view of the ease of learning many of these choice points, and hence evidence for little or no strong competing response tendencies, the theory would have led us to expect that the High A subjects would have made fewer errors on them than the Low A subjects. Obviously the theory was wrong in some respect, but just in what way—an incorrect assumption or failure to include an important relevant variable—was not clear.

At this point in our work we realized that such serial learning tasks are, for a variety of reasons, quite unsatisfactory. Among the most important from our viewpoint was the fact that one has little or no knowledge of the relative strengths of the competing responses in each of the hierarchies. Accordingly we abandoned this type of situation and attempted to develop learning tasks in which it would be possible to specify or manipulate in some known manner the relative strengths of the competing responses in each hierarchy. Probably the chief value of these earlier experiments is that they did point up the fact that a higher anxiety score (and hence possibly a higher drive level) does not necessarily always lead to a higher level of performance.

Among the types of learning problems that we turned to was paired-associates learning. This type of learning task may be conceived as consisting of the formation of a set of more or less isolated S-R associations or habit tendencies. In one type of list, which we have referred to as a noncompetitive list, an attempt is made to isolate as much as possible the paired items by minimizing the degree of synonymity or formal similarity among both the stimulus and response words. As learning proceeds and the habit strengths of the stimulus words to their paired response words increase, high drive subjects should, according to our theory, perform at a higher level than low drive subjects. An important condition in this derivation is that the associative connections between each stimulus word and the nonpaired response words are lower than that to the paired response word.

Two lists of this type have been employed. In one the associative connections between the paired words were initially zero

or at least very low.   In this type of list it would be predicted
that there would be little or no difference between high and low
drive subjects at the start of learning, but that as learning progressed the curve of correct responses would diverge, that for the
high drive group being the higher.   Using nonsense syllables of
low association value and low intralist similarity, Taylor has
reported two experiments in which this type of list was employed (*33, 34*).   The lower pair of curves in Figure 7 present

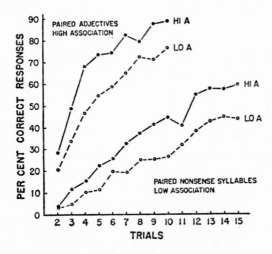

FIG. 7.   Paired-associates learning as a function of A-score
under conditions of unusual interword pair competition.

the data from one of these studies (*34*).   Both curves, it will be
observed, began at a very low level with the curve for the High
A group (solid line) rising above that for the Low A group
(broken line).   An unpublished study from our laboratory employing nonassociated paired adjectives has given similar results,
although the superiority of the High A over the Low A subjects
was significant only on a single tailed hypothesis.

The second type of noncompetitive list differs from the first
in that the associative strengths of the paired words are, as the
result of past experiences, considerably above zero.   Under this
condition it would be predicted that the performance curves
would, on the first anticipation trial, be considerably above 0%

and that the curve for the high drive group would be above that for the low drive group. Employing paired adjectives that had been scaled by Haagen (7) as having high "closeness of association" values, two studies (24, 29) have reported results which support these implications. The upper pair of curves in Figure 7 shows the findings of one of these studies (29). As may be seen, the initial level of performance was well above 0 and the High A subjects started out and continued at a higher level than the Low A subjects. On the other hand, a recently completed doctoral dissertation (6) using this type of list failed to obtain results in accord with the theory. There was little or no difference between the two groups at any stage of practice.

In contrast to these noncompetitive type lists we have also designed a competitive list which includes some paired items in which the initial habit strength of the stimulus word to call out the paired word is weaker than the habit strengths to one or more other response words in the list. In the case of these items it would be predicted from our theory that high drive subjects would at the start of learning perform more poorly than low drive subjects. Here again we should have emphasized that the theory of paired-associates learning has as yet not been developed sufficiently to predict what will happen beyond the first few trials, and it would have been more appropriate, as far as implications for our drive theory are concerned, if we had used at most only the data from the first four or five trials. Precise predictions concerning performance beyond this point must await the development of a more adequate theory of the variables determining the weakening of these stronger, incorrect responses in paired-associates learning. Two published studies (24, 29) and one doctoral dissertation (6) have reported data with respect to the implication of our theory for this type of list; while all three found, as predicted, that the High A subjects were inferior to Low A subjects in the first four trials, none of the results was statistically significant. However, the implication of the theory that there would be an interaction between level of A-score and performance on the two kinds of lists, competitive and noncompetitive, was confirmed.

Summarizing the results with these paired-associates lists, I would say that the batting average of our theory is fairly high but by no means perfect. It is clearly evident from the data that differences in level of A-score (and hence level of D), if it is a factor determining performance on such tasks, is a relatively unimportant one. Certainly individual differences in verbal learning ability play a much more decisive role. Moreover, there are as yet many factors that play important roles in such complex behavior situations, about which we have as yet little or no knowledge. Among those of a motivational nature is the type of task-irrelevant response that Child and his group have studied (3). We think of these interfering responses as being elicited by drive stimuli (s_D), and hence they would be incorporated in a more complete motivational theory of learned behavior. On the basis of evidence in the literature and some recently completed studies of our own, we believe this factor is especially important when shock is introduced into verbal learning situations.

I should like to conclude this presentation by stating very briefly the purpose of such theoretical schemas as has been presented here. As I conceive them, their primary function is to provide for the unification of what, without the theory, would be a multiplicity of isolated or unconnected facts and laws. Thus, in the present instance, such phenotypically different phenomena as behavior in eyelid conditioning under various stimulus conditions, degree of emotionality as revealed by a personality questionnaire and physiological measures, and such opposite performance differentials in paired-associates tasks as just described have been interrelated by means of the theory. That much work, both of a theoretical and experimental nature, remains to be done in this area of behavior study is clearly revealed by the many gaps and deficiencies in the present attempt. It is my firm belief, however, that progress in the development of this, as in any other scientific field of knowledge, is greatly facilitated by such theoretically oriented research endeavors.

REFERENCES

1. AMSEL, A. The effect upon level of consummatory response of the addition of anxiety to a motivational complex. *J. exp. Psychol.,* 1950, *40,* 709–715.

2. ——, & MALTZMAN, I.   The effect upon generalized drive strength of emotionality as inferred from the level of consummatory response. *J. exp. Psychol.*, 1950, *40*, 563–569.

3. CHILD, I. L.   Personality.   *Annu. Rev. Psychol.*, 1954, *5*, 149–170.

4. CRONBACH, L. J., & MEEHL, P. E.   Construct validity in psychological test.   *Psychol. Bull.*, 1955, *52*, 281–302.

5. FARBER, I. E., & SPENCE, K. W.   Complex learning and conditioning as a function of anxiety.   *J. exp. Psychol.*, 1953, *45*, 120–125.

6. FREDENBURG, NORMA C.   Paired-associates learning as a function of anxiety level and shock.   Unpublished doctoral dissertation, State Univer. of Iowa, 1956.

7. HAAGEN, C. H.   Synonymity, vividness, familiarity, and association value ratings of 400 pairs of common adjectives.   *J. Psychol.*, 1949, *27*, 453–463.

8. HILGARD, E. R., JONES, L. V., & KAPLAN, S. J.   Conditioned discrimination as related to anxiety.   *J. exp. Psychol.*, 1951, *42*, 94–99.

9. HULL, C. L.   *Principles of Behavior*.   New York: Appleton-Century, 1943.

10. JESSOR, R., & HAMMOND, K. R.   Construct validity and the Taylor anxiety scale.   *Psychol. Bull.*, 1957, *54*, 161–170.

11. LACEY, J. I.   The evaluation of autonomic responses toward a general solution.   *Ann. N. Y. Acad. Sci.*, 1956, *67*, 123–164.

12. MACDONALD, ANNETTE.   The effect of adaptation to the unconditioned stimulus upon the formation of conditioned avoidance response.   *J. exp. Psychol.*, 1946, *36*, 1–12.

13. MILLER, N. E.   Learnable drives and rewards.   In S. S. Stevens (Ed.), *Handbook of Experimental Psychology*.   New York: Wiley, 1951, pp. 435–472.

14. MOWRER, O. H.   A stimulus response analysis of anxiety and its role as a reinforcing agent.   *Psychol. Rev.*, 1939, *46*, 553–565.

15. PASSEY, G. E.   The influence of intensity of unconditioned stimulus upon acquisition of a conditioned response.   *J. exp. Psychol.*, 1948, *38*, 420–428.

16. ROSENBAUM, G.   Stimulus generalization as a function of clinical and experimentally induced anxiety.   Unpublished doctoral dissertation, State Univer. of Iowa, 1950.

17. RUNQUIST, W. N., SPENCE, K. W., & STUBBS, D. W.   Differential conditioning and intensity of the US.   *J. exp. Psychol.*, 1958, *55*, 51–55.

18. SIEGEL, P. S., & BRANTLEY, J. J.   The relationship of emotionality to the consummatory response of eating.   *J. exp. Psychol.*, 1951, *42*, 304–306.

19. ——, & SIEGEL, HELEN S.   The effect of emotionality on the water intake of the rat.   *J. comp. physiol. Psychol.*, 1949, *42*, 12–16.

20. SPENCE, K. W.   *Behavior Theory and Conditioning*.   New Haven: Yale Univer. Press, 1956.

21. ——, & BEECROFT, R. S.   Differential conditioning and level of anxiety.   *J. exp. Psychol.*, 1954, *48*, 399–403.

22. ———, & FARBER, I. E. Conditioning and extinction as a function of anxiety. *J. exp. Psychol.*, 1953, *45*, 116–119.

23. ———, ———. The relation of anxiety to differential eyelid conditioning. *J. exp. Psychol.*, 1954, *47*, 127–134.

24. ———, ———, & McFANN, H. H. The relation of anxiety (drive) level to performance in competitional and noncompetitional paired-associates learning. *J. exp. Psychol.*, 1956, *52*, 296–305.

25. ———, ———, & TAYLOR, ELAINE. The relation of electric shock and anxiety to level of performance in eyelid conditioning. *J. exp. Psychol.*, 1954, *48*, 404–408.

26. ———, & ROSS, L. E. Experimental evidence on the relation between performance level in eyelid conditioning and anxiety (drive) level. USN office of Naval Research *Tech. Rep.*, 1957, No. 5 (Contract N9 onr-93802).

27. ———, & TAYLOR, JANET A. Anxiety and strength of the US as determiners of the amount of eyelid conditioning. *J. exp. Psychol.*, 1951, *42*, 183–188.

28. ———, ———. The relation of conditioned response strength to anxiety in normal, neurotic, and psychotic subjects. *J. exp. Psychol.*, 1953, *45*, 265–272.

29. ———, TAYLOR, J., & KETCHEL, RHODA. Anxiety (drive) level and degree of competition in paired-associates learning. *J. exp. Psychol.*, 1956, *52*, 306–310.

30. TAYLOR, JANET A. The relationship of anxiety to the conditioned eyelid response. *J. exp. Psychol.*, 1951, *41*, 81–92.

31. ———. A personality scale of manifest anxiety. *J. abnorm. soc. Psychol.*, 1953, *48*, 285–290.

32. ———. Level of conditioning and intensity of the adaptation stimulus. *J. exp. Psychol.*, 1956, *51*, 127–131.

33. ———. The effects of anxiety level and psychological stress on verbal learning. *J. abnorm. soc. Psychol.*

34. ———, & CHAPMAN, J. P. Paired-associate learning as related to anxiety. *Amer. J. Psychol.*, 1955, *68*, 671.

35. ———, & SPENCE, K. W. The relationship of anxiety level to performance in serial learning. *J. exp. Psychol.*, 1952, *44*, 61–64.

36. ———, ———. Conditioning level in behavior disorders. *J. abnorm. soc. Psychol.*, 1954, *49*, 497–502.

9

Learning and Performance in Eyelid Conditioning as a Function of Intensity of the UCS [1]

Experimental studies concerned with the effects upon behavior of variation of the motivational level of S may be grouped into three classes. The first class contains those experiments in which after training in the situation under some constant period of deprivation (T_D) a test or measurement period is given in which T_D is varied. These studies are regarded as providing a measure of the drive factor (D) that determines response strength and the empirical relation $R = f(T_D)$ is taken as a reflection of the relation of D to T_D. The classical obstruction box studies of Warden and his associates (*19*) and more recent investigations (*4, 8, 12, 13, 20*) in which the Skinner box type of situation was used fall into this class.

In the second class of experiments T_D is varied (*i.e.*, is different for different subgroups) during the first training period and then a second test period is given in which T_D is the same for all groups. The objective of these studies has been to ascertain whether the learning factor (habit strength) is a function of the differences in drive strength resulting from different values of T_D during the first period. Instances of experiments designed in this fashion are those of Finan (*3*), Kendler (*7*), and Strass-

[1] The writer wishes to acknowledge the assistance of George Harker, Henry Loess, Wallace McAllister, Donald Swisher, and Janet Taylor who served as assistants either during preliminary experimentation or the present study.

148

burger (15).   All of these studies used simple instrumental conditioning.

A third group of studies has not attempted to differentiate
between the two factors of habit (H) and drive (D) but has
simply studied performance during the training period as a
function of differences in T_D.   Typically these investigations
have involved more complex learning situations such as the
maze (9, 16, 17, 18) or discrimination learning (2, 10).   Recently, however, two studies of this type have been reported in
which classical defense conditioning was employed (11, 14).   In
these studies the experimentally manipulated motivational variable was the intensity of the unconditioned stimulus (UCS)
rather than the time of deprivation of some goal object.

This third group of studies, it should be noted, does not
permit one to identify which factor, learning (habit strength) or
drive strength, lies behind the obtained differences in performance level.   Quite frequently, however, these investigators
have inferred that the acquisition process (habit formation) was
superior under conditions of strong motivation.   Thus, Passey
(11) interpreted his finding that the level of conditioning was a
positive function of the intensity of the UCS as supporting
Hull's assumption (5) that more habit strength was developed
with a stronger drive.   He pointed out that this was in line with
Hull's special reinforcement hypothesis that related the increment of habit strength per trial to the amount of drive reduction
or drive stimulus reduction.

While it is true that this finding is in agreement with the implication of Hull's hypothesis, it should be noted that there are
two other possible interpretations of it even within the framework of Hull's theorizing.   Thus, according to this formulation,
response strength is a function of both habit and drive strength,
i.e., $R = f(H \times D)$.   It is conceivable that the increments of
habit strength (H) do not vary with the intensity of the UCS and
T_D but that only drive strength (D) does.   Finally, there is the
possibility that differences in the intensity of the UCS or in T_D
might result in differences in both of these hypothetical factors,
H and D.   The experimental design employed by Passey does
not permit one to make any decision among these alternatives.

The appropriate experimental design with which to investigate this problem is the factorial type shown later in Table 1. The experiment is conducted in two periods. In the first the *S*s are divided randomly into two groups, one of which is conditioned with a weak UCS and the other with a strong UCS. In the second period these two groups are each divided into two subgroups with half of the *S*s continuing with the same UCS as in the first period and half being switched to the other intensity. There are thus four different subgroups in this second experimental period.

Response measures obtained in the second period provide the data. Comparison of the row means indicates whether response strength during this period varies with the level of intensity of the UCS present in the first period. As the level of intensity of UCS in the second measuring period is controlled, this comparison cannot reflect differences in drive strength (D) resulting from a difference in intensity of UCS. Hence, a significant difference in these row means would be interpreted as indicating that a different amount of habit strength developed in the two groups during the first period. An accompanying significant difference in the column means would be interpreted as reflecting differences in drive strength (D) resulting from the different intensities of UCS present at the time of measurement. Presumably such a difference would also reflect differences in habit strength that would develop during the second period. If, on the other hand, there is no difference in the row means and a significant difference in the column means, this would lead to the interpretation that habit growth was not a function of the motivational level of the organism and that the difference between the groups under different intensities of UCS reflected differences in drive strength (D) only. The absence of a significant difference in the column means and a significant difference in the row means would imply that the difference in response strength reflected different habit strengths with no difference in drive strength.

Attention should be called to the fact that the studies in the first two of our three classes of motivational experiments conform partly in design to the factorial type described above except that they have been incomplete designs. Thus, the investigations in the first group had but a single motivational condition in the first training period and two or more different motivational conditions in the second period. In terms of Table 1 there was but a single row and a number of columns consisting of but a single cell. Studies in the second group, on the other hand, have typically had but a single column with a number of different rows each with but a single cell. Only the Kendler study involved the complete factorial design.

The partial nature of the experimental design employed in these investigations has resulted in a certain amount of distortion in their findings. Thus, in the first class of studies, those concerned with differences in drive strength (D), the typical procedure has been to carry on the original training in the setup with a deprivation interval of approximately 24 hr. Subsequent comparisons of response strength at different deprivation periods, e.g., 3, 6, 12, and 24 hr., do not make proper allowance for the fact that the 3-, 6-, and 12-hr. groups are performing at *different* conditions from those employed in the first period while the 24-hr. group has the *same* deprivation condition. Interpreted in terms of our theoretical constructs H and D, this design provided assurance that a constant amount of H was *developed* in the groups to be run subsequently under the different deprivation intervals. It did not, however, control for the possibility that a significant part of the stimulus complex that acquires habit strength for the response consists in the internal cues from the need state (S_D). If these cues are discriminably different for the different deprivation periods, and there is experimental evidence $(1, 6)$ to indicate that they are, then the stimulus complex for any groups run under a different deprivation condition in the test period from that used in the original training period is changed. This would mean that the effective habit strengths available for the different groups during the test periods would not be constant but would differ from each other in varying amounts that would be a function of the amount of change in the stimulus complex (principle of stimulus generalization). *So far as providing the precise nature of the function relating* D *to* T_D, these studies have been worthless because they have not controlled for these differences in generalized habit strength.[2]

The present experiment attempted to investigate the question as to whether differences in response strength in classical defense conditioning resulting from the use of different intensities of the UCS are to be interpreted as reflecting, in part at least, differences in the strength of conditioning, *i.e.*, habit strength (H), or whether the differences reflect only differences in drive strength (D). The experimental design employed was the factorial type discussed above.

Procedure

Subjects

A total of 97 men from an introductory course in psychology served as Ss. Women were not used as it was found in an exploratory experiment that a very high proportion of them responded with voluntary blinks to the CS under the condition in which the UCS (air puff) was very strong (5.0 lb./sq. in.). Eleven men were eliminated because of the fact that they gave a very high incidence of voluntary closures to the conditioned light signal. Such voluntary responses were distinctly different from conditioned responses both in their form and in their latency distribution. Thus, the voluntary pattern of response, consisting of a smooth, sharp closure which was maintained until after the onset of the air puff, occurred almost exclusively in the period 200 to 460 msec. following the onset of the CS. The responses predominating in the period 460 to 755 msec. were more gradual and much more irregular in their pattern. All Ss who had a high incidence (one-third or more) of responses with latencies less than 460 msec. in either one of the two conditioning periods were eliminated from the experiment. Questioning of these Ss revealed that there was not always awareness that such "voluntary" closures were taking place. Six Ss were

eliminated from the experiment because of error on the part of
E or apparatus difficulties.   Eighty Ss remained for the experiment described below.

Apparatus and method of recording

The S was seated in a dental chair in a semidarkened room
adjoining that in which the recording apparatus and stimulus
controls were located.   Fixed in a reclining position in the
chair, S was instructed to blink on receiving a ready signal, and
then to fixate on a 6-in. circular milk glass disc, placed at a distance of 132 cm.   The brightness of the disc between trials was
.05 apparent ft.-candles.

The CS consisted in an increase in brightness of the disc to
1.51 apparent ft.-candles.   The duration of the CS on each trial
was 825 msec.   The onset and duration of the CS and UCS were
controlled by means of Hunter electronic timers and were recorded on a Brush polygraph by means of a Brush BL-902 penmotor.

The UCS, a puff of air, followed the onset of the CS by 755
msec. and was delivered to the right eye.   The source of the
air puff was a high pressure compressed air line provided in the
building.   Appropriate pressure was obtained by means of a
variable (0–10 lb./sq. in.) air pressure reducing valve.   A pressure gauge was used to provide the two strengths of air pressure
employed, .25 lb./sq. in. in the case of the weak UCS and
5.0 lb./sq. in. in the case of the strong UCS.   A 110-v., 60-cycle
AC operated solenoid valve, controlled by an electronic timer,
limited the duration of the puff to 50 msec.   This represents a
much superior air-puff system than that previously employed in
this laboratory in that the air pressure can be maintained at the
stated pressure for any desired time interval.

The movement of the eyelid was recorded by a system similar
to that described earlier by Spence and Taylor (*14*) except that
a simpler method of amplification was employed.   Briefly the
technique involved the use of (*a*) a lightweight microtorque
potentiometer, (*b*) a direct current amplifier, (*c*) a Brush polygraph, and (*d*) a Brush BL-902 penmotor.

The microtorque potentiometer was mounted on an adjusta-

ble headband just above S's eye.   A very light lever was attached
at right angles to the variable (rotating) arm of the potentiometer and a mechanical linkage was accomplished between it
and a tiny plastic lever fastened to the upper eyelid by adhesive
tape.   A small restoring spring was added to the potentiometer
arm thus permitting it to follow the eyelid's motion.   The system was very light and involved a minimum of work.   Movement of the eyelid, with its accompanying rotation of the potentiometer arm, altered the DC voltage appearing on the grids of
a push-pull vacuum tube amplifier.   The latter was a three
stage push-pull amplifier with a push-pull cathode follower out-
put stage being used to match the impedance of the Brush penmotor.

Conditioning procedure

The experiment was conducted in two periods, the second
following the first by 24 hr.   Following the reading of instructions each S received three presentations of the light alone in
order to check for any initial conditioned response tendency to
the light.   A single air puff was then administered and the eyelid behavior recorded for 40 sec.   All Ss were then given 30
paired presentations of the light and air puff.   Intertrial intervals of 15, 20, or 25 sec., averaging 20 sec. and arranged according to a fixed schedule, were used.

On this first day half of the 80 Ss were conditioned with the
relatively weak air puff (.25 lb./sq. in.) and half with the strong
puff (5.0 lb./sq. in.).   At the beginning of Day 2 the instructions were repeated and a further 70 paired presentations of the
CS and UCS were given.   On this day half of the Ss trained with
the weak puff on Day 1 were trained for 70 more trials with it
and half were shifted to the strong UCS.   Similarly, half of the
Ss trained on Day 1 with the strong UCS had the strong UCS
continued on Day 2 and half were shifted to the weak UCS.
Thus, on Day 2 there were four subgroups of 20 Ss each in terms
of the UCS used in the two conditioning periods: WW, WS, SS,
and SW.

At the end of the session all Ss were asked not to discuss the
experiment with other members of the class.

Results and Discussion

The values in the four cells of Table 1 represent the mean number of CR's made by the four subgroups in the first 20 trials

TABLE 1

MEAN NUMBER OF CR's MADE IN FIRST 20 TRIALS OF DAY 2

| Day 1 UCS (lb./sq. in.) | Day 2 UCS (lb./sq. in.) | | Means Reflecting H |
	.25	5.00	
.25	5.65	8.80	7.23
5.00	7.45	13.00	10.23
Means Reflecting D	6.55	10.90	

of the second day.   This 20-trial period was chosen because a longer period ran into the problem that our measuring scale has a ceiling, i.e., 100%.   The frequency measure of response strength is quite satisfactory only so long as we do not reach this ceiling level.   Once an S has reached 100% any further increase in strength of the S-R tendency (sE_R) with further training cannot be reflected by this measure.   By the second ten-trial block two Ss were responding 100%, and in the next ten-trial block four more Ss reached this level.   Accordingly, it was decided to use the data for the first 20 trials only.   The scores obtained in this period provided quite satisfactory distributions so far as the requirements (variance and form) for statistical analysis are concerned.   Score distributions for longer periods were quite unsatisfactory, for with the ceiling on the measure the distributions became more and more skewed as more Ss attained the 100% level of response.

Returning to Table 1, it will be seen that there are sizable differences both in the case of the row means and the column means.   The statistical significance of these variations was tested by means of analysis of variance, the results of which are presented in Table 2.   It will be noted that there was no significant

TABLE 2

ANALYSIS OF VARIANCE FOR TRIALS 31–50
(DAY 2)

Source	df	Mean Square	F*
Intensity Day 1 (rows)	1	180.00	6.40
Intensity Day 2 (columns)	1	378.45	13.46
Rows × columns (interaction)	1	28.85	1.03
Within groups	76	28.11	
Total	79		

* .05 level, $F = 3.98$; .01 level, $F = 7.01$.

interaction.   The "main effect" of the intensity of the UCS on Day 1, as shown by the difference between the two row means, is revealed to be significant by the F test at a level just short of the .01 level of confidence.   The difference between the column means, which reflects the "main effect" of the intensity of UCS at the time of measurement (Day 2), is also seen to be highly significant by the F test, in this instance beyond the .001 level of confidence.

The significant difference between the row means supports the interpretation, it will be recalled, that different strengths of conditioning (amounts of habit strength) were developed during the first day of training when the UCS was different for the Ss compared.   This result would be in line with the notion that the increment of habit strength (ΔH) is a function of the strength of drive and interpretable as in agreement with the drive-reduction theory of reinforcement; that is, the stronger UCS would produce a stronger drive and with its cessation there would be greater drive reduction.

The significant difference between the column means indicates that response strength varied with the intensity of the UCS employed at the time of measurement.   Presumably this difference reflects the differences in drive strength (D) produced by the different intensities of UCS.   However, if habit strength also varies with intensity of UCS, then there must also be a difference between the habit strengths of the two groups (.25 and 5.0).   This difference in habit strength would be that which developed during this 20-trial period of Day 2 for they were equated in terms of the amount of habit strength developed on Day 1.   While no evaluation can be made of the differences, it is of some interest that the difference between the column means (4.4) is 47% larger than the difference between the row means (3.0).   The former involves only a difference in H based on 30 trials with different intensities of UCS.

A problem that arises in connection with this interpretation of a different amount of habit strength being built up with the different intensities of UCS is the negative evidence that has been obtained in studies employing an appetitional need such as hunger.   Thus, the experiments of Kendler (7) and Strassburger (15), which involved varying the time of deprivation of some goal object (food, water), did not provide comparable significant differences in the row means of the response measures in the second period.   An answer that suggests itself is that the amount of reinforcement (drive reduction) in the food reward situation is the same for different conditions of deprivation.   Indeed, the reinforcement probably is secondary in nature and does not involve any primary drive reduction whatever.   In the conditioning study, on the other hand, the reinforcement was primary (pain reduction) and, presumably, different for the different intensities of air puff.

There are, of course, other possible interpretations as to the factor responsible for the difference in the row means, *i.e.*, the difference related to the intensity of the UCS on Day 1.   One most likely to be offered by the theorist opposed to any kind of reinforcement notion is that a *bigger* response is probably conditioned in the case of the stronger UCS.   The logic is not too clear as to how one gets from this to the predicted greater *frequency* of CR for the group which is making the larger unconditioned response (UCR) although it is evident that a higher average magnitude of CR would be expected.   Presumably it is assumed that the magnitude of the CR increases with successive trials and there is thus a greater likelihood of a response reaching the criterion magnitude (1 mm.) of a CR earlier in the case of Ss with a large UCR than those with a smaller one. An examination of the magnitude of the UCR during the first ten trials of Day 1 did reveal that the mean UCR was larger for the 5.0-lb. group than for the .25-lb. group (18.17 mm. vs. 14.5 mm.). However, an examination of the scatter diagrams relating amplitude of UCR on these trials with the number of CR's on Day 2 (Trials 31–50) showed no evidence of a positive correlation. In fact the relationship was slightly but insignificantly negative.

As a further means of checking on the possibility that amplitude of UCR was a factor, Ss in the four subgroups were matched by selecting ten Ss in each subgroup whose mean amplitude of UCR on Day 1 fell between 14 and 20 mm. The mean amplitudes of the four subgroups when so matched were either 17.3 or 17.4 mm. The mean number of CR's in Trials 31–50 on Day 2 for the WW and WS subgroups and for the SW and SS subgroups were then calculated for these Ss. They were 6.5 for the Ss (WW and WS) who had the weak UCS on Day 1 and 11.5 for the Ss (SW, SS) who had the strong UCS. The difference, 5.0, is even larger, it will be noticed, than that which appears between the raw means in Table 1.

A second possible interpretation of this finding that would not involve the reinforcement principle is that a stronger emotional or fear reaction was established to the cues from the experimental situation in the case of the more intense UCS. As the conditioned fear response is one of the determiners of the drive level (D), it would follow that Ss trained with the more intense UCS would be expected to have a higher D level. According to this formulation, however, the different levels of response are due to this different level of D (from the secondary motivation of fear) and not to a difference in H. The present experiment does not, of course, permit an evaluation of these rival interpretations. Its chief contribution is the experimental finding that performance level in the second period is a function of the differential conditions in the first period. This fact points to the necessity for invoking some kind of historical or learning factor, different habit strength, conditional fear responses, or some such to account for it.

Summary and Conclusions

A factorial type experiment was conducted to investigate the question as to whether a difference in the intensity of the UCS (air puff) during a first training period would lead to differences in the level of eyelid conditioning in a second period in which intensity of the UCS was controlled.

During the first experimental period of 30 trials, 80 Ss, divided randomly into two equal groups, were conditioned. One group was conditioned with a weak UCS and the other with a strong UCS. In a second training period given on the following day the two groups were each divided into two subgroups with half of the Ss continuing with the same UCS and half being switched to the other intensity.

Analysis of variance of the frequency of CR's in the first 20 trials of the second period revealed that there were significant differences in performance in relation both to the intensities of UCS employed in the first period and also in relation to that used in the second period. The fact that response level varied with the intensity of the UCS employed on Day 1 was interpreted as in accord with Hull's theory that the increment of habit strength is a function of the amount of primary drive reduction. The finding that the level of CR varied with the intensity of the UCS at the time of measurement on Day 2 was taken as a reflection of difference in drive level (D). Other possible interpretations not involving the principle of reinforcement were also suggested.

REFERENCES

1. BLOOMBERG, R., & WEBB, W. B. Various degrees within a single drive as cues for spatial response learning in the white rat. *J. exp. Psychol.*, 1949, *39*, 628–636.

2. DODSON, J. D. Relative values of reward and punishment as habit formation. *Psychobiol.*, 1918, *1*, 231–276.

3. FINAN, J. L., & TAYLOR, L. F. Quantitative studies in motivation. I. Strength of conditioning in rats under varying degrees of hunger. *J. comp. Psychol.*, 1940, *29*, 119–134.

4. HORENSTEIN, B. R. Performance of conditional responses as a function of strength of hunger drive. *J. comp. physiol. Psychol.*, 1951, *44*, 210–224.

5. HULL, C. L.   *Principles of Behavior.*   New York: D. Appleton-Century, 1943.

6. JENKINS, J. J., & HANRATTY, J. A.   Drive intensity discrimination in the albino rat.   *J. comp. physiol. Psychol.,* 1949, *42,* 228–232.

7. KENDLER, H. H.   Drive interaction: II.   Experimental analysis of the role of drive in learning theory.   *J. exp. Psychol.,* 1945, *35,* 188–198.

8. KIMBLE, G. A.   Behavior strength as a function of the intensity of the hunger drive.   *J. exp. Psychol.,* 1951, *41,* 341–348.

9. MacDUFF, M. M.   The effect on retention of varying degrees of motivation during learning in rats.   *J. comp. Psychol.,* 1946, *39,* 207–240.

10. MEYER, D. R.   Food deprivation and discrimination reversal by monkeys.   *J. exp. Psychol.,* 1951, *41,* 10–16.

11. PASSEY, G. E.   The influence of intensity of unconditioned stimulus upon acquisition of a conditioned response.   *J. exp. Psychol.,* 1948, *38,* 420–428.

12. PERIN, C. T.   Behavior potentiality as a joint function of the amount of training and the degree of hunger at the time of extinction.   *J. exp. Psychol.,* 1942, *30,* 93–109.

13. SACKETT, R. S.   The effect of strength of drive at the time of extinction upon resistance to extinction in rats.   *J. comp. Psychol.,* 1939, *27,* 411–431.

14. SPENCE, K. W., & TAYLOR, J. A.   Anxiety and strength of the UCS as determiners of the amount of eyelid conditioning.   *J. exp. Psychol.,* 1951, *42,* 183–188.

15. STRASSBURGER, R. C.   Resistance to extinction of a conditional operant as related to drive level at reinforcement.   *J. exp. Psychol.,* 1950, *40,* 473–487.

16. TEEL, K., & WEBB, W. B.   Response evocation on satiated trials in the T-maze.   *J. exp. Psychol.,* 1951, *41,* 148–152.

17. TOLMAN, E. C., & GLEITMAN, H.   Studies in spatial learning. VII. Place and response learning under different degrees of motivation.   *J. exp. Psychol.,* 1949, *39,* 653–659.

18. ———, & HONZIK, C. H.   Degrees of hunger, reward and non-reward, and maze learning in rats.   *University of California Publ. Psychol.,* 1930, *4,* 241–256.

19. WARDEN, C. J.   *Animal Motivation: Experimental Studies on the Albino Rat.*   New York: Columbia University Press, 1931.

20. YAMAGUCHI, H. G.   Drive (*D*) as a function of hours of hunger (*h*).   *J. exp. Psychol.,* 1951, *42,* 108–117.

10

UCS Intensity and the Associative (Habit)
Strength of the Eyelid CR [1,2]

In a recent series of lectures (7) the senior author tentatively suggested the theoretical possibility that classical aversive conditioning is governed by a reinforcement principle, whereas instrumental appetitional (reward) conditioning does not involve such a principle. Contiguity of the stimulus and behavior events was considered to be a sufficient condition for learning, *i.e.*, habit formation, to occur in this latter type of situation. That is, the increment of habit strength (H) of the instrumental response was assumed to depend only on the occurrence of the response and not to be a function of the reinforcer and its properties. In contrast, the increment of H of the conditioned aversive response was interpreted as being a function of the occurrence and properties of the reinforcing UCS. The present study is concerned with evidence as to whether classical aversive conditioning requires the assumption of a reinforcement principle, or more specifically, whether the habit strength (H) of a defense CR is a function of the intensity of the UCS.

On the basis of the experimental finding that level of performance in classical aversive conditioning varies directly with

1 This study was carried out as part of a project concerned with the role of motivation in learning under Contract N9 onr-93802, Project NR 154-107 between the State University of Iowa and the Office of Naval Research.
2 Written in collaboration with D. F. Haggard and L. E. Ross.

the intensity of the UCS it has been assumed that drive strength, D, is a function of the intensity (noxiousness) of the UCS. According to a reinforcement interpretation of this kind of learning the habit strength (H) would also be assumed to be a function of the UCS. Thus, according to this conception, performance differences with different intensities of the UCS reflect differences both in H and in level of D.

The experimental problem involved in testing this theory is to find some way of separating out these two factors. A previous study by Spence (6) attempted to accomplish this by employing the factorial design type of experiment. While the results of this experiment were in agreement with the reinforcement interpretation that different amounts of habit strength develop with different intensities of the UCS, as was pointed out, it was also possible to interpret the findings in terms of a differential drive (D) level based on fear responses of different strength that become conditioned to the cues of the experimental situation.

The present studies represent a different type of attack on this problem. In these experiments an attempt is made to equate S's level of drive during the course of the conditioning and at the same time provide for differential reinforcement. In order to understand the logic of these experiments, it is necessary first to consider further the source of drive in classical defense conditioning. In the other main types of conditioning situations, classical and instrumental reward, and instrumental escape conditioning, the drive level (D) is a function of some relevant need produced by the manipulation of a maintenance schedule or by presentation of a noxious stimulus. The need in these instances is active (present) at the moment of the occurrence of the response and thus provides a certain level of D which, in combination with habit strength, determines the excitatory strength of the response. But what determines the need (drive state) and hence the level of D in the case of the conditioned anticipatory response on a particular trial in the classical defense type of conditioning? One cannot say that it is the noxious UCS on that particular trial for the CR anticipates this stimulus event. Furthermore, one cannot appeal to a conditioned emotional (fear) response that presumably would be established to the CS. The latency of such a response, mediated as it is by the autonomic nervous system, is much longer than the half-second or less interval of time that has typically been used and found optimal for conditioning such defense reactions. Thus in such instances the conditioned skeletal response, occurring as it does in from 200 to 500 msec., and lasting only briefly, has presumably taken place long before the fear response would even get started.

Because of these considerations it has generally been assumed that the level of drive (D) in this type of conditioning experiment is determined by the previous unconditioned stimuli; that is, those given on previous trials. These stimuli, depending upon their intensity, have been assumed to elicit hypothetical emotional responses (r_e) of varying magnitude (7). The latter have been thought of as persisting in their effects, lasting at least until the ensuing trial. As a number of writers have pointed out, this persisting emotional response may also get established as a CR to other cues in the general situation, possibly even to S's own verbal responses. These expectations, of fears, are assumed to keep a persisting level of emotional activity present that is, to an important degree, a function of the intensity of the UCS employed in the experiment. We have assumed that the level of D is directly related to this level of hypothetical emotional activity.

In the two experiments to be reported the drive level (D) of two groups for whom reinforcement was differential was equated by employing two different intensities of the UCS (air puff). For the low-reinforcement group a weak puff always occurred on a conditioning trial, while a strong puff was always presented on a trial on which no conditioning could occur. For the high-reinforcement group these conditions were reversed, the strong puff being presented on the conditioning trials and the weak puff being presented under the conditions in which no learning could take place. Since the two groups received the same average intensity of the noxious puff stimulus throughout the training period, their drive levels would be equal. However, the intensity of the puff on the trials on which conditioning could occur differed for the two groups. According to the present reinforcement interpretation the group that had the strong puff on a trial on which conditioning could occur should develop a greater amount of habit strength than the group that had a weak

puff on a conditioning trial.   Multiplication of these different
H values by the same D values (since drive level was equal) implies that the excitatory potential (E) and, hence, response
strength should be greater for the high-reinforcement group
than for the low-reinforcement group.

Experiment I

Subjects

A total of 164 men and women students from an introductory
course in psychology were used.   Ten of these were eliminated
because they met the criteria employed in previous studies in
this laboratory defining a voluntary responder (*6, 8*).   The data
of four others Ss were discarded, two because they gave CR's in
the pretest trials and two for reasons of equipment failure.   The
remaining 150 Ss provided three groups, each of which contained 25 men and 25 women.

Apparatus and method of recording

The S was seated in a dental chair in a semidarkened room.
The E was in an adjoining room in which the stimulus controls
and recording equipment were located.   The apparatus for recording the eyeblinks and presenting the stimuli was identical
with that used in recent studies from this laboratory (see *6*).

The CS consisted of an increase in the brightness of a 6-cm.
circular disc from a level of .004 to .506 apparent ft.-candle.
The duration of the CS was 500 msec., with the UCS occurring
450 msec. after the onset of the CS.   The duration of the UCS,
an air puff of either .33 or 2.0 lb./sq. in. applied to the right eye
through a .062-in. diameter orifice, was limited to 50 msec., by a
100-V., 60-cycle AC-operated solenoid valve controlled by an
electronic timer.

The word "ready" preceded each presentation of the CS by 2,
3, or 4 sec. according to a prearranged schedule.The Ss were
instructed to blink upon presentation of the ready signal and
then fixate the circular disc in front of them.   A CR was recorded whenever the record showed a deflection of 1 mm. or
more in the interval 200 to 450 msec. following the onset of the
CS.   Responses with a latency of less than 200 msec., which were

infrequent, were classified as original responses and were not included in the data.

Conditioning procedure

Following the reading of instructions, each S received three presentations of the CS alone. A single presentation of the UCS alone was then given. Immediately following these preliminary trials each S received 100 trials, 50 conditioning trials which involved the paired presentation after the ready signal of the CS and the UCS and 50 trials which involved the presentation of only the UCS. The order of presentation of these paired and unpaired trials was prearranged according to an irregular order in which the number of each was equalized in blocks of four trials. Intertrial intervals of 15, 20, and 25 sec., averaging 20 sec. and arranged according to a fixed schedule, were used throughout the 100 trials. At the end of the experiment Ss were warned not to discuss the experiment with other members of the class.

In the case of the high-reinforcement group (Group H) the CS was always paired with the strong puff, whereas the weak puff was always presented alone, *i.e.*, without the CS. The reverse conditions held for Group L (low reinforcement), the weak puff always being paired with the CS and the strong puff always being presented alone. A third group designated Group LL (low reinforcement and low drive) was also run in which a weak puff was used on both the paired (conditioning) trials and the trials on which the air puff was given alone.

Results

Figure 1 presents the frequency curves of conditioning for the three groups of Ss, 50 in each group. As may be seen, the curve for Group H rises well above that for Group L, whereas the latter is above that for Group LL. Evaluation of the performance levels over the last two points of the curves by means of the Mann-Whitney U test indicated that the difference between Groups H and L was highly significant ($P = .0014$), while the difference between Groups L and LL was significant at the .05 level.

Since the level of D, defined in terms of the intensities of the

UCS employed, was equated for Groups H and L, the significant difference in the performance levels of these two groups presumably reflects a differential strength of *H*. The latter is, of course, related to the different intensities of the puff strengths

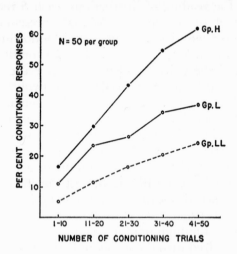

FIG. 1.   Acquisition curves showing the percentage of CR's in successive blocks of 10 conditioning trials.

on the paired conditioning trials. The difference in the curves of Groups L and LL, on the other hand, presumably reflects a difference in the level of *D* only, since these two groups had equated puff strengths on the conditioning, *i.e., H*-producing, trials. The difference between Groups H and LL, which was also highly significant ($P = .0002$), would be interpreted by the present theory as reflecting differences in both habit strength and drive level.

The findings of this experiment are thus seen to be in accord with those reported in a preliminary experiment in which a regular order of presentation of the paired (P) and unpaired (U) trials (repeated blocks of UPPU) was employed (7, p. 177). The irregular order of presentation employed in the present experiment rules out the possibility that the difference between the high- and low-reinforcement groups could have resulted from the conditioning of the S's emotional response to the temporal order.

In order to investigate the possibility that the performance difference between the high- and low-reinforcement groups (H and L) might be due either to a difference in the magnitude of the UCS's made to the different intensities of the UCS on their respective conditioning trials, or to adaptation of the response to the weaker UCS during the conditioning trials, a further analysis of the data was made.   Measurement of the amplitudes of the UCR's made to the air puff on the conditioning trials on which no CR occurred over the first 10 and last 10 paired trials revealed the fact that some Ss did show considerable adaptation of the eyeblink to the puff, and also that there was a marked difference in Groups H and L in this respect.   Accordingly, all Ss whose UCR's during the last 10 paired trials averaged less than 50% of their magnitudes in the first 10 paired trials were eliminated.   On the basis of the criterion 1 S was eliminated from Group H and 11 from Group L, leaving 49 and 39, respectively, in these two groups.[3]

Table 1 gives the mean percentage of CR's made in the last 20

TABLE 1

MEAN PERCENTAGE OF CR'S IN LAST 20 CONDITIONING TRIALS

Group	N	Mean	σ_m
H	49	59.6	4.43
L	39	43.8	5.06

conditioning trials (31–50) by Groups H and L after elimination of these 12 Ss.   While the difference between the two groups was reduced, it was still significant as tested by the Mann-Whitney U test $(.02 < P < .05)$.   Thus the performance differ-

[3] Examination of the amplitudes of the UCR's given by the two curtailed groups during the last 10 paired trials on which no CR's occurred revealed a slight, but insignificant, difference in their mean magnitudes (H = 25.9 mm., L = 24.0 mm.).   Within these groups there was no evidence of any relation between the level of conditioning performance and magnitude of the UCR.

ence in the case of these *S*s is shown not to be accountable for in terms of failure of the low-reinforcement *S*s to respond with adequate UCR's on the conditioning trials.

Experiment II

Instead of using the UCS alone on the nonconditioning trials the CS was presented on all trials in this experiment. On half of the trials the UCS was administered at a CS-UCS interval (500 msec.) known to produce optimal conditioning, whereas on the other half of the trials this interval was 2650 msec., a duration known to produce little or no conditioning, and to result in extinction when introduced after establishing a CR at a shorter, optimal interval (*2, 3*).

It will be seen that this procedure involved a kind of partial reinforcement for both groups, with half of the trials being reinforced and half nonreinforced. In the case of the high reinforcement *S*s the reinforcing, *H*-producing trials (short CS-UCS interval) always involved the strong UCS, whereas the weak UCS was present on the nonreinforcing trials. The reverse conditions held for the low-reinforcement *S*s. According to a reinforcement interpretation the group which received the strong UCS on the short CS-UCS (*i.e.,* reinforcing) trials should show a higher frequency of CR's than the group which received the weak UCS on these trials. Again, since the intensity of the air puffs administered was equated for the two groups during the training period, the performance difference cannot be interpreted as reflecting a difference in *D* and hence would be considered as due to a difference in *H*.

Subjects

The *S*s were 47 women and 44 men from an introductory course in psychology. The data of seven *S*s who were identified by criteria described previously (*8*) as defining voluntary responders were eliminated from the experiment along with that of two *S*s who gave CR's to initial test trial presentations of the CS alone. Two additional *S*s were excluded due to *E*'s error. The remaining 80 *S*s provided two groups, each of which contained 20 men and 20 women.

Apparatus and method of recording

The experimental apparatus and recording procedures used in this experiment were identical with those employed in the first experiment.

Conditioning procedure

The instructions and preliminary trials were the same as those used in Exp. I, as was the employment of a 15-, 20-, or 25-sec. intertrial interval, a ready signal which preceded the CS, again an increase in the brightness of a 6-in. circular disk, by 2, 3, or 4 sec. Each S received 100 trials, 50 reinforcing trials with a 500-msec. CS-UCS interval, and 50 nonreinforcing trials with a 2650 msec. CS-UCS interval. The order of the two kinds of trials was irregular with the number of each type equalized in blocks of four trials. One group of Ss (H-50%) received a 2-lb./sq. in. air puff on the 500-msec. trials and a .33-lb./sq. in. air puff on the 2650-msec. trials, while the other group (L-50%) received the reverse pairing, *i.e.*, a 33-lb. puff on the 500-msec. trials and a 2-lb. puff on the 2650-msec. trials.

Results

The dotted curves in Figure 2 present the data obtained in this experiment. They represent the frequency curves of conditioning in terms of the number of conditioning (*i.e.*, reinforcing) trials for the high-reinforcement group (H-50%) and the low-reinforcement group (L-50%). Also presented for comparative purposes are the frequency conditioning curves obtained for high- and low-reinforcement conditions in Exp. I. Corroborating the results of Exp. I in which 100% reinforcement was involved, the curve for Group H-50% exhibited a gradual divergence from that of group L-50%. Over the last 20 trials the difference in performance level in favor of the high-reinforcement group, tested by means of the Mann-Whitney U test, was highly significant ($P < .01$).

The relative position of the conditioning curves obtained in the present experiment with respect to those of Exp. I is of some interest. Unfortunately, through an error in calibration, the CS-UCS interval employed in the two experiments differed by

50 msec.   The interval employed in Exp. I was 450 msec., while
that used in the present one was 500 msec.   With the exception,
however, of this difference and the difference in reinforcing
procedure, the experimental conditions in the two studies were

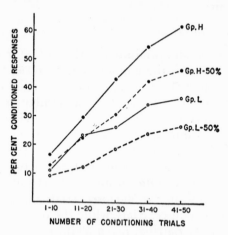

FIG. 2.   Acquisition curves showing percentage of CR's in
successive blocks of 10 conditioning trials for high- and low-
reinforcement groups.   The curves for both Exp. I (solid) and
Exp. II (broken) are shown in order to reveal the decremental
effects of the partial reinforcement schedule used in Exp. II.

the same.   Since we know from other unpublished data obtained in our laboratory that a 500-msec. interval produces just
as high, if not slightly higher, level of performance than 450
msec., the depressed levels of performance shown by the high-
and low-reinforcement groups in the present experiment, as
compared with the groups from the first, reflect the inhibitory
effects of the nonreinforcing trials.

The findings of this experiment further preclude the possibility that the performance difference in the two previous experiments might have been due to the operation of some kind of
differential set with respect to the CS that could have been
established in the two reinforcement groups by virtue of the fact
that the CS was paired with a UCS of different strength.   In the
present experiment there presumably was no possibility of such

a differential set being present since the CS was followed equally often in both groups by the two different puff intensities. Furthermore, S was never aware of which puff intensity would follow the CS on any particular trial.[4]

As in Exp. I, an analysis of the data was also carried out in which Ss who exhibited adaptation to the UCS were eliminated. Thus all Ss whose UCR's during the last 10 reinforcing trials averaged less than 50% of the magnitudes in the first 10 reinforcing trials were eliminated. In the case of the high-reinforcement group these were UCR's made to the 2.0-lb. puff, whereas in the case of the weak-reinforcement group they were responses given to the weak (.33 lb.) puff. On the basis of the criterion of elimination, one S was eliminated from Group H-50% and nine from Group L-50%, leaving 39 and 31 Ss, respectively, in the two groups.

Table 2 shows the mean percentage of CR's made in the last

TABLE 2

MEAN PERCENTAGE OF CR's IN LAST 20 CONDITIONING TRIALS

Group	N	Mean	σ_m
H-50%	39	47.8	5.4
L-50%	31	31.6	3.9

20 conditioning trials (last 40 trials) by the two groups of Ss after elimination of the 10 adapters. Again, as in the previous experiment, the difference between the two groups was reduced, but was still significant at the .05 level. That there was no relation within these Ss between the amplitude of the UCR made to the reinforcing UCS and the percentage of CR's is shown by the fact that the correlation coefficient between them was —.046. In the case of all Ss this coefficient was .245.

[4] It is of some interest to note that Ss did not acquire a set to respond differentially at the longer interval. Thus, there was no difference between the two groups of the present experiment in the number of anticipatory responses occurring 1 sec. prior to the UCS in the long-interval trials. Such responses are, for the most part, random blinks, for we know that there is little, if any, conditioning at this long interval.

This finding thus confirms the previous experiment in showing that the performance difference between the two groups is
not due to a failure of the low-reinforcement Ss to respond with
an adequate UCR on the conditioning trials. Perhaps attention should also be called here to the point that the failure of
the Ss whose UCS adapts out to show conditioning is quite in
accord wtih a reinforcement interpretation that learning (*i.e.*,
growth of H) is a function of the intensity of the reinforcing
aversive stimulus. Such Ss, according to this interpretation,
should show relatively little, if any, conditioning.

Discussion

The evidence of these two experiments and the similar experiment previously reported by Spence (7, p. 177) shows clearly
that, with level of drive (D) equated, performance in classical
aversive conditioning is a function of the intensity of the UCS
occurring on the reinforced trials. This finding may be interpreted as lending support to a reinforcement-type theory that
habit strength (H) in such aversive conditioning is a function
of the intensity of the UCS. One version of such a reinforcement theory is the drive-stimulus reduction conception of Hull
(*1*) and Miller and Dollard (*4*). According to this view the
cessation of a strong UCS in aversive conditioning would provide greater reinforcement than cessation of a weak UCS and
thus should lead to a greater increment of H per trial. The
present writers would prefer to confine their interpretation to
the more general conception that habit strength (H) is some
function of the intensity of the UCS, leaving the nature of the
reinforcing mechanism out of consideration.

In connection with the decremental effects of the partial reinforcement procedure employed in Exp. II, attention should be
directed to the evidence provided in Figure 2 by a comparison
of the upper two curves that the inhibitory effect developed
gradually and consistently over the 50 trials of conditioning and
50 nonreinforced trials. In contrast, the two lower curves suggest that the inhibitory effect reached a maximum much earlier
in the low-reinforcement condition, possibly as soon as 20 conditioning trials or a total of 40 trials. Further data providing

such comparisons are needed so that we may ascertain the nature of the development of such inhibitory effects on performance level during conditioning under partial schedules of reinforcement.

Summary

This study was concerned with the problem of whether habit strength (H) is a function of the intensity of the UCS in classical aversive (eyelid) conditioning. In Exp. I one group (high reinforcement) always had the CS paired with a strong UCS and in the other group (low reinforcement) with a weak UCS. The drive (D) level was equated (on the average) in the two groups by interspersing among the conditioning trials an equal number of trials with the UCS alone. Thus the high-reinforcement group was presented with the weak UCS on such trials and the low-reinforcement group the strong UCS. Comparison of the frequency of CR's in the last 20 conditioning trials revealed a significant difference between the high- and low-reinforcement groups. This result was shown to hold even with Ss equated for the magnitudes of their UCR's.

In Exp. II one group (high reinforcement) had the CS, a light, paired on half the trials with a strong UCS at an optimal CS-UCS interval (500 msec.). On the other half of the trials the CS was paired with a weak UCS at an interval (2650 msec.) known not to lead to conditioning. The conditions for low-reinforcement group were the reverse, the CS being paired with the weak UCS on the conditioning (*i.e.*, reinforcing) trials and the strong UCS on the nonconditioning trials. Performance measured over the last 20 conditioning trials (40 total trials) revealed that the high-reinforcement group gave a significantly greater number of CR's than the low-reinforcement group.

Since the drive levels of the high- and low-reinforcement groups in each experiment were equated, the performance differences between them were interpreted as reflecting a difference in the learning factor (H) and hence as supporting a reinforcement type of learning theory as far as aversive conditioning is concerned.

REFERENCES

1. HULL, C. L.   *Principles of Behavior.*   New York: D. Appleton-Century, 1943.
2. MCALLISTER, W. R.   The effect on eyelid conditioning of shifting the CS-US interval.   *J. exp. Psychol.,* 1953, *45,* 423–428.
3. ———.   Eyelid conditioning as a function of the CS-US interval.   *J. exp. Psychol.,* 1953, *45,* 417–422.
4. MILLER, N. E., & DOLLARD, J.   *Social Learning and Imitation.*   New Haven: Yale Univer. Press, 1941.
5. PASSEY, G. E.   The influence of the intensity of unconditioned stimulus upon acquisition of a conditioned response.   *J. exp. Psychol.,* 1948, *38,* 420–428.
6. SPENCE, K. W.   Learning and performance in eyelid conditioning as a function of the intensity of the UCS.   *J. exp. Psychol.,* 1953, *45,* 57–63.
7. ———.   *Behavior Theory and Conditioning.*   New Haven: Yale University Press, 1956.
8. ———, & TAYLOR, J. A.   Anxiety and strength of the UCS as determiners of the amount of eyelid conditioning.   *J. exp. Psychol.,* 1951, *42,* 183–188.

11

Performance in Eyelid Conditioning Related to Changes in Muscular Tension and Physiological Measures of Emotionality [1,2]

In interpreting some recent studies of classical aversive conditioning use has been made of the basic assumption that the associative factor (H) and the drive factor (D) combine in a multiplicative manner to determine excitatory strength (E), which in turn determines performance. Drive level has been conceptualized in terms of an emotional response (r_e) to the noxious stimulation (UCS) of preceding trials, so that the greater the amplitude of r_e, the higher the drive level (16, 17). Studies in which performance level in eyelid conditioning has been shown to be a function of UCS intensity (15, 20) and a function of extreme scores on a questionnaire designed to select Ss differing in emotionality (18, 20, 22) have been offered in support of this theory. In two recent studies (12, 13), emotional Ss were selected on the basis of either large pulse rate increases *or* skin conductance increases in response to weak noxious stimulation (an air puff to the eye). The performance of these Ss in eyelid conditioning was compared with that of a group which did not

1 This research was carried out as a part of a project concerned with the influence of motivation on performance in learning under Contract N9 onr-93802, Project NR-154-107 between the State University of Iowa and the Office of Naval Research. Thanks is given to John Hunter who served as research assistant.

2 Written in collaboration with W. N. Runquist.

show large increases in these measures. The emotional group performed at a higher level than the nonemotional group. This latter result has been interpreted as supporting the hypothesis that drive level (D) is a function of the intensity of the emotional response (r_e) to noxious stimuli, and as also supporting a hypothesis advanced by Lacey (1956) that the "symptoms" of emotionality are specific to each individual. That is, not all physiological systems are activated by stress or noxious stimulation, but there are individual differences not only in intensity of amplitude of the emotional response but also in the particular autonomic channel through which it discharges.

The concept of level of emotional response as underlying generalized drive level (D) in behavior theory (*17*) corresponds quite closely to the concepts of level of activation and arousal level recently discussed by Duffy (*4*), Schlosberg (*14*), Lindsley (*8*), Hebb (*6*), Freeman (*5*), and Malmo (*10*). These authors refer to arousal level as the intensity dimension of behavior in contrast to its directive aspects. That is, arousal level affects any response being made regardless of what the particular response is. The definition of level of arousal has been in terms of certain physiological measures, such as EEG and autonomic activity (pulse rate, GSR, respiration, etc.). Several recent studies by Malmo and his associates (*1, 9, 10, 21*) have suggested that changes in the level of muscular tension, as measured by muscle action potential (MAP), could also be used to define a level of arousal continuum. In fact, Malmo notes the similarity between arousal level and anxiety as defined by the Manifest Anxiety Scale and suggests the use of physiologically defined arousal level as a possible alternative.

If the emotional responsiveness of an individual is related to MAP changes, then those Ss with large MAP changes should show a higher level of conditioning performance than those Ss with small MAP changes. Moreover, the conditioning curves should diverge with trials. These predictions follow from the hypothesized relation between emotional responsiveness and drive level, D, and the multiplicative relation between D and H. The primary purpose of this study was to investigate the relation between MAP change and level of performance in eyelid conditioning. A second purpose was to check on results obtained in the previous studies (12, 13) relating conditioning performance to level of autonomic activity when pulse rate and skin conductance are measured during the course of conditioning rather than in a pretest series of UCS presentations as was done in the previous investigations.

Method

Subjects

The Ss were 86 volunteers from an introductory course in psychology.   An additional 35 Ss were run but were discarded. Apparatus failure accounted for 22, 5 were classified voluntary responders, and 8 gave initial CRs to the light CS.

Apparatus

The equipment for recording eyeblinks and delivering the UCS, a 1-lb. air puff to the right eye, was the same as that used in previous studies from this laboratory.   The CS was the increase in brightness of a 6-cm. circular disc.   The duration of the CS was 550 msec. with the UCS occurring 550 msec. after its onset.   The air puff was limited to 50 msec. by a solenoid valve controlled by an electronic timer.

The equipment for recording pulse rate and skin resistance was the same as used in a previous study (13).   EKG electrodes were attached to each forearm, and GSR electrodes to the palm and back of the right hand.   The muscle action potentials were recorded with one electrode placed above the sternomastoid muscle about half way up the neck.   The ground electrode was placed on the back of the neck.   The action potentials were integrated by means of a full wave rectifier, then sent through a low pass filter to a second amplifier.   The MAP appears as a low frequency of the order of 10–15 cps, and is recorded by a Brush ink-writing oscillograph.   The amplitude of the record was a summation of the energy generated within each period of time controlled by the low pass filter.   Amplifiers used push-pull circuits with standard high quality broadcast transformers. An over-all amplification of about one million was obtained with this method.

Procedure

After all electrodes had been attached, the standard eyelid conditioning procedure employed in this laboratory was used. All Ss received three trials with the CS alone, plus one trial with the UCS alone, followed by 80 conditioning trials. The intertrial interval was either 15, 20, or 25 sec. in a prearranged order. A verbal ready signal preceded each trial by from 2 to 4 sec., also in a prearranged order. A CR was recorded when a deflection of 1 mm. occurred in the interval 200–500 msec. following the onset of the CS. Measurement of physiological responses was made for a 5-sec. period before the first CS alone trial, on the UCS alone trial, and on trials 10, 20, 30, 40, 50 ,60, 70, and 80 of conditioning. On these trials a continuous record of pulse rate, skin conductance, and MAP was obtained for 15 sec. starting 5 sec. before the ready signal. The intertrial interval preceding the test trials was always 25 sec., and the time between ready signal and CS onset on these trials was always 2 sec.

Measurement of physiological responses

Pulse rate was measured as the speed of two beats at points immediately preceding the onset of the CS and 4 sec. after the UCS. Skin conductance measures were also taken at the same points. The MAP measure was the sum of the magnitude of the deflections during a 500 msec. interval preceding the CS and immediately following the UCS. Measures of all three responses were made at a randomly selected 500 msec. interval while S was resting before the experimental procedure was begun.

Results

Autonomic responses

By selecting samples of emotional and nonemotional Ss on the basis of the two autonomic measures (pulse rate and skin conductance), a comparison may be made between the present study and two previous ones (*12, 13*). Two separate analyses were made. In the first analysis pulse rate increase and skin conductance increase in response to the air puff delivered alone on a single trial were used. The emotional Ss were those who were in the 15% of the sample with the largest pulse rate increase *or* the 15% of the sample with the largest skin conductance increase (N = 20). The nonemotional Ss were the 25% with the lowest combined z score of the two measures (N = 21). The emotional Ss made a mean of 21.8 CRs in the last 40 trials, while the nonemotional Ss made a mean of 13.7 CRs. A t test gave a value of 2.18 which was significant beyond the .05 level. These results are consistent with the findings of the first study (*12*). In a second analysis, the same pulse rate increase measure was used, but the skin conductance measure was the increase in base level conductance over the first 20 trials of conditioning. Samples of 18 emotional and 18 nonemotional Ss were selected according to the same criteria as above.[3] The emotional Ss made a mean of 24.5 CRs and the nonemotional Ss a mean of 14.9 CRs in the last 40 conditioning trials. The t between these two means was 2.47 which was significant at better than the .05 level. These results confirm the findings of the second study (*13*).

Muscle action potential indices

Two measures of MAP activity were employed. The first was the base level of activity as determined by the sum of the MAP deflections in two randomly selected .5-sec. periods during the resting pretest period. Three groups of 20 Ss each, representing high, middle, and low levels of such base level MAP measures were compared as to their conditioning performances. The mean number of CRs over the last 40 trials for these high, middle, and low groups were 22.9, 15.4, and 18.7, respectively. Analysis of variance of these data gave an F of 2.07, which fell short of significance.

The second measure of MAP related to level of conditioning performance was the response to the air puff. While the autonomic responses to the noxious stimulation have a latency of from 2 to 7 sec., it has been demonstrated (*3*) that the latency of the MAP response is between .1 and .3 sec. A measure of MAP

---

[3] The smaller sample of emotional Ss in this analysis resulted from the fact that some Ss met the criterion on both measures. The nonemotional Ss were then selected to keep the samples roughly the same size.

response to the air puff was taken as the summed deflections in a .5-sec. period following the air puff minus the summed deflections in a .5-sec. period preceding the CS. Nearly all Ss gave positive scores indicating an increase in MAP following the presentations of the air puff. By the tenth conditioning trial, however, the responses decrease to almost zero. For our present purposes, the sample of 86 Ss was divided into four groups corresponding to successive quartiles on the basis of the MAP response on the trial in which the air puff was given alone. The top and bottom quartiles contain 21 Ss per group; the two middle groups contain 22 Ss. Curves of acquisition of the CR in terms of percentage of CRs in each block of 10 conditioning trials are shown in Figure 1. The curves clearly rank order themselves in terms of these MAP measures and show the diver-

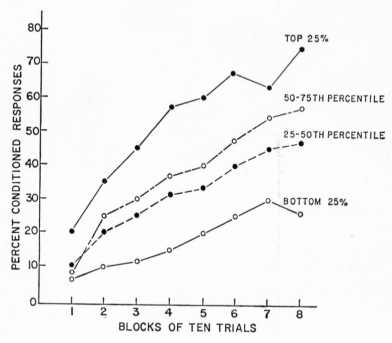

FIG. 1. Percentage of CRs in each block of 10 trials for four groups of Ss selected on the basis of the MAP response to the air puff alone.

gence with trials implied by the theory concerning the interaction between H and D. Analysis of variance based on the total CRs for the last 40 trials gave an F of 8.99 which is significant beyond the .001 level. A rank order correlation between this MAP measure and number of CRs during Trials 41–80 gave a rho of .52.[4]

Discussion

The finding that emotionality as defined by autonomic response measures is related to performance in conditioning provides additional supporting evidence for the hypothesis that drive level (D) is a function of the level of emotional response of the individual. The second significant finding in this experiment is the high positive correlation between MAP response and performance in conditioning. Although the MAP measure may represent merely the magnitude of the skeletal startle response and not a change in any persisting tension level, this finding may, nevertheless, be interpreted as being consistent with the hypothesis that the four groups represent different drive levels. Thus, if it is assumed that the MAP response is some increasing function of the magnitude of this startle response to the air puff, and that the magnitude of the startle response is a function of drive level (D) then individual differences in MAP response should reflect individual differences in drive level. That the magnitude of the startle reflex is related to drive is, in fact, part of the theory of generalized drive, which states that any response will be facilitated by higher drive level. Experimental evidence for the effects of raising D on unconditioned reflexes has been provided by several studies (2, 11, 19) which have shown increased unconditioned reflex amplitude when reflex occurs in the presence of a stimulus previously paired with some kind of noxious stimulus.

The writers who have used the concept of arousal level or

4 The MAP measure could be combined with the autonomic measures to predict performance in conditioning. When this was done the 24 emotional Ss based on the 10 highest on each measure gave a mean of 23.9 CRs. The nonemotional Ss, the 22 Ss with the lowest total score, gave a mean of 14.6 CRs. The t between these means was 2.86, which is significant beyond the .01 level.

activation in much the same manner as drive level has been used here, have postulated an inverted **U** relation between performance and arousal level, and have presented considerable evidence to support this generalization $(1, 9, 10, 21)$. The results obtained here show that the conditioning performance is monotonically related to the magnitude of the MAP. However, the tasks used in the studies cited above have been relatively complex ones, presumably involving competing responses and other factors which are not analyzable according to the present theory. Such results are not contradictory to the theory and, considering that the conditioning situation is very different from those in which the **U**-shaped relationships have been obtained, the difference is not surprising. Furthermore, arousal level was defined in these studies as the increase in MAP occurring during a trial on these tasks, a definition which differs somewhat from the brief response to a noxious stimulus. There is no way to tell from the data of the present study whether these two MAP measures are related. It is felt, nevertheless, that the results are in agreement with the theoretical notions concerning the relation of drive level (D) to performance in eyelid conditioning and the hypothesis relating D to level of arousal as defined by MAP changes.

Summary

Eighty-six Ss were given 80 eyelid conditioning trials. During these trials pulse rate changes, skin conductance, and muscle action potential (MAP) were recorded. Two groups of Ss were selected on the bases of their GSR and pulse rate responses to the UCS. The group classified as emotionally responsive gave significantly more CRs than the group classified as nonemotional. Four groups selected on the basis of the magnitude of the MAP response to an air puff trial, were also compared. Mean number of CRs was found to be an increasing function of MAP response, the rank order correlation being .52.

The results were interpreted as supporting a theory that drive level in classical aversive conditioning is a function of the magnitude of the emotional response to a noxious UCS, and that the magnitude of MAP response is a direct function of drive level.

REFERENCES

1. BARTOSHUK, A. K. Electromyographic gradients as indicants of motivation. *Canad. J. Psychol.*, 1955, *9*, 215–230.

2. BROWN, J. S., KALISH, H., & FARBER, I. E. Conditioned fear as revealed by magnitude of startle response to an auditory stimulus. *J. exp. Psychol.*, 1951, *41*, 317–328.

3. DAVIS, R. C., BUCHWALD, A. M., & FRANKMANN, R. W. Autonomic and muscular responses and their relation to simple stimuli. *Psychol. Monog.*, 1955, *69*(20, Whole No. 405).

4. DUFFY, E. H. The concept of energy mobilization. *Psychol. Rev.*, 1951, *58*, 30–40.

5. FREEMAN, G. L. *The Energetics of Human Behavior.* Ithaca: Cornell University Press, 1948.

6. HEBB, D. O. Drives and the C.N.S. (conceptual nervous system). *Psychol. Rev.*, 1955, *62*, 243–254.

7. LACEY, J. I. The evaluation of autonomic responses: Toward a general solution. *Ann. NY Acad. Sci.*, 1956, *57*, 123–164.

8. LINDSLEY, D. B. Emotion. In S.S. Stevens (Ed.), *Handbook of Experimental Psychology.* New York: Wiley, 1951, pp. 473–516.

9. MALMO, R. B. Anxiety and behavioral arousal. *Psychol. Rev.*, 1957, *64*, 276–287.

10. ——, & DAVIS, J. F. Physiological gradients as indicants of arousal in mirror tracing. *Canad. J. Psychol.*, 1956, *10*, 231–238.

11. MERYMAN, J. J. The magnitude of an unconditioned GSR as a function of fear conditioned at a long CS-UCS interval. Unpublished doctoral dissertation, State University Iowa, 1953.

12. RUNQUIST, W. N., & ROSS, L. E. A preliminary study of the relationship between GSR, heart rate changes and level of performance in eyelid conditioning. *Proc. Iowa Acad. Sci.*, 1958, *65*, 398–404.

13. ——, & ——. The relation between physiological measures of emotionality and performance in eyelid conditioning. *J. exp. Psychol.*, 1959, *57*, 329–332.

14. SCHLOSBERG, H. Three dimensions of emotion. *Psychol. Rev.*, 1954, *61*, 81–88.

15. SPENCE, K. W. Learning and performance in eyelid conditioning as a function of intensity of the UCS. *J. exp. Psychol.*, 1953, *45*, 57–63.

16. ——. *Behavior Theory and Conditioning.* New Haven: Yale University Press, 1956.

17. ——. An emotionally based theory of drive (*D*) and its relation to performance in simple learning situations. *Amer. Psychologist*, 1958, *13*, 131–141.

18. ——, & FARBER, I. E. Conditioning and extinction as a function of anxiety. *J. exp. Psychol.*, 1953, *45*, 116–119.

19. ——, & RUNQUIST, W. N. The temporal relation of conditioned fear to the eyelid reflex. *J. exp. Psychol.*, 1958, *55*, 613–616.

20. ———, & TAYLOR, J. A.   Anxiety and strength of UCS as determiners of the amount of eyelid conditioning. *J. exp. Psychol.*, 1951, *42*, 183–188.
21. STENNETT, R. G.   Relationship of performance level to level of arousal. *J. exp. Psychol.*, 1957, *54*, 54–61.
22. TAYLOR, J. A.   The relationship of anxiety to the conditioned eyelid response. *J. exp. Psychol.*, 1951, *41*, 81–92.

12

The Relation of Anxiety (Drive) Level to Performance in Competitional and Non-Competitional Paired-Associates Learning [1,2]

Conditioning studies involving some form of noxious stimulation have revealed that level of performance is a function of the intensity of the unconditioned stimulus (*13, 17*). One interpretation that has been given of this finding is that the more noxious the stimulus the higher is the level of the emotional response (state of emotionality) of *S* (*21, 22*). Level of emotionality, in turn, is one of the factors assumed to determine the total effective drive level of the organism. This concept of drive level or *D* is one of the important intervening variables determining response strength in S-R theory.

Another line of evidence indicating that noxious stimulation and its after-effects determine level of response are the studies (*3, 15, 16*) which have shown that the level of consummatory response (eating, drinking) is significantly increased for a period of time if *S*s are shocked just prior to being placed in the food or water situation. These investigators have interpreted their findings as reflecting the perseveration of the emotional state produced by the preceding shocks, which is assumed to increase response strength through increase in level of *D*.

[1] This study was carried out as part of a project conducted under contract N9 onr-93802, Project 154-107 between the State University of Iowa and the Office of Naval Research. A portion of the data in the first experiment was collected by Rhoda Ketchel.

[2] Written in collaboration with I. E. Farbar and H. H. McFann.

Similar motivational properties have been demonstrated in the case of non-noxious stimuli which, in the previous history of S, have been associated with a noxious stimulus. Mowrer (12) and Miller (10) have assumed that such prior training establishes a conditioned emotional (fear) response to the previously neutral stimulus. Studies such as those of Amsel (1), Kalish (8), and Brown, Kalish, and Farbar (4) have demonstrated that the presence of these conditioned fear arousing stimuli can intensify coincident stimulus-response tendencies.

Accepting the notion that the degree of emotionality of S, produced either by unconditioned or conditioned stimuli, affects level of response, and interpreting this effect within the framework of our theoretical system as reflecting level of D, a series of experiments was initiated a number of years ago which attempted to manipulate degree of emotionality in a quite different manner (20, 21, 22, 23). In the first of these studies (23) a test was developed which was aimed at differentiating Ss in terms of the degree to which they admitted having overt symptoms of emotionality. The test was in the form of a personality inventory, the items of which were judged by clinical psychologists to differentiate persons in terms of their emotional responsiveness. Unfortunately, the scale was called a test of "manifest anxiety," which has led to all manner of investigations designed to ascertain whether it is a valid test of *real* anxiety! We shall continue to refer to it as an anxiety scale (A scale) but with no assumption other than that it differentiates degrees of emotional responsiveness and level of D.[3]

Turning now to the role of drive in learning situations, the effect of variations in the level of D will, according to the theory, depend upon the nature of the learning task. As has been

[3] One sort of criticism of our experiments has revealed a serious misunderstanding of their purpose and underlying logic. It is that since there is not independent evidence that the test really measures emotionality, and there is evidence that the test scores correlate with other personality indices, it cannot legitimately be *assumed* that differences on the test reflect differences in drive level (D). To repeat again the reasoning of these experiments, the *hypothesis* is set up that the test scores reflect differences in emotionality and hence differences in D. This hypothesis is then tested by deriving, with the aid of other parts of the theory of learning, implications concerning differences to be expected in conditioning and various other types of learning situations. Confirmation of these deductions lends support to the theory, including the hypothesis about the relation of the anxiety scales scores to D. Obviously they don't prove the theory, just as any theory is never proved in science.

pointed out on a number of occasions (*18, 19*), the implications of a theory are a joint function of the laws or hypothetical relations postulated in the theory *and* what are called the initial or boundary conditions of the behavior situation. In simple classical conditioning, in which there is but a single response tendency, an increase in the strength of D results in a higher level of E, and hence implies a stronger response ($R = f(E) = f(H \times D)$. In more complex learning situations involving a hierarchy of competing responses, however, the effect of drive level variation will depend upon this initial response hierarchy and the relative position in it of the response that is to be learned.

In general, the greater the number and strength of the competing, incorrect responses relative to the correct response, the more detrimental should a high drive be to performance level, at least in the early stages of learning. Making use of the known fact that anticipatory and perseverative tendencies in serial learning produce strong competing response tendencies, a test of this implication has been made in three studies, one involving a verbal maze (*24*), one a stylus maze (*6*) and one rote serial learning (*11*). All three experiments provided evidence supporting the implication that the high-anxious Ss would be inferior to Ss scoring at the low end of the scale.

In these serial learning experiments, however, one has little or no knowledge of the relative strength of the correct and incorrect S-R tendencies. On the assumption that the incorrect, competing responses are based on theoretical remote associations or generalized response tendencies, it is possible, as Montague (*11*) did, to vary the similarity of the nonsense syllables employed, and thus to manipulate, theoretically, the strength and number of competing S-R tendencies. We were interested, however, in designing a learning situation in which it would be possible to manipulate in some better known manner the strengths of both the correct and the competing, incorrect S-R tendencies. Minimization of the latter would provide a situation in which Ss with high drive level would be expected to perform better than those with a low drive, whereas if we maximized the relative strengths and number of competing, incorrect S-R tendencies, the opposite result should obtain. The present study describes two such learning situations and presents the findings of a separate experiment with each.

Theoretical Analysis of Paired-Associates Learning

The situation selected for the experiments was paired-associates learning. In this type of learning situation, S is required to learn to respond to a stimulus word or nonsense syllable by anticipating a paired response syllable or word. By using different orders of presentation of the paired words the development of remote associations, so prominent in serial learning, is minimized.

Paired-associates learning may be conceived as consisting of a set or series of more or less isolated S-R associations or habit tendencies ($S_1 - R_A$, $S_2 - R_B$, $S_3 - R_C$, etc.) that become established as a consequence of the training procedure. Theoretically, if these stimulus-response items were entirely isolated from one another so that the only existent associative tendencies were between each stimulus word and its own paired response word, then Ss with relatively high drive would be expected to perform at a higher level in learning such a series than Ss with a lower drive strength. Essentially, the situation is similar to that of classical conditioning, except that instead of one S-R tendency being conditioned, a number of different S-R tendencies are being established simultaneously. While it may not be possible to obtain complete isolation among the S-R items, it is known how, on the basis of existing experimental knowledge, to approach this limiting condition with its minimal competition among S-Rs. Similarly, it is known how to vary the conditions so as to increase the amount of competition among them.

One of the most important factors determining the degree of isolation of the paired S-Rs is that of generalization, which, in turn, is a function of the degree of synonymity and/or formal similarity among the stimulus and response words. If this factor is minimal, there will be little or no generalized tendency for S_1 to elicit other responses than R_A, S_2 to elicit responses other than R_B, etc.

A second factor that enters into such paired-associates learning is the strength of the associative connection between any stimulus word and any response word. As the result of past experience, words tend to become associated with other words to varying degrees, and for each word the hierarchy of associative strengths tends to be similar for individuals in the same culture. Such differences in the strength of associative connections between words in a language are exemplified by the word association data of Kent and Rosanoff (9).

It is readily apparent that one may also take advantage of this factor to control not only the extent to which each stimulus word will tend to elicit its own paired word but also will tend to elicit response words other than the one with which it is paired. Thus, we could pair each stimulus word with a response word with which it tends, as the result of past verbal experiences, to be highly associated and, at the same time, make sure that the associative connections between each stimulus word and each of the nonpaired response words are low or nonexistent. Such a condition would obviously help further to minimize the likelihood of competing response tendencies of any appreciable strength for each stimulus-response pair. A list of paired associates in which the paired words have high initial associative connections and in which the degree of synonymity of the stimulus and response words is minimal would thus provide a learning situation in which high-drive (high-anxious) Ss should perform at a higher level than low-drive (low-anxious) Ss.

Contrariwise, we may construct a paired-associates list with a high amount of competition in which the opposite finding should occur; that is, the high-anxious Ss should perform more poorly than the low-anxious. There are a number of different ways in which such competition may be introduced, one of which will be described here.

Beginning with four stimulus-response pairs having high associative connections, the remaining eight pairs are formed as follows. For each of the four original stimulus words two synonymous stimulus words are selected and paired with response words with which they have little or no associative strength. Thus, for each triad of synonymous stimulus words, two are paired with response words with which they are weakly associated, if at all, and one is paired with a highly associated word, as follows:

$$S_1 \longrightarrow R_A \text{ (strong)}$$
$$S_1' \dashrightarrow R_B \text{ (weak)}$$
$$S_1'' \dashleftarrow R_C \text{ (weak)}$$

The stimulus words S_1' and S_1'', being highly synonymous with S_1, also have a high initial associative connection with R_A. As a result, the learning of the pairs involving these stimuli, *i.e.*, $S_1' - R_B$ and $S_1'' - R_C$ would involve a strong competing response tendency, one, in fact, that is stronger than that to its paired response. In the case of these paired words, then, we would expect the anxious Ss to be poorer than the nonanxious.

The implications of the theory with respect to the relative performance of high and low drive Ss on the four stimulus-response pairs of the list that have strong original connections (*e.g.*, $S_1 - R_A$) are more involved. At the very beginning of learning the performance of the high-drive Ss should be superior to that of low-drive Ss, just as in the case of the first, noncompetitional list. If properly chosen, these stimulus words should have little if any initial associative tendencies to R_B or R_C. However, once Ss begin to learn the other pairs (*e.g.*, $S_1' - R_B$, $S_1'' - R_C$), there should develop a generalized habit for S_1 to evoke R_B and R_C (principle of generalization of associative or habit strength). Since the excitatory potential (E) from S_1 to these responses (R_B and R_C) would reach super-threshold values sooner for the high-drive group than for the low-drive group we should expect these responses to intrude or block the correct response (R_A) earlier (and more frequently) in the case of the high-drive group. Thus, we would be led to predict that the initial superiority of the high-drive group on the strongly associated pairs should tend to disappear during training. Evidence with respect to these theoretical expectations was sought in the following experiments.

Experiment I

Since all of our previous experimental studies with verbal learning had involved comparison of high- and low-anxious Ss, in situations in which there were strong competing responses, we were interested, first, in testing the prediction that a noncompetitive verbal learning situation would reveal a superior performance on the part of high-anxious *S*s, as has been found in the case of simple classical conditioning. Accordingly, Exp. I involved a paired-associates list in which there was a minimum of competition among the paired words and in which the associative connections between the paired words were initially high.

METHOD

Subjects

The *S*s were 20 men and 20 women enrolled in an introductory psychology course, an equal number of each sex having scored in either the upper 20% or lower 20% of scores on the A scale. All were naive with respect to the experimental task.

Apparatus

A Hull-type memory drum was employed to present the lists of paired-associates learning material. The successive stimulus items of each list were exposed every 4 sec., including a 1.67-sec. anticipation interval, with a 4-sec. rest interval between successive presentations of a list. The practice list (15 paired nouns) was used to acquaint *S* with the procedure and to provide maximal and minimal performance criteria. The test list, shown in Table 1, consisted of 15 pairs of two-syllable adjectives from Haagen's word list (7), and was constructed in such a manner as to maximize closeness (strength) of association between paired stimulus-response words. Meaningful intralist associations and formal similarities were minimized. Thus, no beginning letter or suffix was repeated within the stimulus or response list and no stimulus-response pair began with the same letter or had the same suffix. Both lists were presented to *S* in three different orders to avoid serial learning.

Procedure

All *S*s served individually under the same experimental conditions. Immediately following the reading of the instructions describing the method of learning, *S* received six trials on the practice list followed by a 2-min. rest period. During this rest period *S* was moved to a seat before the screen containing the

drum with the test list.   Following this interval, S was run to a
criterion of two successive perfect trials on the test list.

TABLE 1

NONCOMPETITIVE AND COMPETITIVE TEST LISTS USED IN EXP. I AND II

Noncompetitive: Exp. I		Competitive: Exp. II	
Stimulus	Response	Stimulus	Response
Adept	Skillful	*Barren	Fruitless
Barren	Fruitless	Arid	Grouchy
Complete	Thorough	Desert	Leading
Distant	Remote	*Little	Minute
Empty	Vacant	Petite	Yonder
Frigid	Arctic	Undersized	Wholesome
Insane	Crazy	*Roving	Nomad
Little	Minute	Gypsy	Opaque
Mammoth	Oversize	Migrant	Agile
Pious	Devout	*Tranquil	Placid
Roving	Nomad	Quiet	Double
Stubborn	Headstrong	Serene	Headstrong
Tranquil	Quiet		
Urgent	Pressing		
Wicked	Evil		

* S-R terms in the competitive test list that were taken from the noncompetitive
list of Exp. I.

On each trial, correct anticipations, errors, and overt intru-
sions were recorded.   An error consisted in either making no
response or an incorrect response (an overt intrusion) during
the anticipation interval.

The Ss were discarded on the basis of their scores on the practice list if they failed to make a single correct response, or if
they made 50 or more correct responses during the six practice
trials.   Only one S was discarded on the basis of these minimal
and maximal performance criteria, and he was replaced by
another.

RESULTS

The mean number of correct anticipations made on the practice list was 14.0 for the high-anxious group and 13.7 for the

low-anxious group. These values are to be compared with a mean of 14.7 for a more extensive sample of 267 high-anxious Ss that have been run on the same list and a mean of 13.8 for a sample of 255 low-anxious Ss. Thus, it will be seen that the difference between the present samples in favor of the high group is somewhat smaller than in the more extensive samples.

Learning curves on the test list for the high- and low-anxious groups in terms of the mean percentage of correct anticipations made on Trials 2–11 are presented in Figure 1. As may be

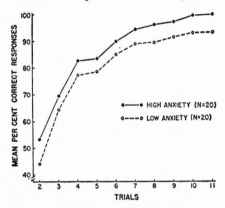

FIG. 1. Paired-associates learning as a function of anxiety under conditions of minimal interpair competition and high initial stimulus-response associative strength.

seen, the curves rise rapidly, with that for the high-anxious group starting and remaining consistently above the curve for the low group.

Data on learning in terms of errors and trials to the criterion of mastery are presented in Table 2. It will be observed that

TABLE 2

PERFORMANCE ON NONCOMPETITIVE TEST LIST

Group	N	Trials		Errors	
		Mean	SD	Mean	SD
High-anxious	20	8.95	2.75	20.95	10.49
Low-anxious	20	12.60	4.67	32.50	20.91

the high-anxious Ss were superior to the low anxious Ss in the case of both measures. The results of an analysis of variance gave Fs for the anxiety variable which were significant at the .01 level for the trial measure and the .05 level in the case of the error measure. In both instances the Anxiety × Sex interaction was less than one, indicating that the difference between high- and low-anxious Ss held for both sexes.

Experiment II

In contrast to Exp. I, a portion of the list of paired associates used in Exp. II involved learning in which competing response tendencies initially stronger than the correct responses were present. Our theory would lead us to expect that the high-anxious Ss would perform more poorly than the low-anxious Ss on these paired associates.

METHOD

Subjects

The Ss were all men, 10 of whom scored in the lowest 20% of scores on the A scale and 9 of whom were above the 80th percentile. Three additional Ss failed to meet the criteria established for the learning of the practice list and were discarded.

Apparatus and procedure

The memory drum, instructions, and practice list were exactly the same as those used in the first experiment. Likewise, the procedure was identical, the Ss first receiving six trials on the practice list and then being shifted to the test list, which they were required to learn to a criterion of two successive perfect trials.

The test list of paired adjectives employed in this experiment is given in Table 1. As may be seen, it consisted in part of four paired adjectives (marked by an asterisk) based on the test list of Exp. I. The associative connections between the words of these pairs were very high. For each of the stimulus words of these four pairs two synonymous adjectives were selected as stimulus words by means of Haagen's study. Each of these

eight stimulus words was paired with an adjective with which
it had little or no associative connection. The data for these
two different kinds of paired associates (those with high and
those with low associative connections) were treated separately,
since the theoretical predictions with respect to them differ.

RESULTS

The high-anxious *Ss* averaged 15.8 correct anticipations on
the practice lists as compared with 14.2 for the low *Ss*. This
difference in favor of the high group was somewhat larger than
that for the more extensive samples (see Results section for
Exp. I). The difference is not, however, a significant one.

Figure 2 presents learning curves for the high and low groups

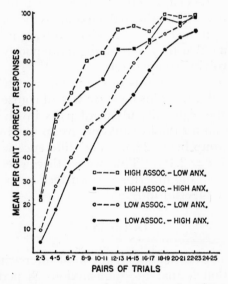

FIG. 2. Paired-associates learning as a function of anxiety
under conditions of high interpair competition. Word pairs
of both high- and low-association value were interspersed within
the same training list, but were analyzed separately.

in terms of the percentage of correct anticipations made on
successive pairs of trials. The two lower curves represent the
performance on the eight weakly associated word pairs that had

strong competing responses, while the two upper curves are for
the four pairs in which the words were initially highly associated.

As our theory predicted, the performance curve for the highly
anxious Ss was below that of the low-anxious Ss in the case of the
eight word pairs that involved competition. However, the
difference in number of errors for Trials 2–23 was not significant
($t = 1.56$). In accord with the deduction concerning the four
stimulus-response pairs of the list that had high associative connections, we find, as predicted, that the performance of the high-
anxious Ss was initially superior to that of the low-anxious Ss,
although the difference was very slight, and, also, that there was
a reversal later in the learning. It should be noted, further,
that the differences between the two groups of Ss for the two
types of paired associates were opposite in nature at the *beginning* of learning. Thus, the high-anxious Ss did better than the
low-anxious Ss on the four word pairs involving no competition
at the same time that they were doing more poorly on the eight
word pairs involving competition.

A final set of data pertains to the number of trials required
to learn the total list. This measure was, of course, determined
primarily by the eight difficult word pairs involving competition. The mean for the low-anxious group was 18.4, with that
for the high group being 23.3. The difference was significant
at the .05 level ($t = 2.48$). Thus we see that, whereas the high-
anxious Ss showed the superior performance in Exp. I, the low-
anxious Ss were superior in Exp. I.

Discussion

From a theoretical standpoint the most interesting finding of
this investigation is that the high-anxious Ss performed in a
superior manner to the low-anxious Ss in Exp. I. In our previous studies that have involved learning situations more complex than classical conditioning (*e.g.*, *7*, *28*), high-anxious Ss
performed more poorly than low-anxious Ss. We ascribed these
results to the presence of strong competing responses (anticipatory and perseverative tendencies) that develop in serial learning tasks. In the first paired-associates task reported here (Exp.

I) such competing responses were minimized by controlling for generalization as described in the introductory section. The fact that the correct responses had high initial associative connections with their respective stimuli also assured a greater initial differential, *with higher drive strength,* between the excitatory strengths of the correct responses and the excitatory strengths of any incorrect, competing responses, *i.e.,* $E_+ - E_- = D(H_+ - H_-)$. The fact that the high-anxious Ss were superior right from the start is in agreement with our analysis. Furthermore, it may be predicted that if the associative connections between the stimulus and response items were low or nonexistent at the beginning of training (and providing competition were minimized by the methods described), there would be no initial difference between anxious and nonanxious groups, but one would develop in favor of the anxious Ss as learning progressed.

On the other hand, when strong response tendencies in competition with the correct response were provided by means of the methods used in Exp. II, this advantage of high- over low-anxious Ss in paired-associates learning disappeared and the low-anxious Ss actually required significantly fewer trials ($P = .05$) to learn than did the high-anxious Ss.

One final series of comments concerns the interpretation of these studies relating anxiety to learning that has been offered by Child (5). Child would explain the inferior performance of anxious Ss in situations involving competing responses elicited by the task stimuli in terms of task-irrelevant responses made to the anxiety, *i.e.,* irrelevant responses that interfere with performance in the task. Although Child has expressed the view that our interpretation had overlooked the role of such responses, we were actually well aware of such a possibility, and have for some time been interested in the role of such task-interfering responses, which we think of as being elicited by the drive stimuli (s_D) resulting from the emotional (drive) state.[4]

That such distracting, task-interfering responses will under

[4] In this connection attention is called to the fact that the series of studies by Amsel and his colleagues (1, 2, 3) which have been concerned with investigating the differential effects of D and the interfering responses elicited by s_D originated in this laboratory.

certain conditions occur we have no doubt. One of the real difficulties is to know when and to what extent they function. From our point of view they are a nuisance, in the sense of a difficult-to-control factor that acts to obscure the role of D in competing response situations. Accordingly, with our primary interest in these studies being in the role of D rather than s_D, we have deliberately attempted to employ conditions in which such interfering responses would be at a minimum. So far as we have been able to observe, our high-anxious Ss have not tended to engage in distracting irrelevant activities to any greater extent than our low-anxious Ss. Possibly the reason for this is that our experimental situations have not been so stressful as to provide the degree of emotionality that would elicit much of this kind of behavior.

The findings of Ramond's study (*14*) are of some interest in this connection. He employed a choice-learning situation in which S had to learn to choose one of two alternative response words for each of 16 stimulus words. In half of the items the associative connection of the correct response word was stronger than that of the incorrect response word, and in the other half, the incorrect response was the stronger. It was found that under the condition in which the incorrect response was stronger, the anxious Ss did significantly worse than the nonanxious Ss, but under the reverse condition there was not a significant difference in over-all performance, although the anxious Ss started out better and subsequently became poorer than the nonanxious Ss in the later portion of the learning. Since the task-interfering behavior, if there was any, would presumably be equal for the two kinds of learning items, which were intermixed with each other in the list, the relatively inferior performance of the anxious Ss with one set of items must be accounted for by some other factor than distracting, task-interfering responses. Our explanation would be that the greater drive level of the anxious Ss increased the unfavorable difference in the competing excitatory potentials in the direction of the incorrect responses and thus led to a greater likelihood of occurrence of such erroneous responses.

It is interesting to speculate in connection with Ramond's findings that both mechanisms (D and s_D) were operative, the two acting jointly to lower the performance of the anxious Ss relative to that of the nonanxious Ss in the case of the items in which the incorrect response was the stronger, while their effects were opposed in the case of the other type of item. Thus, whereas higher D would tend to give an advantage to the anxious Ss in the case in which the correct response was the stronger, interfering responses elicited by the cue aspects of anxiety would favor the nonanxious Ss. If this interpretation is correct, we see that the effects of the interfering activities must have become greater as the learning proceeded.

In concluding, attention should be directed to the point that Child's theorizing is not opposed to ours. Both operate within the framework of Hullian S-R theory. Our experiments have merely been somewhat more restricted in interest, being mainly centered on the role of D in determining behavior, rather than in the other possible functions of anxiety, including its drive cue (s_D) aspects.

Summary

On the basis of the assumption that the A scale measures degree of emotionality and, hence, level of D, and the further assumption that the effect of variations in the level of D upon performance in learning depends upon the position in the response hierarchy of the responses to be learned, different predictions were made concerning the relative performance of high- and low-anxious Ss in two different verbal learning situations. In the case of a list of paired associates having a minimum of generalization among the S-R pairs, and, therefore, little competition among responses, it was predicted that highly anxious Ss would perform better than nonanxious Ss. In the case of a list in which competing, incorrect responses could be expected to be stronger than correct responses, it was predicted that highly anxious Ss would perform more poorly than nonanxious Ss.

In Exp. I, using a noncompetitive list, the anxious Ss made significantly fewer errors and required significantly fewer trials to reach the learning criterion than did the nonanxious Ss. In Exp. II, using a list mainly composed of highly competitive items, anxious Ss required significantly more trials to reach the criterion.

The necessity of minimizing the possible confounding effects of responses elicited by the drive stimuli (s_D) resulting from emotionality when one studies the effects of drive level (D) upon learning performance is strongly emphasized.

REFERENCES

1. AMSEL, A. The combination of a primary appetitional need with primary and secondary emotionally derived needs. *J. exp. Psychol.,* 1950, *40,* 1–14.
2. ——, & COLE, K. F. Generalization of fear-motivated interference with water intake. *J. exp. Psychol.,* 1953, *46,* 243–247.
3. ——, & MALTZMAN, I. The effect upon generalized drive strength of emotionality as inferred from the level of consummatory response. *J. exp. Psychol.,* 1950, *40,* 563–569.
4. BROWN, J. S., KALISH, H. I., & FARBER, I. E. Conditioned fear as revealed by magnitude of startle response to an auditory stimulus. *J. exp. Psychol.,* 1951, *41,* 317–328.
5. CHILD, I. L. Personality. *Annu. Rev. Psychol.,* 1954, *5,* 149–171.
6. FARBER, I. E., & SPENCE, K. W. Complex learning and conditioning as a function of anxiety. *J. exp. Psychol.,* 1953, *45,* 120–125.
7. HAAGEN, C. H. Synonymity, vividness, familiarity, and association value ratings of 400 pairs of common adjectives. *J. Psychol.,* 1949, *27,* 453–463.
8. KALISH, H. I. Strength of fear as a function of the number of acquisition and extinction trials. *J. exp. Psychol.,* 1954, *47,* 1–9.
9. KENT, G. H., & ROSANOFF, A. J. A study of association in insanity. *Amer. J. Insanity,* 1910, *67,* 37–96; 317–390.
10. MILLER, N. E. Learnable drives and rewards. In S. S. Stevens (Ed.), *Handbook of Experimental Psychology.* New York: Wiley, 1951, pp. 435–472.
11. MONTAGUE, E. K. The role of anxiety in serial rote learning. *J. exp. Psychol.,* 1953, *45,* 91–98.
12. MOWRER, O. H. A stimulus-response analysis of anxiety and its role as a reinforcing agent. *Psychol. Rev.,* 1939, *46,* 553–565.
13. PASSEY, G. E. The influence of intensity of unconditioned stimulus upon acquisition of a conditioned response. *J. exp. Psychol.,* 1948, *38,* 420–428.
14. RAMOND, C. K. Anxiety and task as determiners of verbal performance. *J. exp. Psychol.,* 1953, *46,* 120–124.
15. SIEGAL, P. S., & BRANTLEY, J. J. The relationship of emotionality to the consummatory response of eating. *J. exp. Psychol.,* 1951, *42,* 304–306.
16. ——, & SIEGAL, H. S. The effect of emotionality on the water intake of the rat. *J. comp. physiol. Psychol.,* 1949, *42,* 12–16.

17. SPENCE, K. W. Learning and performance in eyelid conditioning as a function of the intensity of the UCS. *J. exp. Psychol.*, 1953, *45*, 57–63.

18. ——. Current interpretations of learning data and some recent developments in stimulus-response theory. In *Learning Theory, Personality Theory, and Clinical Research*. New York: Wiley, 1954, pp. 1–21.

19. ——. *Behavior Theory and Conditioning*. New Haven: Yale University Press, in press.

20. ——, & FARBER, I. E. Conditioning and extinction as a function of anxiety. *J. exp. Psychol.*, 1953, *45*, 116–119.

21. ——, ——, & TAYLOR, E. The relation of electric shock and anxiety to level of performance in eyelid conditioning. *J. exp. Psychol.*, 1954, *48*, 404–408.

22. ——, & TAYLOR, J. A. Anxiety and strength of the UCS as determiners of the amount of eyelid conditioning. *J. exp. Psychol.*, 1951, *42*, 183–188.

23. TAYLOR, J. A. The relationship of anxiety to the conditioned eyelid response. *J. exp. Psychol.*, 1951, *41*, 81–92.

24. ——, & SPENCE, K. W. The relationship of anxiety level to performance in serial learning. *J. exp. Psychol.*, 1952, *44*, 61–64.

13

A Study of Simple Learning Under Irrelevant Motivational-Reward Conditions [1]

Introduction

In the first report (22) of a series of experimental studies concerned with the motivational-reward conditions underlying learning in animals, the sign-gestalt (non-reinforcement) theory of trial-and-error learning as formulated by Tolman (25) and others (12, 29) was subjected to experimental test. According to this theory such selective learning involves the acquisition of sign-gestalt-expectations with respect to the various aspects (signs) of the situation, the alternative responses and the different significates to which each of the latter leads. These expectation-sets (also termed cognitions, hypotheses, etc.) constitute one of Tolman's so-called intervening or theoretical variables which are assumed to be determinants of behavior. Thus, in the alternative choice situation typical of simple trial-and-error learning, the response on any trial will depend upon the state of these cognitions (C) and another intervening variable, motivational state (M) or, more briefly, $B = f(C, M)$.

Cognition (C) and motivation (M) are, in Tolman's system, hypothetical state variables of the organism which are to be specified in terms of certain past experimental operations or conditions. The particular point at issue in our experiment was

[1] Written in collaboration with G. Bergmann and R. Lippitt.

Tolman's hypothesis as to the conditions essential to the development of the cognitive states. Tolman and his group have taken the position that this learning factor (*i.e.*, cognition) develops as the result of mere association by contiguity (sequence in experience) of the sign, the response and the significate, and that such learning is not due, as the opposing reinforcement theorists have claimed, to any rewarding property possessed by a significate. That is, according to this view, the learning of sign-significate expectations is not dependent upon their being a reward or goal object for which the organism is at the moment motivated. Any differential reward values among the significates will, Tolman admits, make for a difference in the response of the organism at any moment, but they play little or no part in the learning *per se*—*i.e.*, the formation of the expectation-sets.

As a test of this theoretical position 10 white rates were run in a simple two-choice Y-maze, one alley (left) of which led to a goal box containing food and the other (right) to a goal box containing a water bottle. The Ss, motivated for water and satiated for food, were given training for 12 days, in which each S was given five trials per day. In two of the five trials the Ss were free to choose either path and the remaining three trials were forced, one to the water and two to the food side.

On the day following the completion of the learning series, a critical test was given in which the motivation of the Ss was shifted from thirst to hunger. According to Tolman's hypothesis, the Ss should have learned what object (food or water) each of the two alleys led to and when motivated for food they should have been expected to reveal this learning by taking the alley leading to the food. The results of the test, however, were entirely negative to this theoretical implication, for every animal, although hungry, chose the water alley. Furthermore, it was found that this group of subjects subsequently were unable to learn to go to the food alley more readily than a comparison group which had had the same previous training experience of 12 days, except that no food had ever been present in the left goal box. Both of these results are in line, it may be noted, with the implications of the reinforcement type of theory such as that of Hull (6) and Thorndike.

A second study in this series essentially similar in design to this investigation has been carried out by Kendler (9). The maze employed in this instance was of the simple T-type and further differentiation of the critical signs was achieved by having one of the alleys painted black while the other remained unpainted. Six of the subjects were trained under thirst, as in the Spence and Lippitt study, and four under hunger drive. In the test series involving a shift of motivation all subjects continued to run to the side which had led to the appropriate reward object during the training series.[2]

While the findings of these experiments were quite contrary to what Tolman's theory would lead one to expect, it was suggested that certain modifications might be made in his formulation that would permit one to maintain a non-reinforcement position and yet account for the present experimental findings satisfactorily. One possibility that suggested itself was that the learning involved, in addition to, or possibly even instead of, the sign-significate expectations with respect to food and water, the formation of the expectations that the right-side alley led to a need-satisfying situation without differentiation as to its specific nature, whereas the left alley led to the expectation of failure of need satisfaction. Such "knowledge," no matter what the motivational state, would presumably lead to the taking of the alley on the right during the test trial.

Statement of Problem

The experiment described in the present report attempted to eliminate the differential need-satisfying character of the two end boxes that existed in our first study. One obvious way of accomplishing this was to have the Ss satiated for both food and

---

[2] The results for Kendler's subjects that were trained under hunger in the learning series and then tested under thirst effectively refute the recent criticism of Hayes (2). The latter claimed that the subjects of Spence and Lippitt had had no experience with a strong hunger drive prior to the test and could not be expected to react appropriately toward food on the test trial. Hayes claims to have shown that rats trained originally on food did respond appropriately to water on the first test trial. He suggested, therefore, that the drive sequence, training on hunger, testing on thirst would be adequate. The identical results of Kendler under both conditions refute Hayes' criticism. Furthermore, the results of the present experiment, as will be seen, seriously call into doubt Hayes' claim that rats will not be able to respond appropriately when tested under hunger.

water during the training runs. A serious difficulty with such a procedure is readily apparent, however, in that one does not have any drive state that will motivate the animal to make the necessary responses in the situation. In the hope that some mild form of motivation (possibly an exploratory drive) might operate long enough to make the animals enter the alleys and end boxes a sufficient number of trials during the training period, a group of Ss was started under this condition of satiation for both food and water. Furthermore, in order not to have the end boxes serve as a possible goal-situation for the animals by reason of the fact that entrance into them led to their being picked up and placed in their home cage or a cage with other animals (social goal), the procedure was followed of placing each S, on removal from the goal box, in the same type of small individual carrying cage that it was in prior to the start of the run. If such a situation would lead to the necessary behavior taking place, it was felt that it would provide the ideal experimental conditions, for the necessary sequence of events (S_L—R_L—S_F, S_R—R_R—S_W) would have occurred without presumably any goal reinforcement at the end boxes.

Unfortunately, the exploratory drive, or whatever the motivation operating at first was, did not persist sufficiently long to provide for an adequate number of experiences in the maze alleys. After making two or three "exploratory" runs into the alleys the Ss refused to run in the maze but instead would lie down in the starting alley and apparently go to sleep. Some attempt was made to keep the Ss moving by gently pushing them, but this was abandoned as unsuccessful.

With this failure to obtain satisfactory runs in the training condition without the use of some goal situation, it was decided to introduce a goal situation that would be identical (equalized) for both end boxes. The goal situation hit upon was a cage similar to the home cage of the animals, in which all except the S run first on the day found one or more of his home-cage mates. As the order of running the Ss was changed each day, all animals found themselves being placed in this "social" situation after reaching one or other of the end boxes on most of their trials. This procedure apparently provided for some type of motivation and goal reward, for under it the subjects did *perform* much more satisfactorily than in the case of the first group of satiated subjects. On the occasions that an *S* would not run in a training trial, it was prodded until the run was completed. There were considerable individual differences in the extent to which the *Ss* were motivated to get to the end box and eventually to the social cage, and on the whole the times taken to run were longer than in the first experiment in which the *Ss* were motivated by thirst.

The fact that the conduct of the experiment required a motivating condition and a goal situation is of no little significance for the theoretical point at issue. For one thing, it meant that the arrangement did not provide for the sequence in experience of the sign, response, and significate *without the occurrence of a reward or goal situation following the sequence.* Thus, the question of whether the mere contiguity of these events in experience without a reinforcing state of affairs is sufficient for the establishment of the sign-gestalt-expectations with respect to food and water cannot be answered by this experimental design. Our experiment can only tell us whether expectation-sets concerning significates for which there is not at the moment any need, can be established on the basis of some other motivating state and accompanying significate which does have reward value. For example, is the white rat able to develop expectations with respect to the food and water while motivated only for the "social" cage which it gets to upon entering either of the end boxes? It is apparent, then, that while we have equalized the reward values of the two end boxes, we are not testing the question of whether sign-gestalt expectations can be established *independently* of motivation and reward.

Experimental Procedure

Subjects

The *Ss*, 39 white rats from the departmental colony, consisted of 15 males and 24 females. Ages at the beginning of the preliminary training varied slightly around 90 days.

Apparatus

A ground plan and detailed description of the apparatus was given in the earlier article (22). It is sufficient to say here that it was a single-choice Y-maze with a relatively large square area at the choice point and a jump of two in. at the entrance to each of the alleys. One of the goal boxes was fitted with a water bottle similar in design and appearance to the type used in the living cages of the animals. The food goal box contained a sliding food tray in the floor but this was more or less completely covered by some six to eight large pellets of Purina Dog Chow spread over the floor.

Vertically sliding doors, operated from behind a one-way screen, prevented the Ss from seeing the objects in the goal boxes and from retracing in the maze. Differentiation of the two alleys from one another was increased by having the floor at the entrance to the left alley covered with fine hardware cloth while the entrance to the right alley was covered with a very much coarser screening.

Preliminary training

After several days of handling, the Ss were given an opportunity to explore and become familiar with the maze. During this experience they were satiated for both food and water. Six to ten Ss were placed in the maze at the same time and were allowed to explore (1) the starting box, choice chamber and one alley, (2) the second alley, and (3) both alleys simultaneously for about 30 to 40 min., respectively. During this period the water bottle was removed and the end of the box containing it covered over. No food was in the food goal box.

On the following day, each S was given two runs alone in the apparatus in order to ascertain information as to a position preference. On the basis of the choices made, each S was classified as a left, right, or neutral animal. The maze was in the same condition as day 1 and the Ss were satiated.

Satiation routines

The following feeding and drinking schedule was begun two days prior to the first day of preliminary training, and was used throughout the training trials. About nine hours prior to the time of running, which began between 4:30 to 5:00 P.M. each day, the water bottles were taken from the living cages. Approximately three hours before the time of running, the water bottles were placed back on the cages and an additional water dish was put into the cage. An abundance of food was also placed in the cage. About one hour before running time an extra dish of small pellets (Purina Dog Chow) was put in the cage and the water dishes refilled. Following completion of the training runs, water was available until the next morning, but no food was given until the following day.

The satiation procedure during the two test trials following the completion of training was as follows. Prior to being tested under hunger motivation, food was withheld for 23 hours. The water bottle was available at all times in the cage and the procedure of placing an additional pan of water in the living cage before the daily run was used. In the case of thirst motivation, the water bottles were removed approximately nine hours prior to the test run. Food was available in the cage at all times and small pellets were placed in the living cage before the test trial.

Learning series

The Ss were given four trials daily for seven days. In the first and third trial of each day the Ss were free to choose either alley. On the second and fourth trial they were forced to take the alley not chosen on the previous trial. An equal number of experiences in each alley was thus provided all subjects.

The animals were run in groups varying in size from six to ten Ss. The same order of running was followed on successive trials of a day but differed from day to day. All Ss of a group were run before the next trial was given, a procedure which provided for a minimum interval of at least 10 min. between the successive trials for each S.

As was described in the section on the statement of the problem, the motivation for running the maze was the "need" to get to the social cage containing cage mates. The Ss were taken to the experimental room in a carrying cage which consisted of a number of small individual compartments (4 in. by 10 in.). S was taken out of this carrying cage and placed directly in the starting box of the maze. At the completion of the trial it was placed in the social cage. In the case of trials two, three and four, each S was taken out of the social cage three runs before its turn to run and placed in one of the narrow compartments of the carrying cage. After the last trial of the day, a five-min.

period elapsed before the group as a whole was returned to its living cages.

Upon entering an end box S was permitted to explore until E was sure that it had examined the food or the water orifice. As the food was spread out over the floor of the goal box, the Ss were forced to walk over it and there was little difficulty in determining whether they sniffed at it. In the case of the water spout, however, S was not so likely to come upon it in the course of its exploration. If at the end of a 15-sec. period the water spout had not been approached, the S was picked up and placed directly before the spout with its nose just a fraction of an inch from it. Typically the Ss moved around the goal box sniffing at either the food or water spout within the 15-sec. period. Care was taken to note whether the animal ate any of the food or drank water. No Ss included in the 39 cases were ever observed to eat or drink.

Test series

Test trials were given on the two days following the training period. On these trials the Ss were motivated on one day for one of the goal objects and satiated for the other. On the following day the motivation was reversed. If the S chose correctly (i.e., chose the alley which led to the goal object for which motivated) on the first trial of the day, it was permitted, depending on its motivation, either to drink for five to ten sec. or to eat for the same period. It was then placed in the social cage and after a 10-min. period returned to the home cage. If the first test trial was incorrect, the S was given further trials until the correct alley was taken. The same procedure was followed on the second test given on the following day.

In the first four groups of subjects run, the decision as to which motivation was to be present in a particular S on the first trial was determined by the preference for the two alleys shown in the fourteen free choices of the training series. In all instances, if an S had chosen one of the alleys less than 50 percent (six times or less), it was motivated for the goal object in that alley. In the last group of ten subjects the reverse procedure was employed. In this group the Ss were motivated for the goal object to be found in the alley for which a preference had been

shown—*i.e.*, eight or more choices of it made.   In the case of
five *Ss* which chose each alley 50 percent of the time on the training trials, three were arbitrarily made thirsty and two hungry.

Results

Figure 1 presents the results for all 39 *Ss* in terms of the percentage of responses made on the first trial of each training day

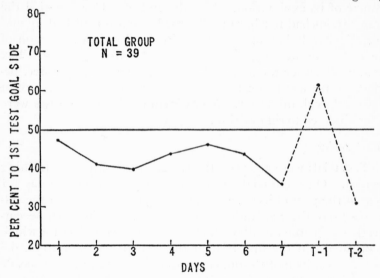

Fɪɢ. 1.   Percentages of *Ss* that chose the side appropriate on test I
during seven training days and two test days

and the two test days to the side containing the goal object appropriate for *the motivation of the first test*.   These values tend
to run below the 50 percent line for the training days because,
as was indicated previously, the majority of *Ss* were motivated
on test one for the goal object on their non-preferred side.

The marked shift in the curve at the first test day suggests that
the subjects had learned something about the location of the
two goal objects during this training period and when motivated
for one of them, tended to take the alley leading to it.   Twenty-
four (61.5 percent) of the *Ss* chose the alley leading to the ap-

propriate goal on this first test, as compared with only 33.3 percent choice of this alley on the first trial of the last day of training. The difference of 28.5 percent between training day seven and the first test day is 2.85 times its standard error, a critical ratio which is significant beyond the one percent level of confidence.[3]

As a further check, a more stable measure of the training preference than that provided by the first trial of the last training day was sought by ascertaining which arm was chosen two or more times on the first trial of the last three training days. Table I presents the comparison of this measure (column 2) with

TABLE 1

PERCENTAGE OF Ss THAT RESPONDED TO THE SIDE APPROPRIATE FOR THE FIRST
TEST ON (a) THE LAST THREE DAYS OF TRAINING, AND
(b) THE FIRST TEST DAY

Motivational Conditions	(a) Last Three Training Days %	(b) Test Day %	Critical Ratio Diff./$\sigma_{Diff.}$
Hungry and Thirsty ($N = 39$)	30.8	61.5	2.98
Thirsty ($N = 23$)	34.7	56.6	1.46
Hungry ($N = 16$)	25.0	68.7	2.64

the test performance (column 3). The critical ratio, determined by the method for dependent samples, is shown in the last column. The critical ratio (2.98) for all 39 subjects is again significant at well beyond the one percent confidence level.

Table 1, it will be seen, presents a further analysis of the data in terms of the subgroups that were hungry or thirsty on the first test. It will be seen that the hungry subjects showed a significant ($P < .01$) shift from their training performance on test one, whereas the shift for the thirsty subgroup was not significant ($P > .14$). It is not unlikely that the poorer result for the latter group was due to the fact that a thirst drive based on only

---

[3] The standard error of the difference between the percentages was computed by the formula for dependent samples as described by McNemar (16, p. 77).

nine hours of water deprivation was used in this experiment. This degree of thirst was selected on the basis of the obstruction box studies as being approximately equal in strength to a 24-hour hunger drive, but these results suggest that this may not be the case.

Looking at the results for the second test, in which the motivation was shifted from hunger to thirst, or vice versa, it will be observed in Figure 1 that the choice point behavior of the subjects shifted markedly again. Only 30.8 percent of the Ss chose the alley leading to the goal object of test one, while 69.2 percent chose the alley leading to the appropriate goal for the second test. While this shift in choice of the two alleys was appropriate to the motivational change, it should be noted that the percentage of appropriate choices on this second test (69.2 percent) did not, as in the first test, differ significantly from the percentage of responses made to the same alley during the first trial of the last training day (66.7 percent).

Table 2 presents the results of the second test in terms of the

TABLE 2

PERCENTAGE OF Ss THAT RESPONDED TO THE SIDE APPROPRIATE FOR THE SECOND
TEST ON (a) THE LAST THREE DAYS OF TRAINING, AND
(b) THE SECOND TEST DAY

Motivational Conditions	(a) Last Three Training Days %	(b) Test Day %	Critical Ratio Diff./$\sigma_{Diff.}$
Hungry and Thirsty (N = 39)	69.2	69.2	0
Thirsty (N = 16)	75.0	68.7	−1.05
Hungry (N = 23)	65.3	69.5	.32

training performance measure based on the last three days of training. It will be observed that neither the group as a whole nor the two subgroups shifted significantly from their training preference to the correct alley. Indeed, the Ss that were thirsty went fewer times to the appropriate side of test day than they had gone on the last three days of training.

Discussion of Results

Since the completion of this experiment in 1940 (*21*), a number of studies (*10, 15, 24*) essentially similar in principle and design to it have been carried out in the Iowa laboratory and one almost identical study has been reported by Meehl and Mac-Corquodale (*17*). We shall first present a summary of the findings of all these experiments and then discuss their implication for the rival theoretical interpretations.

The experiments of Kendler (*10*) and Meehl and MacCorquodale (*17*) gave almost identical results with those of the present study. Both obtained a significant number of appropriate responses on the first test, the results of the Meehl and MacCorquodale study being at the one percent level and that of Kendler at the five percent level of significance. Both studies also agreed with the present one in failing to obtain positive results on the second test in which the motivation of the first test was reversed. From the description of their experiment, the motivational-reward conditions of the Meehl and MacCorquodale investigation closely approximated those of the present study. The chief difference appears to have been that the Ss were put back in the home cage only after the second and fourth trials of the day. Whether they were placed in a cage containing other animals (social goal) after the first and third trials of the day is not clear. These experimenters explicitly recognize the operation of such reinforcements as "being removed from the confinement of the maze, returning to the home cage, etc." (*17*, p. 375).

Kendler's study, carried out in the Iowa laboratory, deliberately attempted to avoid the social goal box and substituted pushing of the S through the maze when it remained in one spot for more than five min. Presumably the motivation for locomotion in this study was the mild, noxious one resulting from the pushing. By proceeding to either end box the S escaped such prodding. It was then picked up from the maze and placed back in the carrying cage to await the next trial. The poorer results of this study might possibly be ascribed to the slower running of the Ss and hence the longer time elapsing between entering an alley and the subsequent experiencing of the food or water.

All three of these studies, then, gave positive evidence of the acquisition of sign-significate expectations with respect to the food and water when not motivated for these objects on the first test, but gave negative evidence on the second test. To complicate the picture even more, the two most recent studies (*15, 24*) in the Iowa laboratory have failed to give any favorable evidence whatever for such learning. Maltzman's (*15*) experiment attempted to improve the social reward conditions employed in the present experiment with a view to speeding up the running of the Ss and thus reducing the time between the occurrence of the cues at the entrance of an alley and the subsequent occurrence of the significates. Other things equal, this presumably should provide better conditions for the acquisition of the essential cognitions. Maltzman did obtain such a speeding up of running at least over the present study and that of Kendler by placing the social cages, which contained a cage mate, at the end of each alley, one foot beyond the boxes containing the significates, food and water. The Ss ran directly by means of a connecting section into the social cage. The latter contained a one-way door that prevented the social animal from entering the maze. Quite in contrast to the previous studies, however, Maltzman found that his Ss did not respond appropriately to the side containing the significate for which they were motivated on the first test. Thus the correct side was chosen only by 17 out of 30 Ss on the first test, a result obviously not significantly different from chance, which the Ss had been running during the last five training days. The second test, involving a reversal of the motivation of test one, also gave results that did not differ significantly from chance, although 19 of the Ss did respond appropriately. Two subsequent tests on the following two days also gave chance results.

So far as the motivational conditions are concerned, our most recent experiment (*24*) represents an extension of the Kendler study. Food and water were again available in one or another of the end boxes. Satiated for these objects, the Ss were motivated to run in the maze by anxiety. Prior to the learning in the maze, the Ss were trained to run down the stem of the maze, the floor of which was an electrified grid, to escape the shock in an empty end box. Following this preliminary training, ten days of training (four trials per day) in the maze situation were given in which the Ss were required to escape by either arm. Shock was not given during this series, the animals presumably being motivated to escape from the maze by fear or anxiety. The experimental question, as in all the above experiments, was whether the Ss would be able to acquire the appropriate cognitions as to the locus of food and water, while motivated by anxiety and rewarded by escape from anxiety.

Despite an even more thorough attempt to satiate the Ss for the food and water than had been necessary to prevent eating or drinking in our other investigations, fourteen of the twenty-four Ss in this experiment either ate or drank or did both. Considering the results of the remaining ten Ss that never drank or ate, six responded appropriately on the first test and four on the second, a purely chance result.

In marked contrast to this test performance was that of the Ss that ate or drank at one time or another in the experiment. Thirteen of these fourteen Ss responded appropriately on the first test and eleven on the second. The results for the first test are significant beyond the one percent level of confidence. The departure from chance expectation (50 percent correct) for the two tests combined is also significant beyond the one percent level of confidence. The success of these latter Ss is rather remarkable in the light of the fact that only about eight reinforcements involving drinking and eating were obtained on the average per S in the forty training trials.

Such results as the above, combined with the findings of our earlier study (22) and its confirmation by Walker (28), Kendler (10), Grice (1), and Kendler and Mencher (11), which have shown that rats are unable to acquire either cognitions as to the locus of food when not hungry but under a thirst drive or cognitions with regard to the location of water when not thirsty but motivated by hunger, have led Tolman to offer a modification of his views concerning the acquisition of sign-gestalt-expectations, or as he now prefers to designate them, field expectancies (27). The extent of Tolman's reversal of viewpoint is shown by the following quotation:

I used to be so impressed by the latent learning experiments of the type invented by Blodgett, in which no reward was introduced during the learning periods, that I was apt to formulate the conditions involved in such field-expectancy learning primarily in terms of frequency alone and as if motivation played no role. However, if I did this, I was in error. It is obvious that completely unmotivated animals will not learn. They will go to sleep or otherwise divorce themselves from the task. So it must be emphasized that in the Blodgett experiments, even though the animals were not rewarded, they *were* motivated. . . . Summing it up then, it appears that motivation conditions *are* very important for the building up of field expectancies (27, p. 150).

While clear and emphatic about the necessity of motivation for learning field-expectations, Tolman is less decisive about the role of reinforcement. He denies the view: "That such learning consists in the stamping in of S-R habits by reinforcements" (27, p. 151). But he goes on to state that: "The presence of reinforcement in a particular locus makes that locus a goal which determines what performance will take place but it does not stamp in S-R connections, though it probably does give a special vividness to that locus in the total field expectancy" (27, p. 151).

So far as the experimental studies discussed above are concerned, they point just as strongly to the necessity for reinforcement as they do for motivation. In every single investigation some form of reinforcement was present, and in one instance the experiment could not be conducted when no reinforcement was provided. However, none of these studies is able to answer the question as to whether learning can occur in the absence of reinforcement. As described earlier, they are concerned only with the question as to whether the learning of the locus of certain kinds of goal objects can occur under motivational-reward conditions not involving these objects.[4]

In terms of Tolman's theory, these experiments attempt to answer the question as to whether the learning involves the formation of cognitions or field expectancies involving the

---

[4] There is no implication that these studies necessarily demand a reinforcement interpretation and are opposed to a non-reinforcement interpretation. While they are in line with a reinforcement assumption, they are not critical with respect to the issue, as none of the studies eliminated completely some form of reinforcement.

stimulus events at the beginning of each alley and the stimulus events (food or water) at the end of each alley. The perception of these events in sequence is assumed to result in the knowledge (cognition) of the relationship between them. Given these cognitions, plus the knowledges that these objects satisfy their respective primary drives, the choice behavior of the subject will depend upon the relative demand value (Δ) of the alternative significates. Thus, if the S is hungry on the test and satiated for water, and assuming food is at the end of the left alley, then the strength of the tendency or force to the left response (B_L) will be greater than that to the right (B_R). Employing the symbols used by Tolman in his article on secondary demands (26), this derivation may be represented as follows:

$$B_L > B_R \text{ if } \Delta_L > \Delta_R$$
$$\Delta_L > \Delta_R \text{ if } \Delta_F > \Delta_W$$

and if hypotheses $H_{L \to F}$ and $H_{R \to W}$ exist,

$$\Delta_F > \Delta_W \text{ if } D_h > D_t$$

and if hypotheses $H_{F \to C_h}$ $H_{,W \to C_t}$ exist.

Where Δ represents secondary demands, such as demand for a particular alley, for food, etc., H represents hypothesis, cognition, equivalence belief, etc., D_h primary demand for consummation of food, $i.e.$, hunger; D_t primary demand for water, $i.e.$, thirst, and C_h and C_t consummation of hunger and thirst respectively.

Taking the results of all of the above experiments, the findings are not too favorable to Tolman's S-S theory. In those instances in which the Ss were motivated for one of the significates, the test data have been uniformly negative. In the experiments in which some motivation other than that for the significates was employed, the findings are ambiguous. In some (Spence, Bergmann, and Lippitt; Meehl and MacCorquodale, and Kendler) one of the tests has agreed with Tolman's theory, whereas a second test has not supported it. In other studies (15, 24) the test data have been uniformly opposed to the implications of Tolman's theory.

Attempting to fall back on the claim that the objective conditions of presentation of the significates in these experiments were not adequate for reception, such as Leeper (*14*) has done, is refuted by the positive instances, as the latter were precisely the same as those in which the results were negative (*33*). Furthermore, such conditions as Kendler and Mencher (*11*) arranged, preclude the possibility that their subjects did not "see" the food. It is at this point, of course, that Tolman introduces the factor of motivation. He writes, "Thirsty animals apparently do not notice food, even though the experiment be rigged as it was by Kendler and Mencher to seem to force them to notice that the cups which did not contain water did contain food" (*27*, p. 150). That is, under the motivation of thirst, the animals did not, he claims, notice (perceive?) the food.

But why, we may ask, did the Ss of our present experiment (accepting the positive results of the first test) apparently notice the food and water while motivated to get to the social cage? And why, when the social goal box was brought nearer to the point of entrance to the alleys, as in Maltzman's study (*15*), did the rats apparently fail to notice the food and water? Again, what lies behind the failure of the Ss to notice the food or water in the experiment in which the Ss were motivated by anxiety and need to escape the anxiety-arousing situation? Under just what motivational conditions will animals perceive or not perceive the presence of the significates? It is obvious that Tolman's theory is as yet totally inadequate to account for these experimental results. Much experimental work remains to be done before any satisfactory theory concerning the role of motivation in perception is achieved. Tolman himself is well aware of the primitive, undeveloped nature of his theorizing, even though some of his more ardent followers are not.

We turn now to the S-R interpretation of these phenomena. So far as we know, neither Hull nor any of his followers have attempted to formulate a *complete* theoretical account of even so simple an instance of trial-and-error learning as is involved in the single T-maze. Many of the critics (*3, 13, 18*) of Hull have either never understood or have forgotten that in his *Principles of Behavior* (*6*) Hull deals only with the basic principles revealed in classical and instrumental conditioning. Hull's basic principles do *not* include all of the principles that are important for all instances of learning, animal and human. By basic he means certain principles revealed in simple instances of learning from which he believes other, just as important, learning principles may be derived. Not treated in his *Principles of Behavior* are such highly important principles as that of the habit-family hierarchy (5), the principle of the fractional anticipatory goal response (4) and a number of others.

The fractional anticipatory goal response is particularly important for all instances of complex learning including the type of problem with which we are here concerned.[5] In the original report of the present experiment (21) and in an unpublished symposium paper presented at the 1941 meeting of the Midwestern Psychological Association (19) an attempt was made to show how this mechanism would operate in the present type of experiment. Before presenting this, however, the necessity for including in the theory some other mechanism than the usual excitatory potentials between the environmental and internal drive cues and the responses may be shown by considering an experiment of Kendler (8). Using a single T-maze, one arm of which had food and the other water, Kendler had his subjects *both* hungry and thirsty during the training series. In the test series only one of the drives, hunger *or* thirst, was operative. Under this test condition Kendler found that his *S*s responded correctly a highly significant number of times. But it is obvious that under the training condition each of the responses was reinforced equally often and hence presumably was of approximately equal strength at the completion of training. How then can one predict the differential strengths under the two test conditions? The explanation suggested by Spence (8, 19) was that the stimulus cues in the water arm and end box become, during training, conditioned to fractional anticipatory drinking acts (r_w) and, in turn, the proprioceptive cues (s_w) resulting from these anticipatory acts become conditioned to the response of entering and continuing locomotion in this alley. In a like manner, conditioned, fractional anticipatory eating responses (r_f) develop in the food alley and these cues (s_f) become conditioned to the behavior of entering this alley. Dur-

---

[5] As one of us (20) has pointed out, the fractional anticipatory goal response is an instance of classical conditioning which itself enters into and plays a role in all the more complex types of learning, including instrumental conditioning.

ing the test series when only one drive is operative, the anticipatory act related to the goal for which the subject is motivated will, because of the greater strength of the particular drive stimulus, Hull's principle of stimulus dynamism (7), be much stronger (more vigorous) than the other and hence will produce stronger proprioceptive cues. Thus, if the S is thirsty, proprioceptive cues from anticipatory drinking responses will be stronger than those from anticipatory eating. As these cues (s_w) will be conditioned to the response of entering the alley leading to water, they will tend to give this response the greater excitatory strength (stimulus dynamism). When the animal is hungry, the proprioceptive cues (s_f) would be stronger and this would give the response of entering the food alley the greater excitatory strength. In other words, the relative excitatory strengths of the competing responses will be a function of the relative strengths of the two fractional anticipatory goal responses, and the latter will be dependent upon which drive is present and which is absent.

The application of this principle to the experiment of the present study is similar. In our experiment, however, the fractional anticipatory goal responses are much weaker as the Ss do not actually eat or drink during the training period. The sight of the food (or water) evokes conditioned fractional eating (drinking) responses. These, as described above, become conditioned to the cues of their respective alleys, the reinforcement being provided by the social goal, or possibly, as in higher order conditioning, by the sight of the food (or water) itself (*i.e.*, secondary reinforcement). The much greater weakness of these fractional goal responses in this experiment as compared with the Kendler experiment, in which eating and drinking actively occurred should lead to much poorer conditioning and hence presumably smaller differences between the excitatory tendencies of their proprioceptive cues. This would nicely account for the poor test results obtained in the present experiment as compared with Kendler's motivated Ss.

Making use of the same explanatory schema, Maltzman (15) has suggested that the explanation of the still poorer results he obtained was possibly due to greater interference with the fractional anticipatory eating and drinking responses by the stronger, anticipatory social goal responses. According to this view, the stronger the motivation operative in the training situation and the stronger the correlated goal response, the poorer will be the test results, as these responses will interfere with the fractional eating and drinking responses. Another implication of this theoretical picture is that the more highly differentiated the fractional anticipatory goal responses elicited by the significates, the better will be the results on the tests.

The failure of the Ss on the second test in the present investigation and in the similar study of Kendler (*10*) would be accounted for by the fact that all of the Ss of our study and those correct on the first test in the Kendler experiment were rewarded on the first test day. This relatively strong reinforcement under motivation for the significate or goal object would tend to strengthen the tendency to enter this alley, thus upsetting the balance of strength in favor of response to this side. As the second response was always to the opposite side there was thus introduced a factor that would be unfavorable to success on this test.

This explanation does not hold, however, in the case of Meehl and MacCorquodale's study, as the goal object for which the S was motivated on the first day's test was not present. Hence, the response to this side would not receive this relatively strong reinforcement, but only the usual reinforcement provided by escape from the maze to the social cage. It may or may not be significant that the shift from the training performance to the appropriate test side was greatest in this study even though not significant.

Finally, the completely negative test findings in the studies of Grice (*1*), Walker (*28*) and Kendler and Mencher (*11*), in which the Ss were thirsty during training and found water at the end of each pathway and food in one can be easily explained in terms of the concept of the fractional anticipatory goal response. In these experiments the drinking response would be dominant in both pathways and hence would become conditioned to the cues at each alley entrance. This explanation assumes, of course, that the drinking and eating responses are incompatible —a not unreasonable hypothesis.

It is readily apparent that this S-R theory, like the rival sign-gestalt theory of Tolman, is much in need of more specific, detailed elaboration. Even in its present stage of development, however, it is more detailed and definitive than that offered by Tolman.   It has, at least, suggested some of the variables, *e.g.*, the various motivations, their relative strengths, the relations among the several goal responses, etc., that are important determiners of the behavior in the situation.   Tolman's original formulation recognized none of these variables and even in his most recent formulation he has only vaguely referred to the role of motivation.   One may suspect that when the sign-gestalt theorists get around to making some definite assumptions, they will become more and more similar to those suggested above.

Summary

The present study is one of a series of investigations undertaken in the Iowa laboratory to test Tolman's sign-gestalt theory of simple trial-and-error learning.   The Ss, thirty-nine white rats, were given seven days of experience (four trials per day) in a single T-maze in which one path led to water and one to food.   The motivational-reward condition employed to get the animals to run in the maze during the training period was that of getting to a social cage containing a cage mate.   In the first of two test series given following the completion of training, twenty-three of the Ss were run under thirst while satiated for food and sixteen were hungry and satiated for water.   In a second test on the following day the motivational conditions for each S were reversed.

The results on the first test showed a significant shift from the pre-test choice of the Ss to the alley containing the goal object for which they were motivated.   The results of the second test, on the other hand, were entirely negative, with little or no shift in the direction of the appropriate alley.

The experimental findings are discussed in relation to both the cognitive theory of Tolman and an S-R theory that makes use of the fractional anticipatory goal response.

REFERENCES

1. GRICE, G. R.   An experimental test of the expectation theory of learning.   *J. comp. Psychol.*, 1948, *41*, 137–143.

2. HAYES, K. J. An experimental criticism of the Spence and Lippitt procedure. *Amer. Psychologist*, 1949, *4*, 223.

3. HILGARD, E. R. *Theories of Learning.* New York: Appleton-Century-Crofts, 1948.

4. HULL, C. L. Goal attraction and directing ideas conceived as habit phenomena. *Psychol. Rev.*, 1931, *38*, 487–506.

5. ———. The concept of the habit family hierarchy and maze learning. *Psychol. Rev.*, 1934, *41*, 33–52, 134–152.

6. ———. *Principles of Behavior.* New York: Appleton-Century, 1943.

7. ———. Stimulus intensity dynamism (V) and stimulus generalization. *Psychol. Rev.*, 1949, *56*, 67–77.

8. KENDLER, H. H. The influence of simultaneous hunger and thirst drives upon the learning of two opposed spatial responses of the white rat. *J. exp. Psychol.*, 1946, *36*, 212–220.

9. ———. An investigation of latent learning in a T-maze. *J. comp. Psychol.*, 1937, *40*, 265–270.

10. ———. A comparison of learning under motivated and satiated conditions in the white rat. *J. exp. Psychol.*, 1947, *37*, 545–549.

11. ———, & MENCHER, H. C. The ability of rats to learn the location of food when motivated by thirst—an experimental reply to Leeper. *J. exp. Psychol.*, 1948, *38*, 82–88.

12. LEEPER, R. The role of motivation in learning: a study of the phenomenon of differential motivational control of the utilization of habits. *J. genet. Psychol.*, 1935, *46*, 3–40.

13. ———. Dr. Hull's *Principles of Behavior. J. genet Psychol.*, 1944, *65*, 3–52.

14. ———. The experiments by Spence and Lippitt and by Kendler on the sign-gestalt theory of learning. *J. exp. Psychol.*, 1948, *38*, 102–106.

15. MALTZMAN, I. A study of learning under an irrelevant need. Unpublished M.A. thesis, University of Iowa, February, 1948. Also *Amer. Psychologist*, 1949, *4*, 352.

16. McNEMAR, Q. *Psychological Statistics.* New York: John Wiley & Sons, Inc., 1949.

17. MEEHL, P. E., & MacCORQUODALE, K. A further study of latent learning in the T-maze. *J. comp. Psychol.*, 1948, *41*, 372–396.

18. RITCHIE, B. F. Hull's treatment of learning. *Psychol. Bull.*, 1944, *41*, 640–662.

19. SPENCE, K. W. Symposium: learning as related to need and the subsequent motivation of such learned behavior. *Psychol. Bull.*, 1941, *38*, 721.

20. ———. Theoretical interpretations of learning. Chapter 18 in: *Handbook of Experimental Psychology.* New York, John Wiley & Sons, Inc.

21. ———, & LIPPITT, R. "Latent" learning of a simple maze problem with relevant needs satiated. *Psychol. Bull.*, 1940, *37*, 429.

22. ———, & ———.   An experimental test of the sign-gestalt theory of trial and error learning.   *J. exp. Psychol.*, 1946, *36*, 491–502.

23. ———, & KENDLER, H. H.   The speculations of Leeper with respect to the Iowa tests of the sign-gestalt theory of learning.   *J. exp. Psychol.*, 1948, *38*, 106–109.

24. THUNE, L., DUSEK, R., & SPENCE, K. W.   Learning under relevant and irrelevant needs.   *Amer. Psychologist*, 1949, *4*, 352.

25. TOLMAN, E. C.   Theoretical interpretation of learning.   Chap. 12 in: Moss, F. A., *Comparative Psychology*, New York: Prentice-Hall, 1934.

26. ———.   Demands and conflicts.   *Psychol. Rev.*, 1937, *44*, 158–169.

27. ———.   There is more than one kind of learning.   *Psychol. Rev.*, 1949, *56*, 144–156.

28. WALKER, E. L.   Drive specificity and learning.   *J. exp. Psychol.*, 1948, *38*, 39–49.

29. WHITE, R. K.   The case for the Tolman-Lewin interpretation of learning.   *Psychol. Rev.*, 1943, *50*, 157–186.

14

The Order of Eliminating Blinds in Maze
Learning by the Rat[1]

One of the most intriguing problems set by the experiments on
animal maze learning is that of explaining or accounting for the
order of difficulty of the blind alleys in a maze. The following paper is an attempt to throw some light upon the nature of
the factors that are operating in the maze situation which determine this order. Before proceeding to this task, however,
a brief review of the past studies concerned with this problem
will be given. The primary purpose of this review is to sum-
marize the outstanding experimental facts that have been obtained, and to discuss certain of the interpretations already
given them.

I

The early studies of maze learning, from the point of view
of the present problem at least, were complicated by the fact
that the mazes used were not uniform in pattern. That is, the
various culs-de-sac differed considerably from one another both
as to their nature and as to the manner in which they digressed
from the true path. The influences of these intra-pattern vari-

1 This article developed out of a paper presented in the Seminar of Professor
Clark L. Hull. The writer is indebted to Professor Hull for his critical reading
of the manuscript.

225

ations are revealed in such studies as those of Hubbert (7), Hubbert and Lashley (8), Peterson (13), White and Tolman (19), Dashiell (3), and Warden (16). Warden, for example, in an analysis of the Carr maze showed that there were three distinct types of culs-de-sac which differed considerably in difficulty. In spite of these complicating factors there appeared in several of these studies a tendency for fewer errors to be made at the food-box end of the maze, which led to the conclusion that the maze is learned from the food-box backward, there being a regressive order of elimination of errors. Carr (2) and Peterson (13), in particular, argued for this point of view and cited evidence in support of it.

With the development of more homogeneous maze patterns such as the Warden U pattern, the Stone multiple T pattern and more recently the Warner-Warden standard unit animal maze (18), many of the variable factors resulting from differences in culs-de-sac within the maze have been eliminated. The ruling out of these irrelevant variables has simplified the problem of interpretation to a considerable extent.

Outstanding in the recent experimental work in which these more uniform maze patterns have been employed is the establishment of the fact that blind alleys pointing in the direction of the goal (food-box) are entered more frequently than blinds pointing away from the goal and are also harder to eliminate. The notion that an orientation towards the goal plays an important part in maze learning is not altogether a recent one as is evidenced by the fact that Hubbert and Lashley (8), in 1917, suggested that the elimination in the Watson circular maze of those errors which consist in running past the right opening was probably due to a general orientation on the part of the animal toward the center where the goal was located. Recent investigations have served to emphasize to a still greater extent the importance of this direction orientation. Dashiell, in one of the most important studies involving this factor has shown that rats, on running a maze, soon develop this orientation in the general direction of the goal. He presents evidence showing that it plays a significant rôle in the learning of the maze. Studies by Yoshioka (20), Gengerelli (6), Tolman and Honzik

(*15a, 15b*) have confirmed Dashiell's findings, all showing the operation of such a goal-orientation tendency.

The evidence of recent studies upon the question as to whether the proximity of the culs-de-sac to the goal end is a factor determining their ease of elimination tends to substantiate the earlier results of Peterson and Carr. There certainly is a general tendency, which is decidedly strong in the case of some mazes, for the blind alleys farthest from the goal to be eliminated with greater difficulty than those nearest to the goal. The evidence for this conclusion is shown in Table 1, which

TABLE 1

RELATIVE DIFFICULTY OF SECTIONS OF MAZE

Investigator	Type of Maze	No. of Blinds	Section of Maze		
			1st	2nd	3rd
Tolman (15a)	Multiple T	14	10.8	6.7	4.8
Tolman (15b)	Multiple T	14	10.8	6.7	4.8
Ruch (14)	Multiple T	12	10.2	4.7	4.5
Ruch (14)	Multiple T	12	9.2	4.7	5.4
Warden (17)	Warner-Warden	10	8.3	4.7	3.7
Husband (12)	Warden U	10	7.0	6.4	2.8
Warden (17)	Warden U	8	6.3	3.5	3.3
Warden (17)	Warner-Warden	8	6.3	3.0	3.7
Corey (2)		8	7.0	4.5	2.0
Warden (17)	Warner-Warden	6	5.5	2.0	3.0
Dashiell (5)	Warden U	6	5.5	3.0	2.0
Dashiell (5)	Warden U	6	5.0	2.5	3.0
Mean			7.66	4.36	3.58
S.D. Mean			.588	.447	.306

gives the results of several of the most recent investigations with homogeneous maze patterns. The values in the table were obtained as follows: In each study the blinds of the maze were ranked in order of difficulty, the easiest being ranked 1, the next easiest 2 and so on. Each maze was then divided into three parts and the average of the ranks of the blinds in each third of the maze computed. The values in the table are these rank averages. It will be seen that the more difficult blinds (high values) tend to be in the first part of the maze and the less

difficult blinds in the latter part, that is, near the goal. At the
foot of the table the mean and the standard error of the mean
of each section of the mazes are given. Table 2 shows the

TABLE 2

SHOWING THE RELIABILITY OF THE DIFFERENCES BETWEEN THE AVERAGE
RANKINGS OF THE THREE SECTIONS

Sections	Difference Between the Means	Standard Deviation of the Difference *	Difference S.D. Diff.
1st and 3rd	4.08	.389	10.49
1st and 2nd	3.30	.346	9.54
2nd and 3rd	.78	.403	1.93

* S.D. difference $= \sqrt{\sigma^2_{M_1} + \sigma^2_{M_2} - 2r\sigma_M, \sigma_{M_2}}$.

reliability of the differences between these means. The critical
ratios $\left(\dfrac{\text{Diff.}}{\text{S.D. diff.}}\right)$ indicate that the chances are 100, 100 and
97, respectively, in 100 that the differences are true ones.

In a report of a study with the Warner-Warden standard unit
maze, Warden and Cummings (17) have denied that there is
any regressive order principle operating. Their own results,
however, offer fairly good evidence that there is such a factor
present as may be seen from Table 3, which is a portion of

TABLE 3

ORDER OF ELIMINATION OF CULS-DE-SAC IN THE WARNER-WARDEN MAZE

Pattern	Culs-de-sac in Order From Entrance to Goal									
	I	II	III	IV	V	VI	VII	VIII	IX	X
2 culs	2	1								
4 culs	4	3	2	1						
6 culs	6	5	3	1	4	2				
8 culs	8	7	4	5	1	6	3	2		
10 culs	10	9	6	3	5	4	7	2	8	1

Warden's Table 4. The two shortest mazes, it is to be noticed,
give a perfect regressive order and the three longer ones show
a strong tendency towards such elimination. Yet in spite of
this evidence Warden writes (17, p. 252):

One theory seems to have been definitely exploded by these results. The notion that the animal maze is learned from the food-box backward (regressive order), which has long been held in some quarters without the slightest positive evidence of a crucial nature to support it, is now seen to be quite erroneous.

TABLE 4

DISTRIBUTION OF MEAN NUMBER OF FORWARD ERRORS PER RAT

Pattern	Culs-de-sac in Order From Entrance to Goal									
	I	II	III	IV	V	VI	VII	VIII	IX	X
2 culs	8.80	6.00								
4 culs	10.44	5.66	4.44	1.66						
6 culs	8.44	5.33	2.33	2.11	3.33	1.55				
8 culs	14.90	6.30	3.10	2.40	1.90	2.30	3.10	2.00		
10 culs	14.25	7.00	4.63	1.25	2.38	1.88	2.65	1.00	3.88	1.0

His argument for this conclusion is that retracings, which were found to occur much more frequently in the section of the maze nearest the entrance compartment, thus increasing the difficulty of that section, disturb the normal order of fixation. The fact that we do not get a perfect regressive order even with this added advantage of the retracing factor is, he claims, evidence against any regressive principle. The perfect regressive order found in the two shorter mazes (2 and 4 culs-de-sac) is dismissed on the "logical consideration" that these very short mazes are limiting cases of serial learning and would not exhibit the true laws of serial learning anyway.

Undoubtedly, as Warden argues, it is true that retracing tends to increase the errors in the blinds nearest the beginning of the maze. But this does not preclude the possibility that there might also be other factors operating that would produce such a result. Again, just because there is not a perfect order of elimination does not necessarily mean that there is not existent some regressive order principle, for, as is evident upon a little reflective consideration, such a principle could be operating without there resulting perfect reverse elimination. Thus if there were any other factor, or factors operating simultaneously with a regressive order factor the reverse order could be disturbed though not completely obliterated. Especially would this be so if this second factor should be in no way related to the order of the blinds in the maze.

That another such factor actually was present in the experiment with the Warner-Warden maze can easily be shown. Warden's own results, in fact, do not justify his belief that all other factors save order (retracing excepted) were properly controlled in this maze pattern. An examination of Table 4, which is a part of Warden's Table 3, will give some indication of what this factor is. It is to be noted in particular that the odd blinds tend to be more difficult than the even blinds. Thus, in the ten culs-de-sac pattern, blinds III, V, VII, and IX are all more difficult than the even blinds IV, VI, VIII, and X. This fact of the greater difficulty of the odd blinds is shown very clearly in Figure 1, which presents in graphical form the data

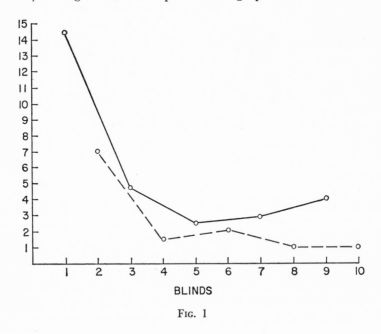

BLINDS

Fig. 1

(errors) for the 10 culs-de-sac pattern. A solid line joins the odd blinds and a broken line the even blinds.

Now the maze pattern employed by Warden (see Figure 2)

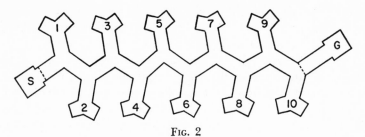

FIG. 2

was a symmetrical linear one that involved a simple right-left alternation of turns. All the odd blinds involved making a *left* turn and all the even blinds a right turn. The final choice (to the goal) consisted in making a *left* turn, the same, it should be noticed, as that involved in the odd blinds which were the more difficult ones. We appear to have here a factor somewhat similar to the goal direction tendency referred to above. That it is probably not the same thing, however, may be seen from the drawing of the maze. At each point of choice it is the true path that points in the direction of the goal. Neither group of blinds points definitely in the direction of the goal. This factor, then, might more aptly be described as an anticipatory goal reaction, considering the turning left into the food-box as a part of the total goal reaction. But whatever the nature of this factor may be, its presence and influence cannot be denied. Moreover, that it would tend to upset a perfect reverse order of elimination can readily be seen.

In summing up the evidence from the recent studies of maze learning, then, there are two outstanding facts: (*a*) Blind alleys pointing in the direction of the goal tend to be entered more often than those pointing away and are harder to eliminate; (*b*) there is a general tendency for the blinds to be more difficult the farther they are away from the goal.

II

From the preceding section it is evident that even in homogeneous maze patterns there is usually more than a single factor operating to determine the difficulty of the blinds. Any attempt, then, to account for the order of difficulty of the blind in maze learning by the operation of a single factor or principle, such as the primary-recency principle is not likely to prove very successful unless that factor plays an extremely important part compared with any others that are operating. The number of such factors and their importance will, in all probability, vary with the different maze patterns and even in the same maze under different experimental conditions.

The evidence from the experimental studies, as have been indicated in the previous section, suggests that there are two particularly important factors operating in the maze situation determining the order of difficulty of the blinds: one of such a nature as to produce, if acting alone, a backward order of difficulty, and a second which operates to increase the difficulty of the blinds pointing in the direction of the goal. Hypothetical accounts of the nature of two such factors have been put forward in the past, as was intimated previously. Particularly is this so with respect to the former factor. Usually, however, they have been conceived in vague pleasure-pain terms with no satisfactory account of their mode of operation being given. Even when these attempts have been in more objective, physiological terms they have proved to be of little value as they did not lead to or even permit the setting up of critical experimentation.

Recently there has been put forward in connection with some theoretical considerations of rat learning an hypothesis from the assumptions of which it may actually be deduced that the blind alleys will be more difficult the farther they are away from the goal. This hypothesis, the goal gradient hypothesis of Hull (*10*), is, moveover, capable of explaining (deducing) a wide variety of rat behaviour phenomena that have already been experimentally established and also some that remain to be investigated, but which in general have never before been shown to possess any organic relationship to each other.

In the following theoretical attempt to account for the order of difficulty of the culs-de-sac in the maze the writer has assumed this hypothetical goal gradient mechanism as one of the factors determining this difficulty. A second factor to be assumed is some (hypothetical) mechanism that tends to produce a particularly strong tendency on the part of the animal to proceed, wherever possible, in a direction towards the goal; thus if at a given choice-point, one path leads directly towards the goal and one in the opposite direction the animal should, as the result of this mechanism tend to prefer the former path. Dashiell proposes a rather general hypothesis as to the possible mode of functioning of this factor. He suggests that, at the time the animal enters the maze a particular implicit process (set or posture) is established or aroused, which persisting in part at least, operates as a guiding factor in the subsequent responses of the animal in the maze, tending to facilitate or strengthen any turns allied with it and to weaken any response antagonistic to it. Such a mechanism acting in a maze would tend to strengthen the excitatory tendencies to take the paths (right or wrong) leading in the absolute direction of the goal, and to weaken the excitatory tendencies to take the paths leading in the opposite direction. Any blind alley pointing in the absolute direction of the goal, then, would be eliminated with relatively considerable difficulty as the tendency to enter it is strengthened while the tendency to take the true path at this point is weakened. Especially is this so in the recent types of maze patterns, in which the true path and the blind alley point in opposite directions.

Hull (11), in an unpublished manuscript kindly made available to the author, has also developed a plausible account of the acquisition of this "Direction Orientation" with respect to the goal in his concept of the habit family hierarchy. It is sufficient to state here that this mechanism, like that suggested by Dashiell would result in a preference on the part of the animal for the path leading in the absolute direction of the goal over the one leading away. For our present purpose the description of this factor in terms of its assumed effects is sufficient.

Although the manner in which the hypothesis of the goal gradient is conceived as functioning need not concern us here in all its details some understanding of it is necessary. According to this hypothesis all stimuli, in particular the drive stimulus, get conditioned to every act of a sequence, the goal reaction being the most strongly conditioned and the other reactions progressively weaker as they are more remote (in time) from the goal reaction. The slope of this gradient Hull assumes to be positively accelerated, being more steep at the goal and becoming less and less steep as the goal becomes more and more remote. As he has shown, a logarithmic curve very accurately fits the experimental results of Yoshioka's careful experiment on discrimination of maze patterns (21). In the present discussion, however, we shall employ a gradient curve of the type

$$Y_N = Y_G(1-1/n)^N$$

in which Y_G stands for the strength of the excitatory tendency of the goal reaction, $1/n$ for the fraction that this tendency becomes weakened at each unit distance from the goal and Y_N for the strength of the tendency N units from the goal.[2] Table 5

TABLE 5

STRENGTH OF EXCITATORY TENDENCIES. $Y_N = 10(1-1/10)^N$

N	Y_N	N	Y_N
0	10.00		
1	9.00	11	3.13
2	8.10	12	2.82
3	7.29	13	2.54
4	6.56	14	2.285
5	5.90	15	2.056
6	5.31	16	1.851
7	4.78	17	1.676
8	4.30	18	1.508
9	3.87	19	1.358
10	3.48	20	1.222

gives the strength of the excitatory tendencies at various unit distances from the goal assuming that Y has a strength of 10 points and that the excitatory tendency is weakened one-tenth of its value at each unit distance from the goal.

The manner in which Hull conceives this goal gradient hypothesis as mediating a backward order of elimination of blinds is as follows (10): Once food has been found and consumed the drive stimulus becomes conditioned to the goal reaction and the several phases of the motor sequence leading to the goal reaction with an intensity progressively weaker according as

[2] This curve is positively accelerated, the slope becoming greater as the goal is approached.

each is farther away (in time) from the goal.   Thus in the maze
in Figure 3, in which each blind and each segment of the true

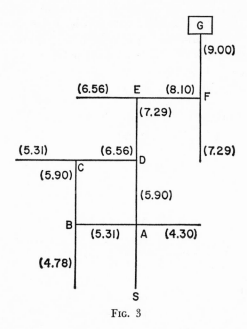

FIG. 3

path is considered as being one unit in length, the excitatory
tendency to each reaction will be as represented by the figure
in the bracket. That is, at the point F the turning movement
to the left (true path) is one unit from the goal reaction.   From
Table 5 it will be seen that the value of an excitatory tendency
of a reaction one unit from the goal is 9.00 points.   At the same
choice-point, F, a turning movement to the right, requiring as
it does going into and coming out of the blind alley, involves
two units more of time and effort.   That is, this right turning
movement is about two units farther from the goal reaction
than the action of turning to the left, making it three units in
all from the goal reaction.   This gives its excitatory tendency
a strength of 7.29 points (Table 5), making a difference of 1.71
points in favor of the left turn, the one into the true path.
This difference in favor of the true path results ultimately in
the elimination of the blind alley.

It is to be noted further that the differences between the
true path and the blind alley reactions at each point of choice
become less and less the farther they are away from the goal
end of the maze. That is, the gradient difference available
to mediate the elimination of blind alleys that are some distance
from the goal is less than is available for blind alley elimination
near the goal. This progressive weakening of the differential
value available for blind alley elimination as distance from the
goal increases would result in a corresponding progressive difficulty in the elimination of blinds. That is, if this factor alone
were operating to determine the order of difficulty of the blinds
there would result a reverse order.[3]

III

Assuming the simultaneous operation of these two hypothetical mechanisms, the goal gradient and the direction orientation mechanism, let us attempt to deduce the order of difficulty
that should occur on some particular maze on which there is
available experimental data. The adequacy of these hypotheses to account for the experimental facts can readily be tested,
then, by comparing the theoretically determined order with the
actual experimental findings. The maze study we have selected
for this purpose is one carried out by Tolman and Honzik (15a,
15b) concerned with reward and maze learning. Their study
is particularly favorable for our purpose as they did not allow
retracing in the maze and the pattern they used had no T's on
the ends of the blinds. These complicating factors, then, are
ruled out. A diagram of their maze is given in Figure 4.

[3] It should be noted that according to the goal gradient hypothesis the differences between the difficulty of the blind alleys at the goal end of the maze should
be greater than these differences at the beginning of the maze. This implication
of the hypothesis does not fit with the facts of Table 1, in which there is shown to
be a greater difference between the beginning and the middle section than between the goal and the middle section. These facts can be accounted for in some
of the mazes as being due to the unequal distribution of goal-pointing alleys in
the three sections; but even when this factor is held constant there is evidence that
the differences do not follow exactly as demanded by the hypothesis. A difficulty
is thus presented that the future development of the theory will have to take
account of.

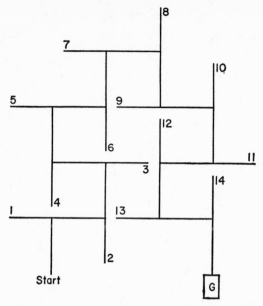

FIG. 4

We shall begin by considering the goal gradient factor. Table 6 shows how the differential value in favor of the true path at each choice-point is derived. Column 1 lists the choice-points from 14 at the goal end to 1 at the start of the maze. The second column gives the unit distance of reactions into the true path and blind at each choice-point from the goal. The blind, it should be noted, always involves traversing 2 more units than the corresponding true path. The third column shows the relative strength of the competing tendencies at each point of choice (based on Table 5), and column 4 the difference between these two tendencies. This differential available for the elimination of the blind alley, it is to be noted, becomes less and less the farther away from the goal a choice is.

Now let us consider the direction orientation factor. This mechanism, as has already been explained, is conceived as tending to favor the reaction pointing in the absolute direction of the goal over the reaction pointing away from the goal. Table

TABLE 6

THE DERIVATION OF THE DIFFERENTIAL VALUE IN FAVOR OF TRUE PATH
BASED ON GOAL GRADIENT HYPOTHESIS

1	2		3		4
Choice Point	Unit Distance From Goal		Relative Strength of Competing Tendencies		Differential Value in Favor of True Path Over Blind
	T. path	Blind	T. path	Blind	
14	1	3	9.00	7.29	1.71
13	2	4	8.10	6.56	1.54
12	3	5	7.29	5.90	1.39
11	4	6	6.56	5.31	1.25
10	5	7	5.90	4.78	1.12
9	6	8	5.31	4.30	1.01
8	7	9	4.78	3.87	.91
7	8	10	4.30	3.48	.82
6	9	11	3.87	3.13	.74
5	10	12	3.48	2.82	.66
4	11	13	3.13	2.54	.59
3	12	14	2.82	2.285	.535
2	13	15	2.54	2.056	.484
1	14	16	2.285	1.851	.434

7 shows the direction of the true path and the blind path at
each choice-point with respect to the goal, T standing for toward the goal and A for away.[4]   The third column shows the
effect of this orientation process upon the tendency to select
the true path.   We have assumed that at each choice-point in
the maze there results from the operation of this factor an increase in strength of 1.00 in favor of the reaction pointing
towards the goal over the reaction pointing away.   The values
in the third column, then, are positive in those cases in which
the true path points towards the goal and negative when the
true path points away.   The unit 1.00, selected as the preferential value resulting from this mechanism was chosen because it is
about midway between the highest and the lowest of the differential values resulting from the operation of the goal gradient
factor, thus tending to give each equal weight.   The direction
orientation mechanism, it should be noted, is conceived as

[4] In this pattern all the blinds pointing toward the right and down point
towards the goal.

TABLE 7

1	2		3	4
Choice Point	Direction With Respect to Goal		Effect Direction Tendency on Reaction into True Path	Relative Strength of Competing Tendencies as Determined by Two Hypothetical Factors
	T. path	Blind		
14	T	A	1.00	2.71
13	T	A	1.00	2.54
12	T	A	1.00	2.39
11	A	T	−1.00	.25
10	T	A	1.00	2.12
9	T	A	1.00	2.01
8	T	A	1.00	1.91
7	T	A	1.00	1.82
6	A	T	−1.00	−.26
5	T	A	1.00	1.66
4	A	T	−1.00	−.41
3	A	T	−1.00	−.465
2	A	T	−1.00	−.516
1	T	A	1.00	1.434

having the same degree of effectiveness throughout the maze, *i.e.*, it operates as strongly at the beginning of the maze as near the goal.

The values in the fourth column of Table 7 show the algebraic summation of the strengths of these two jointly operating tendencies at each choice point, *i.e.*, they represent the combined effect of the two hypothetical factors. At some of these points the two factors are in harmony with each other, both favoring the excitatory tendency to take the true path over the tendency to enter the blind. At others, those in which the blinds point in the direction of the goal, they are opposed to each other, the direction orientation mechanism favoring the tendency to enter the blind and the goal gradient mechanism favoring the reaction of taking the true path. We see that the greatest difference in favor of the true path is at choice 14, the one nearest the goal. The blind at this point, then, we should deduce to be the easiest of the blinds to learn to avoid.

While the absolute values of the figures in this column have not a great deal of significance, the negative values are of some interest. These negative values would imply that at some time in the learning process there would actually be set up a tendency to prefer the blind at these points over the true path. Such tendencies are quite commonly observed in the learning of a maze; rats often persist in running into certain blind alleys for a considerable number of trials. Some other mechanism, then, such as inhibition resulting from frustration must be invoked to explain the final elimination of these blinds.

The first row of Table 8 shows the order of difficulty of the

TABLE 8

SHOWING THE THEORETICAL AND EXPERIMENTAL ORDERS OF
DIFFICULTY OF THE BLIND ALLEYS

	Number of Blind													
	1	2	3	4	5	6	7	8	9	10	11	12	13	14
Theoretical	9	14	13	12	8	11	7	6	5	4	10	3	2	1
Experimental ...... {	9	14	13	10	8	12	4	6	5	3	11	2	7	1
	9	14	13	10	8	12	4	5	6	2	11	3	7	1

blinds in this maze which we should expect to find if two such mechanisms as those assumed were the sole determiners, the easiest blind being given the rank 1, the next easiest 2, and so on. The second and third row of this table give the experimentally determined orders of difficulty of the blinds for two different groups or rats (*15a, 15b*). It will be seen that the order deduced from the two assumed principles or factors corresponds very closely with the experimental results, the correlations (rank difference) in the 2 cases being .90 ± .03 and .91 ± .03. These two hypothetical mechanisms operating jointly would seem, then, to account extremely well for the experimental results on this particular maze.

There are, undoubtedly, other factors than these two operating in this maze which are influential in determining the order of difficulty of the blinds. There is evidence in the experimental literature of such factors. Dashiell and Bayroff (5), for instance, have shown that turns made at choices encountered later in the maze are subject to the influence of preceding choices even in the first trial. Anticipatory tendencies have also been shown to be a factor in determining errors in the maze. In connection with this last type of factor there may be mentioned the hypothesis of the anticipatory goal reaction suggested by Hull (9). According to this hypothesis the goal reaction, or a fractional component of it, tends with practice in the situation to intrude into the very beginning of the behaviour sequence and to persist throughout the cycle. The operation of such a mechanism might be conceived as tending to increase the number of errors in those blinds involving the same direction turn, right or left, as the last turn leading directly to the goal. That is, this last turn might be considered a fractional part of the goal reaction. On the assumption that such a mechanism was operating in Tolman's maze along with the two we have been considering, the theoretical order resulting from all three mechanisms operating jointly correlated slightly higher, .93, with the experimental results than the order deduced from only two.

As has been pointed out the conditions under which Tolman's experiment took place (no retracing and the non-complication of the blind alleys with T's) were particularly favorable to our present purpose, that of determining the extent to which the two above assumed factors are able to account for the order of difficulty of the blind alleys. An examination of the literature failed to reveal any other studies with data bearing upon our problem in which these complicating factors were altogether eliminated. Table 9, however, presents the results of an analysis of what data are available as to the difficulty of blind alleys in the more recent homogeneous maze patterns. The first three columns of this table give information as to the investigator and the type of maze pattern used. The fourth column shows the weight given the direction factor in each maze. In the multiple T mazes the value is 1.00, while in the Warden type mazes this value is only .10 as these patterns are uni-directional, *i.e.,* the goal is neither to the right or to the left but straight ahead. In these uni-directional mazes the mechanism operating is assumed to be that of the anticipatory goal reaction. The fifth column gives the correlation (rank method) between the experimental order and the theoretical order as deduced from the operation of the goal gradient factor alone, and the sixth column the correlation between the experimental results and the theoretical order as deduced from the joint operation

TABLE 9

Investigator	Type of Maze	Number of Blinds	Weight of Direction Factor	Goal Gradient	Goal Gradient and Direction Factor
Ruch (14)	Multiple T	12	1.00	.63	.77
Ruch (14)	Multiple T	12	1.00	.40	.36
Warden (17)	Warner-Warden	10	.10	.48	.77
Warden (17)	Warner-Warden	8	.10	.52	.50
Warden (17)	Warner-Warden	6	.10	.71	.77
Husband (12) ...	Warden U	10	.10	.61	.45
Dashiell (5)	Warden U	6	.10	.80	.80
Dashiell (5)	Warden U	6	*	.60	
Corey (2)	No diagram	8		.88	

* Blind alleys all pointed in the same direction.

of the goal gradient and the direction orientation, or the anticipatory goal reaction in the case of the uni-directional mazes. The correlations, it will be seen, are all positive and with one or two exceptions fairly high. The possibility that such consistently high positive values are merely the result of chance is extremely remote.

Summary

This paper has been concerned with the nature of the factors operating in the maze situation that are responsible for the order of difficulty of the blind alleys, and also, with ascertaining the extent to which certain hypotheses that have been put forward in connection with this problem are capable of accounting for the facts. The following conclusions have been reached:

1. There is considerable evidence of some backward order principle of learning operating in the maze situation. In general, the blinds are more difficult the farther they are from the goal.

2. Such a principle alone, however, is not able to account for the actual order of blind alley elimination.

3. Other factors that appear to be of importance in determining the order of difficulty of blind alleys are an absolute direction orientation on the part of the animal to the goal and a tendency to anticipate, particularly the goal reaction.

4. When the two or three major factors are known, there is reason to believe that the order of difficulty of the blinds in a maze may be deduced or predicted with considerable precision.

REFERENCES

1. CARR, H.   The distribution and elimination of errors in the maze. *Jour. Animal Behav.*, 1917, 7, 145–159.

2. COREY, S. M.   An experimental study of retention in the white rat. *J. exper. Psychol.*, 1931, *14*, 252–259.

3. DASHIELL, J. F.   The need for an analytic study of the maze problem. *Psychobiol.*, 1920, *2*, 181–186.

4. ――――.   Direction orientation in maze running by the white rat. *Comp. Psychol. Monog.*, 1930, 7, no. 2.

5. ――――, & BAYROFF, A. G.   A forward-going tendency in maze running. *J. comp. Psychol.*, 1931, *12*, 77–95.

6. GENGERELLI, J. A.   The principle of maxima and minima in animal learning.   *J. comp. Psychol.*, 1931, *11*, 193–236.

7. HUBBERT, H. B.   Elimination of errors in the maze. *Jour. Animal Behav.*, 1915, *5*, 66–72.

8. ――――, & LASHLEY, K. S.   Retroactive association and the elimination of errors in the maze.   *J. Animal Behav.*, 1917, 7, 130–138.

9. HULL, C. L.   Goal attraction and directing ideas conceived as habit phenomena. *Psychol. Rev.*, 1931, *38*, 487–506.

10. ――――.   The goal gradient hypothesis and maze learning. *Psychol. Rev.*, 1932, *39*, 25–44.

11. ――――.   Habit family hierarchy. (In manuscript.)

12. HUSBAND, R. W.   Comparison of human adults and white rats in maze learning.   *J. comp. Psychol.*, 1929, *9*, 361–379.

13. PETERSON, J.   The effect of length of blind alleys on maze learning: An experiment on twenty-four white rats. *Behav. Monog.*, 1917, *3*, no. 15, p. 53.

14. RUCH, F. L.   Food-reward vs. escape-from-water as conditions motivating learning in the white rat. *J. Genet. Psychol.*, 1931, *38*, 127–145.

15a. TOLMAN, E. C., & HONZIK, C. H.   Degrees of hunger, reward and non-reward, and maze learning in rats. *University of California Pub. in Psychol.*, 1930, *4*, 241–256.

15b. ——, & ——. Introduction and removal of reward, and maze performance in rats. *University of California Pub. in Psychol.*, 1930, *4*, 257–275.

16. WARDEN, C. J. Some factors determining the order of elimination of culs-de-sac in the maze. *J. exper. Psychol.*, 1923, *6*, 192–210.

17. ——, & CUMMINGS, S. B. Primacy and recency factors in animal motor learning. *J. Genet. Psychol.*, 1929, *36*, 240–257.

18. WARNER, L. H., & WARDEN, C. J. The development of a standardized animal maze. *Arch. Psychol.*, 1927, *15*, no. 93.

19. WHITE, A. E., & TOLMAN, E. C. A note on the elimination of short and long blind alleys. *J. comp. Psychol.*, 1923, *3*, 327–331.

20. YOSHIOKA, J. G. Direction as a factor in maze solution in rats. *J. Genet. Psychol.*, 1930, *38*, 307–320.

21. ——. Weber's law in the discrimination of maze distance by the white rat. *University of California Pub. in Psychol.*, 1929, *4*, 155–184.

15

Cognitive Versus Stimulus–Response Theories of Learning[1]

Contemporary learning theorists, whatever their predilections, seem to be in fair accord so far as the general statement of the problem or task confronting them is concerned. Learning psychologists, all seem to agree, are interested, first, in discovering and specifying the experimental variables that determine the observed behavioral changes that occur with practice, and, secondly, in the formulation of the functional interrelationships, *i.e.*, laws, holding between these sets of variables. Most learning theorists agree, furthermore, that this latter task seems to require the introduction and use of some type of theoretical construct.

It will be well at the outset to get clearly before us the problem confronting the learning psychologist. If we consider the behavior of an organism at any moment, the specific response made may be said to be a function of two sets of variables: (1) the particular world situation (physical or social) of the moment, and (2) the particular state or condition of the organism at the moment. The former is represented in Figure 1 by S, and the latter by the oval.

[1] This paper represents the main address, with some modifications, given in a symposium on learning of the Division of Theoretical-Experimental Psychology at the Boston meetings of the American Psychological Association in 1948.

Now the fact that in learning experiments the behavior or response of the organism to the same objective situation changes with successive practice has led the learning theorist to assume

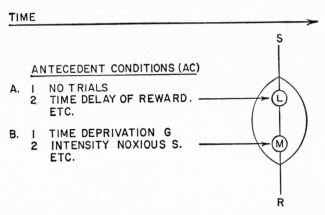

TIME

ANTECEDENT CONDITIONS (AC)

A. 1 NO TRIALS
   2 TIME DELAY OF REWARD.
      ETC.

B. 1 TIME DEPRIVATION G
   2 INTENSITY NOXIOUS S.
      ETC.

Fig. 1. Schematic representation of the experimental variables and theoretical constructs with which the learning psychologist is concerned.

that certain changes must also occur within the organism. Unable to observe these under-the-skin events, he has been led to speculate or theorize as to their nature. In the diagram I have represented these hypothetical learning changes by means of the symbol, L. As represented here, L, or the class of hypothetical learning factors, is assumed, on the one hand, to be the product of the past interactions of the individual with his environment and, on the other, to be one of the set of conditions or factors that determine his present performance. In this sense L is similar to constructs representing other hypothetical states of the organism that are assumed to be among the determinants of the behavior of the moment—*e.g.*, drive, fatigue, drug condition, etc.

Our diagram, then, attempts to show in a schematic way the relations between this hypothetical learning construct (L), other intervening theoretical constructs, such as the motivational (M), and the various experimental variables: (1) present environmental events (S), (2) past environmental events, or antecedent conditions (A.C.) and (3) the response measure (R).

Psychologists have differed widely in the manner in which they have conceived of these hypothetical learning changes, and it is in terms of these different theoretical conceptions that we can designate the main theoretical issues. Turning for the moment to psychological theorists whose main interests have not been in the problem of learning—*e.g.,* the late Professor Lewin —the favorite method has been to infer (define) them from behavior, particularly from the verbal introspections of either their subjects or themselves (*16, 17*). In the case of Lewin, symbols or terms taken from entirely different disciplines—*e.g.,* topology and dynamics—have been employed to represent these introspectively or response-derived notions.

A second group of psychologists who have favored this method of inferring their hypothetical constructs from behavior is the Gestaltist. While primarily interested in problems of perception and the complex problems of thought and reasoning, Köhler (*15*) and Koffka (*14*)—particularly the latter—have given no little attention to the problem of learning. The extent to which phenomenological introspection has entered into the theories of these psychologists is well known.

There is a further characteristic of the Gestaltists' thinking to which attention may be directed at this time. In contrast to Lewin's topological and dynamic constructs, those of Köhler and Koffka have a neurophysiological ring. Thus they introduce such concepts as brain field, neurophysiological traces and trace systems, etc. This tendency to describe the hypothetical response-determining factors in terms of neurophysiological models is a very prevalent one among psychologists, whether Gestalt or otherwise. Apparently it is akin to the physicists' construction of models representing the internal state of the atom. However, unlike the theoretical physicist who typically uses these models merely for expository purposes and who does his real theorizing in terms of mathematical constructs, the psychological theorist is more often likely to have only the model. In such instances one does not usually have any theory at all but only a simple analogy which more often than not explains nothing.

There is still another type of analogy which has been used all too frequently by some psychological writers. I refer to the practice of likening the hypothetical internal events within the organism to a telephone switchboard in which learning is represented as consisting of the alterations in the resistance or conductance of the various connecting switches. Such pictures should never, of course, have been taken as serious, responsible theorizing, but rather what they were most often meant to be— a device often employed by writers of elementary textbooks to try to convey something that even a college sophomore will believe he understands. Elementary textbook writers do not, at least nowadays, attempt to represent, in the best scientific manner possible, the various theoretical aspects of psychology. Everyone knows such books are written to sell, and to sell they apparently must use such simple, familiar analogies.

Unfortunately for the S-R point of view, many of the current elementary textbooks are written in terms of this schema and as a consequence its opponents have come to imply that the switchboard is a necessary part of the S-R position. Thus, recently Tolman (32) referred to the "stimulus-response" viewpoint as the "telephone-switchboard school of psychology." No scientifically oriented person in psychology, however, would ever take such analogies, whether telephone switchboards or map control rooms, as serious attempts at theoretical representation of learning changes.

This brings us to the consideration of the last of the techniques which have been employed for introducing or defining the hypothetical states or conditions in the organism supposed to determine behavior. I have reference here to the method of defining them as mathematical functions of the present stimulus and the antecedent environmental conditions. The best examples of this method are Hull's constructs of habit ($_sH_R$) and drive (D) (10). Tolman's program for theorizing is essentially similar in plan (30, 31).

With this picture of the varieties of psychological theorizing before us, we now turn to the particular issue in hand—namely, cognitive versus stimulus-response interpretations of learning. This distinction is emphasized primarily by the cognitive group and, as we shall see, the psychologists falling into this group are united about as much by their opposition to what they conceive the *S-R* position to be as by the positive notions they have to offer by way of an alternative.

I shall begin by presenting the positive side of the theoretical picture that the cognition, or *S-S*, theorists offer. The essential notion underlying the theorizing of all members of this group seems to me to be that learning is part of a larger problem of organization, including, as a most important aspect, *perceptual organization*. These theorists all agree that learning is to be conceived in terms of the organization into some kind of functional whole of the perceptual systems of the subject. Thus, in referring to the simple type of learning involved in the *CR* situation, Zener writes:

. . . the essential structural modification consists in a reorganization into some kind of functional whole of the perceptual systems corresponding to the conditioned and unconditioned stimuli; and in the functional relation of this organized system to the urge or tension system originally excited by the unconditioned stimulus (*34*, p. 386).

Adams (*1*), Koffka (*14*), Lewin (*17*) and Tolman (*30, 32, 33*) likewise emphasize that learning involves primarily the structuring (or restructuring) of the cognitive field of the subject— *i.e.*, the formation and modification of cognitive patterns representative of the relationships in the environment.

The following statement, quoted from White's article, in which he attempted to clarify the Tolman-Lewin interpretation of learning, is, in my opinion, one of the best brief statements of the cognitive theory of learning:

The perceptual-learning postulate implies the importance of *perceptual "field" conditions at the time of the original perception,* rather than any subsequent reward or "reinforcement." This difference is both an affirmation and a denial. It affirms the importance, in relation to perception, of all those field conditions which have been experimentally shown to influence perceptual organization: temporal contiguity, spatial contiguity, visual continuity, common contrast, embeddedness, exploratory motivation, etc. All of these factors, except temporal contiguity, have been given less emphasis by *S-R* psychologists (*34*, p. 166).

So much for the cognitive theory of learning. Let us turn now to a similar brief survey of the main concepts of the *S-R* theory. Instead of conceiving of learning in terms of perceptual or cognitive changes, the S-R learning theorists refer to such things as stimulus-response connections, bonds, associations, habits, or tendencies. As Hull (*10*) and Thorndike (*28*) have used these concepts, they have had reference to a hypothetical learning state or intervening variable. In effect Thorndike's original three major laws of learning (*27*) provided a definition of his concept of S-R bond in terms of the experimental conditions, variation of which would lead to changes in its strength. Later, in connection with his experimental studies with human subjects, Thorndike (*28*) introduced six further experimental variables that must, he believed, be taken into account in specifying the strength of an S-R bond or association. These variables are belongingness, impressiveness, polarity, identifiability, availability and mental systems (or set). It is rather interesting to note that most of these latter variables are of the type that the cognitive theorists, particularly the Gestaltists, emphasize. They refer to the content of the materials learned rather than to relations—*e.g.*, temporal—between the contents.

Thorndike's major interest has been in the identification of the experimental conditions that are responsible for the occurrence of learning. In particular he has attempted to discover and define the necessary motivational-reward conditions. This task involves primarily the operational definition of a "trial" or "reinforcement" in a learning experiment. Thorndike has never particularly concerned himself with the problem of specifying the nature of the functional relationship between his hypothetical intervening variable, S-R bond, and these antecedent experimental variables.

In sharp contrast to this relatively circumscribed interest of Thorndike, Hull (*10*) has been interested not only in the problem of specifying, operationally, the experimental variables determining his hypothetical learning factor—*habit*—but also, he has attempted to guess at the "law" describing how these variables combine to determine *habit* strength ($_sH_R$). Thus he postulates that *habit* is a specific function (shown in Figure 2) of at least four variables: (1) the number of reinforcements (N); (2) magnitude of the reward (W); (3) time of delay of the reward

(T); (4) time interval between the stimulus and response (T'). Hull then goes on to specify certain further hypothetical relations that habit has to other hypothesized intervening variables

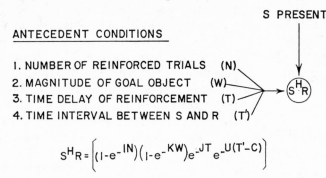

FIG. 2. Hull's mathematical specification of *habit* strength
$(_sH_R)$.

such as drive (D), excitatory potential (E), inhibition (I), etc. He finally ends his theorizing by relating these hypothetical intervening variables to the several empirical response measures used in simple conditioning experiments. Incidentally it is important to note that in his *Principles of Behavior* Hull has dealt almost exclusively with classical and instrumental conditioning. Because of the simplicity of these experimental situations he believes that they provide the best means of revealing the basic learning principles. It is his intention to employ the basic constructs and hypothetical laws discovered there, plus whatever additional ones are necessary to explain more complex learning phenomena. Some anticipations of this program, so far as maze learning and certain other more complex learning situations are concerned, appeared in a series of articles (4, 5, 6, 7, 8, 10, 11) in the 1930's, and the present writer has attempted to extend Hull's principles to simple T-E learning (25), discrimination learning (21) and transposition phenomena (22).

What are the main points of disagreement between these two theoretical positions? My own reaction to this question is that the differences have been greatly exaggerated and, mainly, I fear, by the cognition theorists. Instead of making a serious attempt to understand the essential nature of Hull's and Thorndike's theorizing, the cognition theorists have either seized upon certain unfortunate, secondary and irrelevant features of their treatments, or have taken their conception of *S-R* theory from oversimplified elementary textbook treatments.

It is therefore pertinent to elaborate and comment on some of these differences, supposed and real.

First, it should, I believe, be clear that there is nothing that implies the notion of a telephone switchboard in Hull's *mathematical* specification of *habit*. The meaning of this construct is given by the mathematical function relating it to the antecedent experimental variables and the operational definition of the latter. Any comparison, then, of switchboards with map control rooms is entirely beside the point so far as this theory is concerned.

Secondly, with regard to the neurophysiological models favored by the two opposing camps, there undoubtedly is a considerable difference, but, again, I should like to emphasize that this difference has little or no significance so far as learning theory is concerned. Just why Hull (*10*), after formulating his mathematical theory of *habit,* found it necessary to elaborate a neurophysiological model of receptor-effector connections, has always remained a puzzle to me. Actually he does little more than identify or coordinate this concept of receptor-effector connection with his mathematical construct of habit. I doubt whether a single one of the deductions with respect to learning in his *Principles of Behavior* would be lost or changed in any way if it were eliminated. These implications follow exclusively from his mathematical theorizing and not at all from the superfluous physiological model.[2] The same is true for Thorndike's theory about the alteration of synaptic conductances, and I suspect that the electrical brain fields that Köhler offers as isomorphic counterparts of his hypothetical trace fields add little more to his theory. The picturing of what the neurophysiological processes are *without specifying the hypothetical relations that tie them up with the experimental variables and the response measures* is almost a complete waste of time so far

---

[2] Since the above statement was written Hull has discussed his reasons for adding his neurophysiological speculations to his mathematical theorizing. See footnote 4 in his recent article on the gradient of reinforcement (*11*).

as furthering our understanding of learning phenomena is concerned. I suspect that I am in close agreement with Tolman on this point for he seems, at least so far, to have quite successfully escaped from the compulsion to engage in brain speculation.

My third point is concerned with the problem as to whether the functional tie-up or association established in learning is between sensory and motor processes, or between sets of sensory processes. The cognition theorists appear to be quite united in the view that learning involves the association (they would prefer to say the organization) of sensory or perceptual processes. Thus Zener's statement, quoted earlier, that conditioning involves the "reorganization into some kind of functional whole of the perceptual systems corresponding to the conditioned and unconditioned stimuli" will be recalled. Maier and Schneirla (19) likewise explicitly state that the essential change in conditioning involves a new dynamic relationship between the sensory cortical patterns of the conditioned and unconditioned stimuli. And Tolman's concept of sign-Gestalt-expectation may be thought of as a cognitive pattern in which are associated the successive perceptual processes occurring in a behavior sequence.

On the other hand, the S-R theorists have certainly tended to hold to the conception that the association is between the stimulus and response mechanisms. Thus in attempting to contrast his behavioristic associationism with the older associationistic doctrines, Guthrie wrote as follows:

Our position is that what is associated is a stimulus and a response. It would perhaps be more exact to say that what is associated is some stimulation of sense organs and a corresponding muscular contraction or glandular secretion (3, p. 43).

Thorndike and Hull have also definitely implied that the tie-up in learning is between receptor and effector mechanisms *although it is important to note that Hull's mathematical definition of habit does not identify it either as an S-S or S-R concept. It is only by virtue of his additional neurophysiological theorizing that Hull falls into the S-R group.* So far as I am concerned I do not find it difficult to conceive of both types of organizations or associations being established in learning. Certainly simple types of perceptual learning would appear possibly to involve intersensory associations. I seriously doubt, however, whether learning is exclusively of this type, or even that the majority of it is. Indeed, what little experimental evidence there is on the point, even in the field of such simple learning as conditioning, would appear to support more strongly the *S-R* conception than the *S-S*.

NORMAL CONDITIONING

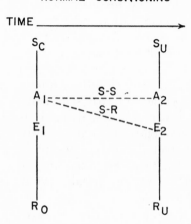

FIG. 3. Schematic representation of the classical conditioned response showing by means of the broken lines the two possible hypothetical associations (*S-S* or *S-R*).

Figures 3 and 4 describe one such experiment. In Figure 3 the typical classical conditioned response situation involving a defense response to shock is represented. The conditioned stimulus (S_c) is indicated as leading to afferent process (A_1) and the unconditioned stimulus to afferent process (A_2). E_1 and E_2 represent the efferent neural processes that result in the original responses, R_o and R_u respectively, to S_c and S_u. The hypothetical association or organization occurring in conditioning may be indicated by either of the two dotted lines, depending upon which theory is held to—*S-S* or *S-R*.

Loucks (*18*) has reported an experiment in which S_u and A_2 were eliminated, the unconditioned flexion response being elicited by applying faradic shock directly to the appropriate area of the motor cortex.   This procedure, of course, by-passed the usual sensory system, pain from shock to limb, involved in normal conditioning (see part A, Figure 4).   Hence the associa-

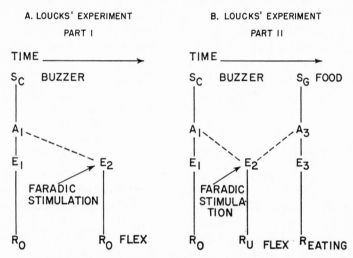

Fig. 4. Schematic representation of two parts of Loucks' conditioning experiment involving by-passing of the afferent system of the unconditioned response.

tion between A_1 and A_2 could not take place, but the association between A_1 and E_2 was still theoretically possible.   Loucks actually found that no conditioning took place under this condition and this result was cited by Maier and Schneirla (19) as evidence in favor of their S-S hypothesis and against the S-R conception.

But there was a second part to the Loucks experiment, as described in part B of Figure 4.   In this part of the experiment Loucks followed each leg flexion with the presentation of food, and conditioning did occur.   Maier and Schneirla's attempt to explain this result away is most unsatisfactory.   I quote them:

Under these conditions foreleg flexion became associated with reward just as string pulling becomes associated with reward in the problem box situation (19, p. 126).

In other words, they are saying, an association between E_2 and A_3 became established and is responsible for the conditioning. Just why this is not an S-R connection is not clear to me, nor why such a backward association would be formed, whereas association between A_1 and E_2 would not be, is also left unclarified.

The explanation of the two parts of this experiment that would be offered by the S-R theorist is probably obvious. He would say that there was no reinforcement in the first part of the experiment and hence the necessary condition for association-formation was not present. When reinforcement was added, the association between A_1 (the sensory mechanism) and E_2 (the effector mechanism) occurred. This explanation would not, of course, work for the S-R contiguity theorist.

The fourth point I should like to discuss presents a very real difference between the two theoretical camps, but the difference seems to me to be one of emphasis rather than of conflict. I refer to the tendency of most cognition theorists to emphasize what may be termed the intrinsic properties of their theoretical constructs, whereas the S-R theorist has tended to emphasize the properties of his concepts that are determined by the antecedent experimental variables. The learning theories of the Gestalt members of the cognition group, in particular, are marked by a very extensive and detailed discussion of the inherent nature of their constructs. Thus Koffka (14) treats at great length the properties of the various kinds of hypothetical factors he assumes, e.g., processes, traces, trace systems, ego systems, etc. While it is true that Koffka also mentions some experimental variables that he believes to be important in determining the properties of his hypothetical learning constructs, for the most part these have consisted of the conditions in the present stimulus situation which play an important part in the perceptual processes. The implication is usually given that analogous relationships (i.e., laws) will be found to hold with respect to traces and, hence, learning. The belief on the part of the Gestalt psychologist that learning is merely a part of the larger problem of perceptual organization provides much of the rationale for this appeal to the laws of perception.

Probably another important factor determining the approach of the Gestaltists to the problem of learning theory is their decided preference for the mediational type of explanation of psychological events. For Köhler, in particular, explanation of psychological events is to be found in terms of the underlying neurophysiological processes. At every point Köhler attempts to indicate the isomorphic relations of his trace fields to electrical brain fields. Unfortunately the properties of these hypothetical brain fields are more often inferred from phenomenological introspections than based on the experimental findings of brain physiology.

Once more I should point out that Tolman's sign-Gestalt formulation represents an exception to this tendency on the part of the cognition theorists to concern themselves extensively with the intrinsic properties of their theoretical constructs. The first psychologist to recognize the role of the intervening variable as an aid to the discovery and formulation of laws in psychology, Tolman has always insisted that these theoretical constructs must be defined in terms of the independent (environmental) variables. It seems to be characteristic of the behavioristic-oriented psychologists that they tend to direct their interests toward explanations that refer to events in the physical and social environment, past and present, rather than to events in the brain.

The fifth point of difference between the two opposed schools of thought has reference to the different independent experimental variables emphasized in the work of the two groups. The cognition theorists have been much more interested in the conditions that determine the reception of the stimulus events and that influence perceptual organization. Thus they have concerned themselves extensively with the effect of such experimental variables as figure-ground conditions, set, visual continuity, embeddedness, belongingness, fusibility, etc., on learning. The S-R psychologists, on the other hand, have been most interested in the effect of various temporal factors, such as time interval between trials, and in the motivational-reward conditions underlying learning, etc. Again the differences with regard to these factors are relative, for the cognition theorists do not confine their studies exclusively to perceptual factors and the S-R theorists have not been concerned only with reinforcement conditions.

Such differences of emphasis, it should be noted moreover, do not necessarily involve conflict. There still remains much to do before we have a reasonably complete understanding of even simple learning phenomena, let alone the more complex types of adjustment. Preoccupation with the reinforcement conditions of learning by the S-R psychologist does not mean, as some cognition theorists appear to have felt, that the former believe stimulus-reception factors are not important. It is merely a reflection of their greater interest in such matters. Similarly if the cognition theorist enjoys speculating about the physiological properties of his hypothetical learning factors, I do not feel that his work is in conflict with non-physiologically oriented attempts at theorizing. I do, of course, think that the latter procedure is more fruitful so far as learning phenomena are concerned *at the present time.*

Sixth, there are a number of other aspects of this problem of stimulus-reception that have been a source of much difficulty and misunderstanding between the two groups of theorists. Perhaps the best way of introducing the discussion of the next point is to paraphrase some of the statements concerning the matter made by Tolman in a recent article entitled, "Cognitive Maps in Rats and Men." Tolman writes: "According to the stimulus-response school, the subject in learning a maze responds helplessly and passively to the succession of external and internal stimuli" (*32*, p. 189). In contrast, he states that while his theory admits that the subject is bombarded by stimuli, he holds that the nervous system is highly selective as to which of these stimuli it will let in at any given time. In commenting on an experiment of one of his students, Tolman writes further:

. . . this experiment reinforces the notion of the largely active, selective character in the rat's building up of his cognitive map. He often has to look actively for significant stimuli in order to form his map and does not merely passively receive and react to all the stimuli which are physically present (*32*, p. 201).

Presumably the last portion of this quotation again has reference to the S-R point of view.

It is difficult to know for sure just what Tolman and others (Krech, Lashley, etc.) who have expressed this same notion mean by this kind of statement but the point comes up so persistently it is time that *S-R* psychologists attempted to clarify their position.   One possible reason for the belief expressed by Tolman is that much of the *S-R* theory is concerned with the classical conditioning situation in which the conditions of stimulation are extremely simple.   No "active looking" for the cue-stimulus in the sense of trial and error receptor-orienting acts is necessary in this situation.   In the case of human subjects a set to orient towards the stimulus, if it is visual, is provided for by preliminary verbal instructions.   In the case of animals an auditory stimulus or change in the general illumination has generally been used.   Receipt of either of these types of stimulus requires no preliminary learning of a special receptor orientation.   The subject receives the stimulus regardless of what it is doing or how its receptor mechanisms may be oriented.

But even in the case of this simple learning situation the *S-R* theorist has not assumed, as claimed, that organisms passively receive and react to all the stimuli that are physically present. In Chapter III of his book, *Principles of Behavior,* Hull distinguishes between the *potential stimuli* of a situation and the actual stimuli being received at any moment by the organism. In the thirteenth chapter he further discusses at some length a number of factors that determine the amount of habit loading acquired by different components of a stimulus compound. Thus he recognizes that such factors as static vs. changing stimulus, intensity, type of receptor, pervasiveness of the stimulus, etc., may lead to different habit loadings.   Very little experimental evidence on these matters is available; hence Hull has not theorized so extensively or as specifically about them as he has about certain other factors.[3]

This misunderstanding of the *S-R* position with respect to stimulus reception has also been chiefly responsible for the controversy known as the continuity–non-continuity issue in animal discrimination learning.   On the one side of this disagreement the cognition psychologists have interpreted the systematic

---

[3] In order to reduce the length of the talk, the remainder of the paper was not presented in the original presentation.

responses that occur during the pre-solution period, when the subject is responding chance to the cue stimuli, as involving a selective concentration on certain other stimulus aspects as the result of "sensory-organization processes." They assume further that no learning or cognitive formation occurs with respect to the cue-differences during this period. Ultimately the animal responds "perceptually" to the cue-aspects and from then on, and then on only according to this view, does it form cognitions about these stimuli. The original experiments on which this interpretation arose and was tested involved discrimination of brightness (12) and weight (20) respectively,—stimulus dimensions, it should be observed, that require no learning of special receptor-orienting adjustments in order to be received. Subsequently a form discrimination situation (13) was employed by Krechevsky in which it was necessary, first, for the subjects to learn certain appropriate visual receptor orienting acts in order to provide for the reception of differential positive and negative cues. Ehrenfreund's recent experiment (2), based on the S-R interpretation of these phenomena, has shown clearly the role that such preliminary receptor orienting acts play in the learning of visual discrimination involving differences such as form.

Quite contrary to its opponents' claims, then, the S-R theory does not assume that the animal passively receives all the physically present stimuli. In more complex learning situations, such as discrimination, simple trial and error and maze learning, etc., the subject cannot possibly receive all of the visual stimulus situation at any one moment. More important still, any particular receptor exposure adjustment that the subject may have picked up in the preliminary training or other prior experiences may be such as not to provide discriminably different stimulation from the positive and negative stimulus-cues. Thus a triangle, the light rays from which strike the periphery of the retina, as the result of the particular fixation habits, will not be discriminated from a circle also in the periphery of vision. The early stages of learning situations more complex than classical conditioning involve, as an important part of them, the acquisition of these receptor exposure adjustments that provide the relevant cue. Such learning is itself an active, trial-and-error process with those adjustments being learned that lead to reception of stimulus-cues, responses to which are followed by reinforcement.

My final comments also relate to an aspect of the problem of perception. Unlike the S-S theorist, the S-R psychologist does not usually talk very much about such things as perception, meaning, knowledge, cognitive processes, etc. I suspect, however, that he deals with pretty much the same things that the cognitive theorists do under different terms. For example, if asked to give an analysis of perception or cognition, the S-R psychologist with his analytical bent would probably proceed very much as follows. First of all he would be likely to distinguish a number of different aspects as shown in the diagram in Figure 5. Time does not permit a detailed elaboration but

Fig. 5. An analysis of perception (cognition) from an S-R point of view.

I will indicate in a most schematic manner the essential nature of each aspect and some of the most pertinent problems that exist concerning them.

Sense reception

This refers to the activity of the receptor mechanisms including presumably their terminal activities in the brain. One problem here is the extent to which organization into units or patterns occurs, and if so, to what extent such organization is innate or learned. The Gestalt psychologists have placed heavy emphasis on the innate factors although other cognition theorists have given more recognition to the possibility of the role of learning in such processes. So far as S-R theorists are concerned, about the only treatment of this aspect of reception is Hull's construct of stimulus trace and his hypothesis of afferent interaction between these traces.

Redintegration

I have chosen this term to refer to the phenomenon that a particular sensory process arouses other sensory experiences, *e.g.*, the sight of ice arouses experience of cold, etc.   There is a suggestion that sensory processes that have been experienced contiguously in the past tend to become associated.   These may involve associations between externally initiated sensory processes or between externally and internally aroused processes. One of the questions to be answered here is whether these associations or habits are between the sensory items as the cognitive theorist would insist or whether each sensory process arouses its particular efferent process and the associations are between afferent-efferent processes.   This is the same question we dealt with before and I should like to repeat that so far as I am concerned I do not feel the need to speculate as to the neurophysiological basis of the habits formed.   I prefer to confine my hypothesizing to certain quantitative properties of these habits that can be defined in terms of the experimental variables, environmental and behavioral.

Signification

Whereas redintegration referred to habit organizations or associations between temporally contiguous sensory processes, signification refers to associations between the stimulus-aroused events that in the past have occurred in temporal succession. The first stimulus event becomes, we say, a sign for the coming of the second event.   Here, of course, the classical example is the Pavlovian-type conditioning situation, but whereas the cognition theorists would be likely again to insist on the association being between the successive sensory aroused events, the *S-R* psychologist is more likely to assume afferent-efferent connections.   As we have already seen, what little experimental evidence there is on this type of learning favors the latter interpretation (*cf.* Loucks' experiment).

Attention should be drawn here to the fact that the emotional significance of environmental events falls into this class of perceptual response.

Manipulation

The meaning of stimulus objects or events is provided not only by the kinds of internal responses (*e.g.*, emotional, anticipatory goal responses, etc.) that are made to it, but also in terms of the overt responses that are made directly to it.   Thus the meaning of "knife" or "ball" is given, in part, in terms of the manipulatory acts (*e.g.*, cutting, throwing) that are learned with respect to them.

Verbal meaning

Finally, in the case of humans there are the meanings provided by learned verbal responses.   The degree of sophistication that has been attained here, particularly in the abstract aspects of language, and the extent to which many of the behavior difficulties of human beings are the result of disorders of verbal behavior, are well known if not as yet well understood. They badly need the attention of all psychologists—cognition, *S-R,* or whatever else.

In concluding this discussion I should not like to leave the impression that I believe the *S-R* psychologist has by any means adequately dealt with the problems of sense reception and perception in learning.   His primary interests, as was indicated before, have been in other areas, *i.e.*, with other variables.   He has not, however, completely neglected the problem, and his point of view is not the naive one that it is usually represented to be in the writings of the cognitive theorists.   Far too prevalent in the writings of current cognitive psychologists is the deplorable technique of misrepresenting the formulations of opposing viewpoints and then showing these erroneous formulations to be inadequate.   One almost gets the impression that the major goal is to prove the other conception wrong rather than to try to arrive at a more comprehensive interpretation of the phenomena.   Psychologists interested and appreciative of the role of theory in the development of a scientific body of knowledge should resist such temptations.   The main result of such theoretical fencing is likely to be the bringing of theory into disrepute.   Already many extremely empirical minded psychologists are thoroughly disgusted with the theoretical debates that go on in this field. Their proposed remedy, elimination of all theorizing, would certainly not help to speed up the acquisition of a scientific body of knowledge about learning.

REFERENCES

1. ADAMS, D. K.　A restatement of the problem of learning.　*Brit. J. Psychol.*, 1931, *22*, 150–178.

2. EHRENFREUND, D.　An experimental test of the continuity theory of discrimination with pattern vision.　*J. comp. Psychol.*, 1948, *41*, 408–422.

3. GUTHRIE, E. R.　Conditioning: a theory of learning in terms of stimulus, response and association.　In *41st Yearbook Nat. Soc. Study Educ.*, Bloomington: Public School Publishing Co., 1942.

4. HULL, C. L.　Simple trial and error learning: a study in psychological theory.　*Psychol. Rev.*, 1930, *37*, 241–256.

5. ———.　Knowledge and purpose as habit mechanisms.　*Psychol. Rev.*, 1930, *37*, 511–525.

6. ———.　Goal attraction and directing ideas conceived as habit phenomena.　*Psychol. Rev.*, 1931, *38*, 487–506.

7. ———.　The goal gradient hypothesis and maze learning.　*Psychol. Rev.*, 1932, *39*, 25–43.

8. ———.　The concept of the habit-family hierarchy and maze learning.　*Psychol. Rev.*, 1934, *41*, 33–52.

9. ———.　The mechanism of the assembly of behavior segments in novel combinations suitable for problem solution.　*Psychol. Rev.*, 1935, *42*, 219–245.

10. ———.　*Principles of Behavior.*　New York: D. Appelton-Century, 1943.

11. ———.　Stimulus trace generalization, "remote" associations, and the gradient of reinforcement.　Unpublished manuscript.

12. KRECHEVSKY, I.　"Hypotheses" versus "chance" in the pre-solution period in sensory discrimination-learning.　*University Calif. Publ. Psychol.*, 1932, *6*, 27–44.

13. ———.　A study of the continuity of the problem-solving process.　*Psychol. Rev.*, 1938, *45*, 107–133.

14. KOFFKA, K.　*The Principles of Gestalt Psychology.*　New York: Harcourt, Brace and Co., Inc., 1935.

15. KÖHLER, W.　*Dynamics in Psychology.*　New York: Liveright Publ. Corp., 1940.

16. LEWIN, K.　*Principles of Topological Psychology.*　New York: McGraw-Hill Book Co., 1936.

17. ———.　Field theory of learning.　In *41st Yearbook Nat. Soc. Study Educ.*, Bloomington: Public School Publ. Co., 1942, Chap. IV.

18. LOUCKS, R. B. The experimental delimitation of neural structures essential for learning: the attempt to condition striped muscle responses with faradization of the sigmoid gyri. *J. Psychol.,* 1935, *1,* 5–44.

19. MAIER, N. R. F., & SCHNEIRLA, T. C. Mechanisms in conditioning. *Psychol. Rev.,* 1942, *49,* 117–133.

20. McCULLOCH, T., & PRATT, J. G. A study of the presolution period in weight discrimination by white rats. *J. comp. Psychol.,* 1934, *18,* 271–288.

21. SPENCE, K. W. The nature of discrimination learning in animals. *Psychol. Rev.,* 1936, *43,* 427–449.

22. ———. The differential response in animals to stimuli varying within a single dimension. *Psychol. Rev.,* 1937, *44,* 430–444.

23. ———. Continuous versus non-continuous interpretations of discrimination learning. *Psychol. Rev.,* 1940, *47,* 271–288.

24. ———. An experimental test of the continuity and non-continuity theories of discrimination learning. *J. exp. Psychol.,* 1945, *35,* 253–266.

25. ———, BERGMANN, G., & LIPPITT, R. A study of simple learning under irrelevant motivational-reward conditions. *J. exp. Psychol.,* 1950, *40,* 539–551.

26. ———. Theoretical interpretations of learning. In *Handbook of Experimental Psychology.* New York: John Wiley & Sons, 1950, Chap. 18.

27. THORNDIKE, E. L. *Educational Psychology,* Vol. II. *The Psychology of Learning.* New York Teachers College, Columbia University, 1913.

28. ———, et al. *The Fundamentals of Learning.* New York Teachers College, Columbia University Press, 1932.

29. ———. *The Psychology of Wants, Interests and Attitudes.* New York: Appleton-Century, 1935.

30. TOLMAN, E. C. Theories of learning. In *Comparative Psychology* (F. A. Moss, Ed.), New York: Prentice-Hall, 1934, Chap. XII.

31. ———. The determiners of behavior at a choice point. *Psychol. Rev.,* 1938, *45,* 1–41.

32. ———. Cognitive maps in rats and men. *Psychol. Rev.,* 1948, *55,* 189–208.

33. ———. There is more than one kind of learning. *Psychol. Rev.,* 1949, *56,* 144–156.

34. WHITE, R. K. The case for the Tolman-Lewin interpretation of learning. *Psychol. Rev.,* 1943, *50,* 157–186.

35. ZENER, K. The significance of behavior accompanying conditioned salivary secretion for theories of the conditioned response. *Amer. J. Psychol.,* 1937, *50,* 384–403.

PART III

Discrimination Learning

16

The Nature of Discrimination Learning in Animals [1]

I

Until recently the learning of a discrimination problem by an animal usually was regarded as an unavoidable nuisance preliminary to the study and determination of sensory capacities, and the experimenter's interest in it was more or less limited to devising means of speeding it up in order to proceed as quickly as possible to the main task of determining sensory thresholds. Largely as the result of a suggestion by Lashley (11), however, there has been a definite shift of interest and the discrimination method is now being employed to considerable advantage in studying the learning process itself, particularly the characteristics of the pre-solution period of learning.

Lashley's suggestion [2] was that the behavioral phenomena

[1] The writer is greatly indebted to Professors Clark L. Hull and Henry W. Nissen for many helpful criticisms and suggestions.

[2] Hamilton (1) and Yerkes (19) had previously called attention to the systematic character of the responses of animals in the solution of multiple and quadruple choice problems. MacGillivary and Stone were the first to make an analysis of the systematic modes of response made by the white rat in the acquisition of the discrimination habit. Their study showed the importance of both a perseveration and an alternating tendency and led them to conclude "that 'trial-and-error learning,' so-called, usually does not depict the operation of chance factors alone but rather displays the operation of one or more directive tendencies other than the one that will eventually lead to mastery of the problem." (13, 489.)

commonly observed in the setting up of discrimination habits, such as persistent responses to position or other irrelevant stimuli, might represent "attempted solutions" of the problem by the animal and that if this were the case then the trials preceding solution were in all probability "irrelevant to the actual formation of the association" (11). Acting upon this suggestion Krechevsky carried out a series of investigations of discrimination learning with the white rat (6, 7, 8, 9, 10), in which he showed, by an appropriate analysis of individual records, that the reactions of the animal during the pre-solution period were not a chance affair but consisted of systematic modes of response—position, alternation, etc., until the correct solution was discovered. He termed these systematic pre-solution responses "hypotheses" and, like Lashley, interpreted them as attempts at solution of the problem by the rat, with the implication that they represented a kind of behavior superior in some manner to that usually described as "trial-and-error." Furthermore, he concluded that these experimental facts offer conclusive evidence of the inadequacy of "trial-and-error" theories of learning, because, as he claimed, they contradict the assumption made by the latter that the learning process is, in its early stages, random and haphazard in nature.

While such facts as Krechevsky presents undoubtedly do not fit the description of the early part of learning as consisting of purely random responses, they do not necessarily refute "trial-and-error" theories of learning for the simple reason that the assumption as to the chance character of the responses in learning is not necessary to this type of theory. The assumption has existed, and for some reason continues to exist, only in the minds of its opponents, for even the earliest crude versions of Thorndike (16) and Watson (18) did not hold that the responses made to a problem situation were really random, but pointed out that they were limited to those that the animal, in its previous experience, had learned were relevant to the situation. Similarly, a more recent formulation of this type of theory of learning very definitely states that "The range or variety of reactions which may be evoked by a given problem situation is limited to the reactions which have become conditioned during the life of the organism to one or another stimulus component of that situation" (2), plus, of course, any native or inherited responses.

In a like manner, a sophisticated "trial-and-error" theory of learning would not hold that the order of sequence of trial acts is a haphazard affair, but rather would conceive it as proceeding according to definite principles or laws. Recent "trial-and-error" learning theories recognize full well that it is an organized, lawful, systematic process. As a matter of fact, the theoretical concepts they employ are put forward on this very assumption. Nevertheless, it must be admitted that as yet no learning theory of this type has presented an adequate account of the phenomena of discrimination learning. For the most part they have merely outlined in very general terms the mechanisms underlying this behavior. It is the purpose of the present paper to attempt a theoretical account of discrimination learning founded on "trial-and-error" principles similar in nature to those recently exploited by Hull in the field of problem-box and maze learning (2, 3, 4).

II

In one of the earliest of his recent series of theoretical articles Hull (2) pointed out that there are several fairly distinct kinds of "trial-and-error" learning. Thus he differentiated the complex type exemplified by maze learning, in which the reinforcement or reward comes only at the end of a series of trial acts, from a simple type in which each trial act is reinforced immediately if successful, but is followed either by no special stimulus or by punishment if unsuccessful. Problem-box learning is an example of the latter, simple type, since there are several alternative trial acts possible to a nonvarying situation, only one of which is correct and thus followed by reinforcement.

Discrimination learning is also of this latter type, *i.e.*, each act is reinforced immediately if correct, and not if incorrect. However, discrimination learning is quite different from problem-box learning as further comparison will reveal. Thus, in problem-box learning only one of the alternative responses is ever followed by reward, the others never being reinforced; whereas in discrimination learning the same response may one time be rewarded and, at another time, not be rewarded, depending upon whether the stimulus aspect that determined it does or does not happen to coincide with the correct or cue aspect of the situation. Discrimination learning does not consist, then, in the strengthening of one response relatively to another or others, as is the case in problem-box learning, but involves, rather, the relative strengthening of the excitatory tendency of a certain component of the stimulus complex as compared with that of certain other elements until it attains sufficient strength to determine the response. By the conditions of the experiment the relevant stimulus component is always reinforced and never frustrated, whereas irrelevant components receive both reinforcement and frustration.

Before proceeding to the analysis of this process, however, a discussion will be presented of the main theoretical principles that are to be employed. The first of these is the principle of reinforcement. This principle, as it will be used here, assumes that if a reaction is followed by reward, which may be defined in terms of the occurrence of a final or consummatory response, the excitatory tendencies of the immediate stimulus components are reinforced or strengthened by a certain increment, I. It will be noticed that the statement of this principle is a general one involving no assumptions as to the nature of the reinforcing mechanism. The second principle to be used is that of inhibition or frustration, which states that when a reaction is not rewarded, $i.e.$, when the final or consummatory response is prevented from taking place, the excitatory tendencies of the active stimulus components are weakened by a certain decrement, D. It assumes that this weakening is due to an active, negative process, inhibition, which, adding itself in algebraic fashion to the positive excitatory tendencies, results in lowered strength values.

Certain further assumptions have also been made as to the relative amounts of strengthening and weakening the excitatory tendencies or $S \cdots R$ connections undergo with reinforcement and non-reinforcement, particularly as to variations in amount in different stages of the learning process. Because of the lack of adequate experimental data bearing directly upon this problem it has been necessary to choose more or less arbitrarily from

among the numerous possibilities. Wherever possible, however, an attempt has been made to select those assumptions that
best fit the available experimental evidence. For example, in
considering the amount of strengthening resulting from reinforcement, the studies of the shape of the curve of acquisition of
the conditioned response have been taken into consideration.
Hull (5), in reviewing the evidence from these studies, concluded that this curve is probably S-shaped, which suggests that
the relative strengthening effect of a single reinforcement is
least at the beginning and end of the learning and greatest in
the middle portion.   If, then, one were to plot the amount of
strengthening resulting for each reinforcement from the beginning of the learning process necessary to produce such an
S-shaped curve it would look like the common bell-shaped distribution curve used by statisticians.   The S-shaped learning
curve is simply the integral of such a normal probability curve,
representing the cumulative effects of successive reinforcements.
Accordingly, the assumption has been made that the strengthening effect of reward varies with the stage of acquisition or
strength of the excitatory tendency in this manner.   Assuming
that the strength of any $S \cdots R$ connection (or excitatory tendency of an S to arouse an R) varies between the limiting values
0 and 100, the strengthening effect of a single reinforcement at
various stages of acquisition is assumed to be as in column 2 of
Table 1, the values of which are determined from the function I
(increment of strength) $= \dfrac{3.99}{e^{(s-50)^2/555}}$ in which the values 3.99
and 555 are arbitrary constants dependent upon the individual
learner and "s" is a variable representing the strength of the
$S \cdots R$ connection at any point in the learning process.   Thus
when an $S \cdots R$ connection has a strength (s) of 20, one reinforcement increases its strength 0.79 giving it a value of 20.79.
   Concerning the weakening effect of an $S \cdots R$ connection of
failure of reward, the little evidence that exists suggests that it
varies directly with the strength of the response, being greater
for strong ones than for weak ones.[3]   Accordingly it has been

[3] It should be particularly noted here that we are referring only to the failure
of reward, i.e., failure of the consummatory response to take place, and not to
punishment such as the administration of electric shock. The latter, according

TABLE 1

SHOWING THE STRENGTHENING AND WEAKENING EFFECTS OF REINFORCEMENT AND
NON-REINFORCEMENT FOR VARIOUS STRENGTHS OF EXCITATORY
TENDENCIES OR S • • • R CONNECTIONS

Strength of Excitatory Tendency (s)	Strengthening Effect of a Single Reinforcement $I =_e \dfrac{3.99}{(s-50)^2}$	Weakening Effect of a Single Failure of Reward $D = .05\,s - .5$
1	.05	.00*
5	.10	.00*
10	.22	.00
15	.44	.25
20	.79	.50
25	1.30	.75
30	1.94	1.00
35	2.66	1.25
40	3.33	1.50
45	3.81	1.75
50	3.99	2.00
55	3.81	2.25
60	3.33	2.50
65	2.66	2.75
70	1.94	3.00
75	1.30	3.25
80	.79	3.50
85	.44	3.75
90	.22	4.00
95	.10	4.25
99	.05	4.45

* "D" is assumed to be zero for all values of "s" less than 10.

assumed that the strength of an $S \cdots R$ connection is decreased
or weakened by failure of reward a decrement, $D = .05\,s - .5$,
in which the values .05 and .5 are constants for an individual
learner and "s" is the strength of the $S \cdots R$ connection. These

to the present view, involves an entirely different mechanism. That is, shock
would not be conceived as weakening an $S \cdots R$ connection it followed, but as
strengthening an opposing one. Thus if a particular stimulus through training
had acquired an excitatory tendency eliciting an approaching response, the introduction of electric shock following its occurrence would not weaken this excitatory tendency but would build up or strengthen the excitatory tendency to the
opposing response of withdrawal.

values are given in the third column of Table 1. The selection of a straight line function is for the sake of simplicity. It is quite possible that the function is some type of curvilinear one, *e.g.,* logarithmic.

The selection of the values for the constants has, of course, been purely arbitrary. It will be observed that the relative effects of these two processes have been arbitrarily weighted by the values given to the constants in the two functions so that the maximum amount of reinforcement, that at the point 50, is not greatly different (3.99 and 4.50) from the maximum amount of inhibition, which occurs at the point 100. It is quite possible, of course, that in some individuals the inhibition will be relatively much weaker than the reinforcing function, while in others the opposite will be the case, inhibition being relatively much stronger. The present case is selected merely for purposes of exposition.

A summary of these two theoretical principles including the assumptions as to the nature of the variation of "*I*" and "*D*" with the stage of the learning process are presented below:

(1) The strength of an $S \cdots R$ connection is increased when followed by reward, *i.e.,* the occurrence of a final or consummatory response, by an increment, "*I*," which varies according to the function $I = \dfrac{K}{e^{(s-50)^2/2t^2}}$, in which K and t are constants dependent upon the individual learner, and s is a variable representing the strength of the $S \cdots R$ connection at any point in the learning process.

(2) The strength of an $S \cdots R$ connection is decreased or weakened by failure of reward by a decrement, "*D*," which varies according to the function $D = as - b$, in which a and b are constants for an individual learner and s is a variable representing the strength of the $S \cdots R$ connection at any point in the learning process.

In addition to these two general principles the following basic assumptions or postulates will also be made:

(3) The strength of an $S \cdots R$ connection or of the excitatory tendency of an S to arouse an R varies between the limiting values 0 and 100.

(4) In the case of antagonistic, *i.e.,* mutually exclusive, stimu-

lus-response connections there will result a competition in which that having the greatest strength will prevail.

(5) The total excitatory strength of a stimulus complex is the sum of the excitatory tendencies of the component stimuli.

III

With these theoretical principles or postulates outlined we may now turn our attention to the analysis of the discrimination problem. The various stimulus aspects in the discrimination situation are, undoubtedly, considerable in number. The essential ones in producing the selective response, however, are the visual appearances of the two boxes or doors containing the incentive, and the two stimuli to be differentiated, *e.g.*, circular and triangular forms. It may be assumed that the organism has acquired, in its past experience, reaction tendencies of orientating towards and approaching each of these stimuli so that we have the following four $S \cdots R$ connections: S_{LB} (left box) $\cdots R_A$ (approaching response), S_{RB} (right box) $\cdots R_A$ (approaching response), S_c (circular form) $\cdots R_A$ (approaching response), and S_t (triangular form) $\cdots R_A$ (approaching response). That is to say, it may be assumed that at the beginning of the discrimination experiment the organism already has these $S \cdots R$ connections established in some degree and that, depending upon the amount and kinds of previous experience, they will each have certain, finite strengths between 0 and 100.[4] The situation may be represented schematically as follows, assuming the circular or position component of the stimulus complex to be situated on the left box and the triangle on the right.

[4] It will perhaps be claimed that when one begins with the assumption that the animal has already acquired this response tendency to each of these stimulus aspects, no real explanation of the learning process has been provided because one has already assumed what was to be explained. It should be noted, however, that our present purpose is to account for the behavioral phenomena characteristic of the learning period of the discrimination habit, *i.e.*, the acquisition of the differential character of the animal's behavior so that it always approaches a certain component of the stimulus complex, and not to give an account of the development of the animal's stimulus-reaction system prior to this period. Observation of the behavior capacities of animals at the beginning of experimental training should make it obvious, moreover, that the assumption that they do have such stimulus-response tendencies established in some degree at least, is not a purely gratuitous one.

$$S_{LB} \dots\dots\dots\dots\dots\dots\dots\dots\dots\dots\dots\dots R_A$$
$$S_c \dots\dots\dots\dots\dots\dots\dots\dots\dots\dots\dots\dots R_A$$
$$S_t \dots\dots\dots\dots\dots\dots\dots\dots\dots\dots\dots\dots R_A$$
$$S_{RB} \dots\dots\dots\dots\dots\dots\dots\dots\dots\dots\dots\dots R_A$$

Examination of this stimulus response scheme will show that the four stimulus components are so arranged or paired that there are only two opposed or competing sets of excitatory tendencies; in this instance, those of the circular form and left box and those of the triangular form and right box. Now which of these opposing sets of stimulus components the animal will respond to on any particular trial by approaching, will depend upon which has the greater aggregate of excitatory tendencies eliciting such a response. Thus if we assume in the case of a hypothetical animal just beginning to learn the problem, that the excitatory strengths of the four stimulus components to the approaching response are as follows: [5] $S_{LB} = 80.20$, $S_{RB} = 80.00$, $S_c = 10.00$, and $S_t = 10.00$, then the combined excitatory tendency of S_{LB} and S_c is 90.20 (*i.e.*, 80.20 + 10.00) while the combined strength of S_{RB} and S_t is 90.00 (*i.e.*, 80.00 + 10.00). The combination of the former two stimuli, S_{LB} and S_c, being the stronger, the animal would, other things being equal, respond by approaching them and, being correct, would receive reward with the result that the excitatory tendencies of these two stimulus components to elicit the approaching response would be strengthened, S_{LB} to 80.97 and S_c to 10.22, according to calculations based on Table 1. If, on the following trial, the positive cue stimulus (S_c) is on the right box, the

[5] The particular values assumed here are more or less arbitrary. They were chosen as probably characteristic of a sophisticated subject, *i.e.*, one that is familiar with the experimental situation as the result of learning a previous discrimination problem. Thus the strengths of the box stimulus components are very high as compared with cue stimuli. Presumably, unsophisticated subjects also begin with the box or position stimuli somewhat stronger than the cue stimuli. At least the large majority of animals show a definite tendency for spatial habits or responses to position to be more dominant than habits based on other sensory characteristics. Possibly this is a function of native or inherited factors, although the cage life of laboratory animals might provide for this difference. Certainly most animals have little opportunity to develop responses to such visual characteristics as triangles, circles, squares, etc. On the other hand they might show fairly strong and differentially developed responses to light and dark stimuli. The past experience of the animal is an extremely important factor in this connection and must always be taken into full account.

aggregate excitatory tendency of these stimuli to the approaching response would be 90.22 (*i.e.,* 80.00 + 10.22), while that of S_t and S_{LB} would be 90.97 (*i.e.,* 80.97 + 10.00) with the result that the animal would go to the latter stimuli. On this occasion, however, the response would be incorrect and with nonreward there would develop inhibition or a net weakening of the excitatory tendencies of these stimulus components.[6] The excitatory tendency of S_{LB} to R_A would be weakened to 77.42, while that of S_t would remain 10.00 as inhibition, according to our assumptions (Table 1), does not develop at this strength.

In Table 2 is presented a complete account of the learning process in this hypothetical case. The first two columns of this table show the number of the trial and the position of the positive stimulus. The third column gives the combined strengths of the excitatory tendencies leading to the response of approaching the stimuli at the left box, which on one trial may be S_c and S_{LB} and on another S_t and S_{LB}, as shown in the following three columns. The same data for the response of approaching the stimuli at the right box are given in the next four columns. The final columns indicate to which set of stimuli the approaching response is made and whether this response is correct or not, an incorrect choice being bracketed. The consequences of the responses upon the strengths of the various excitatory tendencies always appear in the next row beneath, which represents their status for this ensuing trial. With the successive reinforcements of the excitatory tendencies of S_c and the failure of reinforcement of those of S_t, the difference between their strengths becomes gradually larger until sufficiently

6 The attention of the reader is here directed to a very important point, namely, that in our hypothetical case the experimental conditions are arranged such that there is no reinforcement whatever following an error. The incorrect box is either locked or without food, and most important of all, the training procedure does not permit the subject to go immediately to the alternative box after the incorrect one is chosen. Instead, the animal is taken out of the situation and, after an interval, given another trial. There is considerable reason to doubt whether, under the procedure of permitting the animal to respond immediately to the correct box after failure, there would develop an inhibition of the excitatory tendencies to the incorrect response. That is, almost immediate reinforcement of the correct response might be expected to disperse this inhibition; and it is conceivable that it might even result in an actual strengthening of these excitatory tendencies, although to a lesser degree than those leading to the correct response, which is always closer in time to the reinforcement (goal-gradient).

TABLE 2

SHOWING A HYPOTHETICAL CASE OF LEARNING IN WHICH THE INITIAL EXCITATORY
TENDENCIES ARE ASSUMED TO BE AS FOLLOWS: $S_{LB} = 80.20$,
$S_{RB} = 80.00$, $S_c = 10.00$, AND $S_t = 10.00$

Trial	Pos. (+) S	Left	R_A			R_A			Right	Response	
			S_c	S_t	S_{LB}	S_c	S_t	S_{RB}			
1	L	90.20	10.00		80.20		10.00	80.00	90.00	L	
2	R	90.97		10.00	80.97	10.22		80.00	90.22	(L)	
3	R	87.42		10.00	77.42	10.22		80,00	90.22	R	
4	L	87.87	10.45		77.42		10.00	80.80	90.80	(R)	
5	L	87.87	10.45		77.42		10.00	77.25	87.25	L	
6	R	88.45		10.00	78.45	10.67		77.25	87.92	(L)	
7	L	85.69	10.67		75.02		10.00	77.25	87.25	(R)	
8	R	85.02		10.00	75.02	10.67		73.90	84.57	(L)	
9	R	81.77		10.00	71.77	10.67		73.90	84.57	R	
10	L	82.71	10.94		71.77		10.00	75.35	85.35	(R)	
											4
11	L	82.71	10.94		71.77		10.00	72.10	82.10	L	
12	R	83.50		10.00	73.50	11.20		72.10	83.30	(L)	
13	R	80.37		10.00	70.37	11.20		72.10	83.30	R	
14	L	81.84	11.47		70.37		10.00	73.75	83.75	(R)	
15	L	81.84	11.47		70.37		10.00	70.60	80.60	L	
16	L	84.00	11.75		72.25		10.00	70.60	80.60	L	
17	R	83.90		10.00	73.90	12.04		70.60	82.64	(L)	
18	R	80.70		10.00	70.70	12.04		70.60	82.64	R	
19	L	83.04	12.34		70.70		10.00	72.45	82.45	L	
20	R	82.55		10.00	72.55	12.65		72.45	85.10	R	
											7
21	R	82.55		10.00	72.55	12.99		74.05	87.04	R	
22	L	85.88	13.33		72.55		10.00	75.47	85.47	L	
23	L	87.84	13.69		74.15		10.00	75.47	85.47	L	
24	R	85.55		10.00	75.55	14.06		75.47	89.53	R	
25	R	85.55		10.00	75.55	14.45		76.72	91.17	R	
26	L	90.41	14.86		75.55		10.00	77.82	87.82	L	
27	R	86.80		10.00	76.80	15.28		77.82	93.10	R	
28	L	92.54	15.74		76.80		10.00	78.82	88.82	L	
29	L	94.12	16.22		77.90		10.00	78.82	88.82	L	
30	R	88.90		10.00	78.90	16.73		78.82	95.55	R	
											10

great to offset, consistently, any other differences that exist between the two competing sets of stimulus components. Learning is completed only when this stage is reached. Thus at the

seventeenth trial it will be seen that although the difference between S_c and S_t is 2.04 points, this differential is not sufficient to
offset the difference of 3.30 between S_{LB} and S_{RB}. The combined excitatory tendency of the correct stimulus components,
i.e., those of the right box, of 82.64, is not as great as that of the
incorrect ones, *i.e.,* those at the left box, of 83.90, with the result
that the response is made to the latter.

The above account does not, of course, tell the whole story.
In order to simplify the exposition such factors as disuse and
spontaneous recovery from inhibition have been purposely
neglected. These factors undoubtedly operate to complicate
the learning process and they must ultimately be taken into
consideration. Similarly, there are various other factors, functions of the experimental situation, that usually have to be considered. For example, learning may be delayed markedly if
the connection between the relevant stimulus and the required
motor response is not sufficiently obtrusive and clear to the
animal. The mere presence of the cue stimulus somewhere in
the experimental situation does not guarantee its impingement
on the animal's sensorium at or near the critical moment of
response. This was, undoubtedly, an important, if not the
chief reason for the greater difficulty that was experienced in
setting up discrimination habits in the older forms of indirect
apparatus. The more recent types, such as those of Lashley
(*12*) and Munn (*15*), are arranged in such a manner as to insure
to a very high degree that the cue stimulus operates each trial.

IV

In the preceding section a hypothetical picture or logically
possible account of the nature of discrimination learning has
been outlined in terms of "trial-and-error" principles of reinforcement and inhibition. An attempt will now be made to
show how, on the basis of these assumptions, it is possible to
explain (deduce) the various behavioral phenomena characteristic of this kind of learning. This section will be particularly
concerned with such behavioral facts as Krechevsky and others
have found to characterize the pre-solution period of discrimi-

nation learning and also the behavior of animals in an insoluble discrimination problem.

The explanation or deduction of the appearance of systematic responses at the very outset of the learning, such, for example, as the spatial habit of always choosing the left box, is fairly simple and obvious. If the excitatory tendency of one of the position stimulus components, *i.e.*, one of the food boxes, S_{LB} or S_{RB}, is, either because of innate factors or past training, much stronger than the other, the response will consistently be made to the stronger, except as chance factors operate to override the difference. This systematic position habit will persist until the difference between excitatory tendencies of these stimulus components becomes, through the action of reinforcement and non-reinforcement, more or less eliminated, or until the difference between the strengths of the excitatory tendencies of the positive and negative cue components becomes sufficiently great to offset it. In the latter case, it should be noticed, the animals would be expected to fall back to a position response if the cue stimuli are removed, a phenomenon well known to everyone who has carried out such experiments.

Position responses, to the right or left, represent by far the most common systematic responses made by animals when first introduced to the discrimination problem. If, however, the excitatory tendencies of the competing stimulus components are not sufficiently different in strength to result in such a preferential tendency one would expect that a "perseverance" habit would be adopted, the animal tending to repeat the response last correct and to continue choosing it until it is incorrect, when it would shift to the alternative because of the shift in balance of strength of the excitatory tendencies. In a similar manner, other systematic responses at the beginning of learning are explained in terms of innate or acquired differences in the excitatory strengths of one of the position or spatial stimulus components.

More difficult to account for than the presence of a systematic position response at the very beginning of learning is the development of such a habit after an initial period of no apparent preference or of one of an opposite tendency. The occurrence of the positive stimulus on the same side several times in succession, say two or three, might be expected to give a temporary advantage to this particular spatial component of the stimulus complex.   One would expect it to be merely temporary, for with the subsequent greater number of trials on the opposite side this difference in their strengths should again be equalized. However, it should be noticed that whether such equalization will be attained depends upon the stage of acquisition of the $S_{RB} \cdots R_A$ and $S_{LB} \cdots R_A$ connections.   If these latter are relatively weak, as presumably would be the case with unsophisticated subjects, there would be or soon would develop a considerable discrepancy between the strengthening and weakening effects of the reinforcing and inhibitory mechanisms, the former becoming much greater in value than the latter.   Such a discrepancy would soon lead to the setting up of a preferential position habit, for with the presentation of the positive cue stimulus in the same position two or three times in succession the excitatory tendencies of this spatial component of the stimulus would be increased in strength to such an extent over the other that the greater number of subsequent non-reinforcements of responses to it would not reduce its strength sufficiently to equate them once more.   In contrast, with sophisticated experimental subjects, the excitatory strengths of the position stimulus components (S_{LB} and S_{RB}) are relatively high as the result of past experience, and the subject would not tend to develop such strong, persistent position habits, as the inhibitory mechanism is, at this stage, comparable in strength to the reinforcing mechanism, being even stronger beyond a certain point. The balance between these two mechanisms would tend to maintain the equalization of the excitatory tendencies leading to the two boxes and thus prevent the establishment of any great difference between them.

Tables 2 and 3 show these two contrasting cases, the latter representing portions of the hypothetical learning of an unsophisticated subject while the former shows the learning of the experienced subject.   An examination and comparison of these two tables reveals a considerable number of interesting phenomena.   First of all, it will be observed that a persistent position habit does not develop in the case of the sophisticated subject (Table 2), but is broken up immediately with failure

TABLE 3

SHOWING A HYPOTHETICAL CASE OF LEARNING IN WHICH THE INITIAL EXCITATORY TENDENCIES ARE ASSUMED TO BE AS FOLLOWS: $S_{LB} = 35.00$, $S_{RB} = 35.20$, $S_c = 8.00$, $S_t = 7.00$

Trial	Pos. (+) S	Left	S_c	S_t	S_{LB}	S_c	S_t	S_{RB}	Right	Response	
			R_A			R_A					
1	L	43.00	8.00		35.00		7.00	35.20	42.20	L	
2	R	44.66		7.00	37.66	8.17		35.20	43.39	(L)	
3	R	43.28		7.00	36.28	8.17		35.20	43.39	R	
4	L	44.62	8.34		36.28		7.00	37.88	44.88	(R)	
5	L	44.62	8.34		36.28		7.00	36.48	43.48	L	
6	R	46.12		7.00	39.12	8.52		36.48	45.00	(L)	
7	R	44.67		7.00	37.67	8.52		36.48	45.00	R	
8	L	46.37	8.70		37.67		7.00	39.35	46.35	L	
9	R	47.70		7.00	40.70	8.70		39.35	48.05	R	
10	L	49.58	8.88		40.70		7.00	42.61	49.61	(R)	6
11	R	47.70		7.00	40.70	8.88		40.98	49.86	R	
12	L	49.77	9.07		40.70		7.00	44.43	51.43	(R)	
13	L	49.77	9.07		40.70		7.00	42.70	49.70	L	
14	R	51.12		7.00	44.12	9.26		42.70	51.96	R	
15	R	51.12		7.00	44.12	9.45		46.32	55.77	R	
16	L	53.79	9.65		44.12		7.00	50.20	57.20	(R)	
17	L	53.77	9.65		44.12		7.00	48.20	55.20	(R)	
18	R	51.12		7.00	44.12	9.65		46.30	55.95	R	
19	L	53.98	9.86		44.12		7.00	50.18	57.18	(R)	
20	R	51.12		7.00	44.12	9.86		48.18	58.04	R	
Trials 21–80 every response to right with consequent 50 per cent success.											6
81	L	69.01	24.89		44.12		7.00	65.41	72.41	(R)	
82	R	51.12		7.00	44.12	24.89		62.64	87.53	R	
83	R	51.12		7.00	44.12	26.17		65.64	91.81	R	
84	L	71.73	27.61		44.12		7.00	68.22	75.22	(R)	
85	L	71.73	27.61		44.12		7.00	65.31	72.31	(R)	
86	R	51.12		7.00	44.12	27.61		62.55	90.16	R	
87	R	51.12		7.00	44.12	29.23		65.56	94.79	R	
88	L	75.21	31.09		44.12		7.00	68.15	75.15	L	
89	R	54.85		7.00	47.85	33.18		68.15	101.33	R	
90	L	83.43	35.58		47.85		7.00	70.36	77.36	L	7
91	R	58.80		7.00	51.80	38.12		70.36	108.48	R	
92	L	93.01	41.21		51.80		7.00	72.25	79.25	L	
93	L	100.44	44.68		55.76		7.00	72.25	79.25	L	
94	R	66.51		7.00	59.51	48.46		72.25	120.71	R	
95	R	66.51		7.00	59.51	52.43		73.89	126.32	R	
96	L	115.89	56.38		59.51		7.00	75.33	82.33	L	
97	L	122.99	60.08		62.91		7.00	75.33	82.33	L	
98	R	72.86		7.00	65.86	63.40		75.33	138.73	R	
99	L	132.16	66.30		65.86		7.00	76.59	83.59	L	
100	R	75.39		7.00	68.39	68.78		76.59	145.37	R	10

Strength of Component Excitatory Tendencies

on any temporarily preferred side, the response becoming one of perseveration with success and alternation upon failure until the solution of the problem. The unsophisticated subject, however, soon develops a considerable difference in the excitatory strengths of the two position stimulus components and consequently adopts a position habit. It is extremely interesting to note, moreover, that as training continues this difference increases for the reason that the reinforcements have the greater effect, although they equal the frustrations in number of occurrences. It is only when the difference between the excitatory strengths of the positive and negative cue stimuli has reached an amount greater than the difference between the strengths of the position stimuli that the animal breaks over to the non-preferred side. This represents, of course, solution of the problem.

Assuming that such unconsidered factors as forgetting, spontaneous recovery from inhibition, and various chance factors will not change this theoretical picture to any significant extent, we have here an interesting and easily tested deduction, namely, that an animal that develops and maintains a long persistent position habit will, when it finally abandons it, proceed directly to the correct discrimination response. Or, in the terminology of Krechevsky, animals that persist for a considerable time in a position hypothesis will, upon rejecting it, immediately adopt the correct hypothesis without trying others, such as perseveration with success and alternation upon failure.

In his series of experiments on discrimination learning in rats, Krechevsky introduced and made considerable use of an insoluble problem, in which no one stimulus, color, form, or position, was regularly the correct one. The development of a systematic mode of response in such a situation was interpreted by him as evidence that the animal, in part at least, must initiate or originate responses and that they are not simply forced upon it "ab extra." While one must grant that the presence or development of such systematic responses demands that something within the organism itself is differentiated or becomes so, for the experimental situation at no time contains a selective factor, nevertheless, it is not at all necessary to ascribe to the animal the powers that Krechevsky's interpretation suggests.   It can be easily demonstrated that the theoretical structure developed above would lead to the expectation than an animal would adopt systematic modes of response in such an unsolvable situation.   Thus the large majority of these hypotheses are positional, to the right or to the left, which, because of their very quick development, suggests that the excitatory strengths of one of the position stimuli, $i.e.$, S_{RB} or S_{LB}, is stronger than the other at the beginning of the experiment.   The presence of a dark-going habit at the very beginning of the experiment would similarly be explained as a difference in strength between the dark and light stimulus excitatory tendencies.   But even without the advantage of such assumed initial differences between the strengths of the various stimuli, it can be shown that such systematic modes would still be expected.   The demonstration is similar to that in the case of the development of position habits after an initial period of no apparent preference in the regular discrimination problem.

V

In interpreting the results of his studies on discrimination learning, Krechevsky described the behavior of the rat during the pre-solution period as consisting of a series of "hypotheses." This name was chosen, he explains, because it suggested four behavioral characteristics describable by the terms (a) systematic, (b) docile, (c) selective, and (d) self-initiated.   Now obviously such terms merely provide a description and name for the phenomena.   They do not greatly further our understanding of them.   That Krechevsky, himself, recognizes this is indicated by the following quotations from a joint publication by himself and Tolman (17), in which they discuss the relationship between their concepts of "means-end-readiness" and "hypothesis."

Thus it is to be strongly impressed upon the reader that all such terms as those of "desire," "aversion," "expectation," "hypothesis," "means-end-readiness" are merely names, or concepts, for relationships between variables.   They do not say anything about the *vera causa* of these relations. (17, p. 63.)

Finally, in closing, it may be pointed out that this descriptive problem of the behavior of means-end-readiness and hypothesis in learning and unlearning is but one phase of the total problem as to all causal conditions underlying the determination and appearance of means-end-readinesses and hypotheses. What, for instance, brings about the initial appearance of certain subordinate hypotheses rather than others, and what are the causes of the alternations between one subordinate hypothesis and another. (*17*, pp. 68–69.)

One could certainly have no quarrel with this point of view, except, perhaps, to protest the use and redefinition of terms which already have connotations that go beyond the limitations they set upon them, for it is an unfortunate fact that most readers quickly forget the new definition of the terms and very soon are interpreting them in all of their old meanings. In fact, Krechevsky, himself, seems, at times, to have departed from the strict definition of his description and has tended to think of the hypotheses as being purposive and insightfully "attempted solutions" in the more generally accepted sense of such terms. This is most apparent in the attempts he has made to indicate the difference between his view and the old "trial-and-error" interpretations. The latter, he insists, err in viewing the behavior as consisting of blind, non-docile habits to the external situation. According to him the responses of the animal are to be conceived of as something beyond this, in some way superior to it, having the character of insight.

But whatever Krechevsky's view of the matter may be, one can, nevertheless, advance the hypothesis that the animal is an organism, capable of insight, that sets out to solve the problem confronting it by trying out, systematically, one of its repertoire of hypotheses, which, failing of solution, leads it to initiate and try out another and another until the correct one is hit upon. Although such a view ignores such critical questions as to what constitutes failure of a hypothesis, and how this leads to its abandonment and the trying out of another, and what determines the order of attempted hypotheses, it does lead to certain implications which can be tested experimentally. One of these implications is that if the values of the cue stimuli are reversed, *i.e.*, the positive stimulus made negative and vice versa, *before* the animal begins to show any learning whatever, it should not necessarily make for any slower learning of the reversed problem; for, according to this theory, the animal selects and concentrates, in turn, on certain aspects of the experimental situation as offering possibilities of providing a solution and does not react to the real cue aspect until just at or just preceding the time of solution. Certainly the statement by Lashley that "the practice preceding and the errors following are irrelevant to the actual formation of the association" very definitely supports such an interpretation.

The implication of our own hypothesis for such an experiment, on the other hand, is quite definitely opposite in nature. Thus, if we begin with S_t and S_c equal in strength, or approximately so, and provide training as in the first ten trials of our theoretical example in Table 2, such that the excitatory value of S_c becomes greater than that of S_t, but not sufficiently so as to result in the animal reacting to it more often than chance, a reversal of the positive and negative relationship of the stimulus cues will obviously require a greater number of trials for S_t to become sufficiently stronger than S_c to insure a persistent response to it. Whereas in our hypothetical example the last error was made on trial 17, the final error with the reversal of stimulus cues would not be until trial 55.

Fortunately, experimental evidence that makes possible a comparison of the validity of these conflicting implications has recently become available. McCulloch and Pratt (14), in a study of the pre-solution period in weight discrimination by white rats, carried out an experiment that closely approaches the above conditions. The purpose of this particular part of their experiment was to determine whether the assumption "that repeated trials work in a cumulative manner to produce a change in the animal which is necessary for discrimination" (14, p. 271), or whether Lashley's interpretation, quoted above, is correct. The issue is essentially the same as presented here, the present theory being an attempt to indicate the nature of the factors operating to produce the cumulative change in the animal. From the theoretical principles here assumed, the deduction follows that there will be such a cumulative change which leads ultimately to discrimination. The results these experimenters obtained support the deduction of the present theory and are opposed to the implication of the insight hypothesis.

The number of errors for the control group, *i.e.*, the one in which there was no reversal of the cue stimuli, was 52.04 ± 3.28, while the experimental group, in which the stimuli were reversed after 28 trials, made 64.35 ± 2.77 errors even after the shift, and approximately 78 errors during the complete period of training. Another experimental group that was given training (84 trials) until they apparently were just beginning to discriminate subsequently made 94.65 errors before learning the converse problem. The authors interpret this result as further evidence favoring the assumption that the learning process represents a cumulative change and furthermore that, at the point at which the animal is just learning a problem, it is not particularly insightful or docile with respect to the relevant stimulus cues. The present writer is now carrying out further studies testing these conflicting theories with chimpanzees serving as subjects. These animals, with their highly complex behavior systems, might be expected to be particularly favorable subjects from the point of view of the insight hypothesis.

In concluding this discussion the writer would like to anticipate and attempt to answer a form of criticism with which the type of theory presented here almost invariably has to contend. The criticism is that the kinds of concepts employed by it, such as connections or bonds, reinforcement, inhibition, etc., are inadequate to explain the behavioral phenomena characteristic of learning because the learning process, far from being the blind mechanical affair these concepts imply, consists of unified, meaningful, and purposive behavior. Furthermore, the criticism usually continues, learning behavior does not consist of such isolated part or unit responses, but is an organized, integrated process involving the development of insight.

Such a criticism of theoretical concepts reveals an unfortunate misunderstanding of the relation of a theory to the facts it is proposed to explain. It is not, as such critics seem to think, the theoretical concepts themselves and their hypothetical relations (principles) that must necessarily coincide or agree with the facts of experience, but it is the logical consequences or deductions that follow from the theories. The test of the adequacy of any theoretical structure is that the logical consequences that flow from it coincide with the events of experience, *i.e.,* the learning behavior of the animal in this instance. The descriptive characteristics of the facts of behavior do not need to be found in the basic theoretical concepts and principles, and, conversely, the failure to find anything in learning behavior descriptively resembling the theoretical concepts is no disproof of their adequacy as a scientific explanation. Finally the question as to whether the theoretical concepts do or do not correspond with reality is a problem not for science but for philosophy. The scientist can justify such ideal constructs wholly from the pragmatic standpoint that they serve as an aid to the integration and comprehension of the observed phenomena. He is under no obligation to imply nor yet deny the possibility of their correspondence with reality.

VI

In summary, the behavioral phenomena characteristic of discrimination learning, such as the non-random, systematic nature of the pre-solution responses, have been shown to be entirely consistent with a "trial-and-error" type of learning theory. Employing clearly defined principles of reinforcement and non-reinforcement (inhibition), a hypothetical picture or logically possible account of the nature of discrimination has been developed. This theoretical structure provides a rational account of such phenomena as, for example, position responses and the habit of perseveration-with-success-and-alternation-with-failure, and, unlike the so-called insight-hypothesis, which states that the organism, itself, initiates various responses (termed hypotheses) as attempts at solution of the problem until the correct one is hit upon, permits of an account of the conditions determining the appearance and succession of these various modes of response.

While no attempt has been made in the present article to work out in detail the experimental implications of these theoretical principles the following deductions have been made:

(1) Naive, untrained animals will tend to show a more pronounced tendency towards position habits than experienced animals in the solution of discrimination problems.

(2) The response pattern of perseverating on the side which

is correct and of shifting to the other on failure will tend to predominate in the experienced animal.

(3) In naive animals that show a long, perfectly consistent position response in the learning period the solution of the problem will occur simultaneously with the abolishment of the position habit.

(4) If the positive and negative relation of the cue stimuli are reversed before the animal is responding to the correct stimulus more often than chance a greater number of trials will be required to learn the reversed problem than would have been necessary for the original problem. A corollary of this deduction is that this difference will be proportional to the time between the beginning of the training and the reversal of the positive and negative stimuli.

(5) Animals will manifest systematic modes of response in an insoluble problem, in which no stimulus is regularly the correct one.

REFERENCES

1. HAMILTON, G. V., A study of trial and error reactions in animals, *J. Animal Behav.*, 1911, *1*, 33–36.
2. HULL, C. L., Simple trial-and-error learning: a study in psychological theory, *Psychol. Rev.*, 1930, *37*, 241–256.
3. ——, The goal gradient hypothesis and maze learning, *Psychol Rev.*, 1932, *39*, 25–43.
4. ——, The concept of the habit-family hierarchy and maze learning. Parts I and II, *Psychol. Rev.*, 1934, *41*, 33–52; 134–152.
5. ——, Learning: II. The factor of the conditioned reflex, Chap. 9 in *A Handbook of General Experimental Psychology* (ed. by C. Murchison), Worcester, Mass: Clark University Press, pp. 382–455.
6. KRECHEVSKY, I., "Hypotheses" versus "chance" in the pre-solution period in sensory discrimination-learning, *University California Publ. in Psychol.*, 1932, *6*, 27–44.
7. ——, The genesis of "hypotheses" in rats, *University California Publ. in Psychol.*, 1932, *6*, 45–64.
8. ——, The docile nature of "hypotheses," *J. comp. Psychol.*, 1933, *15*, 429–441.
9. ——, Hereditary nature of "hypotheses," *J. comp. Psychol.*, 1933, *16*, 99–116.
10. ——. Brain mechanisms and "hypotheses," *J. comp. Psychol.*, 1935, *19*, 425–462.
11. LASHLEY, K. S., *Brain Mechanisms and Intelligence*, Chicago: University Chicago Press, 1929.

12. ———, The mechanism of vision: 1. A method for rapid analysis of pattern-vision in the rat, *J. genet. Psychol.*, 1930, *37*, 453–460.

13. MacGillivary, M. E. and Stone, C. P., Suggestions toward an explanation of systematic errors made by albino rats in a multiple discrimination apparatus, *J. genet. Psychol.*, 1930, *38*, 484–489.

14. McCulloch, T. L. and Pratt, J. G., A study of pre-solution in weight discrimination by white rats, *J. comp. Psychol.*, 1934, *18*, 271–290.

15. Munn, N. L., An apparatus for testing visual discrimination in animals, *J. genet. Psychol.*, 1931, *39*, 342–358.

16. Thorndike, E. L., *Animal Intelligence*, New York: The Macmillan Co., 1911.

17. Tolman, E. C. and Krechevsky, I., Means-end-readiness and hypothesis: a contribution to comparative psychology, *Psychol. Rev.*, 1933, *40*, 60–70.

18. Watson, J. B., *Behavior: An Introduction to Comparative Psychology*, New York: The Henry Holt and Co., 1914.

19. Yerkes, R. M., The mental life of monkeys and apes: a study of ideational behavior, *Behav. Monog.*, 1916, *3*, No. 1, Serial No. 12.

17

The Differential Response in Animals to Stimuli Varying Within a Single Dimension[1]

I

The differential response of animals to stimuli involving differences of degree, such as intensity, size and wave length, has long been regarded as being based on the relational character of the stimulus situation. Prior even to the emphasis given this interpretation by the new Gestalt movement, early American investigators of the problem (2, 4, 5, 9) had concluded that animals learn to respond to the relative properties of the stimulus situation rather than to the specific properties of one or other of the stimulus objects. They inferred from these experiments that the animals possessed the ability to perceive the relationship, larger, brighter, etc., and to act in accordance with this ability in new situations in which the same relationship entered. Later, the experiments of Köhler with hen, chimpanzee and human child (12) led to a similar emphasis of the relational aspect. The response of the animal in such instances, he insisted, is not to an isolated "sensation-process" but to a "structure-process." It is responding to properties whose character is a function of the situation as a whole and not to any

[1] This paper was presented in a preliminary form before the American Psychological Association, in Hanover, New Hampshire, September 1936.

specific or absolute property of a part or aspect of it.[2]   Both his experiments and the theoretical interpretation he placed upon them have received considerable attention and have greatly influenced thinking on the problem (*12, 13*).

But while the relational viewpoint in one form or another has dominated the attempts at an interpretation of these phenomena, the experimental studies on the problem, almost without exception, have shown that response to relationship is by no means universal.   In the transposition tests, in which stimuli of different absolute value but having the same objective relation to one another are employed, the animals sometimes respond in accordance with the relationship, but in a large number of instances they fail to do so.   These negative results have led certain psychologists who are opposed to the Gestalt viewpoint to be critical of relational interpretations and to deny that the behavior in such experiments necessarily involves either "transposition of structure properties" or "abstract relative judgments" (*7, 18, 19, 20*).   Beyond pointing out, however, that absolute factors, under certain conditions at least, play an important part, they have had little of a positive nature to offer in the way of an explanation.

II

In a recent article (*16*) a theoretical schema based on stimulus-response principles and concepts was proposed to explain the nature of discrimination learning in animals.   According to

---

2 There is, however, a considerable difference between the views of American investigators and the German Gestalters which, unfortunately, has not always been clearly understood by some recent writers on this problem.   In a certain sense, indeed, their views may be said to be quite opposed to each other.   Thus the American group (and this seems to include the current American configurationists) has held to the notion that the response, in such experiments, represents a fairly high order of mental activity, one involving a relational judgment or a definite experiencing of the relationship in the form of some abstract principle expressible as "food-in-the-larger," "always-in-the-brighter," etc.   According to the German Gestalt psychologists (*11, 12, 13*), on the other hand, response to such relations is a very elementary and natural form of reaction rather than an achievement of intelligence.   Its occurrence in animals, particularly the more primitive forms, is conclusive evidence of what is to them the fundamental fact that the stimulus situation is from the beginning organized as a "whole" and that response is based on "whole" properties of the stimulus.

this hypothesis, discrimination learning is conceived as a cumulative process of building up the strength of the excitatory tendency of the positive stimulus cue (*i.e.*, the tendency of this stimulus to evoke the response of approaching it) by means of the successive reinforcements of the response to it, as compared with the excitatory strength of the negative stimulus, responses to which receive no reinforcements. Theoretically, this process continues until the difference between the excitatory strengths of the two cue stimuli is sufficiently large to offset always any differences in strength that may exist between other aspects of the stimulus situation which happen to be allied in their action with one or other of the cue stimuli. That is to say, the difference between the excitatory strengths of the cue stimuli, positive and negative, must reach a certain minimum or threshold amount before the animal will respond consistently to the positive stimulus.[3]

The theory as presented in that article was concerned with the discrimination of stimulus objects which differed, objectively at least, in the single characteristic of form; for example, triangle, circle, or square. It was implicitly assumed that there was no transfer of the excitatory tendency acquired by the positive form-character to the negative form-character, and likewise, that the negative or inhibitory tendency of the latter was not transferred to the former.[4]

---

[3] This is, of course, only a skeletal and purely conceptual outline of the processes that lead to the establishment of the discrimination habit. It is not intended to be, and in no sense should be construed as, a descriptive account of the behavior of the animal in the discrimination situation. Moreover, the animal learns many other responses in addition to the final, selective approaching reaction. Prominent and important among these are what have been termed, for want of a better name, "preparatory" responses. These latter consist of the responses which lead to the reception of the appropriate aspects of the total environmental complex on the animal's sensorium, *e.g.*, the orientation and fixation of head and eyes towards the critical stimuli. That is, the animal learns to "look at" one aspect of the situation rather than another because of the fact that this response has always been followed within a short temporal interval by the final goal response. Responses providing other sensory receptions are not similarly reinforced in a systematic fashion and hence tend to disappear.

[4] In the discrimination of stimulus objects differing only in size, the stimulus aspects which the objects have in common, such as brightness, wave length, etc., receive both reinforcement and non-reinforcement. Their effective excitatory strengths do not, then, change greatly, unless considerable overtraining is given. This problem will be discussed briefly in a later portion of the paper.

In the case of such continuous dimensions as size and brightness, however, it would seem reasonable to assume that there is some transfer of training, at least between nearby members of a series. There is, in fact, direct experimental evidence in support of such a belief. Thus Pavlov reports that when an animal is conditioned to a stimulus, *e.g.*, a tone of a certain wave length, tones of different wave length also acquire the capacity to evoke the response. His experiments suggest further that the more unlike the tone is in wave length from the one employed in the original training, the less will be the transfer or irradiation of the conditioning *(14)*. Bass and Hull *(1)* have also demonstrated such a spread or generalization of conditioned excitatory and inhibitory tendencies in human subjects.

The essential characteristics of our hypothesis, as they pertain to the type of discrimination problem involving a stimulus dimension of a continuous nature, can be presented most briefly and clearly in the diagram of Figure 1. (1) We shall assume

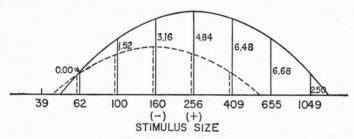

Fig. 1. Diagrammatic representation of relations between the hypothetical generalization curves, positive and negative, after training on the stimulus combination 256 (+) and 160 (−).

that, as a result of training or successive reinforcements, the positive stimulus, 256,[5] of the combination 256+ and 160−, acquires an excitatory tendency to the response of approaching it of the amount or strength represented by the solid line at that point. (2) We shall assume that there is a generalization of this acquired excitatory tendency to stimulus objects of similar size

---

[5] We shall describe the stimulus-object simply by a number which represents its area in square centimeters, ignoring other stimulus characteristics which are the same for all stimuli.

and that this generalization follows a gradient such as that represented by the upper curved line. (3) We shall postulate also that with failure of reinforcement of response to stimulus 160, experimental extinction will take place and a negative or inhibitory tendency will be developed to the amount indicated by the broken line at the point on the abscissa marked 160. (4) Similarly it will be assumed that there is a generalization of this inhibitory tendency according to the gradient shown by the lower curved line. (5) And, lastly, we shall assume that the effective excitatory strength of a stimulus is the algebraic summation of these two positive (excitatory) and negative (inhibitory) tendencies. This value is indicated graphically by the distance between the upper and lower generalization curves and numerically by the number to the right of each line.

The selection of the curves of generalization has been more or less arbitrary as little experimental evidence bearing on the problem is available. There are, nevertheless, one or two general guiding principles that have been followed. One important assumption that has been made is that sensory process is a logarithmic function of the stimulus dimension (size), and accordingly the latter has been plotted on a logarithmic scale. This assumption is in line with the Weber-Fechner relation between sensory and stimulus dimensions. This relationship has, of course, been found to hold only within a certain middle range of stimulus values. Beyond these points certain modifications would have to be made in this relationship. Finally, because elaborate mathematical treatment does not seem to be warranted at the present stage of development, our presentation is essentially graphical. The particular curves have been constructed, however, from mathematical equations relating stimulus values and positive and negative tendencies.[6]

Examination of Figure 1 reveals the fact that the hypothetical, effective strengths of the various stimuli after the original training on the stimulus pair 256+ and 160− are such that in the

---

[6] The curves of generalization of the positive excitatory tendency all have the equation E (excitatory tendency) $= 10 - 20D^2$ in which D is the distance in logarithmic units between the test stimulus and the training stimulus, i.e., $D = (\log S_1 - \log S_T)$. The curves of generalization of the negative or inhibitory tendency have the equation I (inhibition) $= 6 - 20D^2$ in Figs. 1 and 2, $I = 6 - 10D^2$ in Figure 3.

transposition test combinations, 409 and 256, and 160 and 100, the effective excitatory strength of the larger stimulus is in each case the greater. Thus the effective strength of 409 is 6.48, as compared with 4.84 for stimulus 256, and the strength of stimulus 160 is 3.16, while that of 100 is only 1.52. The implication of the hypothesis is that the animal should respond consistently [7] to the larger stimulus in each of these transposition tests. Similarly, as shown in Figure 2, subjects trained positively to the smaller stimulus, 160, and negatively to the larger, 256, should respond in each of the test combinations, 100 and 160 and 256 and 409, to the smaller stimulus.

We have shown, then, that it is possible to deduce from stimulus-response concepts and principles that animals will respond to stimulus differences of degree in a manner which has hitherto been interpreted as involving a perception of a relationship or response to a structure-process (larger, brighter, etc.). According to the present hypothesis, however, the animal is responding in each situation to the particular stimulus object which has the greater effective excitatory strength. There is in the preceding account no assumption of a perception of the relational character of the situation.

III

Now let us consider Figure 1 further. We have seen that after training in the combination 256+ and 160— the animal's response in the transposition tests with 409 and 256 should be to the *larger*, 409. In the next combination, however, 655 and 409, the difference (.20) is only slightly in favor of the larger

[7] Whether the response will be consistently, that is 100 per cent, to the larger of the test stimuli will depend on the size of the difference between their effective strengths. This minimum or threshold requirement for a consistent response is a somewhat difficult matter to handle theoretically. One possible indication of it, however, is the amount of the difference between the strengths of the training stimuli, which, in the present instances, is 1.68. Presumably the threshold value would be somewhat less than this difference as training is usually continued, depending upon the criterion of learning adopted, beyond the point at which the animal is just able to respond with 100 per cent consistency. In the present example we shall arbitrarily assume this threshold value at 1.50. A difference less than this would lead, depending on the amount, to the choice of the stronger stimulus somewhere between 50 and 100 per cent of the trials.

stimulus, and the response should be chance. But, in the still larger combination, 1049 and 655, the effective strengths are such that the response would be expected to favor 655, the *smaller* of the two stimuli. The same result, response to smaller, would be expected for the 1678 and 1049 combination. It is apparent then that the results for the transposition tests depend upon the particular stimulus combination employed. The response may be to the larger in some tests, in some to the smaller, and, in some combinations, to the larger and smaller equally often—that is, a chance response.

In view of the fact that the point (stimulus pair) at which these changes occur depends upon the extent of the individual generalization curves, it is not possible to make any specific deductions concerning them. The somewhat general implication may be drawn, however, that the amount of transfer will be a function of the absolute change in the test stimuli, the transfer decreasing as the test stimuli are made more different from the training pair. A survey of the experimental literature on discrimination behavior reveals evidence which supports this deduction. Klüver (*10*) reports an investigation of size discrimination in two Java monkeys which were trained to choose the larger of two rectangles, 300 and 150 sq. cms. In critical tests each subject was presented with the following four stimulus combinations: 1536 *vs.* 768, 600 *vs.* 300, 150 *vs.* 75 and 8.64 *vs.* 4.32, and in agreement with the general deduction from our hypothesis we find that the percentage of test responses consonant with the training response, that is, to the larger stimulus, were much less in the extreme pairs than in the combinations nearer to the training pair. In the former, both animals responded approximately only 50 per cent of the time to the larger stimulus, whereas their responses to the larger in the 600 *vs.* 300 and the 150 *vs.* 75 combinations averaged 72 and 97 per cent respectively.

Gulliksen's experiment with white rats (*6*) also presents data relative to this aspect of our problem. After training them on circular stimuli 9 and 6 centimeters in diameter, he found that the more similar the test combination to the training pair, the higher was the percentage of responses consistent with the original training. His results for the various test combinations were as follows: 7½ *vs.* 5 = 97 per cent; 12 *vs.* 9 = 74 per cent; 6 *vs.* 4 = 67 per cent; 18 *vs.* 12 = 55 per cent.

In a series of experiments with chimpanzees designed to test various aspects of the theory, the writer also has obtained data bearing on this particular problem. Before presenting these results, however, a brief description of the experimental procedures is given. The discrimination apparatus has been described in detail elsewhere (*17*). Briefly, it consisted of two small stimulus (food) boxes which were presented to the animal by pushing the platform on which they were placed up to a position one inch from the cage wall, so that the animal could reach its fingers through the two-inch wire mesh, push open the boxes and obtain the food. The stimulus forms, squares cut from no. 28 galvanized iron and enameled a glossy white, were fitted with a clamp by means of which they could be fastened to the front of the boxes.

In the training series both positive and negative boxes were loaded with food, but the negative one was locked. When the subject responded correctly by opening the box which carried the positive stimulus, it obtained a small piece of banana as a reward. In the case of an incorrect response, the box was found locked and the apparatus was immediately withdrawn so that there was no opportunity to correct the error. Twenty trials, spaced from 20 to 30 seconds apart, were given in each experimental session. Training was continued on a problem until the subject satisfied a criterion of 90 per cent correct in twenty trials, the last ten of which were all correct.

In that part of the experiment concerned with the particular problem with which we are at present concerned, five adult subjects were used. Three of these individuals were trained originally to respond to the larger of two white squares, 160 and 100, while the other two were trained to respond positively to the smaller square of the combination 256 and 409. Beginning on the day after the learning of these discriminations a series of transposition tests (10 trials each) was given daily, followed by 10 trials on the training combination. The subjects trained positively to the larger were given tests on still larger stimuli, and those trained positively to smaller were tested on smaller combinations. All responses in the test series were rewarded.

Table 1 shows the results for these tests in terms of the percentage of responses consonant with the original training.   The upper half of the table presents the results for the three individ-

TABLE 1

SHOWING THE PERCENTAGE OF RESPONSES CONSISTENT WITH THE ORIGINAL
TRAINING, *i.e.*, TO THE LARGER (OR SMALLER) STIMULUS OF THE COMBINATION

Training Stimuli	*Test Stimuli*		
160 (+) *vs.* 100 (−)	256 *vs.* 160	320 *vs.* 200	409 *vs.* 256
Pati	100% (2) 100% (3)	80% (1) 100% (4)	80% (5) 60% (6)
Mona	50% (1) 100% (4)	40% (2) 70% (3)	80% (5) 60% (6)
Pan	80% (1) 100% (4)	90% (2) 100% (3)	90% (5) 100% (6)
	Mean = 88.3%	Mean = 80%	Mean = 78.3%
256 (+) *vs.* 409 (−)	160 *vs.* 256	100 *vs.* 160	
Soda	50% (1) 70% (4)	40% (2) 50% (3)	
Bentia	40% (2) 60% (3)	30% (1) 40% (4)	
	Mean = 55%	Mean = 40%	

uals trained originally to the larger stimulus.   It will be observed that the average percentage of test responses consistent with the training response decreases from 88.3 per cent to 78.3 per cent as the test combinations are increased in absolute size. The small drop from the second to the third test combination (80.0 per cent to 78.3 per cent) is to be accounted for, in part at least, by the fact that the third test was not given in counterbalanced order, but only after the two series with each of the other two test situaions had been given.   The order in which each test was given is indicated by the bracketed numbers in the table.   If the percentage values in terms of the order of the tests are computed, we find that they increase with each successive test as follows: first—70 per cent, second—76 per cent, third—90 per cent and fourth—100 per cent. The drop to an average of 78 per cent in the fifth and sixth tests is thus seen to be of considerable significance. A more desirable procedure, of course, would be to use only one test for each subject and have a large number of subjects. The present experiment should be regarded as exploratory and not as offering conclusive results.

The results for the two individuals trained to respond to the smaller of the training pair, 256 and 409, similarly show a decreasing percentage of responses as the smaller test combinations are used. However, a markedly different result was obtained with these subjects, in that the amount of transfer dropped off much more quickly. In fact, in the second test combination, 100 and 160, a slight preference was shown for the larger stimulus over the smaller. That the result for these two subjects was not merely accidental is shown by the results of a further experiment reported below.

Six subjects were used in this part of the investigation; three of which were trained to the smaller stimulus and three to the larger. On the day after the learning of the discrimination a test series of 10 trials was given, in which half of the subjects were tested with the larger of the training stimuli and a still larger stimulus, and half, on the smaller of the training pair and a still smaller one. The next day a second series of test trials was given in which the test stimuli were reversed, i.e., subjects which had had the large stimulus combination were given the small stimuli, and vice versa. A retraining series of 10 trials followed each test.

The results for this experiment are shown in Tables 2 and 3. It will be seen that the three subjects trained to choose the larger stimulus (Table 2) responded to the larger stimulus in both test series almost 100 per cent of the time (mean, 93.3 per cent). The data (Table 3) for the subjects trained originally to the smaller stimulus show a different result. While these individuals responded fairly consistently (86.6 per cent) with their original training in the test series involving the negative stimulus of the training pair (256), and a still larger one (512 or 409) such was not the case in the test series involving the positive stimulus (128 or 160) and a still smaller one (64 or 100). Thus, as will be seen from the last column of Table 3, only 16 out of 30, or 53.3 per cent, of the responses were to the smaller

TABLE 2

SHOWING THE PERCENTAGE OF RESPONSES IN THE TRIALS CONSISTENT WITH THE ORIGINAL TRAINING, *i.e.*, TO THE LARGER STIMULUS OF THE TEST PAIR

Training Stimuli	*Test Combinations*	
256 (+) *vs.* 128 (−)	512 and 256	128 and 64
Cuba	90%	100%
Lia	100%	100%
256 (+) *vs.* 160 (−)	409 and 256	160 and 100
Mimi	90%	80%
	Mean = 93.3%	Mean = 93.3%

TABLE 3

SHOWING THE PERCENTAGE OF RESPONSES IN THE TEST TRIALS CONSISTENT WITH THE ORIGINAL TRAINING, *i.e.*, TO THE SMALLER STIMULUS OF THE TEST PAIR

Training Stimuli	*Test Stimuli*	
128 (+) *vs.* 256 (−)	256 and 512	64 and 128
Jack	80%	50%
Nira	100%	60%
160 (+) *vs.* 256 (−)	256 and 409	100 and 160
Bokar	80%	50%
	Mean = 86.6%	Mean = 53.3%

stimulus in this test, none of the subjects responding significantly more than a chance number of trials to the smaller stimulus. A second test series of 10 trials with this combination showed a similar result.

This failure of transposition to the smaller of two stimuli in the direction of smaller sized stimuli is contrary to the implications not only of the relational theories, but also, of course, to the present hypothesis, *at least in so far as the particular curves of Figures 1 and 2 are concerned.* Either some modifi-

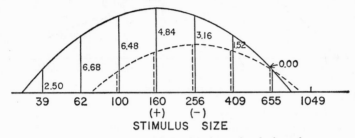

FIG. 2. Diagrammatic representation of relations between the hypothetical generalization curves, positive and negative, after training on the stimulus combination 160 (+) and 256 (−).

cation of these curves is required, or some additional factor must be postulated to account for this phenomenon. One possibility of the latter type is that the larger stimuli have, initially, a greater excitatory value than the smaller ones, or that the larger the stimulus the more rapidly do excitatory and inhibitory tendencies develop with training. Tending to support some such belief is the fact that there was a very slight, although not significant, initial preference shown by the subjects for the larger stimuli. Also the individuals trained to the larger stimulus required fewer trials to learn the discrimination than those trained to the smaller, but again the difference was only slight and not statistically significant. Further experimentation involving relatively slighter changes in the size of the test stimuli is required in order to obtain more adequate data on this problem.

In Figure 3 is presented a modification of our irradiation curves which fits the experimental data very satisfactorily. The assumption has been made in this figure that the extent of the generalization varies with the size of the stimulus, being greater for large than for small stimuli. Thus, while the positive curve of 160 in Figure 3 is the same as that for 160 in Figure 2, the negative curve for 256 in Figure 3 drops off more slowly than the corresponding curve in Figure 2 and, of course, extends farther.

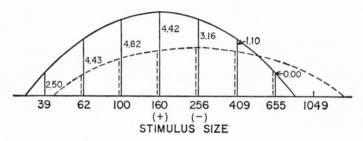

Fig. 3. Diagrammatic representation of relations between the hypothetical generalization curves, positive and negative, after training on the stimulus combination 160 (+) and 256 (−). This diagram differs from Figure 2 in that the negative generalization curve has a more gradual slope and extends farther.

After positive training to 160 and negative to 256, the effective excitatory strengths of 100 and 160 in Figure 3 are respectively 4.82 and 4.42. The difference of .40 is considerably below the minimum value for a consistent response to one of the stimuli, which in the present instance is assumed to be 1.00, an amount which is slightly less than the difference (1.26) between the training pair, 100 and 160. With such a small difference the response to the smaller test stimulus might be expected to be only a chance one, or possibly slightly more. Such a result, it should be noticed, is more closely in line with the data obtained in the present experiments (see Tables 1 and 3).

IV

In concluding this paper there are several further points of a theoretical nature that require at least passing mention. A problem of no little importance is the part played by stimulus characteristics other than the cue difference. Stimulus objects have various other aspects, such as form, intensity, wave length, in addition to the cue dimension, size in the present experiments. In so far as these characteristics are the same for both stimulus objects, only one member of each dimension (square form, white, etc.) is present, and, as they receive both reinforcement and non-reinforcement, their effective excitatory strengths are not greatly increased. If, however, a considerable amount of overtraining is provided, all of the stimulus characteristics are increased in excitatory value since all responses are correct and consequently followed by reinforcement. Just what effect such differences in the level of strength of these non-cue stimulus characteristics may have, it is not possible to say a priori. Possibly they would not affect the differential nature of the response but only the vigor of the reaction. On the other hand, it is possible that the amount of difference between excitatory strengths of the cue aspects necessary to produce a differential response is related to the level of strength of the remaining stimulus aspects. This point is of particular importance in connection with the problem of equivalence of stimuli when more than one stimulus aspect is changed.

Another question that is important from several points of view is the nature of the development of the curves of generalization during training. The theoretical implications of the effects of overtraining would depend to a considerable extent on what happens to these curves, that is, whether the range narrows, broadens, or remains unchanged with continued training. The effects to be expected from employing larger differences between the training stimuli would also depend most importantly on the manner in which the generalization curves develop. It is planned to take up the various theoretical aspects of this problem in a subsequent paper.

Similarly, there are very likely numerous other factors that play more or less important parts in this kind of discrimination behavior. As yet, however, only the barest beginning has been made in the experimental analysis of these phenomena. In this connection one cannot help but be struck by the relatively small amount of progress that has been made in this field of research since the initial work of Kinnaman in 1902. While it is true that the problem was a more or less incidental one in the investigations of the early American psychologists, to the Gestalt or configuration psychologists it has been of crucial importance. Instead, however, of a really systematic investigation, the latter seem to have been satisfied to demonstrate the commonness of response on the basis of relational properties as compared with response to absolute factors. Instances of failure of relational response have either been ignored as merely chance occurrences, or vaguely accounted for in terms of a threshold of equivalance of structure-properties.

The Gestalt theories have failed to furnish either a satisfactory explanation of these phenomena or an adequate experimental formulation of the problem.[8] The present theoretical scheme, on the other hand, does provide a basis for a systematic experimental attack in this field of study. It possesses, moreover, that most important attribute of a *scientific* theory—the capacity to generate logical implications that can be experimentally tested.

REFERENCES

1. BASS, M. J. AND HULL, C. L., The irradiation of a tactile conditioned reflex in man, *J. comp. Psychol.,* 1934, *17,* 47–65.

2. BINGHAM, H. C., Visual perception in the chick, *Behav. Monog.,* 1922, No. 20, Baltimore, Md.: Williams & Wilkins, pp. 104.

3. CASTEEL, D. B., The discriminative ability of the painted turtle, *J. Animal Behav.,* 1911, *1,* 1–28.

4. COBURN, C. A., The behavior of the crow, *Corvus Americanus Aud, J. Animal Behav.,* 1914, *4,* 185–201.

5. JOHNSON, H. M., Visual pattern discrimination in the vertebrates, *J. Animal Behav.,* 1914, *4,* 319–339, 340–361; *6,* 169–188.

6. GULLIKSEN, H., Studies of transfer of response. I. Relative versus absolute factors in the discrimination of size by the white rat, *J. genet. Psychol.,* 1932, *40,* 37–51.

7. GUNDLACH, R. H. AND HERINGTON, G. B., JR., The problem of relative and absolute transfer of discrimination, *J. comp. Psychol.,* 1933, *16,* 199–206.

8. HELSON, H., Insight in the white rat, *J. exper. Psychol.,* 1927, *10,* 378–396.

9. KINNIMAN, A. J., Mental life of two Macacus rhesus monkeys in captivity, *Amer. J. Psychol.,* 1902, *13,* 98–148, 173–218.

[8] The writer does not wish to deny the possibility that a theory of this type may be developed which will be capable of accounting for these experimental facts satisfactorily. Such dogmatic denials have no place in the realm of science. At the same time, however, we would emphasize the fact that the burden of the proof devolves on the theory. Its only claim to consideration lies in the extent to which it leads logically to consequences which coincide with empirical events.

10. KLÜVER, H., Behavior mechanisms in monkey, Chicago: University of Chicago Press, 1933.

11. KOFFKA, K., The growth of the mind, New York: Harcourt, Brace, 1928, 153–159, 233–242.

12. KÖHLER, W., Aus der Anthropoidenstation auf Teneriffa. IV. Nachweis einfacher Strukturfunktionen beim Schimpansen und beim Haushuhn: Über eine neue Methode zur Untersuchung des bunten Farbensystems, *Abh. preuss. Akad. Wiss.*, 1918, Berlin, 1–101.

13. ——, *Gestalt Psychology.* New York: Liveright, 1929.

14. PAVLOV, I., *Conditioned Reflexes.* London: Oxford Press, 1927.

15. PERKINS, F. T. AND WHEELER, R. H., Configurational learning in the goldfish, *Comp. Psychol. Monog.*, 1930, 7, 1–50.

16. SPENCE, K. W., The nature of discrimination learning in animals, *Psychol. Rev.*, 1936, 43, 427–449.

17. ——, Analysis of formation of visual discrimination habits in chimpanzee, *J. comp. Psychol.*, 1937, 23, 77–100.

18. TAYLOR, H., A study of configuration learning, *J. comp. Psychol.*, 1932, 13, 19–26.

19. WARDEN, C. J. AND ROWLEY, J. B., The discrimination of absolute versus relative brightness in the ring dove, *Turtur risorius, J. Comp. Psychol.*, 1929, 9, 317–337.

20. —— AND WINSLOW, C. N., The discrimination of absolute versus relative size in the ring dove, *Turtur risorius, J. genet. Psychol.*, 1931, 39, 328–341.

18

Continuous Versus Non-Continuous Interpretations of Discrimination Learning

I

Some few years ago the writer (*14*) presented a theoretical interpretation of discrimination learning based upon stimulus-response concepts and association principles which he contrasted with a purely descriptive picture of the behavioral phenomena of the pre-solution period of such learning offered by Krechevsky (*5*). Considerable care was taken in the article to point out that Krechevsky's discussion of the problem was entirely a descriptive affair and as such had a different purpose than the present writer's interpretation. That Krechevsky concurred with this difference in approach is shown by the following quotation from a subsequent note of his:

> In the first place I should like to point out that as far as Spence's original contribution is concerned there need not be any point of conflict between what he has to offer and anything I may have said in my previous papers. This does not mean that I necessarily accept Spence's proposed theoretical "explanation" of my data, but simply that we are really talking about two different things. I have contented myself with an attempt at a description of the learning process on a given behavioral level (*6*, p. 97).

After pointing out this purely descriptive characteristic of Krechevsky's interpretation, the present writer went on to propose and elaborate a second, alternative theory as to the nature of pre-solution behavior which, it was believed, was in line with the original statement by Lashley that "the practice preceding and the errors following are irrelevant to the actual formation of the association" (8, p. 135). This theory [1] was that the animal sets out to solve the problem confronting it by trying out, systematically, one of its repertoire of hypotheses. If this fails of solution, the animal is led to initiate and try out another and another until the correct one is hit upon (14, p. 444). In other words, this theory assumed that the animal *selects* and responds, in turn, to certain aspects of the experimental situation as offering possibilities of providing a solution and that it does not react (pay attention) to the relevant cue aspect until just at or just preceding the time of solution. Although incomplete in many respects, this conception leads to the implication that if the values of the cue stimuli are reversed, *i.e.*, the positive stimulus made negative and vice versa, before the animal begins to show any learning, it should not necessarily make for any slower learning of the reversed problem.

The present writer proposed this extension of Lashley's suggestion as one which disagreed with the implications of his own association type of theory and then proceeded to examine the experimental evidence bearing on the issue. Since that time several articles have been published by Krechevsky (7) and Haire (2, 3) which have dealt in one way or another with this problem. While in some instances these have provided valuable experimental contributions, they have, unfortunately, been marred by a tendency to misinterpretation of the opposing viewpoint, with the result that a very misleading picture has developed as to the status of the issue. It is the purpose of the

[1] This theory which the writer dubbed the insight hypothesis is referred to here as the Lashley theory because it is based upon Lashley's original statement quoted above. Krechevsky (6, p. 98–100) mistakenly believed that the writer ascribed the theory to him and somewhat indignantly denied such responsibility. This was a misinterpretation on his part. The writer's statement was: "But whatever Krechevsky's view of the matter may be, one can, nevertheless, advance the hypothesis that . . . ." (14, p. 444). The subject of this sentence was "one," not "Krechevsky." Furthermore, the theory or hypothesis was referred to as the insight hypothesis, not as the Krechevsky hypothesis. It is the writer's belief that the theory as outlined is merely a simple, logical extension of Lashley's brief statement.

present paper to attempt to clarify these confusions and also to examine the experimental data, old and new, which bear upon the problem.

II

We may begin with the results of the original McCulloch and Pratt experiment on weight discrimination with white rats (*13*), which the writer has already cited as supporting his association theory of discrimination learning and as being in conflict with the Lashley theory (*14*). These investigators found that when the significance of the cue stimulus was reversed before the subjects were responding more than 50 per cent to the positive cue stimulus, the subsequent learning of the converse problem required a longer time than a control group, continued on the original problem. A second experimental group which was trained originally until it was just beginning to discriminate, subsequently required even more trials than the first group to learn the converse problem. McCulloch and Pratt interpreted this to mean that instead of being docile and insightful at the moment of discovery of the relevant stimulus cues, the rats, before solving the problem, continued on the now incorrect cue and even went back to responding systematically to stimuli (position) that had previously been given up.

But Krechevsky (*6*), writing later, raised an important point, which, if found to be true for these data, would render them indeterminate so far as the Lashley theory is concerned. His point was that the animals might have been responding to more than one hypothesis at a time, one of which was the correct stimulus. He wrote:

An animal *may* (and in many cases probably does) select only one cue out of the stimulus field, and in such cases a change in the value of the cue stimulus may be without effect on the learning speed, but he may also (and that I have demonstrated) before dropping one hypothesis entirely, or to any great extent, select another cue and continue to divide his responses between the two. In this latter case, obviously, a reversal of the meaning of the second cue (if it happened to be the correct one) would interfere with the learning speed of the animal. Nothing that I have said rules out either of the two possibilities—actually from the data I have presented, *both* of those possibilities would be expected (*6*, p. 103).

If the animals had been responding to two stimuli or hypotheses, position and weight, at the same time, then reversal of the significance of the stimuli, it is true, should be expected to interfere with the converse problem. But to prove his point it was necessary for Krechevsky to show that the animals actually were responding to a weight cue. This he made no attempt to do despite the fact that there was a perfectly simple method of checking for it. Since McCulloch and Pratt reported that with the exception of one case their subjects did not respond more than 50 per cent of the time to the positive weight cue before the reversal, it is obvious that they could not have been responding to either one of the weight stimuli in combination with any other stimulus.

More recently, however, Krechevsky (7) has presented experimental evidence in visual discrimination which is contrary, in part, to McCulloch and Pratt's data and thus in support of the Lashley theory. Apparently encouraged by this turn of affairs Krechevsky was himself led to propose a Lashley type theory similar in its essential details to that previously suggested by the present writer. According to Krechevsky's formulation of this theory, which he called the non-continuity hypothesis,[2] each time the animal, while "paying attention" to a particular set of discriminanda, makes a correct or incorrect response he learns something about the particular stimulus to which he was reacting or paying attention. But he does not learn anything during such trials about the to-be-finally learned stimuli. He eventually gives up responding to the first set of stimuli and responds to another and another until he hits upon the relevant set. A corollary of the theory, Krechevsky further indicated, is that "if the significance of the stimuli are reversed before the animal begins to 'pay attention to' them (*i.e.*, during the presolution period), it should not necessarily make for any slower learning of the reversed problem" (7, p. 112).

---

[2] To avoid confusion the terms continuity and non-continuity suggested by Krechevsky will be used hereafter to designate the rival theories. Thus, what has been referred to as the Lashley theory, whether in the form elaborated by Krechevsky (7) or by the present writer (14) is a non-continuity theory. The writer's association theory of discrimination learning (14) is one of several versions of the continuity theory. Other theories included in this class by Kreschevsky are those of Gulliksen and Wolfle (1) and Wiley (19).

In contrast to his version of the Lashley theory, Krechevsky presented what he called the continuity hypothesis, citing as one example the association theory of discrimination learning proposed by the writer (*14*). His statement of the continuity theory was as follows:

> Simply restated the former assumption (which we shall from now on refer to as the "continuity" assumption) says that once an animal is immersed in a given problem situation (more specifically, discrimination-box) *each time* the animal makes a choice an effect is recorded on his nervous system. This effect is specific and constant. Every time, from the very first trial on, the animal makes a "correct" response the strength of the tendency to respond positively *to the specific stimulus the experimenter has in mind,* is strengthened; each time, also from the very beginning, he makes an "incorrect" response, the strength of the tendency to respond positively to the specific stimulus the experimenter has in mind is weakened, and further, these increments (or decrements) are constant throughout the learning process. Nothing is said about the "attention" of the animal, nothing about the "awareness" of the animal with respect to the important stimuli (7, p. 111).

Insofar as the above statements are supposed to apply to the present writer's version of the continuity type of theory, there are three major deviations. First, the effects of each trial (correct or incorrect) have not been assumed to be constant. It is difficult to understand how Krechevsky could have made such a mistake, for the writer very explicitly postulated that the increments of reinforcements and decrements of non-reinforcement varied with the strength of the associative connection, and a table showing these relationships was published (*14*). Apparently Krechevsky missed the significance of the writer's theoretical account of the pre-solution phenomena in discrimination learning, for it is only on the basis of these assumed *variable effects of reinforcement* that they can be explained.

Secondly, the writer did not assume that, from the very first trial on, the strength of the tendency to respond to the specific stimulus the experimenter has in mind is necessarily strengthened. The following quotation reveals the inapplicability of this statement. "The mere presence of the cue stimulus somewhere in the experimental situation does not guarantee its impingement on the animal's sensorium at or near the critical moment of response. This was, undoubtedly, an important, if not the chief reason for the greater difficulty that was experienced in setting up discrimination habits in the older forms of indirect apparatus" (*14*, p. 438).

The third discrepancy between the writer's particular version and Krechevsky's outline of the continuity hypothesis is his complaint that nothing is said about the attention of the animal, nothing about the awareness of the animal with respect to the important stimuli. This statement of Krechevsky's, when written, was accurate, but was not at the time of its publication. In September, 1937, almost six months prior to the publication of Krechevsky's paper, the writer attempted to deal with this question in a brief footnote (*16*, Footnote 3). The problem is an important one, particularly for the experiment being considered here, which is crucial for the continuity type of theory only if one can be sure the relevant stimuli are received on the animals' sensorium each trial from the very first. A more extended discussion of it will be given here in order to clarify the writer's view.

Insofar as the discrimination situation is such that the animal's sense organ is not forced to receive the relevant aspect of the stimulus from the very first trial, associations would not be formed between the response and this particular stimulus aspect. Obviously, if the stimulus does not occur for the animal, it cannot acquire any associative connections. The design of discrimination apparatus has been directed towards the forcing of the reception of the relevant stimulus aspects from the beginning of training. In the case of weight discrimination and, in the field of vision, at least, in brightness discrimination, the modern types of apparatus and procedures have been more or less successful in this respect, for it is practically impossible for the animal to make a response in such situations and not receive the relevant stimulation. In the case of visual discrimination of forms or figures, on the other hand, this condition does not necessarily hold. In these instances the animal is required to learn, in addition to the final selective approaching response, the appropriate (perceptual) response which leads to the reception of the relevant stimulus aspects. That is to say, the animal must learn to orient and fixate its head and eyes so as to receive the critical stimuli. These reactions are learned for the very same reason that the final approaching response is learned, *i.e.*, because they are followed within a short temporal interval by the final goal response. Responses providing other sensory receptions are not similarly reinforced in a systematic fashion and hence tend to disappear.

Anyone who has ever observed white rats performing in the jumping style of apparatus or any type involving locomotion (walking) can well appreciate what little likelihood there is that the animal will from the first respond to (look at) a small figure or form in a vertical plane in front of it on each and every trial. The white rat, in particular, runs with its head lowered to the floor and, even in the Lashley jumping apparatus, jumps to, and hence presumably fixates, the lowest portion of the stimulus cards.

Another matter of importance is the brightness relation of the figure and ground. Because animals (white rats, at least) apparently tend to orient visually more readily towards the lighter region of the stimulus complex (*10*) they are more likely to "see" or will come to respond more quickly to the form or figural aspect of a stimulus pattern if the figure is light with the background dark than vice versa. All these factors must be considered when dealing with the particular type of critical experiment being considered here. Obviously, conditions can easily be arranged so that the animal will not look toward the relevant stimulus aspect at first, with the result that it will have no effect.

The problem of perception in the discrimination situation is not a simple matter, as Lashley (*9*) has recently so well demonstrated, and the above treatment does not make any claim to being exhaustive. The motor responses involved in the orientation of the animal's head and eyes probably play, through their proprioceptive consequences, a much more important part in determining behavior than has been realized. Experimentation should be specifically directed to this important problem. Furthermore, the manner in which complex patterns are reacted to is not dealt with at all. Indeed the whole problem of patterning is omitted from discussion because our present interest is centered on the learning process *in situations where the perceptual response is as simple as possible.*

III

Turning now to Krechevsky's experimental results (7), it may be noted first that the experiment was essentially the same as that of McCulloch and Pratt, except that it involved visual instead of weight discrimination.   Briefly, it consisted of training 3 groups of rats with the Lashley jumping technique.   A control group (I) was trained throughout to a stimulus card (A) containing horizontal rows of black squares on a white background, the negative stimulus (B) consisting of vertical rows of black squares.   Two experimental groups were trained positively to stimulus B, Group II for 20 trials and Group III for 40 trials and were then reversed to stimulus A and trained to learning on it.   The critical experimental question was whether the animals which were originally trained on stimulus B would show retardation in their learning of the converse problem.

Krechevsky presented the data in two ways.   He first compared the learning data of the reversed groups (II and III) after reversal with the total learning record of the control group (I), and secondly, he compared the data of the reversal groups with the learning of the control group after 20 and 40 trials, respectively.   The first method of comparison is not valid because the experimental groups have had the benefit of 20 (or 40) trials of training by a technique which leads to rapid elimination of position preferences.   This technique is the one which was employed by Lashley and consists of placing the animal, when it responded incorrectly, back on the jumping stand with the same orientation it had before the jump and with the stimuli in the same position until the correct choice was made.[3]

Its most important effect is to break down or eliminate any position preference or, in the terminology of our theory, it leads readily to equalization of the excitatory tendencies of the two position stimuli (left and right positions), for the continued incorrect response to this stronger position stimulus leads to the weakening of its excitatory strength.   That is to say, any animals with position preferences tend to have them equalized by this procedure.   But the rate of learning of a discrimination

3 Krechevsky limited the number of such wrong responses to 5 on the first day.

problem is in part a function of the presence and extent of differences in the excitatory strength of the position stimuli. A much smaller difference between the positive and negative cue aspects is required, and hence fewer reinforcements (trials), when the position stimuli are equal in strength than if they are very different. To compare the learning of the experimental groups, which have had their position preferences at least partially eliminated, with the control group which has not, from the beginning of its training, does not take into consideration this factor. The more usual experimental procedure of not permitting such repetitive responses would not tend so readily to result in such elimination of position preferences and hence comparison of such data would not be so seriously affected. But even in such cases the better procedure would probably be to have neither stimulus cue consistently positive during the first 20 (or 40) trial period of the control group. Comparison could then be made from this point on, the experimental group being reversed from stimulus *B* to stimulus *A* and the control group having stimulus *A* made consistently positive.

Confining oneself, then, to these latter data, we find that Group II did not require any more trials or errors (in fact, required fewer) than the control group (I) to learn the reverse problem, a result which is in agreement with the non-continuity (Lashley) theory and appears, on the surface, to contradict the writer's continuity theory (as well as all of the other variations of the continuity theory). On the other hand, Group III did require more trials than the control group to learn the converse problem, a result which would appear to be opposed to the non-continuity theory and in support of the continuity theory.

At this point the "explanations" of the inconsistencies of fact with theory make their appearance. Krechevsky thinks the results for Group II are quite all right; they indicate to him that the animals learned nothing in the two days with respect to the specific cue stimuli. On the other hand, the results of Group III were not, he claims, in disagreement with his theory because, as he states, the results to be expected here on the "non-continuity" assumption were indeterminate. Everything depended upon whether or not four days (40 trials) were or were not too long for the pre-solution period. Here we encounter one of the most important points in the whole issue.   Indeed, whether there is an issue or not depends upon what is meant by such a term as "pre-solution period," or the expression "before the animals begin to react to or pay attention to the significant set of stimuli."   In his earlier articles, Krechevsky seemed unequvocally to mean by pre-solution period, the period of trials before the animal began to respond *systematically* to the correct stimulus aspect.   Thus, responding with an hypothesis or "paying attention to" a particular stimulus aspect was indicated by the fact that the response to it occurred systematically, *i.e.*, beyond chance expectancy.   The pre-solution period marked that period before the animal responded systematically to the relevant stimulus.   This was Krechevsky's original concept of hypothesis behavior, being based upon his attempt to find a method of operationally identifying Lashley's "attempts at solution" on the part of the subject.   It was in this sense that the writer originally proposed that the McCulloch-Pratt experiment provided a critical test of the non-continuity (Lashley) theory and the continuity theory proposed by himself.   The whole issue was whether or not the presence of the cue stimulus had any effect before the animal began to respond *systematically* to it. Lashley's suggestion implied that it did not; the writer's theory, that it did.[4]

The fact that Group III learned more slowly following reversal than the control group is definitely opposed to the non-continuity theory in the above sense of the word pre-solution period, *unless* it can be shown that the animals had already begun to respond systematically to the cue stimuli during the 40 trials.   Krechevsky presents no evidence to show that they were doing so.   As McCulloch (*11*) has pointed out that the control group showed no evidence of responding even above chance (50 per cent) to the positive stimulus in trials 21–40, let alone re-

---

[4] More recently Haire has suggested abandonment of this strict operational definition of an hypothesis on the truly surprising grounds that "too strict operationism clouds the real issue" (*3*).   In effect, with this restriction removed, Haire is free to posit single or multiple non-operationally defined hypotheses to suit the occasion.   Such a theory, whatever its implications, has nothing to do with the type of Lashley theory proposed by Krechevsky and the writer.   It is entirely irrelevant to the present issue and, as McCulloch (*12*) has pointed out, altogether invulnerable to disproof.

sponding systematically to it, it is not unlikely that Group III were not responding more than chance to either of the cue stimuli. This result then, is, definitely opposed to a non-continuity theory involding the systematic conception of hypothesis.

Returning to the consideration of the results of Group II from the point of view of the writer's continuity theory, the alibi is, of course, that the relevant cue aspects simply were not received at first by the subjects. They did not "see" the rows of black squares because they were fixating other aspects of the stimulus complex. And in support of this argument attention is directed first to the fact, pointed out above, that the Lashley technique predisposes the animal to fixate and jump to the very bottom of the card, and secondly, that the stimulus patterns involved black figures on white ground. It is the writer's belief that if white squares on a black ground had been used the results for the experiment might have been quite different. However, repetition of the experiment would best be done with white and black stimuli, for in such a situation, with proper precautions, it is practically impossible for the animal to fail to receive the significant stimulation. Clearly, this experiment has its difficulties as a means of testing these two opposing theoretical views.

IV

We turn now to the consideration of an experiment which the writer carried out with chimpanzee subjects (15). The experiment was not at the time of its inception regarded as a critical one for a decision between the association or continuity type of theory and the non-continuity theory, but was designed primarily to test certain additional implications of the writer's own particular theory of discrimination learning. In his paper Krechevsky (7) considers this experiment briefly, and cites various reasons for his belief that it does not have any data relevant to the present problem. In the opinion of the writer, however, Krechevsky has overlooked several points at which this experiment present data of considerable significance for the present issue.

Briefly, and in part, the experiment was as follows: The subjects were required to learn a series of discrimination problems involving four different stimulus forms, which may be designated $A, B, C,$ and D respectively. Each subject was first taught two preliminary discriminations: A (+) versus B (−) and, after the completion of this, C (+) versus D (−). Following the learning of these two preliminary problems, the animals were presented with five tests consisting of five new learning problems in which the same stimuli were used in different combinations. Only the first test need be considered for the moment. It involved the positive stimuli, A and C of the two preliminary problems, half the subjects having A positive and half C positive.

Commenting on this experiment, Krechevsky remarks that the learning of the preliminary problems meant that the animals had been trained to "pay attention to" or "react to" the relevant discriminanda, and that transferring the animals after this to another set of problems involving these same stimuli cannot give us any data on what had gone on during the *pre-solution period*. But is this so? The main point brought out by these experimental data was that there was a definite positive correlation between the responses of the animals to the two stimuli (hypotheses if one wishes) in this new test problem and the relative number of times they had been previously reinforced on them. This result was entirely in accord with the writer's continuity theory. But it is not to be expected on the non-continuity view, for each "hypothesis" had received an equal amount of training after being adopted. The differences exhibited in the preferences of the animals in the test problem must thus be ascribed to the *differential number of reinforcements received during the pre-solution period*. But according to the non-continuity theory these differential experiences should have had no effect. This fact is thus not only relevant to the non-continuity theory, but very embarrassing for it.

Similarly, the remainder of the experimental data showed that a very close relationship existed between the relative number of reinforcements (and after once being reinforced, the number of non-reinforcements) the two stimuli of any problem had previously had, and both the initial response and the rate of learning in the new problems. It was possible to predict which "hypothesis," if any, the subject might be expected to exhibit at the beginning of each new test problem and the relative speed with which each would be learned. In this connection, Kerchevsky's statement that "There is no longer a pre-solution period for the 'test' problems in the sense that the animals might reasonably be expected to react to any other set of discriminanda such as spatial differentia, etc." (7, p. 127), is flatly contradicted by the facts. The data indicate that if the two stimuli to be discriminated in the new test problem happened to have received about the same number of reinforcements in previous, earlier problems, the subject would respond in purely chance fashion so far as the cue aspects were concerned, and would exhibit a position preference (hypothesis) or some other *systematic* spatial response, *e.g.*, perseveration response. When one of the stimuli had previously received many more reinforcements than the other, no such spatial hypotheses would be exhibited, but, depending on the amount of difference in the number of previous reinforcements, would respond predominantly to the stimulus previously reinforced most. The scatter diagrams of these data indicated a continuous function, not a discontinuous one.

V

Haire (2) has recently carried out an experiment under the direction of Krechevsky which is supposed to furnish still further support for the non-continuity (Lashley) theory and yet another disproof of the continuity (particularly the writer's) theory. By altering the jumping stand of the Lashley apparatus so as to give the animal two separate promontories instead of the same central position from which to jump, it was found that a marked speeding up in learning was attained. According to Haire, the explanation of this result was that the change in apparatus design provided a clearer spatial articulation which in some unexplained way aided the rat to discard and avoid more readily interfering spatial hypotheses.

The writer's version of the continuity theory was then ex-

amined by Haire.   He was unable to see how it could explain
the facts; ergo, as usual, it could not possibly do so.   Haire's
reasoning was based upon the statement of the writer that "The
difference between the excitatory strengths of the cue stimuli
must reach a certain minimum before the animal will respond
consistently to the positive stimulus" (*16*, p. 432), plus the further assumption, taken on his own initiative, to the effect that
in the single and double platform groups "the difference between the excitatory strengths of the cue stimuli are equal at
the moment of 'learning' since they both display the same behavior characteristic (*i.e.*, 90 per cent or better performance)"
(*2*, p. 88).   Apparently Haire believed that the latter of the two
above assumptions followed necessarily and logically from the
first.   Such is not the case, however, for the size of the difference between the excitatory tendencies of the positive and negative cue aspects of the stimulus situation necessary for consistent
response to one of them (*i.e.*, completed learning) *depends upon
the presence of any systematic or variable differences among the
excitatory tendencies of other aspects of the stimulus situation
which are allied in their action with the cue aspects.*

As has been brought out in the writer's previous articles (*14,
15*), a greater difference between the excitatory strengths of the
positive and negative cue would be required for the attainment
of learning if there is a difference in the excitatory strengths of
the position stimuli than if no such difference is present.   Similarly, to the degree that variable stimulus factors are operative
in the situation, now favoring (allied with) the positive aspect
and now the negative aspect, a greater difference between the
excitatory strengths of the cue stimuli would be required.   The
presence of such differences between the other stimulus aspects
in the situation necessitates the building up of a sufficiently
great difference between the cue aspects so that the stimulus
complex of which the positive cue is a member is always (or in
90 per cent of the trials, or whatever the learning criterion is)
greater in strength than that containing the negative aspect.
Accordingly, although it is accurate to say that at the attainment
of the learning criterion the differences between the stimulus
complex containing the positive cue and that containing the

negative cue must be the same for the two groups of subjects, the differences between the excitatory strengths of the cue aspects themselves need not necessarily be the same.

The explanation of Haire's results according to the writer's interpretation, then, would begin with the assumption that a bigger difference between the excitatory strengths of the positive and negative cue aspects is necessary with the single platform for the reason that any original difference in the excitatory strengths of the two position stimuli, S_L and S_R, would tend to be broken down more slowly under this condition than with the divided platform. The derivation of the latter part of this statement is, in turn, based upon assumptions as to generalization of reinforcement and non-reinforcement effects similar to those employed by the writer in his article (16) on the discrimination of stimulus differences of degree, e.g., brightness and size. Thus the two position stimuli would be conceived of as members of a single spatial continuum or dimension. In the single platform, S_L and S_R would be close together, while in the double platform they would be farther apart. The effects of reinforcement and non-reinforcement of a response to one of these stimuli, it is assumed, would generalize more to the other in the case of the single than in the double platform. But it may be shown that the greater the degree of generalization the less would the difference between the excitatory strengths of the position stimuli be reduced per non-reinforcement.[5] To restate more briefly, then, the slower learning of the single-platform group as compared with the dual-platform group is explained as due to the circumstance that the greater generalization of the training effects on the position stimuli in the single situation would make for slower reduction of differences in the excitatory strengths of the position stimuli which in turn, according to the theory, would require a bigger difference between the excitatory strengths of the cue stimuli and thus more trials.

[5] This may be shown very simply by assuming hypothetical values, e.g., that $S_L = 70$ and $S_R = 50$, and further that the decrement from non-reinforcement is 5 points, with generalization to S_R of 3 points in the single platform and 1 in the double. After 5 successive non-reinforcements of responses to S_L the hypothetical strengths would be as follows: $S_L = 45$, $S_R = 35$ for the single platform and $S_L = 45$, $S_R = 45$ in the case of the double platform.

A test of the adequacy of this explanation as opposed to the "hypothesis" view would be nicely provided by comparing the learning of the single and double-platform groups in the converse discrimination problem, half of the subjects in each group now being run on the single and half on the double platform. The reversal learning of the two original groups according to the view supported by Haire presumably should be the same. But according to the theory proposed by the writer a greater difference between the positive and negative cue stimuli was developed in the original learning problem in the case of the single platform group than in the double platform group. Hence, it should take longer for the former group to learn the reversal problem.

VI

In conclusion, one further characteristic of the pre-solution responses of animals in learning situations needs clarification. That systematic response tendences or "hypotheses" occur in pre-learning periods is by now a well established experimental fact.   In addition to Krechevsky's evidence from discrimination learning experiments with white rats, the writer has recently presented data showing similar phenomena in the solution of multiple choice problems by chimpanzees.   And much earlier Hamilton (4) had revealed similar kinds of "reaction tendencies" exhibited to varying degrees by several mammalian forms ranging from the white rat to man in the insoluble quadruple choice problem.

A major difference exists, however, as to interpretation.   Krechevsky has interpreted the hypotheses as being insightful, or intelligent responses, revealing something quite different from a "blind process of trial and error" adjustment.   According to the writer's theory, on the contrary, these pre-solution phenomena appear to be a typical example of what has been described as trial and error learning, while hypotheses are far from what he understands by the terms insightful and intelligent.   Only *persistent* non-adaptive responses can attain the distinction of being hypotheses—for, in order to classify as a hypothesis, a response, although ineffective, must continue to be persisted in a certain minimum number of times. A maladaptive act which is speedily (intelligently?) abandoned cannot ever be a hypothesis.

Degrees of intelligence as revealed in learning problems would, from the writer's point of view, be indicated by two main characteristics: (1) the readiness and persistence with which an ineffective response is avoided, and (2) the readiness and persistence with which the appropriate response is made, once hit upon. In the writer's opinion differences in these two characteristics are continuous. High degrees of readiness and persistence in each case do not differ in kind from low degrees. What has been termed intelligent or insightful learning in animals differs only in degree from blind or slow learning.[6]

REFERENCES

1. GULLIKSEN, H., & WOLFLE, D. L. Theory of learning and transfer. *Psychometrika*, 1938, *3*, 127–149; 225–251.

2. HAIRE, M. Some factors influencing repetitive errors in discrimination learning. *J. comp. Psychology*, 1939, *27*, 79–91.

3. ———. A note concerning McCulloch's discussion of discrimination habits. *Psychol. Rev.*, 1939, *46*, 298–303.

4. HAMILTON, G. V. A study of trial and error reactions in mammals. *J. Animal Behavior Monogr.*, 1911, *1*, 33–66.

5. KRECHEVSKY, I. "Hypotheses" in rats. *Psychol. Rev.*, 1932, *39*, 516–532.

6. ———. A note concerning "The nature of discrimination learning in animals." *Psychol. Rev.*, 1937, *44*, 97–103.

7. ———. A study of the continuity of the problem-solving process. *Psychol. Rev.*, 1938, *45*, 107–133.

8. LASHLEY, K. S. *Brain Mechanisms and Intelligence.* Chicago: University of Chicago Press, 1929.

9. ———. The mechanism of vision. XV. Preliminary studies of the rat's capacity for detail vision. *J. gen. Psychol.*, 1938, *18*, 123–193.

10. MAIER, N. R. F. Qualitative differences in the learning of rats in a discrimination situation. *J. comp. Psychol.*, 1939, *27*, 2, 289–331.

[6] The writer is not including here certain higher forms of adjustment such as are mediated by the complex symbolic mechanisms of man. He has reference to the usual type of learning situation employed with non-articulate, infra-human organisms, *e.g.*, discrimination, problem box, maze, multiple choice situation, etc. Another manner of saying the same thing as above is that sudden jumps in the learning curves of these problems are different only in degree from the more gradual acquisitions.

11. McCulloch, T. L. Comment on the formation of discrimination habits. *Psychol. Rev.*, 1939, *46*, 75–85.

12. ———. Reply to a note on discrimination habits. *Psychol. Rev.*, 1939, *46*, 304–307.

13. ———, & Pratt, J. G. A study of the pre-solution period in weight discrimination by white rats. *J. comp. Psychol.*, 1934, *18*, 271–290.

14. Spence, K. W. The nature of discrimination learning in animals. *Psychol. Rev.*, 1936, *43*, 427–449.

15. ———. Analysis of the formation of visual discrimination habits in chimpanzee. *J. comp. Psychol.*, 1937, *23*, 77–100.

16. ———. The differential response in animals to stimuli varying within a single dimension. *Psychol. Rev.*, 1937, *44*, 430–444.

17. ———. Gradual versus sudden solution of discrimination problems by chimpanzees. *J. comp. Psychol.*, 1938, *25*, 213–224.

18. ———. Solution of multiple choice problems by chimpanzees. *Comp. Psychol Monogr.*, 1939, *15*, no. 3, serial no. 75.

19. Wiley, L. E., & Wiley, A. M. Studies in the learning function. *Psychometrika*, 1937, *2*, 1–19, 107–120, 161–164.

19

Gradual Versus Sudden Solution of Discrimination Problems by Chimpanzees

Introduction

The occurrence of sharp rises in the learning curves of animals at or just preceding the solution of a problem has led to the critical view that the learning process, at least in such instances, is not aptly described or explained in terms of the building up of associative connections between stimuli and responses by means of appropriate rewards and punishments.   Instead, a picture of learning is offered in terms of such concepts as "insight," "seeing into" or "reorganization of the sensory field." The Gestalt psychologists, in particular, have insisted upon the necessity of viewing the learning process in these terms and they have placed considerable stress upon the instances of sudden solution in the learning of animals as evidence of its insightful nature (*1, 3*).   Thus Perkins and Wheeler (*4*), American proponents of the Gestalt views, concluded, on the basis of the sudden jumps in the learning curves they obtained with goldfish, that these animals learned a brightness discrimination in an insightful manner and not through changes effected by repetition and satisfaction.

Köhler, in his 1925 Powell lectures (*2*), likewise considered sudden solutions in the learning of discrimination problems.

While he pointed out that discrimination learning is usually a slow, gradual process even in the anthropoids, he nevertheless claimed that the learning is probably quite different in cases in which the solution is sudden. The occurrence of such sudden solutions is, moreover, evidence to him that the learning involves more than mere associative processes or, to quote him: "We do not well describe experiments of this type by saying, as we usually do, that an animal in such a situation learns to connect certain stimuli with certain reactions and that the connection is 'stamped in.' This formulation of the process gives too much importance to the memory or association side of the problem, and it neglects another side of it which may be even more important and more difficult" (2). This neglected aspect of the problem, according to him, is the process by which the sensory field becomes organized, or rather reorganized, during learning, and it is this part that is responsible for the sudden solutions or insights in learning.

But are such instances of sudden jumps in the learning curves of animals evidence either for the existence of an insightful factor in learning, or for the inadequacy of the view that learning consists in the formation of stimulus response connections by a repetitive process of reinforcement and non-reinforcement? In the opinion of the writer, both parts of the question are, as yet, to be answered in the negative. To say, as the Gestalt psychologists do, that such learning involves the development of insight is merely to restate the problem in new terms. No satisfactory theoretical account of how such an insight factor operates to produce such sudden learning in discrimination problems, or for that matter any other type of problem, has ever been given by its Gestalt proponents. The association theorists, of course, are in exactly the same position, for they have never given a satisfactory theoretical account of this phenomenon. It does not logically follow, however, that an adequate theory cannot be developed on association principles.

The writer has presented a theory of the nature of discrimination learning, based on association or conditioning principles which was shown to be capable of explaining the various phenomena known to be characteristic of the pre-solution period of learning (5). Quite in contrast to the Gestalt or configuration interpretation, this theory conceives discrimination learning as a cumulative process of building up the strength of the excitatory tendency of the positive stimulus cue (*i.e.*, the tendency of this stimulus to evoke the response of approaching it) by means of the successive reinforcements of the response to it, as compared with the excitatory strength of the negative stimulus, responses to which receive no reinforcements.   Learning is completed when the difference between the excitatory strengths of the two cue stimuli is sufficiently large always to offset any differences in strength which may exist between other aspects of the stimulus situation that happen to be allied in their action with one or other of the cue stimuli; for example, such differences as may exist between the excitatory strengths of the food boxes on which the cue stimuli are placed.   In the presentation of this theory, no consideration was given to the problem of the occurrence of sudden solution in discrimination learning. It is proposed in the present paper to examine the relation of the theory to this problem.   Our discussion will be based largely on the results of an analysis of discrimination learning curves of chimpanzees.

Description of Experiment

The experimental data employed were obtained from an investigation with chimpanzees which was designed to test certain aspects of our theory of discrimination learning (6).   The subjects were required to learn a series of discrimination problems involving four different stimulus forms, which may be designated A, B, C, D respectively.   Each subject was first taught two preliminary discriminations: A (+) versus B (—) and, after the completion of this, C (+) versus D (—).   Following the learning of these problems the animals were presented with five tests consisting of five new learning problems in which the same stimuli were used in new combinations.   Table 1 shows the sequence of the problems, including the two preliminary habits.

According to our theory of discrimination learning, a definite relationship should have been found between the learning of each of these test problems (both the initial response and the total learning score, *e.g.*, number of errors) and the relative

number of reinforcements and nonreinforcements the stimuli
had in previous problems. Thus, in the case of a particular
subject, if the positive stimulus of a particular test has received

TABLE 1

SHOWING THE SEQUENCE OF DISCRIMINATION PROBLEMS

The animals were divided into two groups, the A group and the C group, on
the basis of the stimulus, A or C, that was made positive in the first test problems.
These two groups are each divided again in the third test problem according to
the stimulus made positive.

Sequence of Problems	Group	Stimulus	
		Positive	Negative
Preliminary habits	Total group	A	B
		C	D
Test 1	A	A	C
	C	C	A
Test 2	A	D	B
	C	B	D
Test 3	A-1	A	D
	A-2	D	A
	C-1	C	B
	C-2	B	C
Tests 4 and 5	Total group	B	A
		D	C

a greater number of reinforcements and fewer non-reinforcements in the learning of previous problems than the negative
stimulus, the excitatory strength of the former should be greater
than that of the latter and the animal should respond from the
first predominantly to it; possibly even choosing it exclusively
if the difference is sufficiently great for complete learning.   On
the other hand, if the negative stimulus has had a greater number of reinforcements than the positive in previous problems,
it should have the greater excitatory strength and, consequently,
the animal should at first tend to respond predominantly to it.
In such cases a greater amount of time (number of trials and
errors) should be required to complete the learning, as this dif-

ference in strength of the excitatory tendencies must first be reduced to zero through non-reinforcement of the response to the negative stimulus and a difference developed in favor of the positive stimulus.

The results of the experiment were in substantial agreement with the theoretical expectations. It was found that the learning of form discrimination problems by our chimpanzee subjects was directly dependent on the relative excitatory strengths of the positive and negative stimuli as determined by the relative number of reinforcements and non-reinforcements each had received in previous problems.   This relationship held not only for the initial response of the animal in each new problem, but also for the entire learning period.   The data of the experiment are of particular interest in the present connection because of the fact that a number of the learning curves of the chimpanzee subjects, which began at chance or, because of a greater amount of training in earlier problems to the negative stimulus, less than chance, showed sudden jumps to solution.

Discussion of Results

The twelve chimpanzee subjects were presented in all with 76 discrimination problems.   In twenty of these cases there was little or no learning involved as the subjects had previously had a greater number of reinforcements on the positive than on the negative stimulus.   Consequently they responded from the beginning predominantly to the correct stimulus.   Table 2 presents the numerical data for the fifty-six remaining cases.   It shows the sharpness with which the curves of learning rise to solution in terms of the size of the increase in the percentage of correct responses from the period of twenty trials preceding to the period of twenty trials in which the criterion of learning (90 per cent correct) is satisfied.   The larger the size of this increase the more sudden is the learning.   An increase of 40 per cent or more, it will be seen, represents a jump from a chance score to completed learning.

Examination of the data contained in this table reveals several interesting facts.   First of all, arbitrarily adopting an increase of 40 per cent as a criterion of sudden or "insightful" learning, there were 19 instances in which this criterion was met and 37 in which the learning was more or less gradual. The question immediately arises as to whether the cases involv-

TABLE 2

SHOWING THE SUDDENNESS WITH WHICH THE CURVES OF LEARNING RISE TO SOLUTION
IN TERMS OF THE SIZE OF THE INCREASE IN THE PERCENTAGE OF CORRECT
RESPONSES FROM THE PERIOD OF TRIALS PRECEDING TO THE PERIOD
IN WHICH THE LEARNING CRITERION WAS ATTAINED

Subject	Preliminary Problems		Test Problems				
	P-1	P-2	T-1	T-2	T-3	T-4	T-5
1. Mimi	15	30	50	45	A	40	A
2. Lia	30	15	A	45	60	40	A
3. May	25	60	80	A	60	70	A
4. Jack	25	30	30	A	A	40	40
5. Pan	35	15	40	20	A	50	A
6. Bokar	40	25	25	A	40	90	A
7. Mona	30	25	30	A	A	25	30
8. Nana	20	20	A	15	25	20	A
9. Wendy	20	10	30	A	A		
10. Josie	20	10	A	25	45		
11. Cuba	25	15	30	A			
12. Nira	10	30	30	30	25	40	
Mean	24.6	23.7	38.3	30	42.5	44.0	

A = Little or no learning involved because of initial preference for positive stimulus.

ing sudden solution were the result of some novel process, *insight,* and as such, *quite independent of associative changes resulting from selective reinforcements and non-reinforcements.* If this is true there should not be in these instances any relationship between the learning or solution of the discrimination problem and the relative excitatory strengths of the stimuli as determined by cumulating the number of reinforcements and non-reinforcements each had previously received. As was reported in a previous paper (6), however, the learning of the test problems (tests 1, 3, 4 and 5) was very closely related to the relative excitatory strengths of the stimuli, as determined by

the number of past reinforcements and non-reinforcements.[1]
The fact that the cases of sudden solution constituted a part of
these data suggests that they were not altogether independent
of these associative processes. This conclusion is further
strengthened by the observation that this relationship was greatest in test problems 4 and 5, in which the proportion of cases
showing sudden solution was also greatest.

In Table 3 is presented a further analysis of the cases of sudden learning in test problems 1, 3, 4 and 5. The first two
columns of this table show the number of the test and the sub-

TABLE 3

SHOWING THE RELATIVE EXCITATORY STRENGTHS OF THE POSITIVE AND NEGATIVE
STIMULI AT THE BEGINNING AND END OF THE EXPERIMENTAL
PERIOD PRECEDING SOLUTION

Test	Subject	20 Trials Preceding Solution	20 Trials on Which Solution	Relative Excitatory Strengths of Positive and Negative Stimuli (P-N)	
				Beginning	End
1	Mimi	50	100	+21	+41
1	May	15	95	+24	+44
1	Pan	55	95	+10	+30
3	May	35	95	−2	+18
3	Bokar	60	100	−14	+6
3	Josie	50	95	−1	+19
3	Lia	40	100	−20	0
4	Mimi	55	95	−67	−45
4	May	20	90	−16	+4
4	Jack	60	100	−4	+16
4	Pan	50	100	−14	+6
4	Bokar	60	100	−14	+6
4	Nira	55	100	−3	+17
4	Lia	50	90	−10	+10
5	Jack	50	90	+14	+34

[1] The stimuli of test 2 have received no previous reinforcements as they were
the negative stimuli of the two preliminary problems. No relationship was
found between the number of non-reinforcements these stimuli had received and
the learning of this test. A more extended discussion of this result is given in
the previous report (6).

ject. The third and fourth columns give, respectively, the percentage of responses to the positive stimulus in the period of 20 trials preceding and the period of 20 trials in which the learning criterion was attained. The final two columns show the relative excitatory strengths of the positive and negative stimuli at the beginning and at the end of the period of 20 trials preceding that on which the learning occurred.

The first point to be observed in the table (see final column) is the fact that at the point of solution, the excitatory strength of the positive stimulus, in terms of previous reinforcements and non-reinforcements, was greater than that of the negative stimulus in all but one instance (Mimi, test 4). Moreover, in ten of eleven cases which involved the reversal of an initial preference, the learning occurred *immediately* following a shift in the relative strengths of the stimuli, the positive stimulus becoming stronger than the negative, as shown by the fact that the P-N values shifted from negative to positive. The probability of a large number of such cases resulting from chance is extremely remote.

Still another indication of a definite relationship between the learning of the discrimination in these cases and the relative associative strengths of the two stimuli is the rank order correlation of $-.79$ between the number of errors made in learning and a measure of the relative excitatory strengths $(R = P - N)$ of the stimuli at the beginning of the learning. This coefficient compares favorably with similar correlations obtained with all of the subjects, which, as reported in the previous study (6), were $-.65$ for test 1, $-.79$ for test 3 and $-.96$ for combined tests 4 and 5.

The above evidence strongly indicates, then, that sudden learning *in discrimination problems* is not to be distinguished from gradual learning by the presence of a novel factor or process (insight), which is independent of associative changes effected by repeated satisfactions and frustrations. The sudden solutions, just as the gradual ones, occurred only after the positive stimulus had attained greater excitatory strength than the negative, and the time taken to learn (number of errors) was closely correlated with the original relative excitatory strengths of the two stimuli as determined by previous training. Again, the curves of discrimination learning of our subjects (see Table 2) reveal no evidence of discontinuity, but range all the way from very gradual to very sudden learning. Our criterion of 40 per cent was a purely arbitrary one, and in no sense marked off two different types of functions. Apparently the learning in both cases was of the same kind.

We turn now to a consideration of the relation of the theory of discrimination learning which we have proposed to the experimental facts presented in this paper. According to this theory (5) the animal responds, other things being equal, to the cue stimulus which has the greater excitatory strength. The discrimination situation is complicated, however, by the fact that there are other stimulus aspects present, some of which, on any particular trial, are allied in their action (*i.e.*, their excitatory tendencies lead to the same response) with one of the cue stimuli, and some of which are allied to the other. The stimulus or food boxes are two such stimuli which are always present. Further, depending upon the extent to which the experimental conditions cannot be rigidly controlled, there may be other variable (chance) factors, or stimulating agents, which coincide in their action with one or other of the cue aspects. When the excitatory strengths of the cue stimuli do not differ greatly, the subject responds sometimes to one and sometimes to the other (approximately 50 per cent), depending on which has the greater excitatory support from other stimuli. With training (reinforcement of responses to positive cue and non-reinforcement of those to the negative cue) the difference between the excitatory strengths of the cue stimuli gradually increases until it becomes sufficiently great to offset always the effects of differences in the excitatory strengths of other stimulus aspects. At such a point the learning is completed, that is, the subject responds consistently (100 per cent) to the positive stimulus aspect.

Now whether the subject's response will shift suddenly or gradually from a chance performance to the consistent choice of the positive stimulus will depend upon several factors. First is the extent to which variable stimulus factors (both environmental and internal or physiological) are operative in the situation. Irregular control of such factors will lead to a more or less gradual and irregular curve of learning, for some of these irrelevant (distracting) stimuli will by chance favor the incorrect, negative stimulus, with the result that the subject will respond to it despite the fact that the positive cue aspect, *per se*, is stronger than the negative.   As the difference between the excitatory strengths of the stimuli increases with training, however, the interfering effect of this factor of variability gradually lessens, until it finally ceases altogether.

A second and more fundamental factor determining the slope of the discrimination learning curve is the rapidity with which the *difference* in the excitatory strengths of the cue stimuli develop.   This, in turn, may be a function of several factors. One very important determiner is the excitatory strength of the cue stimuli, for according to the postulates of the theory, the amount of increase in strength of an excitatory tendency (S-R connection) with each reinforcement and the amount of weakening with each non-reinforcement, varies according to its strength.   This relationship in the case of the positive stimulus is assumed to be similar in shape to the normal probability curve, the increment of strength being relatively small for a weak excitatory tendency, increasing to a maximum, and finally becoming small again as the limiting, maximum strength of the excitatory tendency is approached.   In the case of the negative stimulus the amount of weakening is assumed to be directly proportional to the excitatory strength of the stimulus with no effect occurring below a certain minimum strength (5, p. 433). If the subject has had little or no previous experience with either of the cue stimuli, we should expect the learning to be gradual, for the increment of reinforcement is small and there is little or no weakening effect from non-reinforcements.   On the other hand, if the cue stimuli have previously been reinforced, the effects of both reinforcement and non-reinforcement should be greater, with the result that the difference between them should develop more rapidly and the learning of the discrimination should be more sudden.   Experimental evidence supporting this theoretical implication is provided in the final row of figures of Table 2, which gives the average increase in the percentage of correct responses for the several tests.   Thus it will be seen that there is a definite tendency for the learning to be more gradual, as shown by the smaller average increase under the condition of the two preliminary problems and test problem no. 2, in which the excitatory tendencies of the stimuli were presumably very slight since the subjects had little or no previous positive experience with them. In tests 1, 3, 4 and 5, the learning was more sudden, which is in accord with the fact that either one or both of the cue stimuli had been previously reinforced.

Another factor determining the rate with which differences in the strengths of the cue stimuli develop, is that of individual differences in the effects of reinforcements and non-reinforcements. A subject whose rate of acquisition of excitatory tendencies with successive reinforcements is relatively slow, or one in whom inhibitory tendencies from non-reinforcement are relatively slight, is not likely to exhibit sudden jumps from chance to solution. It follows from this that individuals who learn slowly are not likely to learn suddenly, *i.e.*, jump abruptly from chance to solution, while, on the other hand, quick learners should tend to show such sudden solutions. Evidence in support of this implication is shown in the results presented in Table 4. The twelve subjects were divided into two groups according to the mean number of trials required to learn the

TABLE 4

SHOWING THE RELATIONSHIP BETWEEN THE RATE OF LEARNING OF THE TWO
PRELIMINARY DISCRIMINATIONS AND THE PERCENTAGE OF SUDDEN
SOLUTIONS IN TEST PROBLEMS 1, 3, 4 AND 5

Group	Trials		Percentage of Sudden Solutions		
	Mean	Range	Tests 1 and 3	Tests 4 and 5	Total
Quick learners ...	65	50–85	6/8 or 75%	7/7 or 100%	13/15 or 86%
Slow learners	135.8	130–150	1/7 or 14.2%	1/4 or 25%	2/11 or 18%

two preliminary discriminations. It will be seen from the table that the rapid learners showed a markedly greater tendency to learn the subsequent test problems suddenly than did the slow learners; whereas the former learned 13 out of 15 (86 per cent) of the test problems suddenly the latter learned only 2 of 11 (18 per cent) in this manner. No such logical connection between rapid learning and the tendency to learn suddenly has ever been demonstrated by any type of insight theory.

In concluding this part of our discussion attention is directed to the contrast provided by the "insight" account of these sudden solutions and that offered by the present theory. The former, in so far as it attempts to be explanatory, does little more than introduce us to a new set of terms. When an animal learns a discrimination problem suddenly there undoubtedly occurs a "reorganization of its sensory field." But such a statement may with equal applicability be made of gradual learning. The problem still remains as to why the reorganization appears suddenly in certain instances and not in others. The theory of discrimination learning we have proposed, on the other hand, is able, in some degree at least, to state the conditions which determine the occurrence of sudden solutions and to indicate how these factors differ from those which lead to more gradual learning of this type of problem.

Summary

Analysis of the learning curves of chimpanzees for discrimination problems indicates that sudden learning, like gradual, is closely correlated with the relative associative strengths of the cue stimuli as determined by the number of their previous reinforcements and frustrations. This result fails to support the interpretation that sudden solutions in the case of discrimination learning are marked by the presence of a novel process (insight) which is independent of these associative changes.

As alternative to the insight interpretation an attempt has been made to show how the occurrence of these sudden solutions may be accounted for in terms of a theory of discrimination learning based on association principles of reinforcement and non-reinforcement. This theory, which permits a description of the circumstances under which sudden learning should and should not occur, is supported by the experimental results.

REFERENCES

1. KÖHLER, W. *The Mentality of Apes.* (Trans. by E. Winter.) New York: Harcourt Brace and Co., Inc., 1925. Pp. viii + 342.

2. KÖHLER, W. Intelligence in apes. *J. genet. Psychol.*, 1925, *32*, 674–690.

3. KOFFKA, K. *The Growth of the Mind.* London: Kegan Paul, 1924. Pp. 382.

4. PERKINS, F. T., AND WHEELER, R. H. Configurational learning in goldfish. *Comp. Psychol. Monog.*, 1930, *7*, no. 1, 50.

5. SPENCE, K. W. The nature of discrimination learning in animals. *Psychol. Rev.*, 1936, *43*, 427–449.

6. SPENCE, K. W. Analysis of the formation of visual discrimination habits in chimpanzee. *J. comp. Psychol.*, 1937, *23*, 77–100.

20

The Basis of Solution by Chimpanzees of the Intermediate Size Problem*

Theoretical Introduction

Almost from the beginning of its discovery in monkeys by Kinnaman (*8*), the phenomenon of transposition has been interpreted as being somehow a relational matter. As the writer pointed out in a previous paper (*15*), however, two somewhat different "relational" interpretations have been put forward. Köhler (*10*) has distinguished between these two conceptions in the following manner. He speaks of the differential response of the animal to such stimulus situations as two greys as being to their "togetherness" and he then distinguishes two ways in which this "togetherness" can occur and be effective: (a) as stimulus wholes or "Gestalt perceptions" and (b) as perceived stimulus relationships or "relational-perceptions." He goes on to state that "it is impossible to explain the former in terms of the latter because the characteristic Gestalt-effect is often at its maximum when nothing whatever of relations is experienced" (*2*, p. 220). According to Köhler, then, the animal is not necessarily responding on the basis of a relational-perception, but only to a structure-function or "togetherness." The earlier American investigators, on the other hand, were of the belief

* From the Yale Laboratories of Primate Biology.

that the response was on the basis of a relational-perception (*1, 7, 8*), and several recent American psychologists (*11, 13*) have offered interpretations which more nearly follow the relational interpretation than the Köhler Gestalt theory.

In their recent theoretical article dealing with the problem of discrimination and transposition, Gulliksen and Wolfle (*4*) make a similar distinction between these two theoretical assumptions. They list three hypotheses which have been suggested regarding the aspect of the stimulus to which the animal responds in such experiments: (a) that it is the total stimulus configuration, consisting of two stimuli presented simultaneously in a given spatial order (Gestalt theory); (b) that it is the relationship between the stimuli, *i.e.*, brighter, larger, etc. (relational theory); and (c) that the animal responds positively to one of the (absolute) stimuli or negatively to the other. Their own theory is based on the first hypothesis and so is in effect a Gestalt or configuration theory so far as the definition of the stimulus is concerned. However, they depend on the "law of effect," which is unacceptable to most Gestalt theorists, in dealing with the problem of learning.

While the majority of experimental findings have shown that the tendency to react to the test situation in a manner which could be interpreted as involving either relational- or Gestalt-perception has been dominant, there has been a considerable number of instances of response contrary to these views. In general, experimental results have shown that transposition tends to fail (a) when the ratio between the original training stimuli is fairly large; (b) when the distance between the training stimuli and test stimuli increases; and (c) in the case of size, when training is to the smaller stimulus and the test is with still smaller stimuli. These inconsistent results have been either entirely ignored by the relational and Gestalt theorists or vaguely accounted for in terms of being beyond the range of equivalence with the training stimuli. To say concerning the failure of transposition at extremes of the size series, as Lashley does, that a pinhead and a cartwheel, unlike a dime and a quarter, just do not belong in the same size series (*11*), describes the experimental finding in a very picturesque manner. However, it explains nothing. A satisfactory theory must be capable of stating, at least in some degree, the factors which limit the range of transposition of response within a stimulus series. Whether or not the relational theory or the Gestalt theory can or ever will be able to do this, is not our present concern. All that can be stated here is that in their present forms neither has as yet done so. Both find themselves confronted with experimental facts which contradict them.[1]

In the course of attempting to formulate an S-R theory of discrimination learning based on association or conditioning principles, the writer found that the theory, when extended to the problem of discrimination between cue members of a stimulus series such as brightness, size, etc., was able to deduce the phenomenon of transposition. Moreover, the theory led to the further prediction that under certain conditions transposition should fail to take place. While not completely in agreement with all the available experimental evidence as to the limitations of transposition, the theory was at least a little more capable in this respect than either the Gestalt or relational theories.

The theory of discrimination learning and transposition proposed by the writer has been presented in two previous articles (14, 15). The first dealt primarily with the learning problem, particularly the phenomena of the pre-solution period, while the second paper elaborated the transposition problem. Briefly, the theory proposes that discrimination learning is a cumulative process of building up the excitatory tendency or association between the positive stimulus cue and the response of approaching it as the result of successive reinforcement, as compared with the excitatory tendency of the negative stimulus to evoke the response of approaching it, which receives only non-reinforcement. This differential training continues, theoretically, until the difference between the excitatory strengths of the two stimulus cues is sufficiently great to overshadow always any differences in excitatory strength that may exist between other aspects of the stimulus situation which happen to be allied in their response-evoking action with one or the other

---

[1] Exception must be made here to the Gestalt theory of these phenomena recently elaborated by Gulliksen and Wolfle (5). Their well-worked-out formulation has shown considerable promise of being able to account for many of the experimental data.

of the cue stimuli on a particular trial, *e.g.,* the two food boxes or food alleys, which may be allied on one trial with one of the cue aspects and on the next with the other.

In extending the theory to differential response to two members of a stimulus series, certain further assumptions were made. A somewhat modified formulation of the essential characteristics of the hypothesis is presented with the aid of Figure 1. For purposes of exposition, the experimental situation is

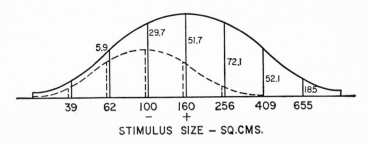

STIMULUS SIZE — SQ.CMS.

Fig. 1. Diagrammatic representation of the relations between the hypothetical generalization curves, positive and negative, after training on the stimulus combination 160(+) and 100(−).

assumed to be a size discrimination, the subject being required to learn to go to a stimulus square 160 sq. cms. in area to obtain food, and not to a square of 100 sq. cms. It is postulated:

(a) That, as the result of training or reinforcement, the positive cue aspect (square 160) acquires a super-threshold excitatory tendency (E) to the response of approaching it of the amount represented by the solid line at that point.

(b) That there is a generalization of this excitatory tendency to other members of the size series, and that this generalization follows a gradient such as that represented by the upper curved line.

(c) That with failure of reinforcement of response to the negative cue aspect (stimulus 100), experimental extinction will take place and a negative or inhibitory tendency (I) will be developed to the amount indicated by the broken line at the point on the abscissa marked 100 sq. cms.

(d) That there is a generalization of this inhibitory tendency to other members of the size series according to the gradient shown by the lower curved line.[2]

(e) That the effective excitatory strength of the size cue at any point in the series is the algebraic summation of these positive (excitatory) and negative (inhibitory) tendencies. This value is indicated by the magnitude of the distance between the upper and lower generalization curves.

(f) That the remaining attributes or dimensions of the two stimulus figures being identical, their excitatory and inhibitory tendencies will cancel each other and hence need not be considered in determining the differential excitatory strengths of the stimulus pair (e.g., square 160 and square 100).

An examination of the hypothetical effective strengths of various stimulus members after learning on the original training pair, which the graph is supposed to represent, reveals that transposition tests with stimulus pairs 256 vs. 160 and 100 vs. 62 should lead to the predominant choice of the larger stimulus in each case. Thus a deduction of a response which has usually been exclusively interpreted as involving a relational-perception or response to a configuration is shown to be possible on the basis of conditioning or association principles.[3]

As was pointed out in the earlier article (14), we lack sufficient knowledge to make specific postulates as to the nature of the generalization curves, e.g., how they vary with the number of reinforcements, from individual to individual, etc., and hence it is not possible to make very specific deductions as to exactly what the nature of the results in the transposition tests will be at each point in the stimulus continuum under various conditions of original training and testing. Nevertheless, certain more general implications follow and thus permit an empirical test of the theory. Two such, (a) that the amount of transfer

---

[2] It will be observed that the stimulus dimension (area) has been plotted on a logarithmic scale, as shown by the fact that the different members (squares) are equidistant from each other. The ratio of the stimulus areas to each other is constant at 1.6 to 1.0. The curves of generalization of the positive excitatory tendency have the equation $E = 100 \times 10^{-cX^d}$, while the equations for the inhibition generalization curves have the form $I = 60 \times 10^{-kX^d}$, where X is the distance in logarithmic units between the test and training stimuli.

[3] The reader is referred to the original article for other details, such as the effect of magnitude of differences between the effective excitatory strengths of the two stimuli, etc.

will decrease as stimulus pairs farther removed from the test pair are employed in the transposition test, and (b) that transposition will be less the greater is the difference between the original training pair, have received confirmation in several different experiments involving different conditions and organisms (*3, 8, 15, 20*).   More recently, the writer presented the results of experiments involving the effects of special training with isolated stimuli on previously learned responses to stimulus pairs.   These data were in striking agreement with the present conditioning theory and not a little embarrassing to the various relational or Gestalt interpretations (*17*).

The Present Problem

The present study reports the results of further experiments concerned with this problem of the basis of differential response by animals to members of a stimulus series.   The learning to choose the intermediate of three members of a stimulus series has also been interpreted by some psychologists as involving either response to the relational properties of the positive member or Gestalt-perception.   Thus Perkins and Wheeler (*13*), upon finding that goldfish could learn to choose the medium of three different brightnesses, interpreted their behavior as involving perception of the relationship.   McCulloch (*12*), employing a somewhat different type of situation in that the animal was required to learn to respond to the intermediate of a series of three weights with only the intermediate and either extreme being presented on any given trial, likewise inferred that his subjects (white rats) reacted, in part at least, on the basis of the membership properties of the positive stimulus, and partly to its absolute properties.   Perkins and Wheeler have explained this latter type of discrimination not as involving any absolute judgment, but as involving "two relative judgments forming a complex temporal configuration."

Warden and his co-workers (*18, 19*) and Wolfle (*20*), on the other hand, have interpreted their experimental results with this intermediate problem, involving the presentation of the intermediate stimulus with only one of the extremes at a time, as indicating that response was to the absolute properties of the stimulus cue. Wolfle nicely showed Perkins' and Wheeler's "two relative judgments" interpretation to be incorrect by demonstrating in a special test involving the simultaneous presentation of all three stimuli that response to the absolute (intermediate) stimulus occurred in 142 of 150 choices by five subjects.

The present investigation was carried out in the Yale Laboratories of Primate Biology and employed chimpanzee subjects in an experimental situation which involved learning to choose the intermediate of three different sized squares, *e.g.,* 256, 160, 100 sq. cms. Tests for transposition to another setting, *e.g.,* 409, 256, 160, were then given at the completion of learning. Our primary interest was to discover whether the chimpanzee would respond to the absolute stimulus of the training combination or to the Gestalt or relational properties of the original stimulus situation.

Experimental Procedure

A. Subjects

Six adult chimpanzees were used in this study. Each had previously been used in multiple-choice experiments and also in various discrimination experiments, including response to size differences. The latter experience consisted, so far as four of the subjects were concerned, in being trained to respond to either the larger or smaller of two stimulus squares differing in area and then, after being tested for transposition, being given reversed training, *i.e.,* to choose the larger if previously trained to the smaller, and vice versa, and a set of further transposition tests.[4] Of the remaining two subjects, Pati learned only a single size discrimination problem and was never given reversal training, while May was never trained differentially to size dif-

[4] The results of these latter transposition tests were reported at the Dartmouth meeting of the American Psychological Association but have never been published. Briefly, it was found that of twelve transposition tests given six subjects, nine were not in accordance with their most recent (*i.e.,* reversed) training, as the relational theory would presumably expect, while three scores ranged from 60 percent to 90 percent in accord with it. Examination of the data from the point of view of the theory proposed by the writer revealed that eleven of the twelve test results were closely in line with it.

ferences, but was merely run in a situation in which responses
to both sized squares were rewarded.   During this period, May
chose the larger predominantly for a while and then shifted to
chance response.

The present experiment was instituted from about five to ten
weeks after the completion of the above described work.   Just
what effect such prior training experiences might have had on
the results of the present experiment cannot, of course, be
known for sure, as no naïve subjects were available as controls.
Presumably, however, the relational or Gestalt interpretation
would be that the subjects had first learned to respond in one
manner to the Gestalt- or relational-perception and had then
learned to make the opposite response to the same stimulus configuration.   Training to the new combination of three differ-
ently sized squares required the learning of a new response.
The relation of the earlier training to the results of the present
experiment from the point of view of the writer's theory will be
discussed in connection with the results.

B. Apparatus and Method

The discrimination apparatus has already been described in
some detail (15, 16).   Briefly, it consisted of three small food
boxes to the front of which were clamped the stimulus forms,
white enameled squares cut from No. 28 galvanized iron.   The
stimulus boxes were presented to the subject by pushing the
platform on which they were arranged to a point one inch from
the living cage screen, where it was possible for the subject to
poke its fingers through the two-inch wire mesh, push open
the box, and obtain the food.   The incorrect boxes were
locked.   No corrective response was permitted; instead, the
platform was immediately pulled back beyond the reach of the
subject and preparations were made behind an opaque screen
for the next trial.

Fifteen trials were given each day during both the learning
and testing series.   The different sized squares were shifted
about so that each appeared equally often (five times) at the
three spatial positions within each daily series.   Training continued until the criterion of learning, fifteen correct choices of

the intermediate or medium sized square within a daily series of trials, was attained.

Half of the six subjects were trained originally on squares 256, 160, and 100 in area and half on squares 409, 256, and 160. Those trained on the first combination were tested for transposition on the second and vice versa. Transposition tests were given immediately following learning. One was given ten minutes after the completion of the criterion series and a second approximately twenty-four hours later. The subjects were then given further training on the original learning combination until the criterion was again met, whereupon a further transposition test was given twenty-four hours later. All responses were rewarded throughout the transposition trials.

The experiment was further continued by having the subjects learn to respond to the medium sized square of the combination previously used in the transposition tests and then testing for transposition with the original learning combination. Thus a subject which originally learned with the 256, 160, 100 square combination and was tested with the 409, 256, 160 setting, was now trained to choose square 256 of the latter and was tested for transposition on the former, etc. Two transposition tests, a ten-minute and a twenty-four-hour one, were given subsequent to this latter reversed learning. The experimental work was carried out daily, usually in the forenoon.

Experimental Results

The experimental data for the individual subjects pertaining to the original learning and the transposition tests following it, are contained in Table 1. The first column gives the name of the subject and the second the total number of trials, including the criterion series, required to learn. The next three columns show the distribution of the responses to the three squares of the training setting on the first day of the learning series. The remainder of the table shows the distribution of responses to the various squares, largest (L), medium (M) and smallest (S), in the several transposition tests.

All subjects successfully learned the original problem with-

TABLE 1

Showing the number of trials to learn original problem of choosing medium square, the distribution of responses on the first day of learning series to the three stimulus squares employed in original learning, and the number of choices in subsequent transposition tests involving a different setting of the largest (L), medium (M), and smallest (S) square. The first three subjects learned on setting: L—256, M—160, S—100, and were tested on setting: L—409, M—256, S—160. For the remaining three subjects were the settings were the reverse.

Subject	No. Trials	Learning			Transposition Tests								
					First 10-Minute			First 24-Hour			Second 24-Hour		
		L	M	S	L	M	S	L	M	S	L	M	S
		256	*160*	*100*	*409*	*256*	*160*	*409*	*256*	*160*	*409*	*256*	*160*
May	225	4	6	5	0	1	14	0	5	10	0	1	14
Bokar	75	9	4	2	0	5	10	3	9	3	5	8	2
Pati	135	9	4	2	0	1	14	0	6	9	0	6	9
		409	*256*	*160*	*256*	*160*	*100*	*256*	*160*	*100*	*256*	*160*	*100*
Lia	165	6	5	4	15	0	0	14	1	0	15	0	0
Mimi	135	0	3	12	13	1	1	15	0	0	15	0	0
Cuba	135	4	3	8	12	3	0	15	0	0	13	2	0
	M = 145				% Medium —12.2 % Absolute—86.6			% Medium —23.3 % Absolute—73.3			% Medium —18.9 % Absolute—75.5		

out too great difficulty. The number of trials, averaging 145 for the six subjects, compares with an average of eighty trials for seven subjects learning to choose the larger or smaller of two squares, the areas of which were in the same ratio as those in the present intermediate problem, *i.e.*, 1.6 to 1.

The results for the group as a whole on the transposition tests are shown most clearly by the data at the bottom of each table. It will be observed that the subjects responded overwhelmingly in the transposition tests to the absolute or specific square to which they were trained on the original learning setting.   Thus in the first ten-minute test the subjects responded 86.6 percent of the trials to the specific (absolute) stimulus and only 12.2 percent to the medium or intermediate sized stimulus of the new test combination.   Twenty-four hours later their responses were again predominantly to the absolute square (73.3 percent), although the percentage of relational responses to the medium squares increased to 23.3 percent.   The final transposition test, given twenty-four hours after further training on the original setting, once more showed a large margin of response in favor of the absolute over the relational response.[5]

Examination of the individual data reveals a very marked difference in the percentage of responses made to the absolute stimulus square when it was the smallest and when it was the largest square of the test combination.   There was a much greater tendency to respond absolutely when the absolute stimulus was the largest of the combination than when it was the smallest.   This is most easily seen by comparing the data for the individuals in the upper half of the table with those in the lower.   The latter, it will be seen, responded in a much higher proportion of trials to the absolute stimulus than the former (94 percent as compared with 62.9 percent).   This finding may be related to the fact that these subjects were originally trained to choose the larger of a pair of stimuli although attention should also be called to the fact that the chimpanzees have consistently shown a tendency to respond to the larger rather than smaller member of a pair.

Only one subject, Bokar, showed a greater tendency to re-

[5] Three subjects performed perfectly on the first learning series, while three required three days to again meet the criterion of fifteen correct responses.

spond to the medium square, 256, in the transposition tests than to the absolute square, 160. Particularly was this the case in the twenty-four-hour tests. It should be noted, however,

TABLE 2

Showing the number of trials to learn the reversal problem and the number of choices in the transposition tests involving a different setting of the largest (L), medium (M), and smallest (S) square. The training and transposition settings were just the reverse of those in Table 1.

Subject	Relearning		Transposition Tests					
	Trials to Learn	Positive Square	10-Minute			24-Hour		
			L	M	S	L	M	S
			256	160	100	256	160	100
May ..	75	256	15	0	0	15	0	0
Bokar .	60	256	7	8	0	10	5	0
Pati ...	75	256	15	0	0	15	0	0
			409	256	160	409	256	160
Lia ...	105	160	0	12	3	0	12	3
Mimi .	120	160	0	0	15	0	0	15
Cuba .	40	160	0	15	0	0	15	0
	M = 80		% Medium —38.9 % Absolute—61.1			% Medium —35.5 % Absolute—64.4		

that both this subject and also Pati, another animal that tended to respond to the medium square, 256, showed a fairly strong tendency to respond to this square (256) in the original learning.

The data for the relearning problem, which involved the shifting of the settings of the original learning and transposition tests, are presented in Table 2. There it will be seen that the learning of the original transposition setting was quite rapid, the group average for the number of trials to reach the learning criterion being 80.

The results of the transposition tests after this reversal training reveal a much lessened tendency to respond absolutely and a corresponding increase in the responses (relational) to the medium square. The results for the group as a whole, however, still favor response to the absolute square.

Discussion and Interpretation of Results

A. Transposition Tests Following Original Training

While our primary concern in the discussion of these results will be with their relation to the conditioning type of "absolute" theory elaborated by the writer in connection with the two-stimulus-member problem, we may briefly consider them in connection with the rival interpretations. We begin with Köhler's version of the configurational or Gestalt-perception theory. Köhler implies that the organism responds (in some way?) to the structure-function or whole properties of the stimulus situation.

Turning to the present "intermediate" problem, the question for this theory is whether the whole properties which the training and test configurations have in common are discernible by the chimpanzee. Insofar as the new test situation has the same whole properties, the organism will respond in the same manner to it that it did to the original configuration. Unfortunately, Köhler does not provide us with any specific postulates that will permit stating in any precise manner what the limit of equivalence of new test situations is. However, one possible basis for reasoning might be the known results on the two-stimulus-member situation. Employing the same size-difference ratio (1.6 : 1.0) as used in the present experiment, it was found that after training on squares 160(+) vs. 100(−) transposition (88.3 percent) took place to the new test combination 256 vs. 160 and to the 409 vs. 256 combination (78 percent) (15). Also, after training on the combination 256(+) vs. 160(−), transposition (80 percent) took place in the test combination 160 vs. 100. One might be led to hazard the guess, then, that these stimuli were within the range of perceptual equivalence and that after training on the configuration 256, 160, 100 there would be transposition to the test configuration 409, 256, 160; and that after training on the 409, 256, 160 combination transposition would occur to the 256, 160, 100 setting. The experimental results (Table 1), however, failed to confirm this expectation for, it will be recalled, the subjects responded predominantly to the absolute stimulus and much less than chance even to the stimulus member that this configuration theory would predict.

The Gestalt or configuration theory of Gulliksen and Wolfe is much more highly developed than the primitive Köhler version. These theorists define the response in spatial terms as response to the left or response to the right. Thus, in the two-stimulus size problem in which response to the larger of the two stimuli is always reinforced and response to the small never reinforced, the subject is assumed to be learning to make a left response on those trials in which the configuration "large on left and small on right" is presented and a right response when the configuration "large on right and small on left" is presented. The effective strength of each configuration to elicit its appropriate response is a function of the number of correct and incorrect responses made to it and the number of these same responses made to the other configuration. The effects of training on each configuration are assumed to generalize to other similar configurations according to a gradient very much as postulated by the present writer. By means of certain assumptions as to the learning and generalization parameters, Gulliksen and Wolfe are able to deduce a considerable number of propositions about discrimination learning and transposition phenomena.

Turning to the three-stimulus problem, their theory becomes rather complicated. Such a situation would involve six different configurations. Using S for small, M for medium, and L for large, these six configurations would be as follows: SML, LMS, MLS, MSL, LSM, and SLM. The animal would learn, in the present type of problem, to select or respond to the middle position (door or box) in the case of the first two configurations; to the left for the next two; and to the right for the last pair of configurations. Prediction as to what should occur in a transposition involving a new combination of stimulus numbers, such as in the present experiment, depends upon how far one shifted on the stimulus dimension from the training combination. A slight shift would lead to the expectation that the animal would continue to respond to the medium-sized stimulus. As the test combination shifted farther away from the training one, the transfer would become less. Until specific postulates are made about the degree of generalization, it is not possible to state how far transposition will occur, except to say that it will be less in the three-stimulus than the two-stimulus problem. So far as the present results are concerned, however, they do not offer much encouragement to this theory, for not only was there no transfer to the test situation, but the subjects responded predominantly to the absolute stimulus. Such a result is definitely not in line with expectations based on this theory.

Little or nothing need be said about the relational interpretation. Like the Köhler Gestalt theory, it suffers from the fact that it has no specific postulates from which any deduction can be made.

In applying the conditioning or absolute theory to the present experimental situation, we shall use the same postulates that were involved in the treatment of the two-stimulus problem situation. Moreover, the particular form and empirical constants of generalization curves which predict the transposition that actually occurs on the test situation 409 *vs.* 256 after training on 256(+) *vs.* 160 and on test situation 256 *vs.* 160 after training on 160(+) *vs.* 100 will be used. The question we are primarily interested in is what are the implications of such a theory as to the kind of result to be expected in the transposition test after training to the intermediate-sized of three squares.

Figure 2 represents the intermediate discrimination situation

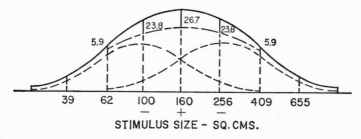

Fig. 2. Diagrammatic representation of the relations between the hypothetical generalization curves, positive and negative, after training on the three-stimulus combination 256(−), 160(+), and 62(−).

in which the subject's responses to the medium-sized square, 160, are reinforced, whereas responses to squares 100 and 256 are not reinforced. It will be observed that the positive, medium-sized square, 160, receives generalized inhibitory tendencies from both negative stimuli. As two errors are made by chance for each correct response, as compared with one error for each correct response in the two-stimulus situation, it will be seen that there is as much inhibition developed at each point as at the single point in the two-stimulus situation. The positive stimulus thus receives generalized inhibition from two sources instead of one. On the assumption that there is a summation of these generalized inhibitory tendencies, it will readily be seen that the learning of such an intermediate problem should be much more difficult than learning in the two-stimulus situation.[6]

With regard to the results to be expected on the transposition test, it is necessary to make some postulate as to the summation of the inhibitory tendencies. The assumption made here is essentially patterned after that made by Hull in a similar connection (6). The rule implies that the inhibition developing with non-reinforcement approaches a limiting value according to an exponential function instead of increasing infinitely according to the straight-line function. The formula is:

$$I_1 + I_2 = I_1 + I_2 - \frac{I_1 \times I_2}{A},$$

where $I_1 =$ inhibition or generalized inhibition at any stimulus resulting from frustration of response to stimulus 100;

6 In this connection, attention should be called to the claim made by Lashley that an experiment by him in which he showed that white rats learned to choose the largest (or smallest) of three different sized circles much more easily than the intermediate problem (indeed, no progress towards learning was exhibited in the latter) was evidence that the rats responded on a relational basis and not absolute. His argument was based upon an assumption to the effect that "on an absolute basis this (the problem of 'intermediate size') should have been no more difficult than reaction to the largest or smallest" (11, p. 165). Whatever "absolute" theory Lashley may have had in mind, it is obvious that the present formulation does not imply that the "intermediate" problem would be no more difficult to master than reaction to the largest or to the smallest. His results, far from being contradictory, lend still further support to the present "absolute" theory.

I_2 = inhibition or generalized inhibition at any stimulus resulting from frustration of response to stimulus 256;

A = threshold or limit of inhibition at any point on stimulus dimension. It has been assumed that the maximum amount of inhibition cannot exceed the strength of the excitatory tendency at that point.

The variable dash curve in Figure 2 represents the theoretical values of inhibition calculated according to the above postulate.

The effective excitatory strength of a stimulus member is taken to be the difference between the excitatory strength and the strength of the inhibition. This value is indicated at the experimental points by the solid vertical lines drawn between the two curves, with the numerical values being given to the right of them. The situation shows that the intermediate stimulus has a strength of 26.7 points and each of the other two stimulus squares strength of 23.8. If this is taken as representative of the state of affairs at the completion of learning, it will readily be seen that the presentation of such a stimulus combination as 409, 256, 160 would lead theoretically to continued choice of the absolute stimulus, 160. Similarly, it may be shown that training to the intermediate square, 256, in the combination 409, 256, 160, would lead to continued response to this same stimulus (256) in the transposition combination 256, 160, 100. This is the type of result, it will be noticed, that was actually obtained in the present experiment.

It is recognized, of course, that the previous experiences of the subjects in the present investigation complicate the theoretical representation of the positive and negative (inhibitory) tendencies they have acquired and that the picture presented in Figure 2 is not entirely accurate because it omits from consideration the effects of earlier training. Obviously, it is impossible to attempt, in the present state of our knowledge, to represent the effects of such training. It is interesting to note, however, that the single subject, May, that had not received any prior differential training on size discrimination responded very decidedly (38 out of 45 trials) to the absolute square in the transposition tests. Indeed, she responded more definitely to the

absolute properties than did either of the other two subjects
trained on the same original setting.   Also, of no little significance is the fact that Lia, the only other subject that did not
exhibit a decided bias for either the largest or smallest member
of the original training combination (see Table 1), also showed
a very clear-cut absolute response in the transposition tests,
choosing stimulus 256, to which it was trained originally, in 44
out of the 45 transposition test trials.   Both of these cases suggest that the more closely are the theoretical conditions approached, the greater is the agreement between the implications
of the theory and the experimental findings.

B. Transposition Tests Following Reversal Training

The second part of the experiment was primarily exploratory
in nature.   Its object was to ascertain what the effect of the
reversal training on the transposition setting of the first part
of the experiment would have upon response to the original
learning setting.   Would the subjects now respond to the intermediate square to which they had originally been trained, i.e.,
to the configurational properties, or would they continue to
choose the absolute stimulus to which they had been last conditioned?   Such contrary training in which first one square,
e.g., 256, is the positive cue and later it becomes supplanted
by a different square, e.g., 160, might lead to a tendency on the
part of the organism to adopt a different basis of response than
an absolute one.[7]

The results of the transposition tests following this "reversal"
training reveal that there was some tendency to shift from response on an absolute basis, although the results for the group
as a whole still favor response to the absolute stimulus.   The
data of two subjects, Lia and Cuba, suggest that response might
have been on the basis of configurational or relational properties of the stimulus complexes.   Cuba chose the medium
square 256, on all 15 transposition trials after just learning to
choose square 160 in the setting in which it was the medium

[7] The factors which make for response on the part of animals to the absolute
or configurational properties of stimulus complexes will be discussed in a subsequent paper, reporting further experiments with chimpanzees on the intermediate-sized problem.   The present investigation merely attempted to ascertain
the effect of a single such "reversal" of training.

stimulus.   Lia chose the medium stimulus on 12 occasions in each of the two transposition tests.

In order to test further the possibility that these two subjects might be responding on some configurational basis, two further transposition tests were given.   The first involved switching back after the two transposition tests to the most recently learned setting, *i.e.*, 256, 160, 100.   In this test Cuba responded eleven times to the intermediate square, 160, three times to square 256, and once to square 100.   This result again suggested that this subject was responding to some configurational property.   On the other hand, Lia responded in this test predominantly (10 times) to the largest square (256) and only five times to the medium square (160).   A still further test was provided by means of an entirely new setting, consisting of squares 160, 100, and 62.   The absence of any widely generalized configurational response to the medium-sized of three stimuli was clearly revealed by the choice of the largest square, 160, by both subjects on all fifteen trials.

Summary and Conclusions

The basis of differential response by chimpanzees to the intermediate member of three different-sized squares was investigated.   After learning to choose the medium-sized of three squares (*e.g.*, 256 sq. cms. in the stimulus combination 409, 256, 160), it was found that the chimpanzees continued to choose the same (absolute) stimulus when it was no longer the intermediate member of a new test combination, *e.g.*, 256, 160, 100.   Reversal training to the intermediate member of the test combination led to some evidence on the part of two of the six subjects of limited response on a configurational basis.   The remaining four subjects continued to respond definitely on an absolute basis.   The results are shown to support the writer's "absolute" type of theory of transposition and to contradict, insofar as it is possible to do so, the Gestalt and relational interpretations.

REFERENCES

1. BINGHAM, H. C. Visual perception in the chick. *Behav. Monogr.*, 1922, no. 20.   Baltimore, Md.: Williams & Wilkins, p. 104.
2. ELLIS, W. D. *A Source Book of Gestalt Psychology.*   New York: Harcourt, Brace and Co., Inc., 1938.

3. GULLIKSEN, H. Studies of transfer of response. I. Relative versus absolute factors in the discrimination of size by the white rat. *J. genet. Psychol.*, 1932, *40*, 37–51.

4. ——, & WOLFLE, D. L. A theory of learning and transfer. *Psychometrika*, 1938, *3*, 127–149, 225–251.

5. ——, ——. Correction of an error in "A theory of learning and transfer." *Psychometrika*, 1939, *4*, 178.

6. HULL, C. L. The problem of stimulus equivalence in behavior theory. *Psychol. Rev.*, 1939, *46*, 9–30.

7. JOHNSON, H. M. Visual pattern discrimination in the vertebrates. *J. animal Behav.*, 1914, *4*, 319–339, 340–361; *6*, 169–188.

8. KINNAMAN, A. J. Mental life of two Macacus rhesus monkeys in captivity. *Amer. J. Psychol.*, 1902, *13*, 98–148, 173–218.

9. KLÜVER, H. *Behavior Mechanisms in Monkeys.* Chicago: University of Chicago Press, 1933.

10. KÖHLER, W. Aus der Anthropoidenstation auf Teneriffa. IV. Nachweis einfacher Strukturfunktionen beim Schimpansen und beim Haushuhn: Über eine neue Methode zur Untersuchung des bunten Farbensystems, *Abh. preuss. Akad. Wiss.*, 1918, Berlin, 1–101.

11. LASHLEY, K. S. The mechanism of vision. XV. Preliminary studies of the rat's capacity for detail vision. *J. gen. Psychol.*, 1938, *18*, 123–193.

12. McCULLOCH, T. L. The selection of the intermediate of a series of weights by the white rat. *J. comp. Psychol.*, 1935, *20*, 1–11.

13. PERKINS, F. T., & WHEELER, R. H. Configurational learning in the goldfish. *Comp. Psychol. Monogr.*, 1930, *7*, 1–50.

14. SPENCE, K. W. The nature of discrimination learning in animals. *Psychol. Rev.*, 1936, *43*, 427–449.

15. ——. The differential response in animals to stimuli varying within a single dimension. *Psychol. Rev.*, 1937, *44*, 430–444.

16. ——. Analysis of formation of visual discrimination habits in chimpanzee. *J. comp. Psychol.*, 1937, *23*, 77–100.

17. ——. Failure of transposition in size-discrimination of chimpanzees. *Amer. J. Psychol.*, 1941, *54*, 223–229.

18. WARDEN, C. J., & ROWLEY, J. B. The discrimination of absolute versus relative brightness in the ring dove, *Turtur risorius. J. comp. Psychol.*, 1929, *9*, 317–337.

19. ——, & WINSLOW, C. N. The discrimination of absolute versus relative size in the ring dove, *Turtur risorius. J. genet. Psychol.*, 1931, *39*, 328–341.

20. WOLFLE, D. L. Absolute brightness discrimination in the white rat. *J. comp. Psychol.*, 1937, *24*, 59–71.

21

The Nature of the Response in Discrimination Learning

In a recent article in this JOURNAL Weise and Bitterman (*11*) raise the question as to what the response is in the typical discrimination learning situation. As they point out, two different conceptions have been put forward. One, proposed by Nissen (*7*) and the writer (*9*), holds that the subject learns to orient towards and approach the stimulus complex (path, door, alley, window) containing the positive stimulus cue (white, form, etc.) rather than to approach the stimulus complex containing the negative cue.[1] The other, held by Gulliksen and Wolfle (*2*), conceives of the problem in terms of learning to turn right to one spatial arrangement of the stimulus cues (*e.g.,* black-white) and to turn left to the other spatial arrangement (*e.g.,* white-black). The latter conception assumes that the subject responds to the total stimulus configuration whereas the former assumes that the subject responds to one part of the stimulus complex without regard *necessarily* to the other.

Admitting that the writer's version of the "approach'" interpretation was able to handle certain facts which they believed refuted the Nissen version, Weise and Bitterman suggested that

---

1 Nissen speaks of avoiding the negative cue. The writer's theory of discrimination learning (*9*) specifically avoided consideration of the condition of punishing a response to the negative cue, and for that reason does not specify avoidance.

a further test could be provided by comparing the rate of learning two different types of discrimination problems. One of these they designated the *simultaneous* problem. Essentially it is the standard discrimination problem in which on 50 per cent of the trials, one of the cues (*e.g.*, black) is on the left and the other (*e.g.*, white) on the right. On the other half of the trials the positions of the cues are reversed. In the second problem, termed the *successive* problem, only one of the cues is present on each trial. If the apparatus is an alley, both paths are either white or both black. The subject must learn to go right when the white cues are present and left when the alleys are black, or vice versa.

Now this latter problem involves a type of discrimination learning which the present writer has never dealt with in any published article. It represents a situation in which no one of the cue elements S_W, B_B, S_L, S_R is consistently reinforced as compared with the others. Unlike the standard situation in which the excitatory strength of the positive cue (S_W) to evoke the approach response becomes steadily greater than that of the negative cue (S_B), so that eventually response is always made to the stimulus complex (alley, window, etc.) that contains it, no one of the stimulus elements or cues in this successive situation acquires greater excitatory strength than the others. How then, in terms of this theory, can one explain the learning of such a problem? The interpretation that the writer has held for some years and has presented at a number of colloquia is essentially the same as that given by Nissen (6). Instead of referring to it as involving a conditional reaction, however, the writer has referred to it as patterned discrimination. According to this conception the response of approaching certain patterns (combinations) of the stimulus components is consistently reinforced, whereas response to certain others is not. Thus on half the trials the situation is shown below as in A and half as in B.

A. $\left.\begin{array}{l} S_W \\ S_L \end{array}\right\} \rightarrow R_A\ (+)$ $\left.\begin{array}{l} S_W \\ S_R \end{array}\right\} \rightarrow R_A\ (-)$

B. $\left.\begin{array}{l} S_B \\ S_L \end{array}\right\} \rightarrow R_A\ (-)$ $\left.\begin{array}{l} S_B \\ S_R \end{array}\right\} \rightarrow R_A\ (+)$

The stimulus compounds, S_W-S_L and S_B-S_R, acquire excitatory tendencies to the response of approaching, the other two (S_B-S_L and S_W-S_R) do not. We can speak here, as experimenters, of a relation, the brightness, *i.e.*, black or white, in connection with the position or spatial cue. The writer would prefer to identify each as discriminable patterns or stimulus compounds *per se*. Discrimination will involve such patterning according to this conception only when no one of the cue members is systematically reinforced more than the others.

There is nothing new, of course, in this conception of stimulus compounds and their differentiation for, as will be recalled, Pavlov (8) demonstrated that one can set up differential conditioned responses to stimulus compounds involving the same elements in different order. Undoubtedly Hull (4) would interpret these different compounds in terms of his afferent interaction hypothesis, and S_W in combination with the cues from the left alley (and the proprioceptive cues from orienting and looking to the left) would now become S_W', whereas it would be S_W'' when combined with S_R. According to this conception the subject learns to approach S_W' and not S_W'', the competing stimulus on the particular trial. Likewise on the alternative trials it learns to approach S_B'' and not to approach S_B'.

It is apparent from the above discussion that the discrimination would be more difficult in the case of this *successive* discrimination problem than in the *simultaneous* problem, for the stimulus compounds to be discriminated on each trial are more similar than in the simultaneous problem. Thus S_W-S_L is more different from S_B-S_R than it is from S_W-S_R. At least on this point everyone seems to be in agreement, as Nissen and Weise and Bitterman all reach the same conclusion. On the other hand, according to Weise and Bitterman the Gulliksen-Wolfle interpretation would predict that the reverse would be the case, *i.e.*, that the *simultaneous* problem would be more difficult.

As there was no evidence directly available comparing the relative difficulty of the two types of situations, Weise and Bitterman conducted an experiment in which they employed a multiple (four-unit) discrimination box. Their data clearly showed that the *simultaneous* problem was the more difficult, and they interpreted the finding as opposed to the interpretations of Nissen and the writer which implied that the *successive* problem would be the more difficult.

The finding of Weise and Bitterman was certainly a surprise to the present writer, for in the course of the last 15 years a number of studies had been run in the Iowa laboratories that had tended to suggest that the *successive* problem was relatively the more difficult of the two situations. Thus the Grice (*1*) and Smith (*10*) theses had been run under somewhat similar conditions, the former being a *simultaneous* discrimination and the latter a *successive* one. Whereas Grice's subjects learned in some 20 trials, Smith's took 70 or more. A number of our exploratory experiments had also pointed in the same direction. Furthermore, Lawrence (*5, 6*) has reported two experiments that permitted comparison of the two learning situations by the same subjects.[2] After learning first on the *simultaneous* discrimination problem, the subjects subsequently learned the same *successive* problem. If transfer affects the results in this instance, it certainly favors the *successive* problem. And yet an examination of the error curves reveals that the curve reached zero at about 25 trials in the case of the *simultaneous* problem whereas it had not yet reached zero by 85 trials in the *successive* problem. In a subsequent study in which the *successive* problem was learned first and the *simultaneous* problem was learned second, the *simultaneous* discrimination was again much easier: The curve reached zero by 18 trials whereas the *successive* problem showed errors still being made at 70 trials. In accord with these results a doctor's thesis just completed along the lines of the Lawrence experiments by Heyman (*3*) in the Iowa Laboratory showed much quicker learning on the *simultaneous* problem.

Nevertheless the Lawrence and Heyman studies involved certain additional irrelevant stimuli that might have been in some way responsible for the disagreement of their findings with those of Weise and Bitterman. Accordingly we instituted an experiment in which an elevated T-maze was employed with black and white cues. It is not necessary to go into detail as to the

---

[2] Weise and Bitterman cite the Lawrence studies in connection with the description of the successive problem, but fail surprisingly to point out the opposing nature of their results.

apparatus and procedure except to state that (a) the maze was a simple T in which the stem was an intermediate gray and the arms of the T were white or black; (b) the non-correction method was used, as this is the procedure specified in the writer's theory (the correction procedure is too complicated); (c) the trials were spaced with a minimum of about five minutes occurring between trials; and (d) the subjects were hooded rats.[3]

The results are shown in Table 1, which presents the mean number of errors and trials required in the *simultaneous* and

TABLE 1

DATA COMPARING LEARNING OF *Simultaneous* AND *Successive* DISCRIMINATION PROBLEMS

Type of problem	Errors		Trials	
	Mean	σ_M	Mean	σ_M
Successive	53.8	7.54	143.0	16.80
Simultaneous	16.6	1.27	59.0	2.77
Difference	37.2		84.0	
t	4.86		4.94	
P	<.001		<.001	

successive situations. The finding, it is readily apparent, points in a direction diametrically opposed to that of Weise and Bitterman and is in line with our previous exploratory studies and with the data of Lawrence and Heyman.

As for the type of discrimination experiment with which the writer's theory is concerned (non-reinforcement and non-correction), he is inclined to believe that the approach interpretation will work. Just why Weise and Bitterman got opposite results is not clear, as it is difficult to interpret the very complex type of discrimination set-up they employed. The simple discrimination situation is sufficiently difficult to deal with theoretically without adding all of the problems that arise as the result of the serial nature of the multiple discrimination set-up along with the fact that it involves a gradient of reinforcement.

3 The writer wishes to acknowledge the assistance of Henry Loess and George Moeller in conducting the experiment.

The writer would like to take this opportunity to discuss further the type of patterning that the Gestalters and Gulliksen and Wolfle are talking about when they say that the subject is responding on each trial in the typical discrimination situation to the total configuration.   The present writer does not believe this to be the case for, as was pointed out earlier, in such discrimination situations, response to the positive cue member (white, triangle, etc.) is being differentially strengthened over response to the others, and hence no conditioning to a pattern is forced.

In discrimination situations not involving differences of degree in the cue stimulus there is little evidence to support the contention that the response is to such a figure-figure pattern. Thus if an animal has been trained to choose a triangle over a circle to get food, substitution of some other form for the negative stimulus does not interfere in any manner with continued response to the positive stimulus so long as no avoidance to the negative stimulus as result of shock or punishment from negative stimulus is involved.   That is to say, changing the nature of the total stimulus pattern does not interfere with the response, which would make it seem reasonable to conclude that the response was not necessarily to a pattern or to one of the cues in relation to the other cue.

According to the theoretical view proposed here, response on the basis of such cue-cue relations, or what might be called *transverse* patterning, would take place in non-articulate organisms, but only under conditions that would not permit learning on the basis of a single reinforced component or some simpler type of cue-position pattern (*e.g.*, the type of patterning involved in the successive problem).   An experiment that would require a response to the relation of the two cues (*e.g.*, two figures) in the stimulus complex would involve three different stimulus figures being presented in pairs.   Thus the animal might be required to learn the following discriminations simultaneously.

$$\triangle + \text{ vs } \bigcirc -; \quad \square + \text{ vs } \triangle -; \quad \bigcirc + \text{ vs } \square -$$

Or in the field of brightness discrimination:

$$20+ \text{ vs } 10-; \quad 5+ \text{ vs } 20-; \quad 10+ \text{ vs } 5-$$

Successful learning of such problems would require that the animal on each trial respond (by approaching) or not respond to a particular figure depending on what the other figure was. Presumably white rats should be able to learn such a pattern discrimination problem; certainly it could be solved by monkeys or chimpanzees. The learning of this type of problem would require a different set of preliminary receptor-exposure acts than simpler discrimination problems involve, and one would expect the first solution to be relatively difficult. Subsequent problems of a similar type, however, should show considerable transfer and be learned without too great difficulty.

REFERENCES

1. GRICE, G. R. The relation of secondary reinforcement to delayed reward in visual discrimination learning. *J. exp. Psychol.*, 1948, *38*, 1–15.

2. GULLIKSEN, H., & WOLFLE, D. A. A theory of learning and transfer. *Psychometrika*, 1938, *3*, 127–149.

3. HEYMAN, M. Transfer in discrimination learning following three conditions of initial training. Unpublished Ph.D. thesis, State University of Iowa, 1951.

4. HULL, C. L. *Principles of Behavior*. New York: D. Appleton-Century, 1943.

5. LAWRENCE, D. H. Acquired distinctiveness of cues: I. Transfer between discriminations on the basis of familiarity with the stimulus. *J. exp. Psychol.*, 1949, *39*, 770–784.

6. ———. Acquired distinctiveness of cues: II. Selective association in a constant stimulus situation. *J. exp. Psychol.*, 1950, *40*, 175–188.

7. NISSEN, H. W. Description of the learned response in discrimination behavior. *Psychol. Rev.*, 1950, *57*, 121–131.

8. PAVLOV, I. P. *Conditioned Reflexes* (trans. by G. V. Anrep). Oxford: Oxford University Press, 1927.

9. SPENCE, K. W. The nature of discrimination learning in animals. *Psychol. Rev.*, 1936, *43*, 427–449.

10. SMITH, M. P. The stimulus trace gradient in visual discrimination learning. *J. comp. physiol. Psychol.*, 1951, *44*, 154–162.

11. WEISE, P., & BITTERMAN, M. E. Response-selection in discriminative learning. *Psychol. Rev.*, 1951, *58*, 185–195.

22

Conceptual Models of Spatial and Non-Spatial
Selective Learning

I

The attempts by psychologists to offer theoretical accounts of selective (discrimination) learning have led to a variety of conceptual formulations or models that have differed widely both in terms of their nature and their origins. In some instances the theoretical schema has been quite unrelated to theories about other forms of learned behavior, while in others the model has been built upon a theoretical structure originally developed on the basis of quite different phenomena. The behavior theories of selective learning phenomena offered by Hull and the writer fall in this latter category; they involve a network of interrelated theoretical and empirical constructs based upon the empirical findings obtained in simple types of classical and instrumental conditioning experiments. The present paper reviews the different types of models of selective and discrimination learning suggested in the past by Hull and the writer and describes in a preliminary manner a new type of model that the writer has favored for a number of years.

The course of development of behavior theory as represented by the formulations of Hull and the writer presents an interesting pattern in regard to the investigation of different kinds of

366

learning situations. When he first turned his attention to the phenomena of learning in the early thirties, Hull's initial theoretical efforts were concerned primarily with various types of selective or trial and error learning. Borrowing Pavlov's concepts of excitation and inhibition and making use of the empirical law of effect, over a period of years Hull developed a number of miniature theoretical systems aimed at accounting for the behavioral phenomena observed in various kinds of selective learning tasks such as the problem box, simple T maze, and the serial maze (7, 8, 9, 10, 13). This type of theorizing was also extended to serial (verbal) learning in human subjects (12, 16). Paralleling these theoretical attempts and closely coordinated with them were the efforts of the writer to formulate a theoretical schema that would provide for the derivation and hence explanation of behavioral phenomena exhibited by animals in the type of learning situation known as the discrimination problem (23, 24, 25).

An important characteristic of these theories was the stress they placed on quantification, an emphasis that led not only to more precise measures of the observed behavioral phenomena, but also to attempts to employ mathematically specified theoretical concepts. Instances of these latter were Hull's logarithmic goal gradient hypothesis (8) and the various quantitative assumptions made by the writer (23, 24) concerning the manner in which S-R tendencies increased or decreased in strength with reinforcement and non-reinforcement. By means of such mathematical assumptions it was possible to derive quantitative implications concerning behavior to be expected in these various situations. Thus in the case of the serial maze Hull was able to derive such phenomena as: (a) that long blind alleys will be more readily eliminated than short ones; (b) that the order of elimination of blind alleys will tend to be in a backward direction; (c) that the readiness of choosing the shorter of two alternative paths whose ratios of lengths remains constant will be independent of the absolute difference between them.

That these theoretical formulations were quite fruitful in generating investigations that helped to advance our understanding of these selective learning situations is amply supported by a survey of the experimental literature of the thirties and forties. Nevertheless, first Hull and later the writer temporarily abandoned interest in these relatively complex phenomena and shifted the focus of our theoretical and experimental efforts from selective learning tasks to the simpler behavior situations represented by classical and instrumental conditioning.   The explanation of this shift in strategy is to be found in the nature of our theoretical program.   It will be recalled that the attempt was made to base the quantitative theoretical concepts employed in these selective learning theories, in so far as possible, on the findings of conditioning experiments.   For example, on the basis of the admittedly meager data available as to the form of classical conditioning curves, the writer (26) assumed that the strength of the excitatory tendency of a stimulus cue to elicit a response increased as an S-shaped function of the number of successive reinforcements.

The basic premise on which we operated was that the laws revealed in these simpler behavior situations provided the best source of information for specifying the quantitative concepts representing the hypothetical associative and inhibitory processes assumed to underlie the behavior changes occurring in different learning situations.   In contrast to the more complex, selective learning problems in which the response measures (e.g., per cent choice of correct response) are a function of two or more competing response tendencies, the conditioning experiment, we believed, provided a situation in which the response measure or measures reflected the strength of an S-R tendency (E in our present terminology) more or less in isolation from other S-R tendencies.   Consequently, we assumed that the empirical functions relating the changes in response measures with reinforcements and non-reinforcements in this type of experiment reflected more directly these hypothetical processes than did selective learning.

As matters turned out, however, the task was not as simple as we had hoped.   First, it soon became apparent that there was not available from conditioning experiments a satisfactory body of quantitative laws relating response measures to the various kinds of variables manipulated in selective learning experiments.   Experimental studies, such as the Perin-Williams (23, 4) investigations, had to be conducted for the purpose of discovering the needed laws. But as more information concerning these laws became available a further complication presented itself. It was found that the different response measures (frequency, speed of running, resistance to extinction, etc.) often gave different laws, particularly from one experimental situation to another. As a consequence of this it became necessary to attempt to develop a theoretical schema which, in combination with the initial and boundary conditions of the different experimental arrangements, would permit the derivation of the empirical functions obtained in these conditioning studies. These laws, it should be noted, were concerned not only with the training variable, N, but also with such other variables as magnitude (W_g) and delay (T_G) of the reinforcement, time of deprivation (T_d) of the incentive object in instrumental reward conditioning and intensity of the unconditioned stimulus (S_u) in classical aversive conditioning. The theory, as developed, involved not only the laws relating behavior to these variables considered singly, but also the manner in which they acted in combination to determine response strength.

Once a theoretical schema was formulated that would be able to explain, in the sense of derive, the empirical laws of these conditioning experiments, it was our hope that it could be employed, along with whatever composition rules were required, to account for behavior phenomena observed in selective learning. During the forties most of Hull's research endeavors were concerned with the development of this conditioning theory (14). In his last book, *A Behavior Theory,* Hull finally returned to more complex behavioral phenomena, attempting to extend his conditioning theory to such tasks as simple trial and error learning, discrimination learning, maze learning, and problem solving. Similarly, for the last ten years the present writer's research endeavors have been primarily devoted to the job of developing an adequate theoretical base for the simpler kinds of behavior found in classical and instrumental conditioning experiments. While much remains to be done as far as the development of a complete theory of simple conditioning behavior is concerned, considerable progress has been made and it would now appear that a sufficiently extensive and precise basis is available to warrant further attempts to extend the theory to more complex behavior. As implied in the opening paragraph of this paper the writer has been engaged during the past three or four years in revising his earlier theory of selective (discrimination) learning on the basis of our latest theory of simple conditioning phenomena.

In the following section a brief presentation of these new developments will be given along with a review of our previous conceptions. Before proceeding to the presentation of these theories, however, an important methodological matter remains to be discussed. It is concerned with the relation of our simple conditioning theory to the more comprehensive theory that attempts to encompass selective learning as well as simple conditioning. Bergmann (2) has pointed out that such comprehensive theories involve a number of fundamental laws, principles or axioms. As he writes, "Some of them [laws, etc.] describe so-called elementary situations, in which only a very limited number of variables interact. At least one is a composition rule, stating how to obtain the laws of complex situations in which many variables interact from those of the elementary situations into which any complex situation can be conceptually decomposed" (1, p. 445).

The elementary situations that constitute one portion of our theory are concerned with single conditioned responses and how they change in strength with reinforcement or non-reinforcement. In order to extend the theoretical schema so as to encompass selective types of learning involving more than a single response, it is necessary, as Bergmann says, to introduce one or more composition rules. In the present instance this requires that statements, rules, or models be formulated to indicate how the several S-R's involved in the different kinds of selective learning situations interact with each other.

II

In simple conditioning experiments an attempt is made to have but a single stimulus complex or discriminandum present on each trial occasion to which, ideally, a single response or response class occurs. In selective learning, on the other hand, two or occasionally more critical discriminanda are deliberately presented simultaneously in some spatial relation to each other and in such a manner that response to one precludes concurrent response to the other. While behavior with regard to other aspects of the total stimulus configuration than the critical discriminanda may occur, usually only responses to the latter are observed and studied. The response of orienting and approaching one of the two discriminanda is reinforced, whereas response to the other is not reinforced and/or is punished. As a consequence of this differential reinforcement procedure the subject comes to respond selectively, shifting from equal choice of the two discriminanda if there is no initial bias, to 100% choice of the positive (*i.e.*, reinforced) stimulus complex at the completion of learning.

In the spatial types of selective learning situations such as the simple T maze and the dual lever box (*18*) the subject is required to orient towards and approach a stimulus complex in a particular locus in space rather than one in a different part of the situation. While the two alternative discriminanda may differ in other respects (*e.g.*, visual properties), in the simplest form of spatial discrimination situation the alternative S-R chains are made as identical as possible. Thus the same type of lever is present at both loci, or the two arms of the maze are made as physically similar as possible. Under such conditions the learning presumably is based primarily upon the discrimination of kinesthetic cues.

In contrast to this spatial type of selective learning the traditionally designated "discrimination learning problem" involves experimental arrangements in which the subject must learn to respond differentially to certain non-spatial, visual aspects of the environment. In other words, the to-be-discriminated objects or discriminanda are *varied* in their relation to the fixed spatial cues. Thus the positions of the white and black alleys in the discrimination apparatus (*e.g.*, Yerkes-Watson box) or the cards with different forms in the windows of the Lashley jumping apparatus are shifted from left to right, each appearing equally often in each position. Responses to the spatial cues are thus not differentially reinforced, being equally often reinforced and not reinforced at the beginning of such discrimination learning and both always being reinforced with mastery of problem. As we shall see the discrimination problem really involves the presentation of two different stimulus configurations, each on half of the trials. The spatial problem, in contrast, involves the same stimulus configuration on every trial occasion.

Turning now to the theories of these two kinds of selective learning we shall begin by considering an early type of schema that Hull (7, 11) and others suggested. As applied to the simple T maze this model may be represented as in Figure 1. Here the total stimulus configuration consisting of the aggregate of cues at the choice point was assumed, as a consequence of past experiences, to have competing excitatory tendencies to two incompatible responses, *turning left* (R_L) and *turning right* (R_R). Learning was conceived in terms of changes in the relative strengths of the excitatory tendencies to these two competing responses. Thus the excitatory strength of the positive, left-

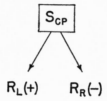

Fig. 1. Competing response (R) model of spatial selective learning.

turning response was assumed to increase with each successive reinforcement, whereas the tendency to make the negative, right-turning response was conceived to become weaker with non-reinforcement.

It was this particular conception of spatial (T-maze) learning that Tolman took as representing the S-R view and which he pitted against his cognition type theory in the series of "place versus response" experiments initiated by him and his students in the middle forties (*cf.* 35, 36, 37). While it is true, as Kendler (17) has contended, that these experiments were conceived by Tolman as being primarily concerned with certain non-essential, intuitive elaborations of the intervening variables of the rival theories, *e.g.*, receptor-effector connections versus cognitive maps, they nevertheless were also relevant to a purely empirical question. This question was whether the learning of such spatial problems is to be conceived in terms of learning to make a left (or right) turning response or whether it consists in learning to orient in relation to some particular set of discriminanda (stimuli) in the environment.

As may be seen the particular model represented in Figure 1 assumes the first of these two response conceptions. However, it is not necessary for an S-R theory to adopt this alternative. As a matter of fact it is interesting to note that Hull did not use this conception very extensively, and the writer has never employed it. In his first treatment of simple trial and error learning Hull (7) introduced a somewhat more general schema that could be interpreted in terms of this particular conception. Only in one other article concerned with problem solving involving spatial cues (11) however, did Hull specify the alternative responses at a choice point as left turning (R_L) and right turning (R_R). Actually, because of his concern with simpler kinds of conditioning phenomena, Hull did not get around to elaborating his theory of selective learning until his book *A Behavior System* (15). In this instance he did not deal with spatial selective learning *per se,* but presented his treatment of simple trial and error learning in the context of an apparatus in which the animal could push one bar to the left or press a second one downward. He identified the stimulus configuration as consisting of two stimulus components (S+ and S—) and identified the responses as R+ (pushing a vertical bar to the left) and R— pressing downward a horizontal bar). While Hull did specify the two different motor patterns, it should be noted that these acts are the terminal ends of two competing response chains, locomoting towards the vertical bar (S+) and locomoting towards the horizontal bar (S—). In effect Hull specified the two competing responses in terms of which stimulus (S+ or S—) was approached and responded to. Even in his treatment of maze learning (15, Chapt. 9) Hull hedged on this question. Thus he referred to the response of turning left *or* choosing path Y, instead of turning right *or* choosing path X. The reason for this was that in terms of the particular molar phenomena that interested Hull it made no difference which type of response description was employed.

In contrast to Hull's indecisiveness on this matter the writer (*23, 26*) has strongly favored the second of the two alternatives mentioned earlier—that is, the response of the subject in such problems was specified in terms of aproaching, *i.e.,* orienting and locomoting towards, one or other of the two discriminanda (paths, objects, etc.). Figure 2 represents this model of the spatial discrimination problem. The stimulus configuration is conceived as consisting of two spatially separated discriminanda, each of which on the basis of past experience, has excitatory tendencies for evoking receptor-orienting and locomotor responses towards them. Since the two response chains are incompatible they are in competition with each other, with the likelihood of the occurrence of one over the other depending upon the magnitude of the difference in their excitatory strengths. For convenience we shall refer to this type of schema as the competing S model (stimulus differentiation) in contrast to the first type which may be designated as the competing R model (response differentiation).

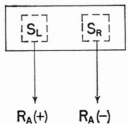

FIG. 2. Competing stimulus (S) model of spatial selective learning.

This competing S schematization of spatial learning followed directly from the writer's earlier formulated theory of nonspatial (visual) discrimination learning. In the latter type of situation the "left-turning" and the "right-turning" responses are not differentially reinforced. Depending on the location of the positive discriminandum the correct, reinforced responses sometimes involve turning left, sometimes turning right. A theory based on the assumption, as the writer's was, that the subject responds to discrete parts or specific aspects of the situation and not to the stimulus configuration as a whole, could not assume that one of the spatial responses, *e.g.*, turning left, became associated with the positive stimulus cue and the other with the negative.   Hence the assumption was made that the response acquired was that of approaching on each trial the positive stimulus complex on whichever side it was and not the negative.

The relation of this theoretical schema for visual discrimination learning to the similar one for spatial learning is seen in Figure 3 which represents a black-white discrimination problem.   This non-spatial problem, it will be noted, has two different stimulus configurations (A and B) each of which is present on half the trials.   Each of these configurations is conceived of as containing two stimulus complexes or discriminanda, *e.g.*, white (S_W) on the left (S_L) and black (S_B) on the right (S_R), or black on the left and white on the right.   Assuming white is the positive reinforced cue, the subject learns to respond to (locomote forward, approach) the discriminanda with the white

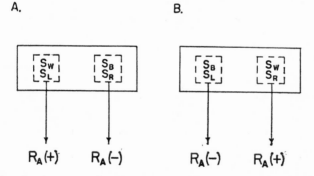

A.   **B.**

Fig. 3.   S type model of non-spatial selective (discrimination) learning.

cue ($S_W S_L$ and $S_W S_R$) and not to respond to the stimulus complexes with the black cue ($S_B S_R$ and $S_B S_L$).   This learning was conceived to be a cumulative process of building up with successive reinforcements the excitatory tendency of the positive cue (S_W) to evoke the approach response as compared to the excitatory tendency of the negative cue (S_B) to evoke this response.   Non-reinforcement of response to the negative cue was assumed to develop inhibition, thus weakening the effective

excitatory strength of this stimulus. These processes were assumed to continue until the excitatory strength of the positive
cue was sufficiently greater than that of the negative cue to
offset any differences that existed between other members of
the two stimulus complexes. Thus the difference in excitatory
strengths of the brightness cues must be greater than the difference between the excitatory strengths of the position cues (S_L
and S_R) before learning would be complete, *i.e.*, before the response would always be to the stimulus complex containing the
positive cue (S_W).

This competing S type of discrimination theory was necessitated, as was indicated earlier, by the writer's assumption that
the animal responded in such learning to specific aspects or parts
of the stimulus situation and not to the stimulus configuration
as a whole. However, if one assumes that the response of the
subject is to the total stimulus configuration consisting of the
two discriminanda in a given spatial order, it is possible to develop an R type theory of this kind of discrimination learning.
Figure 4 represents this type of theoretical schema as suggested
by Gulliksen and Wolfle (*6*). It shows the two stimulus configurations, A and B, which differ in that the two discriminanda,
white and black squares, are in opposite spatial arrangements.
The diagram also indicates that two responses, identified as a
left turning movement (R_L) and a right turning movement (R_R)
may be made to each stimulus configuration. The left turning
response to configuration A is always correct and consequently
increases in strength with each reinforcement. Non-reinforcement of the incorrect right turning response is assumed to
weaken the tendency of this configuration to evoke it. These
relations are reversed in the case of configuration B. As a result
of this differential training the subject is said to learn to turn
left when confronted with configuration A and to turn right
when presented with configuration B. In addition to these
assumptions about the stimulus and response in discrimination
learning, Gulliksen and Wolfle also presented an elaborate
mathematical model based on an earlier theory of simple learning developed by Gulliksen (*5*).

Returning now to the writer's theory of discrimination learning it should be realized that it was formulated almost 25 years

ago. At most it represented a bare outline or beginning of specifying the manner in which the variables might interact and, at the time, it was the intention of the writer to proceed with

A.   **B.**

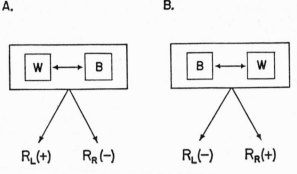

FIG. 4.   R type model of non-spatial selective (discrimination) learning.

the further development of the theory in conjunction with experimental studies of discrimination learning.   For reasons described above, however, interest shifted to the simpler types of conditioning behavior and, except for formulations in seminars, the writer has never found the time to prepare the theory for publication.

In the meantime on the basis of our experimental studies of conditioning phenomena a much more precise and detailed theoretical framework of simple learning has been elaborated. One aspect of this later theoretical development that has been of considerable importance for behavior situations involving more than one response possibility is the notion of oscillatory inhibition (I_o) introduced by Hull in his *Principles of Behavior* (*14*). As the present writer has conceived this concept, I_o represents the effects of uncontrolled factors affecting the strength of a response tendency at any moment.   Applied to selective learning involving two alternative response possibilities, it permits one to derive the probability of occurrence of either one of the responses as a function of the difference in their theoretical excitatory strengths.

The manner in which this concept and its associated properties may be applied to the problem of choice behavior is

exemplified by the writer's treatment of selective spatial learning in the Silliman Lectures (*28*, Chapt. 7).   As developed there
the S type of model was employed, the behavior situation being
represented in the manner shown in Figure 2 as consisting of
two incompatible S-R tendencies conceived to be in competition
with each other.   By means of a composition rule which stated
that in such situations the response that has the greater excitatory potential at the moment will be the one that will occur
and the laws or postulates concerning the variables in the individual response systems, particularly those relating to oscillatory inhibition (I_o), it was possible to derive the implication
that the per cent occurrence of the response of approaching the
positive stimulus is a normal integral function of the magnitude
of the difference between the strengths of the excitatory potentials of the competing approach responses.   While the S type of
model was used in this presentation the R type could just as well
have been employed.   About the only difference between them
as far as the use of the oscillatory inhibition concept is concerned
is that the S type of schema requires that the two discriminanda
be so arranged that they both provide *effective stimulation* at
the moment of choice, whereas the R type theory does not require that this condition be met.

As has been brought out in previous discussions (*28, 29*) these
models employing the conception of competing and oscillating,
momentary, effective excitatory potentials lead not only to the
implication that the per cent occurrence of the stronger of two
competing responses is a function of the difference between
their excitatory strengths (E), but also that it will vary with the
absolute level of the excitatory strengths above the threshold.
Thus it was shown that a given difference in the competing E's
at very low absolute levels of E produces a higher per cent occurrence of the stronger response than at a high absolute level.
The nature of this relationship was derived by an approxima-
tion method employing the normal probability tables (*28*, p.
237).[1]

The concept of oscillatory inhibition (I_o) could also be em-

[1] Unfortunately, space does not permit a more elaborate discussion of these
matters here. They are especially important for making derivations as to the
effects of manipulating drive and incentive factors on performance level at dif-

ployed with the S type model in a similar manner to develop a more sophisticated theory of discrimination learning than the 1936 formulation (23). However, the writer has not attempted this for the reason that he has preferred to work with a more complex schema which, in a sense, includes features of both the S and R type models.

There are a number of reasons for this preference of what will be referred to hereafter as the compound SR model of selective learning to distinguish it from the previously described S and R types. Mention has already been made that the R type model would not work for non-spatial (visual) discrimination learning, particularly within the framework of a position that assumed that the subject's response in some situations at least, is to discrete aspects of the situation and not to the stimulus configuration. Secondly, the S type model presents real difficulties as far as the requirement that the critical discriminanda be so arranged that they *both* provide effective stimulation at the moment of choice. While conditions can be arranged so that this is the case, such as, for example, in a black-white discrimination, there is no question but that in many spatial and non-spatial discrimination situations this is not the case; hence this model will not be sufficiently comprehensive. Finally, the SR model not only surmounts these difficulties, but also leads to implications concerning so-called vicarious trial-and-error behavior (VTE) that occurs at the choice point as well as derivations concerning the per cent of responses made to the two discriminanda. A number of investigations from the laboratories of Muenzinger, Tolman, and others have shown that this kind of "looking back and forth" behavior is lawfully related to the changing proportion of correct responses that occurs with practice (4, 33). It has seemed more worthwhile to attempt to develop a more comprehensive theory that would be able to encompass this type of behavior as well as the per cent of successes. The following section briefly describes this new model, first as it applies to spatial selective learning and then to visual discrimination learning.

---

ferent stages of selective learning. As yet only very preliminary treatments of these implications of the theoretical schema have been published (28, 29).

III

Figure 5 represents the SR type of model that the writer has been using for the spatial learning problem. As may be seen the animal is assumed to respond at the choice point (S_{CP}) by

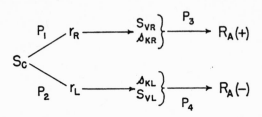

FIG. 5.   SR type model of spatial selective learning.

making either a right orienting (r_R) or a left orienting response (r_L). This response may be specified as a turning of the eyes, head and/or body to the left or right so that the visual discriminanda to the left (S_{VL}) or to the right (S_{VR}) are fixated and thus received.[2]   The subject also provides itself with differential proprioceptive stimulation (s_{KL} or s_{KR}) as a consequence of making one or other of these turning responses.

As in the case of the responses in the R model, these orienting responses are conceived as being in competition with each other, the probability of their occurrence being a function of the difference between their excitatory strengths as determined by the assumptions concerning oscillatory inhibition (I_o).   With train-

[2] One must understand that as a consequence of past experiences in its cage and preliminary training in the experimental situation, an animal brings with it a well organized set of receptor-orienting acts.   In this instance we are interested only in those orienting responses of turning the eyes, head, and body to the left or to the right.   If the animal has been reinforced frequently in its past life to orient towards the top of the cage it is very likely to make the same response in the experimental situation.   Presumably in its past life animals have made many left and right orienting responses and hence the habit strengths of both are fairly high.   It is also possible that the circumstances of the home cage (e.g., position of the food box) could be such that the habit strength of one of the orienting responses is considerably stronger than the other.   Presumably, through transfer, this would result in an initial bias in favor of one of the orienting responses.   So-called position habits are probably, in part, a function of such differences, although other factors may also be responsible.

ing in the spatial discrimination situation the effective excitatory potential ($\bar{E}$) of the correct, or reinforced, orienting response (r_R in the example) becomes stronger, while the effective strength of the non-reinforced response is weakened. As the difference between these competing potentials increases with training, the probability (P_1) that the subject will make the correct, right orienting response on reaching the choice point increases. The probability of making the incorrect left orienting response (P_2), of course, decreases since $P_1 + P_2 = 1$ and $P_2 = 1 - P_1$.

At this point an assumed property of such orienting behavior originally suggested by Tolman in connection with his theoretical sowbug (*33, 34*) is introduced. It is that these receptor-orienting acts are relatively refractory or easily fatigued and can be maintained for only a limited period of time. That is, an animal is able to keep its head and eyes oriented and fixated on the right alley or lever for only a brief period at a time. Work inhibition, or some such refractory factor, weakens it so that another orienting response becomes stronger and takes its place. In the present instance the animal would likely turn its head and body to the left.[3]

Now whether the animal will shift its orientation in this manner on a particular trial will depend upon whether or not it makes the response of locomoting forward to the combination of alley cues (S_{VR}) and the kinesthetic cues (s_{KR}) *before* the orienting response becomes fatigued or refractory. The likelihood of occurrence of this latter, forward going response during this period will, in turn, depend upon the strength of its effective excitatory tendency. This latter probability, P_3 in the diagram, is thus calculated in terms of the extent to which this excitatory potential ($\bar{E}$) is above the threshold (L) necessary for the response to be elicited. In a similar manner the probability (P_4) of the occurrence of the response to the negative cues (S_{VL} and S_{KR}) would also depend upon the extent to which the effective excitatory potential ($\bar{E}$) of these cues to evoke R_A

---

[3] Presumably stimuli from the left portion of the stimulus field also play a role in this shifting of the orienting response. In the light of the spontaneous alternation studies, the more different the new stimuli, the more likely they would be to elicit the new orientation.

is above L. As described in the Silliman Lectures (31, p. 103–106) in connection with the calculation of the theoretical frequency of occurrence of a classical conditioned response, these probability values (P_3 and P_4) are normal integral functions of the extent to which the values of $\bar{E}$ are above the threshold L. This relation follows from the assumptions made concerning the distribution of oscillatory inhibition values (I_o) from trial to trial.

Given the theoretical $\bar{E}$ values for the four responses and hence the four values of P (*i.e.*, P_1, P_2, P_3, and P_4), the probability (P_R) that the subject will sooner or later on a particular trial complete the right going response chain may be shown to be: [4]

$$(1) \qquad P_R = \frac{P_3 (1 - P_2 P_4)}{P_3 + P_4 - P_3 P_4}$$

The probability that the subject will respond by completing the alternative left going response chain is 1 minus the above, or:

$$(2) \qquad P_L = \frac{P_4 (1 - P_1 P_3)}{P_3 + P_4 - P_3 P_4}$$

These expressions yield exact solutions for all values of P_1, P_2, P_3, and P_4 except when *both* P_3 and P_4 equal zero. In this latter event the subject will not make, *i.e.*, complete, either response chain. Position habits, as may be seen, will result either from a zero value for P_3 or P_4. Presumably, however, past experience leads through transfer of training to superthreshold values for these response tendencies in most instances.

Before proceeding to a consideration of how this model is applied to discrimination (non-spatial) learning, attention may be directed to the point that according to this conception what Tolman and his colleagues (22, 35, 36, 37) have called *place* learning and *response* learning both take place in the standard single choice T maze. There is an important difference, how-

[4] The following equations for combining the probabilities of the orientation and approach responses were derived independently by Sheldon White and Paul Games, who at the time (1956) were students in the writer's seminar.

ever, in the present interpretation and that of Tolman and his group.   In the present model the animal is assumed to learn in the standard T maze to make one spatial orientation (*e.g.*, turning right) and not the other, but it is not assumed to learn to *orient towards one place or locus* and not some other place. Rather it learns to *approach* one place and not to *approach* the other.   In the standard spatial situation the two different kinesthetic cues, s_{KR} and s_{KL}, acquire differential excitatory strengths for the approach response.   Hence the problem can be described as involving, in part, a kinesthetic discrimination. But if the visual stimulation from the two arms or the external visual cues associated with the two arms are different, the discrimination will also be based on differential excitatory tendencies established to the two sets of visual cues (S_{VL} and S_{VR}). Only in the type of experiment that Tolman and his group introduced in the so-called series of place versus response studies, in which the subject starts from two opposed positions (*e.g.*, north and south) does the problem become a pure kinesthetic discrimination problem.   In such a situation responses to the visual cues from the east and west alleys are equally often reinforced and not reinforced and hence do not acquire differential excitatory tendencies to the response of approaching.

In the so-called place learning situation in which the subject, starting from both the north and south positions, must learn to turn always to one place, *e.g.*, the west alley, the problem becomes a visual (non-spatial) discrimination problem in which the excitatory strengths at the choice point (S_{cp}) to the two orienting responses are not differentially reinforced and the kinesthetic cues, s_{KR} and s_{KL}, are also non-differential, since both are equally reinforced and not reinforced.   The learning of such a problem involves, according to this theory, the differrential building up of the excitatory potential of the visual cues on the reinforced side (*e.g.*, S_{VR}) to evoke the approaching response as compared to the excitatory potential of the visual cues, S_{VL}, on the non-reinforced side.

Quite in contrast to the formulation of Tolman *et al.*, who interpreted the faster learning of their place group as indicating that the disposition to orient toward the goal (place) was simpler and more primitive than the disposition to make right or left turns, the present theory would state that neither type of learning, orienting spatially and approaching the subsequent stimulus pattern, is more primitive or basic than the other. Rather the speed of learning will depend upon whether the differences between s_{KR} and s_{KL} are greater than the differences between S_{VL} and S_{VR}. Specification of the relative magnitudes of these differences independent of the rate of learning is not, as yet, feasible since they are in two quite different stimulus dimensions.

A number of interesting implications concerning these two types of learning problems, place and response learning, can be derived from the present theoretical model. One example is that, whereas response learning would not be affected by the magnitude of the different visual cues associated with the two arms of the maze, place learning would be. In the latter type of problem learning would be a positive function of the magnitude of the difference between these visual cues. On the other hand a factor that would affect response learning would be the time interval between trials. Unfortunately, the limitations of space do not permit a further elaboration of these theoretical implications here.

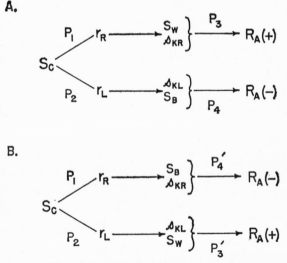

Fig. 6.   SR type model of non-spatial selective (discrimination) learning.

Returning now to the non-spatial discrimination situation, it will be recalled that two different configurations of the discriminanda are presented, each on half of the trials. As may be seen from Figure 6 in configuration A, in which white card or alley is on the right and black on the left, the probability that the response chain leading to white will be completed is given by the probability of completing the right going response chain. This probability, which will be designated as P_{RA}, is given by the following:

$$(3) \qquad P_{RA} = \frac{P_3 (1 - P_2 P_4)}{P_3 + P_4 - P_3 P_4}$$

In the case of configuration B the probability that the response will be to the white stimulus is the probability that the left going response chain will be completed. This probability, designated as P_{LB}, is as follows: [5]

$$(4) \qquad P_{LB} = \frac{P_3' (1 - P_1 P_4')}{P_3' + P_4' - P_3' P_4'}$$

The probability (P_W) of responding to the white discriminandum in both configurations considered together will, of course, be the mean of these two probability values. Thus

$$(5) \qquad P_W = \frac{P_{RA} + P_{LB}}{2}$$

As is well known, the two probability values of a white-going response (P_{RA}, P_{LB}) may have very different values at one time for the same subject. Thus in the case of a strong position preference to the right, the subject may respond in a particular block of trials 100% to white in configuration A and 0% in configuration B. This provides an average of 50% to the white discriminandum.

In the case of subjects that do not exhibit a position preference it may be assumed that $P_1 = P_2 = .5$ and that $P_3 = P_3'$ and $P_4 = P_4'$. For such subjects equations for P_{RA} and P_{LB} may be simplified to the following:

---

[5] Because of the possibility that the habit loadings of s_{KR} and s_{KL} are different, the P_3 and P_4 values may be different for configurations A and B. For this reason primes (P_3', P_4') have been employed in the case of these values for configuration B.

(6)
$$P_{RA} = \frac{P_3 (1 - .5\,P_4)}{P_3 + P_4 - P_3 P_4}$$

(7)
$$P_{LB} = \frac{P_3 (1 - .5\,P_4)}{P_3 + P_4 - P_3 P_4}$$

(5)   Since
$$P_W = \frac{P_{RA} + P_{LB}}{2}$$

(8)   Then
$$P_W = \frac{P_3 (1 - .5\,P_4)}{P_3 + P_4 - P_3 P_4}$$

Depending upon the assumptions made concerning the growth fo E and I_n with reinforcements and non-reinforcements, theoretical curves of per cent of choice of the positive (right going) response in the spatial situation and of the positive (white going) response in the non-spatial situation could be determined. Such derivations are not, however, particularly valuable as there are many different combinations of assumptions concerning the growth of E and I_n that can be made and presumably a number of different such combinations would provide equally satisfactory fits to any set of empirical curves. Nevertheless, this model is of considerable theoretical value and can be employed to make testable deductions concerning the effects of various kinds of experimental manipulations. Again, an example, concerned in this instance with the theoretical effect of widening the gap between the choice point and the white and black platforms in a visual discrimination situation after the subjects have been partially trained in a small gap situation, will be presented.

Table 1 presents the derivation and results of a theoretical experiment in which the excitatory potentials of the responses S_W——E_3——$\rightarrow R_A$ and S_B——E_4——$\rightarrow R_A$ of three groups of subjects after a given amount of differential training are assumed to be 3.7 and 2.5 σI_o units (see Column II). At this point the gap between the choice point and discriminanda platforms is varied for the three groups, and it is assumed that the threshold value (L) of excitatory potential necessary to elicit the response of locomoting forward (*i.e.*, jumping) after orienting to the white or black platforms is .5, 1.0, and 1.5 σI_o units for groups A, B, and C, which have increasingly larger gaps (see Column III). The superthreshold values of the excitatory potentials of the

TABLE 1

THEORETICAL EFFECTS OF INCREASING GAP BETWEEN THE CHOICE
POINT AND DISCRIMINANDA ON (P_W) AND $(\overline{V})$

I	II		III	IV		V	VI	VII
	$E/\sigma I_o$			$E\text{-}L/\sigma I_o$				
Group			L			P_3	P_4	P_W	$\overline{V}$
	S_{W+}	S_{B-}		S_{W+}	S_{B-}				
A	3.7	2.5	.5	3.2	2.0	.75	.30	.77	.79
B	3.7	2.5	1.0	2.7	1.5	.57	.15	.83	1.59
C	3.7	2.5	1.5	2.2	1.0	.37	.06	.88	3.38

competing stimuli under these different conditions are shown in Column IV, and the P_3 and P_4 values of our theoretical equation corresponding to these latter values appear in Column V. Column VI gives the proportion of responses that will theoretically be made to the positive white discriminandum by the three groups [6] and Column VII the mean number $(\overline{V})$ of VTE responses per trial that each group should make.[7] As may be seen the implication of the theory is that the level of choice of the positive stimulus will increase as a positive function of the size of the gap as will also the number of VTE's.

Similarly, derivations may be made concerning the effects of manipulating a number of other variables, such as the drive level, magnitude of reward, spatial angle between the discriminanda, similarity of the discriminanda, etc., on these two performance measures. One further example that may be mentioned is of interest because its effects are just the opposite of those of increasing the distance of the discriminanda from the

[6] The values for P_W were calculated by means of formula (8) and hence applies to subjects that do not exhibit a marked position habit.

[7] $\overline{V}$ was calculated by means of the following equation derived from the model by Allan R. Wagner:

$$V = \frac{2 - .5\,(P_3 + P_4) - (P_3 + P_4 - P_3\,P_4)}{P_3 + P_4 - P_3\,P_4}$$

choice point. If the drive level is increased at a stage late in
training when the subject is responding at a high level to the
positive stimulus, the implication of the theory is that there
will be a decrease both in the per cent of correct responses and
the number of VTE's. The stage of training must be specified,
for in the early stage of learning, when the subject is responding at a relatively low level to the positive reinforced stimulus,
the effects of increasing the drive are much more complex and
cannot be described in such a simple fashion.

IV

In this final section consideration will be given to a number
of points about such theorizing that appear to require repeated
emphasis. The first can be disposed of briefly. The *continuity* assumption is held to in all of these different theoretical
models. Thus it is assumed in the SR model, as in the earlier
types, that the excitatory strength of the correct orienting response (*e.g.*, r_R) is increased in cumulative fashion with each
increment of habit strength resulting from a reinforcement,
while the effective excitatory strength of the incorrect orienting
response (*e.g.*, r_L) is decreased with each increment of inhibition
(I_n) resulting from non-reinforcement. Likewise the excitatory
strengths of the positive and negative stimulus complexes to
evoke R_A in the second portion of the chains also change in a
cumulative manner with successive reinforcements and non-
reinforcements.

Unfortunately the use of the term "reinforcement" in connection wth such theorizing has often led to some misunderstanding. As employed here "reinforcement" refers to an experimental operation and not to such theoretical notions as
Thorndike and Hull have espoused. The issue of reinforcement versus contiguity theory does not, or at least need not,
arise in this area; for, as the writer has pointed out (27), his
original formulation of discrimination learning theory could
have been conceived either as a reinforcement or a contiguity
theory. The essential feature of this theory was its quantitative
nature, particularly the notion of cumulative change in the
property of the effective stimulus cue, however conceived, to

elicit some specified response. As revealed in a number of previous writings (28, 29, 30) the writer tends to favor a contiguity principle in the case of learning involving some form of appetitional motivation and a reinforcement principle in the case of aversive motivation.

The particular quantitative assumptions concerning the increments of habit strength (H) with reinforcement and increments of inhibition (I_n) with non-reinforcement are based in this type of theory on the empirical findings of conditioning experiments. The data of differential instrumental conditioning studies are especially relevant as the writer has attempted to show (29, 30). In this connection it should be noted that the particular assumption made in the discrimination theory concerning the development of inhibition is quite different from that made as to the development of a withdrawal (avoidance) response to the negative stimulus when shock is employed instead of non-reinforcement. Unfortunately, if one may judge from the psychological literature, this does not always seem to have been appreciated, and one finds instances in which a theoretical set involving assumptions about non-reinforcement have been tested by situations involving shock and vice versa.

With regard to discrimination learning the discussion has so far not called attention to the point that visual discrimination situations differ greatly in the extent to which they require the animal to learn special receptor-orienting acts in order to receive differential stimulation from the two discriminanda. In the case of the Yerkes-Watson type of brightness discrimination apparatus involving entrance and passage through a lighted or darkened alley there is no question as to whether the subject receives differential stimulation. Only if it kept its eyes tightly closed could it avoid receiving the differential stimulation. In the case of form discrimination, however, the animal does not necessarily receive different effective stimulation from the inception of training. In such situations the animal usually has to learn first to make the appropriate receptor-orienting acts that will provide it with discriminably different stimulation from the two stimulus forms so that differential excitatory tendencies can be developed with respect to them. In an experiment involving form discrimination Ehrenfreund (3) showed that when conditions were arranged so that there was differential effective stimulation from the inception of training, differential excitatory tendencies were established to the form cues from the beginning of training as the continuity assumption demands. All too often, again, psychologists have neglected to take this matter into consideration. Because of the added complexity of these problems it would appear that the most effective way to proceed to the development and testing of a theory of discrimination behavior would be to employ the simpler type of stimulus cue such as brightness rather than form.

A final aspect of our discussion of discrimination learning is that it has been confined to the relatively simple situation in which the stimulus configuration contained two discriminanda differing in a single attribute or dimension such as brightness, size, form, etc. Space will not permit here treatment of the more complicated types of discrimination learning involving successive, conditional and transverse patterns such as have been employed by Nissen *(19, 20)* and Bitterman and his associates *(cf. 2, 32, 39)*. These complex types involve what the writer has called the principle of patterning. Only a very preliminary discussion of these complex types of discrimination learning has been given by the present writer *(26)*.

REFERENCES

1. BERGMANN, G.   Theoretical psychology.   *Ann. Rev. of Psychol.,* 1953, *4,* 435–452.

2. BITTERMAN, M. E.   Approach and avoidance in discrimination learning.   *Psychol. Rev.,* 1952, *59,* 172–175.

3. EHRENFREUND, D.   An experimental test of the continuity theory of discrimination with pattern vision.   *J. comp. Psychol.,* 1948, *41,* 408–422.

4. GOSS, ALBERT E., & WISCHNER, GEORGE J.   Vicarious trial and error and related behavior.   *Psychol. Bull.,* 1956, *53,* 35–54.

5. GULLIKSEN, H.   A rational equation of the learning curve based on Thorndike's law of effect.   *J. gen. Psychol.,* 1934, *11,* 395–434.

6. ———, & WOLFLE, D. L.   A theory of learning and transfer.   I and II.   *Psychometrika,* 1938, *3,* 127–149, 225–251.

7. HULL, C. L.   Simple trial and error learning: a study in psychological theory.   *Psychol. Rev.,* 1930, *37,* 241–256.

8. ———.   The goal gradient hypothesis and maze learning.   *Psychol. Rev.,* 1932, *39,* 25–43.

9. ———. The concept of the habit family hierarchy and maze learning: Part I. *Psychol. Rev.*, 1934, *41*, 33–52.

10. ———. The concept of the habit-family hierarchy and maze learning: Part II. *Psychol. Rev.*, 1934, *41*, 134–152.

11. ———. The mechanism of the assembly of behavior segments in novel combinations suitable for problem solution. *Psychol. Rev.*, 1935, *42*, 219–245.

12. ———. The conflicting psychologies of learning—a way out. *Psychol. Rev.*, 1935, *42*, 491–516.

13. ———. Mind, mechanism, and adaptive behavior. *Psychol. Rev.*, 1937, *44*, 1–32.

14. ———. *Principles of Behavior*. New York: D. Appleton-Century Co., 1943.

15. ———. *A Behavior System*. New Haven: Yale University Press, 1952.

16. ———, HOVLAND, C. I., ROSS, R. T., HALL, M., PERKINS, D. T., & FITCH, F. B. *Mathematico-Deductive Theory of Rote Learning*. New Haven: Yale University Press, 1940.

17. KENDLER, H. H. "What is learned?"—A theoretical blind alley. *Psychol. Rev.*, 1952, *59*, 269–277.

18. LOGAN, F. A. The role of delay of reinforcement in determining reaction potential. *J. exp. Psychol.*, 1952, *43*, 393–399.

19. NISSEN, H. W. Description of the learned response in discrimination behavior. *Psychol. Rev.*, 1950, *57*, 121–131.

20. ———. Sensory patterning versus central organization. *J. Psychol.*, 1953, *36*, 271–287.

21. PERIN, C. T. Behavior potentiality as a joint function of the amount of training and the degree of hunger at the time of extinction. *J. exp. Psychol.*, 1942, *30*, 93–113.

22. RITCHIE, B. F. Studies in spatial learning. III. Two paths to the same location and two paths to two different locations. *J. exp. Psychol.*, 1947, *37*, 25–38.

23. SPENCE, K. W. The nature of discrimination learning in animals. *Psychol. Rev.*, 1936, *43*, 427–449.

24. ———. The differential response in animals to stimuli varying within a single dimension. *Psychol. Rev.*, 1937, *44*, 430–444.

25. ———. Continuous versus non-continuous interpretations of discrimination learning. *Psychol. Rev.*, 1940, *47*, 271–288.

26. ———. The nature of the response in discrimination learning. *Psychol. Rev.*, 1952, *59*, 89–93.

27. ———. Mathematical theories of learning. *J. gen. Psychol.*, 1953, *49*, 283–291.

28. ———. *Behavior Theory and Conditioning*. New Haven: Yale University Press, 1956.

29. ———. Behavior theory and selective learning. *Nebraska Symposium on Motivation*, 1958, pp. 77–107.

30. ———, GOODRICH, K. P., & ROSS, L. E. Performance in differential conditioning and discrimination as a function of hunger and relative response frequency. *J. exp. Psychol.*, 1959, *58*, 8–16.

31. ——, HAGGARD, D. F., & ROSS, L. E.   UCS intensity and the associative (habit) strength of the eyelid CR.   *J. exp. Psychol.*, 1958, *55*, 404–411.

32. TEAS, D. C., & BITTERMAN, M. E.   Perceptual organization in the rat. *Psychol. Rev.*, 1952, *59*, 130–140.

33. TOLMAN, E. C.   Prediction of vicarious trial and error by means of the schematic sowbug.   *Psychol. Rev.*, 1931, *46*, 318–336.

34. ——.   Discrimination vs. learning and the schematic sowbug.   *Psychol. Rev.*, 1941, *48*, 367–382.

35. ——, RITCHIE, B. F., & KALISH, D.   Studies in spatial learning.   II. Place learning versus response learning.   *J. exp. Psychol.*, 1946, *36*, 221–229

36. ——, ——, & ——.   Studies in spatial learning.   IV. The transfer of place learning to other starting paths.   *J. exp. Psychol.*, 1947, *37*, 39–47.

37. ——, ——, & ——.   Studies in spatial learning.   V. Response learning vs. place learning by the non-correction method.   *J. exp. Psychol.*, 1947, *37*, 285.

38. WILLIAMS, S. B.   Resistance to extinction as a function of the number of reinforcements.   *J. exp. Psychol.*, 1938, *23*, 506–522.

39. WODINSKY, J., & BITTERMAN, M. E.   Compound and configuration in successive discrimination.   *Amer. J. Psychol.*, 1952, *65*, 563–572.

Index

A

A-score, 143, 144, 145
Abstraction, science as, 45, 73
Agreement, intersubjective, 75
Analysis, operational, 5
Anger, 97, 98
Anxiety
  and paired-associates learning, 189–200
  and response hierarchy, 140, 141
  as motivation for maze learning, 214, 215, 218
  cue aspects of, 199
  performance curves of conditioning and, 131–37, 139, 141, 158, 178–82
  scale of, 129, 130, 176, 186, 199; see also Drive, Emotionality
Apparatus
  chimpanzee, 326–37, 339–45
  discrimination, 346–47
  dual-platform, 320–23
  eyelid experiments, 131–38, 148–59, 164–72, 175–82
  jumping, 314
  maze, 187, 362, 363, 371, 372, 383
Arousal level, 176, 181, 182
Association, 309, 327, 343
  and cue aspect of situation, 287
  and reception of stimulus, 313
  discrimination and, 310–24
    theory of, 337
  non-continuity theory of, 318
  principles, 308
  remote, 188; see also Conditioning
Associative connections, 188, 191, 197
  building of, 326
  verbal, 189, 190
Associative strengths, 333
Autonomic nervous system, 163
Axioms, 370

B

Behavior
  choice, 217

determinants of, 202, 222
  proprioceptive, 314
disorders of, 27
effect of motivational level of S on, 148
intensity dimension of, 176
language, 80
phenomenological approach to, 27
pre-solution, theory of, 309
psychological investigation of, 79, 80
quantitative laws of, 92
simple adaptive, mathematical expression of, 35
task-interfering, 198
theory of, 18, 36, 98
  graphic expression of, 12–13
Behaviorism, 72
  and operationism, 44
  data used in, 43
  laws sought by, 48, 49, 50
  methodological position of, 78, 79
  varieties of, 39
Biases, ontological, 72
Blind alleys, 367
  maze experiments and, 225–27, 230, 231, 233–34, 242
  order of difficulty of, 243; see also Maze learning

C

CR, 155, 158, 159, 162, 163, 167
  acquisition curves of, 166, 170, 180
CS, 154, 162, 164, 165, 168, 169, 170, 173
Categories, ontological, 74
Chimpanzee, 288, 292, 299, 318, 323, 337
  discrimination learning by, 326–37, 339–57
Choice, 68, 377
Choice-learning, 198
Choice point, 140, 141, 142, 207, 212, 231, 233, 235, 238, 239, 373, 379, 383
  gap between discriminanda and, 387; see also Maze learning

393

400

INDEX

determination of, 175
level of, 185
  high drive as detrimental to, 187
Personality, 76, 77, 78, 79, 80, 83
Phenomenology, 27; *see also* Behaviorism
Physics, 41, 72
  field theory in, 54
  inductive generalization in, 47
  laws in, 38
  role of theory in, 48, 81, 82, 87
Position
  effect on discrimination learning of, 281, 282, 290, 315, 320, 321, 322
  preference, 207; *see also* Habit
Positivism, 77; *see also* Logical empiricism
Postulates, 113
  behaviorist, 40
  role of in psychology, 9, 11
Postulational technique, 9
Pragmatism, 3
Predicates, dispositional, 20, 22n, 78
Predicates, psychological, 74
Prediction, 21, 28, 352, 353
  intervening variables and, 85
  perceptual behavior, 26
  performance
    by anxious subjects, 199
    conditioning, 181
Problem-box learning, 271, 272
Problem solving, sudden solution in, 330–34, 336
Problems
  discrimination, 329, 361–73
  dynamic, 23
  insoluble, 284, 290
    systematic response in, 285
Proprioception; *see* Cues, proprioceptive
Psychoanalysis, 55
Psychological events
  nature of, 41–43
  neurophysiological processes and, 257
Psychology
  behaviorism, 39–55, 72, 78
  clinical, 80n
  concepts, 6, 10, 18, 19, 22, 30, 31, 46, 47, 49, 60, 76, 81
  delimited by pointer-reading observations 75–76
  empirical language in, 14n

introspection and, 24–26, 36, 39, 43, 44, 72, 74, 77, 80, 81
laws in, 19
material of, 6, 43
mathematical expression of basic task of, 12
of personality, 76, 77, 78
private experiences as data for, 75
problems of, 11
role of immediate experience in study of, 41–43, 72
role of intervening variables in, 28–37
scientific method in, 9, 76
status of knowledge of, 83
subject matter of, 42, 45, 72, 79
task of, 15
theory in, 38, 40, 47, 48, 51, 55, 58, 59, 82, 83, 85
  constructs, 18–20
  ultrapositivistic approach to, 32–39
types of laws in, 48, 49
verbal sources of data for, 27, 40, 43, 53
vocabulary of, 75
Punishment, 326, 347; *see also* Conditioning

R

Reaction threshold, 114
Realism, common-sense, 71
Reality, correspondence of constructs with, 289
Redintegration, 261, 262
Reduction chain, 6n, 7n
Reinforcement, 149, 173, 204, 215, 216, 258, 277n, 278, 280, 294, 305, 319, 328–31, 335, 342, 354, 360, 361, 383, 388, 389
  absence of in appetitional conditioning, 161
  as experimental operation, 388
  associative changes and, 331
  changed interpretation of, 92, 94, 95
  definition of, 388
  delay of, 91
  drive-reduction theory of, 156, 157
  effect of varying schedules of, 99
  empirical law of effect in, 92, 93, 96